British Flag Officers in the French Wars, 1793–1815

Also available from Bloomsbury

The English Armada, by Luis Gorrochategui Santos
Modern Naval History, by Richard Harding
The Royal Navy in the Age of Austerity 1919–22, by G. H. Bennett

British Flag Officers in the French Wars, 1793–1815

Admirals' Lives

John Morrow

BLOOMSBURY ACADEMIC
LONDON • NEW YORK • OXFORD • NEW DELHI • SYDNEY

BLOOMSBURY ACADEMIC
Bloomsbury Publishing Plc
50 Bedford Square, London, WC1B 3DP, UK
1385 Broadway, New York, NY 10018, USA

BLOOMSBURY, BLOOMSBURY ACADEMIC and the Diana logo
are trademarks of Bloomsbury Publishing Plc

First published 2018
Paperback edition first published 2020

A catalogue record for this book is available from the British Library.

Library of Congress Cataloging-in-Publication Data
Names: Morrow, John, Ph. D., author.
Title: British flag officers in the French wars, 1793-1815: admirals' lives
/ John Morrow, University of Auckland, New Zealand.
Other titles: Admirals' lives
Description: London ; New York : Bloomsbury Academic, 2018. | Includes
bibliographical references.
Identifiers: LCCN 2017040941 | ISBN 9781474277679 (hardback) | ISBN
9781474277686 (ePUB ebook) | ISBN 9781474277673 (PDF ebook)
Subjects: LCSH: Admirals--Great Britain. | Great Britain.Royal
Navy--Officers. | Great Britain--History, Naval.
Classification: LCC VB315.G7 M67 2018 | DDC 359.0092/241 [B] --dc23 LC record available at
https://lccn.loc.gov/2017040941

ISBN: HB: 978-1-4742-7767-9
PB: 978-1-3501-2777-7
ePDF: 978-1-4742-7769-3
eBook: 978-1-4411-2382-4

Typeset by Newgen KnowledgeWorks Pvt. Ltd., Chennai, India

To find out more about our authors and books visit
www.bloomsbury.com and sign up for our newsletters.

In loving memory of my father, Henry (Harry) Morrow, 1919–2014

Contents

List of Illustrations

List of Figures and Tables

Figures

Tables

Preface

In the French Wars of 1793–1801 and 1803–15 the government and the nation relied heavily on the resilience and leadership of those who commanded the Royal Navy's fleets. Some of these officers were celebrated in nineteenth-century 'lives and letters' produced by relatives or admiring subordinates. A significant number of them have been the subjects of modern scholarly biographical studies and essays, and aspects of their careers have been examined in books and essays on naval history during the war period. This book draws upon these works, on biographical and thematically focused collections of printed primary materials, and official and private archival sources to explore the attitudes, challenges and professional interactions that shaped the lives of British admirals during the French Wars. Its focus is not primarily biographical, operational or organizational, although these considerations are important in determining how flag officers understood their role and how that was reflected in professional aspirations, attitudes, behaviour and engagements. Some of the men discussed in this book are still household names but their professional lives are set here within the context of a broader group of flag officers now known only to those versed in late Georgian Naval history. The approach is thematic, with a range of individual officers being discussed in relation to particular themes. Men such as Earl St Vincent, Admiral William Cornwallis, Lord Keith, Viscount Nelson, Lord Collingwood, Sir James Saumarez and Sir John Duckworth, who held key positions for prolonged periods, or who were in some ways emblematic of significant attitudes and developments, play prominent roles in a number of chapters. Other officers make more occasional and fleeting appearances.

I have tried to avoid technical terms which are likely to be foreign to some readers, but for the sake of convenience, I have sometimes adopted the contemporary practice of referring to the members of a ship's crew by the plural form of their ship's name, hence *Victories* or *Caesars*, or simply 'the people'. The term 'subordinate flag officer', which I was pleased to find in a contemporary Admiralty record after I had adopted it, refers to admirals on active service who were not commanders-in-chief and were thus subject to a more senior flag officer.

Four officers' names changed when they became peers during the course of the wars and this can cause confusion in referring to them. Except where the context particularly requires it, John Jervis is referred to by the title (St Vincent) he took when he became an earl in 1797, and George Keith Elphinstone by his title in the Irish peerage from 1797 (Keith) and the United Kingdom peerage in 1801. William Waldegrave appears as (Lord) Radstock in references to his career after he acquired this Irish title in 1801. Charles Middleton, who became Lord Barham very late in his career, is treated in the same manner. Sir Edward Pellew, who became Lord Exmouth at the end of the wars, is referred to by his family name. As a general practice, admirals are given their full rank when first mentioned in a chapter and are then referred to by their name or name and title. That is, unless the context requires it, no attempt is made to track their rise in rank over chapters in which they make a number of appearances over extended periods of time. Dates of promotion are recorded in the biographical notes appended to the conclusion. When details of an officer's life, connections and career are salient to a particular line of discussion, they are included in the text.

I would not have been able to write this book without the generous support of Professor Stuart McCutheon, the vice chancellor of the University of Auckland. He has encouraged me to pursue a project that lies beyond the scope of my day job, and provided funds through the Vice Chancellor's Office that have made it possible for me to undertake research in archives and libraries in England and Scotland. I am also indebted to other colleagues at the University for their advice and practical assistance. Dr Bill Barnes (Classics), Associate Professor Erin Griffey (Art History) and Professor Warren Swain (Law) have been most helpful on questions relating to their scholarly expertise. Bridget Cameron and Claire Walters, colleagues in the Vice-Chancellor's Office, helped organize the presentation of data and produced the tables and graphs. Ms Celestyna Galicki undertook some useful initial data work. Susan McDowell-Watts, my executive assistant, has helped to keep my library affairs in tolerable order. She has also provided patient, expert assistance in arranging travel and finding time in my diary to finish this book. Work on this project has been assisted greatly by the University of Auckland Library. I have made very full use its rich resources and have benefited from an exceedingly liberal interpretation of its borrowing policy. Staff members have responded with courteous efficiency to requests to purchase recently published books and to secure older ones on inter-loan. These debts are general but I particularly wish to acknowledge the sustained assistance of Simona Traser, the arts subject librarian, and Mathew Morton from Interloans.

When undertaking archival and library research in England and Scotland I have benefited greatly from the kindly professionalism of archivists and librarians at a number of county records offices and research libraries. I wish to record my thanks to staff at the Cambridgeshire Records Office, Cambridge University Library, the Derbyshire Records Office, the Devonshire Country Records Office, Dundee City Archives, the Hampshire Records Office, the Suffolk Records Office, Ipswich, the Somerset Heritage Centre, the West Sussex Records Office, the Wiltshire and Swindon History Centre, Keele University Library, The United Kingdom National Archives at Kew, the British Library, the Caird Library at the National Maritime Museum, the Library of the Museum of the Royal Navy, Portsmouth, the National Library of Scotland and the National War Museum of Scotland, Edinburgh. As in the past, I am grateful to the Warden and Fellows of Robinson College, Cambridge, for accommodating me in college when I worked in Cambridge and to Mr Colin Barnes, the head porter, for making the arrangements. I have been most fortunate to be given access to manuscript material in three private archives and to quote from these papers. I must thank the Marquis of Lansdown for allowing me to read typescripts of some of Lord Keith's letters at Bowood House and to Ms Jo Johnston, the Bowood archivist, for her most courteous and helpful assistance in arranging my visit to Bowood. I am most grateful to the Duke of Northumberland for granting me access to papers relating to Sir John Duckwork and Sir Edward Pellew at Alnwick Castle. Dr Christopher Hunwick, the Alnwick archivist, offered very valuable advice in advance of my visit and he and his assistant, Isabel Keating, were most helpful during the course of it. I have also consulted the papers of Sir Hyde Parker in the archive at Melford Hall, Suffolk. Sir Richard Parker very kindly allowed me access to this material and permission to quote from it. Sir Richard and Lady Parker's generous hospitality made my visit a particular pleasure. Dr Lyn Boothman, the archivist, was most helpful in arranging the visit to Melford Hall and identifying material of interest to me. Finally, I am grateful to the National Library of Scotland, Edinburgh, the National Maritime Museum, Greenwich, the National Galleries of Scotland and the West Sussex Record Office, Chichester, for permission to reproduce illustrative material from their collections.

Over the past few years I have contacted private individuals for help in securing publications and other materials, and for advice. I am most grateful to Peter Hopkins of the Merton Historical Society, Bob Braid of the Milton-on-Sea Historical Record Society and Alan Green of the Murray Club, Chichester, for their prompt and most helpful responses. Daphne Austin most obligingly supplied me with the text of her lecture on admirals from Lymington. Elsie Ritchie of Ermington, New South Wales, a descendent of Vice Admiral Moriarty, invited me to her home and gave me a copy of material from her work on the family relevant to my book. Dr N. A. M. Rodger of All Souls, Oxford, kindly clarified a query on Admiralty papers. Finally, my former colleague Professor Glyn Parry of Roehampton University kept me company when I was batching at Kew and most kindly followed up on a couple of details from papers in the National Archives. I would also like to record my thanks to Dr James Gazzard and Paul Ireland of the Institute of Continuing Education at the University of Cambridge, Alan Green from the Murray Club, Chichester, Katrina Duncan and Andrew Long of Auckland University Press, for their help in securing some of images for this book.

My old friends and colleagues Colin Davis and Jonathan Scott have generously set aside time from their own work to read earlier drafts of all the substantive chapters of this book. I am most grateful to them for their warm encouragement and incisive criticism. Mark Francis, an old friend and collaborator, kindly loaned me a rare book on the mutinies of 1797 and encouraged my work on this project.

It has been a pleasure to work with the History team at Bloomsbury Academic. Frances Arnold was initially encouraging about the project and passed it on to Emily Drewe when she returned to her role as History editor. Emily and her assistant Beatriz Lopez have been very helpful and efficient. I have benefitted greatly from the advice of the Press's readers who helped me shape the project and have saved me from numerous blunders. The errors that remain are my own responsibility.

My wife Diana, who has lived with this book for a number of years, has been of inestimable help in bringing it to fruition. She allowed me to sacrifice part of an English holiday in archives and libraries and lent her significant research and critical skills to the cause. Di has read many drafts of all the chapters with a sympathetic but sharp eye, helped draft the biographical notes, and accommodated my absence on research trips and virtual absence on weekends with good humour. When our daughter asked her to tell me that 'that book will not look after you when you're old', she passed on the comment but tactfully refrained from endorsing it.

John Morrow
Auckland, New Zealand
July 2017.

Abbreviations

The following abbreviations are used in the endnotes. Full details of titles appear in the Bibliography.

Aspinall, *Correspondence of George III* (Aspinall, ed., *Later Correspondence*)
Barham Papers (Laughton, ed., *Letters and Papers ... Barham*)
Blockade of Brest (Leyland, ed., *Dispatches and Letters ... Blockade*)
Channel Fleet (Morriss, ed., *Channel Fleet ... Brest*)
Clowes, *History* (Clowes et al., *The Royal Navy: A History*)
Collingwood's Correspondence (Hughes, ed., *Private Correspondence ... Collingwood*)
Keith Papers (Perrin, ed., *Letters ... Keith*)
Markham's Letters (Markham, ed., *The Correspondence of ... Markham*)
Martin's Letters (Hamilton, ed., *Letters and Papers of ... Martin*)
MM (*Mariners' Mirror*)
Nicolas, *Dispatches* (Nicolas, ed., *Dispatches ... Nelson*)
NRS (Publications of the Navy Records Society)
ODND (Matthews, ed., *Oxford Dictionary of National Biography*)
Rodger, *Command* (Rodger, *Command of the Sea*)
Saumarez Papers (Ryan, ed., *Saumarez Papers ... Baltic*)
Spencer Papers (Corbett, ed., *Private Papers ... Spencer*)
St Vincent's Letters (Bonner-Smith, ed., *Letters ... St Vincent*)
Tracy, *Naval Chronicle* (Tracy, ed., *Naval Chronicle*)

Introduction

From early 1793 until mid-1815 Britain was almost always at war.[1] France was the principal and persistent enemy, with significant support from Spain and Holland, and Denmark and Russia playing cameo roles at sea. A range of European allies and victims of French arms, including Austria, Prussia, Russia and Sweden, did much of the heavy lifting in the land wars in Europe. The first major phase of this protracted and bloody conflict, the 'French Revolutionary Wars', ended on 1 October 1801, although the Treaty of Amiens was not concluded until late March 1802. The second stage, the Napoleonic Wars, which began on 18 May 1803, coincided with Napoleon Bonaparte's reign as emperor of France. In mid-1812 Britain also stumbled into a war with the United States that continued after the emperor's abdication in the spring of 1814. War against Napoleonic France resumed briefly on 1 March 1815 before coming to a decisive end a hundred days later at Waterloo. Although these wars originated in Europe, the global interests of the European powers ensured hostilities engulfed their colonies and other dependences in the East and West Indies, South America and southern Africa. The Royal Navy was involved in all theatres and in the final act of Napoleon's career. The captain of a British man-of-war took him on board after his flight from Waterloo, and he remained in the custody of the Royal Navy while his fate was determined. Then, one of its ships conveyed him to final exile at St Helena.

The Navy's numerous fleets and home ports were under the command of senior officers who held 'flag' rank. They were usually admirals but might sometimes be 'commodores', a rank that lasted only for a particular appointment. Commanders-in-chief reported to the lords commissioners of the Admiralty in London (known variously as the 'Admiralty Board', 'Admiralty' or just 'the Board'). Three of the five commissioners were either senior captains or admirals. The Board was headed by the 'first lord' who was a member of the Ministry. He was often a civilian politician but during the war two admirals headed the Board, John Jervis, Earl St Vincent, from 1801 to 1804, and Charles Middleton, Lord Barham, from 1805 to 1806.

Flag officers were recruited through periodic promotions from the officers at the top of the post captains' list. The system was heavily governed by considerations of seniority, although, as we shall see, there were significant and persistent exceptions. Over the course of their careers, these men had moved with very variable rates of rapidity through the lower ranks of commissioned officers, serving as lieutenants and (masters and) commanders. Admirals were organized in four hierarchically ordered ranks, headed by an admiral of the fleet. Four men held this rank during the French Wars, all of whom were elderly and saw no active service. There were three other flag ranks: 'admiral', 'vice admiral' and 'rear admiral', each subdivided in descending seniority into Red, White and Blue squadrons.[2] When admirals were appointed to a fleet or a port, they were ordered to hoist the flag designated to their rank and squadron on their 'flag' ship. At the end of their appointment they received orders to 'strike' their flags and 'go ashore'.

A few senior captains received commissions as 'superannuated rear admirals'. They were entitled to the half-pay of a rear admiral and were not liable for employment on active service or for promotion. In common parlance and in newspaper reports, these officers were, like their colleagues on the active list, often referred to as 'admiral'. Formally, these officers were rear admirals 'in general terms', that is, without designation to a squadron.[3] Informally within the service, and probably also among those acquainted with its ways, they were jokingly assigned to the 'yellow squadron', a reference to complexions ravaged by harsh climates, old age and illness and not an imputation of timidity in the face of the enemy.

Depending on the size and frequency of promotions, flag officers moved more or less quickly up through the divisions and ranks on the basis of seniority. On each promotion they received a new commission, for which they paid a fee (£2 12sh 6d between squadrons and £5 7sh 6d when they stepped up a rank) for the legal stamp attached to the document.[4] Officers of a given rank received the same pay, regardless of the squadron to which they belonged, but each step in rank involved a significant increase in pay. Admirals' pay was twice that of rear admirals, with vice admirals sitting on the midpoint of this scale.[5] Senior captains usually gained flag rank as rear admirals of the Blue but if particularly large promotions occurred, the more senior of them could be appointed directly to the white squadron. All admirals, vice admirals and rear admirals were regarded formally as being on the 'active' list, whether employed or not. This designation meant that they were eligible for appointment as a commander-in-chief, or as a subordinate flag officer. Flag officers who did not hold an appointment at sea or in a port were described officially as being 'unemployed'. They received a proportion of full pay, denoted as 'half-pay' but amounting to rather more than that after an increase was approved in 1802.[6]

The French Wars had a profound impact on the career prospects of post captains and admirals. If these wars had not occurred, most of those on the captains' list at the beginning of 1793 would have faced a painfully long wait to become rear admiral, and those who already held flag rank would have had to resign themselves to a very slow progression to the crowning dignity of full admiral. At the start of the French Wars in 1793 the admirals' list numbered only 49, but after the big valedictory promotion of 1814 it stood at 223.[7] Over the course of the wars, 323 officers were promoted to flag rank. Those who were already admirals in 1793, or were promoted in the first two years of the wars, enjoyed unprecedented advancement through the ranks as a result of frequent and often large promotions. Adam Duncan and Sir John Jervis, flag officers since 1787, waited until 1793 to be made vice admirals but were admirals by 1795. Some promotions reached deep down into the captains' list. The average for wartime promotions was twenty-eight positions, but in 1799 and 1804 the Board reached down more than fifty places on the list.[8] In the Revolutionary Wars newly promoted rear admirals had between thirty-one and sixteen years of service as post captains with an average of twenty and a half and a median of just under nineteen years. By the Napoleonic Wars the average had dropped below twenty years and the range had reduced greatly from twenty-two and two-thirds to seventeen years of service as post captain.[9] Not only were many more officers promoted during the wars, but those who were moved more quickly through the flag ranks. Thus William Cornwallis was promoted directly into the White Squadron in early 1793 and was an admiral six years later. So too was Sir Alan Gardner who became a rear admiral of the Blue in the same year. This rate of advancement was unusually fast but even the wartime cohort that advanced at the slowest rate (that of 1801) took less than thirteen and a half years to move through the flag ranks. Some officers who had not even been post captains at the end of the American War were admirals of the Blue by 1814.

But while the wars provided radically enhanced opportunities for promotion to flag rank, they did not produce proportionate increases in the number of 'active' appointments. This imbalance meant that as the wars progressed an increasingly large majority of flag officers were 'unemployed', residing ashore on half pay. Some admirals had no desire to take up active duties, but there was still sharp competition for employment and the material and honorific rewards that might flow from it. As we shall see, a significant number of men lost out in this competition and though *in* the flag-officer cadre and formally holders of commissions on the 'active' list, were only nominally *of* it.

This book draws on aspects of the careers of a relatively wide range of flag officers to explore their professional attitudes, ambitions, anxieties and interactions during a period of protracted and often desperate warfare. While many admirals longed to establish their reputations by commanding brilliant 'fleet actions', these opportunities were very few and far between. Flag officers commanded at sea in fifteen actions during the wars, only ten of which were large scale.[10] Of these ten battles, six resulted in conclusive victories. Less than 10 per cent of wartime admirals fought in these actions. The last really significant fleet action occurred in early 1806, nine years before the wars ended. This did not mean, however, that the Navy ceased to be important. To the contrary, the gross tonnage of its forces reached its peak in 1809 and remained at about 90 per cent of that level until the end of the wars.[11] It was engaged throughout the period in persistent and extensive blockading, trade protection and amphibious and army support operations that were critical in defeating Napoleonic France.[12]

Since few flag officers commanded fleets or divisions in battle, it was exceedingly rare for them to die from, or suffer, serious wounds. Nelson was the only admiral to fall to enemy fire and it is significant that he was at the centre of four of the major fleet actions. Rear Admirals George Bowyer and Thomas Pasley lost legs during the Battle of the First of June 1794 and Rear Admirals Sir Thomas Troubridge and Robert Reynolds were drowned on service during the Napoleonic War. A handful of other flag officers (including Cuthbert, Lord Collingwood, Sir Charles Cotton, Lord Hugh Seymour, Sir Samuel Hood and Sir John Laforey) died of natural causes while on, or returning from, active service. By and large, however, Admirals were far more likely to die in their beds at home, or in a watering place such as Cheltenham or Bath, than on board their flagship.

Although admirals rarely experienced the personal dangers and leadership challenges of fleet action, the reality of their lives on active service was in many ways more persistently taxing on the body and the mind. Commanding fleets blockading enemy ports posed severe tests of flag officers' seamanship, fleet management and logistical skills. It was also extremely physically and psychologically demanding. Blockades reduced but did not eliminate the threat to British merchant shipping around the globe. The 'protection of the trade' was a particularly onerous responsibility of flag officers in the seas around Britain's West and East Indian possessions, the Atlantic fisheries, the Channel approaches and the Baltic. Finally, admirals were involved throughout the wars in joint operations with land forces and, as British troops took on Napoleon's armies in Spain and Portugal, in supporting armies ashore. To this awesome range of operational activities were added those arising from flag officers' diplomatic responsibilities and the perpetual logistical challenges of keeping fleets at sea. Even their routine administrative duties were onerous and pressing. The pressures under which admirals worked was exacerbated by the expectations of superiors and inferiors within the service, the professional and political imperatives of Admiralty Boards and governments, and exposure to organs of public opinion that were quick to applaud and even quicker to condemn. After the initial stages of the wars, when major commands had been held by elderly flag officers whose understanding of their role reflected past practices, the demands placed on admirals on active service increased as a new ethos of discipline, fleet management and personal vigour emerged. At the beginning of the war Captain Cuthbert Collingwood wrote as if there had been a falling-off from past standards but his more senior colleague Sir John Jervis had been critical of the energy and focus of his superiors since the late 1770s.[13] An increase in urgency was to be expected in the move from war to peace but the need for it became an article of widely shared and declaimed faith in the Revolutionary and Napoleonic Wars.

This book focuses on a range of important aspects of flag officers' lives. Partly because the major naval actions of the period have been subject to such close attention, and also because, as indicated in the previous paragraphs, they occupied so little of the professional lives of admirals, they are considered here only in relation to their impact on career aspirations and professional interactions. Although some indicative aggregate data is summarized in figures and tables and referred to in the text, the book does not attempt to offer a comprehensive treatment of those on the flag officers' list. However, many of the officers discussed here were prominent in their profession and immersed fully in it for significant periods of the wars. They were exposed to the physical and psychological demands of naval high command, grappled with its logistical and disciplinary challenges and with intra-service tensions prompted by these demands and by personal and professional rivalries. They were well-positioned to shape the careers of their subordinates through the disposal of 'interest' derived from patronage and from their standing in the service, and shared ambitions for 'honourable and profitable' employment and material and honorific recognition from the state. From time to time, their experience is contrasted with those of more obscure and less successful admirals.

Over the course of the two wars, 49 pre-war admiral whose post rank dated back to 1737 were joined in the flag ranks by 323 officers who had been appointed post captains between 1762 and 1795.[14] Age on promotion (which depended almost entirely on when post rank was gained) varied greatly but there was a tendency for it to drop as the wars progressed.[15] The oldest wartime appointees, Robert McDougall (72 years), Smith Child (70 years), Thomas Hicks and John Hunter (69 years), had delayed starts to their careers as commissioned officers. McDougall did not become a lieutenant until he was 30, while Hunter had extensive service as a master's mate and master before gaining a lieutenant's commission. Henry Hotham, Alan Gardner (the younger), Thomas Martin and Richard King were at the other end of the range. Early promotion to post captain and a career span that was well-aligned with the wars saw them achieve flag rank in their mid-to-late thirties. The overwhelming majority of wartime promotions, however, benefited officers of between 40 and 50 years of age.

A recent analysis of a large random sample of all commissioned naval officers during this period shows about 3 per cent of their fathers were titled, 18 per cent were landed gentry, 45 per cent were members of the professional classes and 27 per cent engaged in business and commerce. However, an earlier study suggests that those from the upper classes of late Georgian society were over-represented in flag ranks – 45 per cent of the 131 peers' sons who entered the Navy in 1793–1815 had attained flag rank by 1849, with figures of 34 per cent of 85, 21 per cent of 494 and 22 per cent of 899 for the sons of baronets, landed gentry and professional men. Moreover, 18 per cent of those whose fathers were in business and commerce became admirals but their numbers (71) were small relative to those from other classes.[16] Of the officers considered in this study, 9 were the sons of peers. Three (Collingwood, Rear Admiral Sir Thomas Troubridge and Vice Admiral Sir George Murray) came from business and commercial backgrounds, with the balance having fathers in the professions. St Vincent (whose father was a lawyer), Nelson, Sir John Duckworth and Sir Richard Keats (minor clergy), Admiral Sir James Saumarez (a doctor) and Admiral Sir Hyde Parker (an admiral) reflect the range of professional backgrounds from which flag officers sprang. These distributions are entirely unexceptional given the role of patronage in late Georgian society. Influence ('interest') derived directly or indirectly from politics played a significant role in advancing commissioned officers' careers and so the prospects of reaching flag rank were likely to be better for those whose fathers came from titled and landed gentry backgrounds. Clergymen often had personal and family connections with those above them in the social hierarchy, while parents in the military and civil services were also likely to have political links that would assist their sons' careers. As we shall see, those with fathers and close relatives in the Navy were able to benefit from the consideration paid to 'sons of the service'.[17]

The book opens with a chapter that sets the working context in which flag officers operated and considers the extraordinary demands placed on them. It sketches the roles they performed on active service and the professional and political pressures they faced. As the wars progressed, the ethos of the upper echelons of the service evolved to take account of these demands. Chapter 2 examines flag officers' understanding of their authoritative role in the service, their ideas on how this authority was to be exercised and the personal dispositions that were necessary to maintain it. It was a paradox of the wartime service that burgeoning numbers of admirals and keen competition between them did not always generate confidence about the supply of flag officers with the required levels of strategic and managerial competence and mental strength. These reservations notwithstanding, outright failures were rare. In a few cases, however, extreme anxiety demotivated and demoralized otherwise competent officers, or serious failures of judgement brought careers to premature, and sometimes, ignominious conclusions. Chapter 3 considers a number of such cases.

Although the disciplinary ethos of the Navy laid great stress on obedience to superiors, flag officers did not always sit quiet under the authority of the Admiralty Board, and they, in their turn, sometimes faced challenges from their subordinates. Chapter 4 looks at a range of significant clashes that occurred between commanders-in-chief, subordinate flag officers and their captains, while chapter 5 considers some flag officers' fractious relationships with the first lord of the Admiralty. Actual or perceived insubordination of those at the head of the service was seen by senior officers as threats to the entire fabric of naval discipline. These views gained apparent credence from serious mutinies that occurred in the late 1790s. Chapter 6 discusses flag officers' responses to these threats to their authority and to the overall discipline of the service.

Admirals' professional achievements and reputations were important assets when advancing their careers and those of others. These matters are considered in chapters 7–10. Increased opportunities for promotion, employment and the riches and honours that might result from active service enhanced the Navy's value in the Georgian patronage network. Flag officers were both clients and patrons, advancing the careers of their 'friends' through interest derived from personal, familial and political connections, and benefitting from the exercise of other players' interest. However, the distinctive skills and temperament necessary for naval leadership meant that patronage imperatives had to be integrated to some degree with the needs and values of the Navy. This requirement was facilitated by the deployment of 'service interest'. Interest derived from the patronage system and from within the service had a role in advancing the career of flag officers as well as their clients. Ambitious admirals sought to secure 'honourable and advantageous' employment that accorded with their sense of worth, provided ongoing access to prize money and opportunities to distinguish themselves, and laid the groundwork for further recognition and rewards, including royal honours, sinecure appointments and pensions.

Admirals' lives were divided between the time spent afloat on active service and the often far more extensive periods when they were unemployed and lived ashore on half pay. Indeed, a significant number of flag officers were never employed as admirals and spent their entire careers ashore. Aspects of these phases of admirals' lives are explored in the last two chapters. Chapter 11 considers the distinctive domestic economy of admirals afloat and the role this played in creating a social-professional environment providing opportunities for companionship that allayed to some degree the separation from their family and friends ashore. It thus supplemented the physically remote but emotionally treasured family life sustained through correspondence. When admirals struck their flags and went ashore, they resumed their place in their families and the niche in the social hierarchy from which they sprang, or to which they had been elevated through ennoblement, fortunate marriages or timely inheritances. Even in a material sense, however, their lives and status were influenced significantly by their naval careers. Fortunes gained through prize money, and comfortable provisions from pensions and sinecures, made it possible for some flag officers to buy landed estates and London townhouses, and to live in a style to which they had not been born. But while the lives of admirals ashore were similar in many respects to those of other men of their ascribed or achieved social status, they remained subject to the requirements of the service, and could also continue to actively sustain connections that had developed over the course of their careers.

1

The Challenge of Command

*I will endeavor to get through the various duties of this extensive command as well
as I can, but my Eyes begin already to fail me from the Constant Correspondence
I am obliged to keep and the details of the wants and defects of the different ships as
well as the completing them as far as our resources extend.*
— Sir Charles Cotton, Mediterranean Fleet, to Charles Yorke,
First Lord of the Admiralty, October 1810[1]

The *Regulations and Instructions Relating to His Majesty's Service at Sea* (1806) specified the responsibilities of commanders-in-chief in broad but emphatic terms. They
were required to report to the Admiralty on the condition of their ships and maintain
them in a state of 'readiness', acknowledge the Board's orders, pass on intelligence and
not resign their command or quit their station without permission unless suffering
from debilitating ill health. When serving as port admirals they were responsible for
the defence of the port, and the 'speedy and perfect equipment of all Ships, and ... the
punctual execution of all Orders'. The *Regulations* made it clear that maintaining discipline was a fundamental background condition of naval efficiency and a primary duty
of flag officers. They were expected to give 'most implicit obedience to their Orders',
discharge their duties with the 'utmost zeal and alacrity' and provide an example of
'morality, regularity and good Order'.[2]

During the French Wars these imperatives applied to a range of highly demanding
duties: maintaining blockades; pursuing enemy fleets at sea with a view to bringing
them to battle; assisting the army in support of amphibious expeditions against enemy
positions; protecting convoys; harassing and destroying the maritime trade of the
enemy; policing ostensibly neutral shipping; and, in many cases, performing front-line
roles in Great Britain's diplomatic representation. The scope of these responsibilities
varied widely. Sometimes, as on the Irish station in the 1790s, commanders defended
the coast and the trade with a dozen ships.[3] At the other end of the spectrum, the naval
commander of the Scheldt expedition in 1809 had 266 armed ships and 352 transports under his command.[4] Key commands (the Channel and Mediterranean and from
time to time the North Sea) almost always employed three or four subordinate flag
officers. Significant variations on these and other stations reflected the number of ships
deployed and shifting strategic significance. Thus Earl St Vincent had ten admirals

under him in the Channel Fleet in 1800, and at the height of the war with the United States in 1814–15 six admirals and two commodores were employed in Sir Alexander Cochrane's enlarged North American command. By contrast, Sir William Parker served alone on that station in 1800 and Sir Richard Kingsmill and Lord Gardner were usually the only flag officers on the Irish command in the Revolutionary Wars.

Weighty responsibilities did not mean that admirals ignored other, apparently minor, matters. St Vincent's blood pressure climbed when he saw officers momentarily tipping their hats to their superiors and inferiors rather than lifting them properly.[5] He believed such casual disregard for the outward signs of respect set a poor example and weakened the fabric of discipline within the service. When Lord Keith commanded in the North Sea he instructed captains on the issue of beer, and on preventing damage to decks when splitting wood for the galley fire.[6] Admiral Lord Gambier responded to complaints that sailors of the Channel Fleet had stolen apples at Paignton by ordering captains to enquire into the matter.[7] When Sir John Warren commanded the North American Squadron during the war with the United States, he was ordered by the Admiralty to instruct his captains *not* to require their crews to scour iron work on their ships. These useless chores distracted the men from more important tasks and 'cannot fail to harass and disgust the Seamen of His Majesty's Navy'. The Board instructed Warren to ensure that this direction was seen to come from the captains rather than from him.[8]

This chapter will provide a context for the aspects of admirals' professional lives discussed later in the book by considering the major ongoing challenges they faced on active service. These challenges arose from the logistical demands of keeping fleets at sea under wartime conditions, from interservice operations, overarching disciplinary responsibilities and flag officers' roles as diplomatic representatives.

Physical and mental challenges

Many flag officers embarked on demanding wartime appointments at a time when age and ill health had already begun to erode their physical resilience. A range of age-related maladies hindered Earl Howe's and Lord Bridport's service in the Channel Fleet in the 1790s. Howe suffered persistently from general ill health and was particularly concerned about his increasing deafness, and by 1794 Bridport was so crippled by gout he doubted whether he could continue in service: 'I have so much pain in my hands, that I find difficulty in holding my pen, and so much in my Hip, that I can with difficulty turn in my bed, or walk when I am out of it.'[9] St Vincent was plagued by inflammation of the eyes and circulatory malfunctions that swelled his legs. When Lord Spencer praised his powers of exertion in mid-1799, he responded that they were 'unhappily ... sapped to the very foundation, by such a rapid decline of health, as to bereave me of all powers, both of body and mind'.[10] Lord Duncan was credited with having an iron constitution but his health gave way in the closing stages of his North Sea command.[11] Nelson reported that Sir John Orde was a 'martyr to the gout', which might in part explain his irascibility.[12] Lord Keith suffered from a persistent gastric disorder and Lord Collingwood struggled through his Mediterranean command afflicted by the symptoms of an increasingly debilitating undiagnosed stomach cancer. In the later stages of his second North American command, Sir John Warren's struggles with the Americans and the Admiralty Board took place against a background of failing health, with rheumatism and optical dysfunction being particularly troubling.[13] Nelson's severe wounds adversely affected his general health and weakened his capacity to withstand the rigours of service at sea. Other flag officers shared his fate. Sir Thomas Pasley and Admiral Bowyer both lost legs on the Glorious First of June, and by the time Sir Richard Keats was in his early fifties, wounds and the rigours of prolonged service so undermined his physical constitution that he had to go ashore to restore his health.

If elderly admirals were particularly vulnerable to the unavoidable physical demands of service at sea, all flag officers had to face the remorseless mental challenges arising from it. As we shall see, St Vincent was particularly attuned to these demands and regarded the capacity to cope with them as the touchstone of effective leadership. Though Collingwood passed these tests with flying colours, he felt the extreme strains that arose from them. As a subordinate flag officer commanding the inshore squadron off Brest he slept fitfully in his clothes for days on end, acutely aware of his responsibility for keeping constant watch on more than twenty large French ships in the port: 'an anxious time I have of it, what with tides and rocks, which have more of danger in them than a battle once a week.' Duty of this kind was demanding, dull and dangerous. St Vincent thought well of Sir James Saumarez but he told Spencer that he felt the strain of commanding off Brest and had grown 'thin as a shotten heron.'[14] His commanding officer suffered too. St Vincent's mental fragility, manifest in the blindly self-righteous vehemence of his correspondence with subordinates and the Board, no doubt reflected the pressures he faced in both his Mediterranean and Channel commands.[15] Sir Alan Gardner's spells as Bridport's deputy in the Channel command also exacted a heavy toll. Rear Admiral Berkeley reported that when Gardner came into Plymouth in July 1799, 'I never saw him so low & dejected, and absolutely grown a skeleton with vexation.'[16] Despite the best efforts of Berkeley and other friends, Gardner languished in low spirits for several weeks. The impact of mental stress on Admiral Cornwallis's well-being and personal and professional relationships was even more marked. Early in the Napoleonic War his successful deployment of the Channel Fleet won plaudits from the public and the profession. In the third year of his command, however, when there was significant political comment on the efficacy of year-round blockades, Cornwallis's relationships with the Admiralty and his colleagues deteriorated sharply. By late 1805 he was exhibiting signs of manic depression. As his protégé Captain John Whitby graphically put it, '[O]n one side of him he is a Sun, shining in all its splendor and possessing all that Blazed Brilliancy of Quality in Heart, Soul and Body – on the other an Eclipse clouded with all its Darkness and Obscurity, from which no Ray is emitted that can afford Consolation or clear the vapourish and disordered Atmosphere.'[17]

As the war progressed, a number of flag officers – Sir Alexander Cochrane in the West Indies, Vice Admiral Peter Rainier in the East Indies and Nelson and Collingwood in the Mediterranean, for example – held long-running commands and often spent months, and sometimes years, at sea. In the mid-1790s Bridport had complained of having to serve ten weeks at sea in the Channel and being without 'a clean shirt upon my Back, or a Morsel of Fresh Meat to place on my Table'. He also expressed concerns about the health of the 10,000 men under his command.[18] The length of Bridport's spell at sea palled into insignificance against the experiences of Nelson, Collingwood and Keats. Nelson's letters from his last command report a number of milestones in a period of continual service at sea that finally extended to 720 days. Collingwood waited even longer for relief from this command. Having taken over on Nelson's death in late October 1805, he did not relinquish it for four and a half years. He had asked to be relieved in 1808, but when Lord Mulgrave said he could not be spared Collingwood declined to act on the suggestion that he should command from ashore.[19] Keats's extended sea service was a direct consequence of his very strong reputation and the Duke of Clarence's patronage. He served nine continuous years at sea through promotion to post captain, commodore and rear admiral.[20]

Eighteenth-century drinking habits posed a threat to the health and temper of sea officers, as they did to other members of the population. Flag officers invariably purchased large quantities of wine and spirits, though as they were expected to entertain other officers on a regular basis that is not necessarily a reliable guide to their personal intake.[21] Some admirals were notably abstemious. Nelson drank very little, and Cornwallis mitigated the effect of tropical climates by avoiding wine and spirituous liquor.[22] It would not be surprising, however, if some flag officers resorted to the bottle in an attempt to relieve stress and blunt the pain of separation from their families. If St Vincent is to be believed, and alcohol abuse was a major issue among junior officers at sea, many of the dipsomaniacal may have succumbed to liver disease or ruined their careers before they came in range of promotion to the flag.[23] It is unclear how far flag officers in general merited the disdainful comment that Lord Keith passed on Rear Admiral John McBride, commanding in Scotland: he was 'seldom himself after dinner, besides opinionated and ill-tempered.'[24] Vice Admiral Sir Richard Onslow, who served with distinction as Duncan's second at Camperdown, was reputed to be 'too fond of his grog' but that seemed to reflect a low tolerance for alcohol and a love of company rather than the morose overindulgence hinted at by Keith.[25] Drink was not the only source of risk arising from flag officers' dining habits. There is no indication that Vice Admiral Peter Rainier drank to excess, but the attractions of East Indian cuisine may have shortened his life. He was so obese that it was not possible to remove a festering abscess in his thigh.[26]

As noted earlier, flag officers were forbidden to quit their commands without permission except in cases of extreme illness. Given the demands of commanding at sea and the impact that serious ill health would have on a flag officer's ability to deal with them, it is not surprising that requests to be relieved appear quite often in correspondence of first lords and flag officers. Howe, Bridport, Cornwallis, Gardner, Rear Admiral Robert Man, St Vincent, Sir George Berkeley, Nelson and Collingwood all asked to come ashore to recover their health. Rear Admiral George Murray sought prior approval on the grounds that he might have already succumbed by the time a response reached him on the other side of the world.[27] This was a wise precaution because, unless the Admiralty had other reasons for wishing to recall flag officers, such as lacklustre service, or a pressing need to find employment for a particularly well-connected admiral, it was often slow and reluctant to respond to these requests.

First lords complained of the small pool of real talent available to them, and they were probably unwilling to face the logistical difficulties of replacing effective senior officers unless it was absolutely necessary. It also seems likely that the Board might have reasoned that the impulse prompting a request for recall could well have passed before it came to their attention.

Ships, provisions and manning

Flag officers were expected to pay close attention to the condition of the vessels under their command and to ensuring their 'readiness', that is, that they were provisioned, manned and ready for whatever service might be required. Wooden men-of-war, highly vulnerable to wear and tear, needed constant attention and frequent refits with the annual maintenance bills for a first rate ship running at about 40 per cent of its construction costs.[28] Sir James Saumarez's *Caesar* had thirteen topmasts carried away in the Channel between February 1798 and June 1799, and Collingwood reported in 1805 that a cruise on that station 'disabled five large ships'.[29] Blockade service was particularly punishing since it involved frequently repeated evolutions that taxed hulls, spars and rigging far more than prolonged runs of ocean sailing. After several years' service in the Channel Fleet and overseeing the blockade of Brest, Sir Robert Calder formed the view that ships should not be at sea for more than four months. St Vincent thought that a ship should not be kept in close blockade during winter weather for more than six weeks.[30] Errors in human judgement and inexperience compounded the unavoidable impact of natural forces and the hazards of operating in very demanding conditions. In the state of perpetual high dudgeon that marked his final command, St Vincent reported to Rear Admiralty Markham of the Admiralty Board that 'if we continue to throw away topmasts at this rate the forests of the north will not furnish an adequate supply. There is a great lack of seamanship in the service'.[31]

Commanders-in-chief worked with officials of the Navy Board and used their own initiative to ensure supplies of cordage, sails and spars and other ships' stores. They also organized the ships at their disposal in ways that allowed for the most battered to return to port for refits while ensuring that they commanded sufficient force to contend with the enemy. These deployments, which had to be integrated with the Admiralty's requirements to augment or reduce the resources available to particular commands-in-chief, meant flag officers had to manage streams of vessels leaving or joining the squadrons or divisions under their command. As a commander-in-chief, St Vincent claimed that some captains exaggerated the extent of damage to their ships to justify long spells in port, and carried this concern through to the Admiralty Board when he chaired it. He harassed his flag officers and captains, holding up Collingwood as an exemplar of rectitude, and pulled no punches in characterizing the approach required: it involved a 'painful employment of *Negro driving*'. By his last spell as commander-in-chief in 1806–1807, St Vincent specified a six-day turnaround for victualing, watering and paying crews in Cawsand Bay in Plymouth Sound, insisting that repairs should be made at sea or at anchorages off the coast whenever possible.[32] He enforced these requirements with characteristically authoritarian relish but the concerns that lay behind them were widely endorsed among the younger generation of flag officers, and practiced as a matter of course.[33] As Collingwood told a correspondent in 1805: 'In the middle of last month we put into Torbay, where we were a week; but the being in Torbay is no great relief, for no person or boat goes on shore. We visit our friends and neighbours in the fleet, but we have no communication with the rest of the world, without they come on board and take the chance of a cruise.'[34]

Under the hands of Spencer and St Vincent, the Navy began to resemble a high pressure system, with the demands of first lords and commanders-in-chief being transmitted to subordinate flag officers, and captains, and then down through their commissioned and non-commissioned officers. Intense pressure was also brought to bear on dockyard and victualing officials and members of other ancillary services. Thus when Rear Admiral John Purvis was preparing his ship for extended service off Ushant in the spring of 1800, he found it necessary to harass the Agent Victualler at Plymouth, his own purser and the naval commissioners so that affairs were settled without incurring his commander-in-chief's displeasure.[35] Four years later, when St Vincent was first lord, an Admiralty Minute pressed the port admiral at Plymouth and Sir Charles Cotton to brook no delays in ensuring ships rejoined Cornwallis's Channel Fleet. The minute prompted the commander-in-chief to pressurize Sir Thomas Graves, a subordinate flag officer, and to warn him and his captains that they would be answerable for any delay in leaving Plymouth.[36] When Sir John Warren insisted on waiting for the Board's notification that Sir Alexander Cochrane had been ordered to supersede him in command of the North American squadron in 1814, his successor (who had already arrived on the station with his commission) was careful to immediately report this difficulty to the Board. He regarded Warren's stance as obstructive and presented it in anticipatory exculpation of any career-limiting consequences that might have arisen from delays in launching an expedition against Portsmouth NH.[37]

Flag officers' obligations to ensure the readiness of their ships included responsibility for procuring and managing ships' stores, manning and provisioning. The first of these responsibilities seems to have fallen to subordinate flag officers. Thus as a junior rear admiral in the Mediterranean in 1799, Duckworth dealt with the issue of cables, and the acquisition of glass, grindstones, iron and lead sheets. He also authorized surveys on rat-eaten bread on transports and on the 'sour, thick, unwholesome' wine issued to unfortunate patients at the hospital at Gibraltar.[38] Manning issues generated significant volumes of paperwork as it was necessary to seek Admiralty confirmation of acting appointments and officers' requests for leaves of absence. While seamen were generally drafted in and out of ships in batches, it was not unusual for flag officers to be asked to order enquiry into the circumstances of individual recruits to the lower deck and discharge them if necessary.[39] Deaths in action, sickness, desertion, the rotation of ships for refit and the movement of officers and their followers from ship to ship exacerbated manning challenges.

A fleet, or even a division of a fleet, consumed huge quantities of food and drink, and if the ravages of scurvy were to be avoided, careful attention had to be paid to the nature, quality and condition of these victuals.[40] It was possible to supply the Channel and North Sea Fleets directly from British ports, although that required careful planning and juggling of ships of war and transports. Commanders-in-chief on more distant stations had to be constantly alert to the availability of supplies in local markets and the means of paying for and shipping them. Thus when St Vincent commanded on the Mediterranean station in 1796, he weighed up the relative merits of Sardinia and the Kingdom of Naples as sources for cattle, and took comfort from the thought that while the fragile peace with Spain lasted he might rely on that market for lemons and onions, both excellent sources of anti-ascorbic nutrition.[41] Keith, Nelson and Collingwood faced similar challenges and devoted considerable correspondence to meeting them. Keith paid minute attention to securing local food stuffs to supplement those supplied from England.[42] When Nelson commanded in the Mediterranean in 1804 the volume of correspondence on logistical and supply issues far outweighed that on strategic matters. It included letters on the sourcing and purchase of material to make replacement bedding for the crew of *Hindoustan* after theirs was lost when the ship was destroyed by fire, the purchase of 30,000 gallons of lemon juice from Messina and the health risks of substituting salt beef for fresh meat in the diet of prisoners of war.[43] Nelson realized that procurement needed to be systemized on this station and persuaded the Victualling Board to appoint an 'agent victualler afloat'.[44] With Lisbon closed to British ships in early 1808, Collingwood's fleet became heavily reliant on supplies from England but he looked to the Barbary states for fresh beef, and to Malta for wine and lemon juice. The exchange of information on securing, packing and shipping supplies is a significant component of Collingwood's correspondence with Rear Admiral Purvis, his most trusted subordinate flag officer.[45] When Saumarez commanded in the Baltic in 1808, the appalling physical condition of crews on Swedish ships alerted him to the risk of relying on local resources. Many supplies were not available and vast quantities had to be shipped from home. He managed to secure beef from Swedish sources, however, and captured a Danish island to ensure a reliable supply of fresh water.[46] Flag officers were closely engaged in the detailed arrangements for provisioning on their station. When Warren commanded at Halifax, he was involved in approving exchange rates, as well as the victuals being purchased. He was answerable to the Victualing Board in London for both sets of transactions and signed off on pages and pages of tenders of purchase, initialing each line.[47]

When admirals approved large payments for provisions and repairs, they risked exposure to significant personal financial liabilities. In 1809, for example, bills of close to £150,000 were drawn on the Victualling Board in the Mediterranean and West Indies, £200,000 in the East Indies and £50,000 on the small but very remote Brazil station.[48] Responsibility for payments rested with the officer who authorized them and was imposed through a legal device by which the Admiralty (usually acting on information from the Navy, Transport or Victualling Boards) set unresolved payments as an 'imprest' against pay, allowances and half pay. The legislative basis of this requirement was an Act for Wages and Pay of Certain Officers, 1795: 'Bills drawn for pay by any Officer will remain as a charge (or imprest) against him till his accounts or journals for the ship are passed.' The provisions of the act were incorporated in the *Regulations and Instructions* of 1806.[49] Settlement was supposed to occur annually but this part of the instruction was rarely complied with. It was the Board's general practice to withhold payment of all monies due to an officer regardless of the sum in question, or the magnitude of the arrears of pay and allowances. By these means it placed pressure on flag officers to settle outstanding business by ensuring that if they had a mind to wrangle, they did so at their own cost and inconvenience. There were few imprests in the early years but as more flag officers returned home from active service more of them had to contend with the Board's onerous accountability demands. Ten flag officers' half pay was subject to an imprest in 1803, more than the total for the entire Revolutionary War period. Thereafter, the annual figures rarely dropped below this level and climbed to more than a dozen in the closing years of the Napoleonic Wars. As at the conclusion of the earlier war, the numbers climbed when admirals gave up their commands and came ashore. Eighteen officers' half pay was remitted against outstanding charges in 1815.[50]

In some cases significant sums of money were at stake over transactions that had taken place years before. For example, Sir Hyde Parker faced a claim of £4,011 for Transport Board bills drawn at Jamaica in 1800 that not been settled until mid-1802.[51] During 1802–1805 Sir John Duckworth engaged in long-distance wrangling from Jamaica over a range of financial issues, including payments to local collaborators when he led the successful attack on Minorca in 1798. Not unreasonably, in this case, he pointed out that he could not have been expected to secure receipts in the course of an opposed landing. Duckworth's difficulties over disputed payments persisted until the closing stages of the war.[52] Nelson's commendable attention to the plight of the *Hindoustans* left him facing an imprest that took more than a year to resolve.[53] Sir Alexander Cochrane had a protracted correspondence with the Board in 1813 over an imprest of £750 incurred for wine supplied from a store ship on the Leeward Islands' Station in 1805.[54] Even mundane posts carried financial risk. In August 1808 Admiral Alymer faced an imprest arising from payments of £1,800 that he authorized when commanding the Sea Fencibles. He complained that although this was a very small sum relative to the total disbursements he authorized, his entire pay was being withheld.[55]

These sums paled into insignificance against claims made (but not ultimately pursued) against Vice Admiral Rainier during his prolonged command in the East Indies. In early 1803 he faced as an 'enormous' charge of £20,059 19sh 2d for unauthorized repairs to a ship damaged in action. Rainier was so rich he could have met this cost but the other person implicated in it (a lieutenant) certainly could not have done so. This officer had been acting under the orders of a maverick captain who had incurred these costs without any reference to his commander-in-chief.[56] Four years later, Rainier's retirement was disturbed by an even more extraordinary claim for all bills drawn against the Victualling Office during his command by the Indian victualing agent, the brother of Sir Alexander Cochrane. No cash figure was attached to the claim at this stage, but since six months' provisions for ships on the Molacca station included more than 60,000 pounds of biscuit, 50,000 pounds of meat and more than 50,000 pounds of flour, rice, peas, sugar and tea, the charge would have wiped out Rainier's quarter-million-pound fortune.[57]

Rainier dealt with demands that seemed to verge on the vexatious with remarkable equanimity. Lord Keith was far less patient with amounts that were trifling in relation to his fortune. In July 1807 he sent a closely written letter of twenty-two foolscap pages challenging an imprest against payments totaling £109 16sh 5d. A significant portion of this sum arose from agents' fees for the urgent purchase of 24,000 pairs of shoes in

1800 for sailors and soldiers on the Egypt Expedition. Keith complained bitterly of the Naval Board's injustice towards him and its failure to provide the Admiralty with a full account of the transactions: 'it is not possible for me to believe that, after a lapse of seven years, their Lordships will allow me to *be fined*, and *discredited* at the capricious will of the Navy Board.' Perhaps in retaliation against such language, the Board let the game run for a further year and three-quarters. By that time an admission on Keith's part had reduced the sum outstanding to just under £100. However, his unpaid arrears in pay and allowances had climbed to £2,000 and the interest foregone on what was due to him exceeded the sum in dispute. Finally, after further lengthy correspondence in March 1809, the Admiralty Board removed the imprest, believing 'after the most mature consideration that under all the circumstances of the case, his Lordship is entitled to this relief'.[58]

As Keith was known to place a particularly high value on his money and had already had prolonged correspondence with the Navy Board over the Palermo purchase, it is easy to see why he thought its actions were motivated by vexatious intransigence.[59] Both he and Vice Admiral Berkeley, who faced similar challenges to expenditure made as part of his diplomatic responsibilities at Lisbon in 1808–12, would doubtless have been provoked to further strong statements of outrage if they had known that imprests against St Vincent were removed within days.[60] Neither, however, suffered financial hardship as a result of these wrangles.[61] Keith's spectacular prize money made him exceedingly wealthy and Berkeley was a comfortably off younger son of the aristocracy. The case was so different for Rear Admiral Alymer that the Board made a rare exception to its practice of blocking all pay until an imprest had been settled. Having applied unsuccessfully for employment in late May 1805, Alymer wrote to the Admiralty Board two weeks later claiming that he was reduced to 'absolute Beggary' as a result of an outstanding imprest charge of £3,611 1sh 5d which prevented him drawing half pay. The Board gave some credence to these claims and indulged him to the extent of withholding only half of his half pay until the charge was cleared. Two-thirds of the outstanding sum was approved a month later, but when Aylmer subsequently attempted to come to a settlement with the Admiralty, he was met with the brusque response that his request 'cannot be complied with'.[62]

The challenges of interservice collaboration

A significant amount of the Navy's wartime work involved amphibious rather than purely maritime operations. These exercises required the coordination of disparate fighting and support units, and often culminated in opposed landings from ships' boats and flat-bottomed barges on open beaches and enemy ports.[63] Sometimes, as in early 1809 when Sir John Moore's army was forced to retreat to Coruna, the Navy managed difficult evacuations. The scale of some landings was vast, requiring armadas of small boats to ferry and land men, horses, artillery, munitions and supplies. When he served as a commodore under Lord Keith in the Mediterranean in 1801, Alexander Cochrane was given charge of the arrangements for landing Lieutenant General Sir Archibald Abercromby's troops and equipment on the coast of Egypt. His plans provided for 250 transports and flat-bottomed boats to carry the first wave of troops ashore, and for the supply of 20,000 pounds of bread and 15,000 pounds of meat per day to feed the entire expeditionary force.[64]

Military and logistical difficulties were compounded by interservice misunder-standings and antagonisms, exacerbated by unclear lines of command and in some cases by the need to work with allied forces with different strategic imperatives.[65] Tensions came to a head when expeditions ran into difficulties and gave rise to bitter *ad post hoc* disputes over the adequacy of planning and accusations of over-sanguine expectations or lukewarm commitment. Lord Hood clashed with Sir John Moore over command of the expedition against Corsica in early 1794 and was vili-fied by his army rival as being 'so false and unmanageable that it is impossible for any general to carry on service with him'.[66] Perhaps with this experience in mind, Lord Spencer was concerned whether Vice Admiral Sir John Laforey was capable of working with the army when an expedition to the West Indies was being planned in 1795–96.[67] Similar considerations informed St Vincent's thinking on who should partner General Stuart in attacking Minorca in late 1798. The general had many virtues, but was 'a niggard in his praise to the Navy, and there are few seaman who would work with him'. St Vincent suggested Commodore John Duckworth for the role on the telling grounds that he possessed 'a large share of forbearance, which he acquired under the high hand of Captain Fielding'.[68] This judgement was astute and Duckworth went on to take part in a range of successful amphibious operations. His interservice difficulties tended to be indirect and retrospective, arising from a perception that the Admiralty failed to ensure the Navy's rewards matched those of the Army. At Minorca, Duckworth was aggrieved that Stuart declined to make him a signatory to the capitulation.[69]

Keith and Abercromby's collaboration in the Mediterranean in late 1800 and early 1801 illustrated the risks of joint operations for flag officers' careers and the ways in which they could be managed. Keith complained to Spencer that 'the military seems to think they are so perfectly masters of our profession it is not easy to give them sat-isfaction however much it has been my study'.[70] The two commanders smoothed over animosities arising from an aborted attack on Cadiz in October of 1800 but not before news of it had reached London and raised questions about whether Keith should com-mand the naval forces in the Egyptian expedition.[71] Thomas Grenville complained to his brother about these squabbles while acknowledging that the ministry had lit-tle room for maneuver: 'With such commanders what hope is there of carrying on any operations to advantage? And yet where are we to find better?'[72] Henry Dundas seemed inclined to give Abercromby the option of working with Keith or asking for another flag officer to be appointed in his stead, but Spencer resisted the suggestion.[73] In the event, Keith and Abercromby worked together effectively in the planning and initial execution of the mission. Following the general's death in the early stages of the landing, however, Keith faced ongoing difficulties in working with his testy and less able successor, Major General Help-Hutchinson.[74] By the later stages of Collingwood's Mediterranean command, his experience of the army had driven him to exaspera-tion. He told Sir Charles Cotton, his second-in-command, that 'I have seen so much of expeditions that indeed I would never let a soldier out of England – they are dead weights on the necks of those who have to care for them'. Saumarez was pleased to be 'disembarked from so great a clog' when Sir John Moore's army left the Baltic.[75]

These millstones eventually dragged Sir Richard Strachan down to the nether regions of permanent unemployment. Early in his career Strachan had served with distinction on the North American station, and was a successful frigate captain in the early years of the Revolutionary War. While commanding a detached squadron in the Bay of Biscay in late 1805 he captured four French ships-of-the-line that had escaped after the Battle of Trafalgar. Although not present at that action, Strachan was included in a parliamentary vote of thanks to Collingwood and those who had survived it. He was made rear admiral in the Trafalgar promotion, and in January 1806 was voted a pension of £1,000pa and made a knight of the Bath. Strachan was continuously employed as a flag officer and was appointed in June 1809 to command the huge naval force to be used in the expedition against the island of Walcheren in the mouth of the Scheldt. The Earl of Chatham, a lieutenant general who had been first lord of the Admiralty in the early stages of the wars, commanded the land forces. The expedition, which has been seen as very ill timed, was a wretched failure.[76] By its latter stages relations between Chatham, who lacked energy and imagination, and Strachan, who had a violent temper and a foul mouth, were toxic. Historians of the expedition deemed neither of these commanders up to the job and 'conspicuously ill-matched'.[77] When Chatham sought to exonerate himself by blaming Strachan and the admiral replied in kind, his erstwhile colleague got by far the better of the exchange. One of his captains reported that Strachan 'slaved like a Dray Horse during the whole offensive operations on the Scheldt, but he never troubled his head about documents, being always more ready to accept blame than to prepare to meet accusation'.[78] As an experienced politician, Chatham knew how to defend his corner and although he felt obliged to give up his cabinet post as Master of Ordnance, his earldom was supported with lavish pensions. He was promoted general in 1812, and later became governor of Gibraltar. Strachan, although brave, energetic and able, was never employed again.

Cochrane was able to utilize his experience off the Egyptian coast when he commanded in the West Indies and North America in the later stages of the war. He avoided major disputes with the army but, like Duckworth before him, complained about the uneven distribution of rewards between the services.[79] This issue also ruffled Vice Admiral Berkeley's feathers when he supported Viscount Wellington's prolonged and fraught operations in the Peninsula from his command at Lisbon. Wellington was a demanding colleague and Berkeley prone to irascibility but they generally worked so well together that the Board sometimes thought the vice admiral too ready to commit resources in support of the army.[80] Towards the end of Berkeley's command, however, the hydra of interservice envy raised its ugly head. He noted acidly that the Navy's contribution to an assault on Villa Velha 'may possibly entitle them to the thanks of the Commander-in-chief, if he has any to spare, from those which are so very deservedly bestowed upon his gallant army'.[81]

In the closing stages of the war in Europe, Keith, who was commanding in the Channel, worked closely with Wellington's land forces in northern Spain. The general became increasingly demanding as his campaign reached a climax, and complained to Lord Bathurst, the secretary of state for war, about the Navy's failure to support him adequately. Lord Melville, the first lord, wrote a long memorandum to Keith which he was directed to use to brief Rear Admiral Sir Thomas Byam Martin when liaising with Wellington. The declared purpose of Melville's paper was to stress what was practicable for the Navy to do in the circumstances and 'what is impossible on such parts of the Coast as are connected with his operations'.[82] He may also have wished to harden the resolve of his flag officers to withstand Wellington's demands when they were inconsistent with their orders.

Diplomacy

In addition to coping with the delicacies of interservice relationships, admirals were occasionally given formal diplomatic and political appointments. Warren was the ambassador at St Petersburg from 1802 to 1804, St Vincent was the accredited ambassador to Portugal for six weeks in 1806, Lord Gambier was responsible for negotiating an end to the conflict with the United States in 1815 and Byam Martin was appointed as the British commissioner dealing with the French and Dutch governments over the disposal of naval stores at Antwerp under the fifteenth article of the Treaty of Paris.[83] Throughout the wars, commanders-in-chief routinely conducted diplomatic business on their stations. They often worked with local consular officials, and where necessary, delegated negotiations to subordinate flag officers and captains. When doing so, they sometimes thought it necessary to provide their delegates with very detailed briefings. For example, St Vincent's instructions to Vice Admiral Waldegrave on the approach to be taken in a negotiation with the Regency of Tunis in early 1796 ran to four closely written folio pages. This level of direction was not just a reflection of St Vincent's controlling personality and his skeptical view of Waldegrave's capabilities. Nelson, who was an effective delegator, briefed Captain Keats very closely before he went ashore to seek redress from the Dey of Algiers for insulting the British consul and seizing shipping from Malta. He was provided with a script outlining scenarios that might emerge in the course of the negotiation, and urged to uphold the dignity of the British Crown in the face of prevarications to which the Dey was expected to resort. Saumarez issued equally detailed directions to subordinates when he commanded in the Baltic later in the war.[84] Flag officers did not always welcome close levels of oversight. Duckworth, for example, complained on the basis of his experience at Constantinople in 1807 that subordinate flag officers were hamstrung by their lack of autonomy and power. This complaint was probably unmerited as Collingwood had been asked by the Admiralty to give Duckworth considerable discretion and had, perhaps against his better judgement, done so.[85]

Diplomatic issues were particularly complicated and demanding in the Mediterranean and Baltic theatres. Nelson, St Vincent, Keith and Collingwood dealt with a range of allies, potential allies, undeclared enemies and neutral states when they held flag rank in the Mediterranean. St Vincent found dealing with the Portuguese frustrating – 'the ways of the Court … will be the death of me' – but relished the prospect of engaging with the rulers of states on the Barbary coast.[86] He joked about the beneficial impact of a captain's intimidating appearance – 'his figure and countenance are made for the occasion, for his highness is very timid, and if the Captain wore Mustachio's, he would have made still greater impression'[87] – and when these props proved ineffectual was quite prepared to adopt a direct and forceful approach. St Vincent contemplated with relish an exercise in what later became known as 'gun-boat' diplomacy:

> I am of opinion that before I quit the Mediterranean, it will be highly proper for me to visit the Regents of Tripoli, Tunis and Algiers, accompanied by a respectable squadron, in order to leave a lasting impression on the minds of these people of the vigour of our character, and the decided pre-eminence we have over all other maritime Powers, in skill, discipline and subordination.[88]

Although Collingwood did not hold any formal diplomatic position, he played a key role in the Mediterranean over five years. He aligned strategic and diplomatic objectives with great skill and patience, dealing with the Turks and their nominally subject rulers on the coast of North Africa, the Spanish, Portuguese, the King of Naples and Sicily, the Pope and other Italian rulers.[89] Collingwood's papers in the British Library include a series of elaborate original documents in Arabic, with translations in English and French, physical remains of complex, demanding and eventually unsuccessful transactions with Ali Pasha, the ruler of Turkey, in September 1807.[90] The British government relied heavily on Collingwood's judgement and gave him an unusual degree of autonomy. While St Vincent had wished to bombard the capitals of the Barbary states, Collingwood made a point of keeping his frustrations in check and expected his subordinate flag officers to follow his lead. Thus in early 1808, for example, he advised Rear Admiral Purvis to 'use every means to keep on good terms with the Emperor of Morocco' and told the British consul that by using 'the most conciliating language in all his intercourse with the Moorish Government he maintains their friendship'.[91]

When Admiral Duncan commanded the North Sea Fleet in the Revolutionary Wars, he had to be careful not to offend the senior officers of a Russian squadron that was attached to his fleet. He arranged for them to receive a share of prizes and also ensured that he paid attention to their sensitivity to rank and seniority without slighting his own officers. Duncan's success in dealing with the Russians played a role in Lord Spencer deciding that he should stay in the North Sea command rather than replacing Admiral Lord Hotham in the Mediterranean.[92] By the time Sir James Saumarez assumed command in the Baltic 1808, the Russians were no longer allies and were attacked by his fleet early in his command. Saumarez had given an early demonstration of his diplomatic capabilities in 1795 when serving as a captain off Cadiz.[93] As commander in the Baltic he had to navigate the hazards of northern diplomacy. Conditions were made significantly more treacherous by France's dominant position, the strength of Baltic trade interests at home, the importance of the region as a source of naval supplies and the unstable policy of Britain's only ally, Sweden.[94] Saumarez handled these challenges with great skill and was rewarded with the plaudits of the sovereigns of the region and the thanks of the descendants of the ordinary people. The inscription on a plaque unveiled in 1975 recalled that through Saumarez's 'wise political foresight Gothenburg was spared the ravages of war'.[95] He was fortunate in having two subordinate flag officers (Keats and Martin) who were highly effective diplomats. Keats's diplomatic contribution in the Baltic was particularly impressive. He was made a Knight Companion of the Bath for negotiating for Spanish troops who were serving in Denmark to change sides, and arranging their return to Spain to take part in the war of liberation.[96]

Admirals occasionally found themselves drawn into politically fraught diplomatic transactions that threatened their reputation in the service and beyond. Nelson's close personal involvement with the Hamiltons, his partiality towards the Queen of Naples and his involvement in what was widely seen as dishonourable treatment of republican prisoners at Naples laid him open to criticism that tarnished to some degree the laurels he had won off Cape St Vincent and at the Battle of the Nile.[97] His conduct at Naples and Palermo was criticized by Lord Keith, his commander-in-chief, and by Vice Admiral William Young of the Admiralty Board who told Keith that Nelson was 'a little too old to be led away by a woman'.[98] It was the subject of a particularly damning observation by Lieutenant General Sir John Moore: 'He is covered with stars, ribbons and medals, more like the Prince of an opera than the Conqueror of the Nile. It is really melancholy to see a brave and good man, who has deserved well of his country, cutting so pitiful a figure.'[99] Later when Nelson commanded in the Mediterranean, he took a significant risk in deciding, on his own initiative, that Genoa had become a French ally and ordering his captains to seize its shipping, pending a determination from the Admiralty.[100]

Other prominent flag officers also faced difficulties arising from their diplomatic duties. Warren found his ambassadorship at St Petersburg a significant financial burden and not without reputational risk.[101] Lord Granville Leveson Gower, who succeeded him in the post, relayed scathing commentary on what he presented as Warren and his wife's reputation for self-importance in their public dealings and unscrupulous ambition in their private ones. In correspondence with friends in London, Gower accused Warren of fawning on the imperial family in a desperate attempt to forge an Anglo-Russian convention and to secure a peerage as a reward.[102] In mid-1812, when Britain's relationship with the United States was highly precarious, Warren was given the very nearly impossible job of attempting to ensure peace while making effective preparations for war.

Transactions with liberators could be as fraught as those with royal autocrats. When Cochrane commanded on the Leeward Islands' Station, he held a series of negotiations with the Latin American patriot General Francisco de Miranda, one of the founders of Venezuela. Lord Howick wrote to Cochrane in early June and early July 1806 to warn him not to give any undertakings to Miranda that would tie the government's hands.[103] In mid-June, however, at a time when he could not possibly have seen the first of these communications, Cochrane supported Miranda's armed landing at Port Cavallo in the Spanish territory of Texas and entered into an understanding to assist him. When news of this development reached London, it brought a swift rebuke from the Admiralty Board. It 'highly disapproves of your having taken upon yourself, without Instructions, to assist General Miranda'.[104] Within a year the government was prepared to ship troops to assist Miranda, but in the meantime Cochrane was left to dwell upon the Board's forcefully stated displeasure.[105]

On at least two occasions flag officers found themselves drawn into highly conten-
tious diplomatic transactions they feared would damage their reputations. In late June
1806 Major General Beresford and Captain Sir Home Popham launched an unauthorized assault on Buenos Aires. When troops acting on behalf of its inhabitants subsequently retook the city, the British seized Montevideo and made a disastrous attack on
Buenos Aires. Rear Admiral George Murray, the naval commander, was not a party to
the negotiations that followed, but was put on the spot by having to sign a humiliating
capitulation agreement.[106] In the following year, Vice Admiral Sir Charles Cotton faced
a potentially more damaging dilemma. Cotton's small squadron was moored in the
Tygrus off Lisbon when the army commanders ashore were framing the terms of the
notorious 'Convention of Cintra'. This agreement, which permitted a defeated French
army to withdraw on highly favourable terms, was widely condemned in parliament
and in the press. Cotton, who was bolder in these matters than Murray, and had more
room for maneuver, refused to ratify the Convention as first proposed. He insisted
on inserting a number of stiffening provisions, including ones preventing the French
departing with property taken from the Portuguese and their allies.[107] Even so, his
friends in England thought it wise to take steps to limit collateral damage. Lady Cotton
secured a statement from Vice Admiral Sir Richard Bickerton, a professional member
of the Board, that Sir Charles's conduct had received 'the greatest approbation from all
the departments of Government'.[108]

Communications and reporting

Flag officers spent much of their time at sea grappling with a welter of correspondence. This aspect of their role is symbolized by one of Duncan's first acts in taking
up the North Sea command in March 1795. Even before telling the secretary of the
Admiralty Board the names of officers whom he wished to appoint, Duncan wrote
to the commissioners of the Navy Board requesting 'directions to ... supply me with
Stationary to enable me to carry on His Majesty's Service entrusted to my care'.[109] The
Admiralty paid the salaries of secretaries who dealt with commanders-in-chiefs' busi-
ness and financial matters and generally acted as executive directors of their offices.
These positions were very demanding but eagerly sought after because flag officers
often gave their secretaries potentially lucrative roles in prize business. Clerks assisted
secretaries with routine correspondence, and made copies of letters and reports to the
Admiralty, and of the orders issued to the officers under their admiral's command.
Some admirals formed very close relationships with their secretaries. Benjamin Tucker
was a purser and then became St Vincent's secretary at sea before following him ashore
to the Admiralty where he prospered. John Scott was Nelson's secretary during his last
command and, as was common, took a hand in the prize business of his fleet. Scott
died at Nelson's side on the quarterdeck of *Victory* at Trafalgar. Keith relied heavily on
his Secretary Nicholas Brown, who had a flair for financial management, but while this
spared Keith much detailed work, it became a source of embarrassed difficulty when
some senior officers accused his secretary of sharp practice over the purchase of slops,
rates of exchange and prize money. These charges were sheeted home to Keith, thus

demonstrating that while able and active secretaries might relieve their admirals from some of the press of routine business, the weight of responsibility rested squarely on their shoulders.[110]

Even with assistance, flag officers' correspondence and administrative business were significant and time-consuming burdens. When St Vincent commanded in the Mediterranean he rose at 2:00 a.m. in order to try to keep up with what he called 'pen and ink work'. He thought his incapacity to cope with it was a clear sign that he should resign his post.[111] Collingwood later complained he worked fourteen- to sixteen-hour days dealing with the press of administrative business and only came on deck once a day to take some fresh air. He told a correspondent that 'I have more confinement at my table and letters than an attorney's clerk'.[112] Sir Charles Cotton, who was Collingwood's successor in the Mediterranean command, quoted him as having said that 'the day was not long enough for the current business'. The weight of correspondence could be a problem for subordinate flag officers as well as their chiefs. In late 1803 Robert Montague asked to be relieved from his position in the Downs on the grounds that the 'intense application and multifarious writing' was ruining his health.[113]

Commanders-in-chief were obliged to provide a pro forma return to the Admiralty of the 'Weekly Disposition of the Fleet Under the Command of ...' including the names of commanding officers, the orders under which they operated and the date when these orders expired. The Board treated the obligation to complete these returns as a serious matter because it relied upon them in making decisions on ship deployment. Not surprisingly, flag officers were sharply intolerant of subordinates who failed to forward necessary information, or failed to keep their ships on their allotted station. Thus in June 1798 Duncan upbraided five captains for failing to report to him and ordered them to immediately inform him and the Secretary of the Admiralty Board 'where you now are and what you are now doing'.[114] When Keith commanded in the North Sea during the early years of the Napoleonic War, he had to contend with the wayward but well-connected Captain Sir Sidney Smith, 'that restless spirit and ungovernable vanity', whose attempt to excuse his failure to report on the grounds of more important preoccupations, met an indignant response from Keith, who forwarded their exchanges to the Admiralty Board.[115] Sir John Orde's airy, self-important reference to his reporting responsibilities off Cadiz in mid-1805 – 'I will not trouble their lordships again with a statement of the forces under my command and of the numerous duties I have to perform with it' – was unlikely to have endeared him to the Board.[116] When Warren failed to report from the North American station in the first half of 1813, he was subject to a stern rebuke couched in one of the Board's standard terms of strong disapprobation. John Wilson Croker was instructed to convey to Warren their Lordship's 'great surprise' at the commander-in-chief's dereliction of duty.[117]

A great deal of flag officers' official correspondence was reactive. That is, commanders-in-chief responded to instructions and other communications from the Admiralty Board, passed on intelligence and diplomatic information that came into their hands and forwarded accounts of actions, operational matters and strategic developments. Subordinate flag officers responded to orders and requests from commanders-in-chief, often in very formulaic terms that acknowledged the instructions they had received, reiterated the main points and confirmed giving effect to them. The volume of correspondence generated by instructions from the Board varied according to distance and the criticality of the strategic and operational situation. Thus for most of Duncan's command in the North Sea he wrote to the Board several times a day. By the time he asked to come ashore in 1800, however, there was little to do and the volume of correspondence had dwindled to a trickle.[118] When Lord Barham headed the Board in 1805 and the situation in the Channel and Mediterranean was critical, his correspondence with the flag officers concerned was even more onerous. Over the course of nine and a half months Nelson wrote at least 330 letters on official business.[119]

In response to the challenges of global war and direct threats to the territorial security of Great Britain, the Board's grip on its scattered fleets tightened. Whatever its intentions, however, the ability to exercise close control was conditioned by distance. Shutter and semaphore telegraphs linking the Admiralty to Deal, Harwich, Plymouth, Sheerness and Spithead carried messages in a matter of minutes if visibility allowed, thus minimizing delays at one end of the chain of command. With clerks, senior officials and the first lord in residence at the Admiralty, urgent incoming business received immediate attention.[120] Beyond the shores of Britain, the Admiralty used a wide range of overland and marine communication routes, sending duplicate dispatches to reduce the risk of loss through accident or interception. These facilities allowed the Admiralty to play an increasingly direct role in blockades of the Texel, Brest, the French Channel ports and, to a lesser extent, Toulon, Cadiz and the Baltic.[121] Its immediate impact on more distant stations was necessarily far more limited. Lord Spencer candidly told Rainier in the East Indies that poor communications 'leave us so much in the dark with respect to the course of your operations that it is very difficult to write anything upon the subject of them'.[122] Nevertheless, a turnaround time of up to sixteen months did not remove Rainier's reporting obligations. In addition to meeting the Admiralty's demands, the senior flag officer on this station had also to engage closely with the East India Company and its servants in the region and with the Transport, Sick and Hurt and Victualing Boards in London.[123] In a period of two and a half years between February 1798 and July 1800, Rainier's official correspondence amounted to about 600 items. He also issued about the same number of written commands to those who reported to him.[124]

Lapses in communication might be a source of uneasiness, eating away at the confidence of the most accomplished officers, exacerbating their sense of isolation and generating a gnawing sense of insecurity. St Vincent bemoaned the lack of direction when his confidence was sapped temporarily by exhaustion and ill health at the end of his Mediterranean command. Keith, who had waited impatiently to take over from him, was unsympathetic, but faced a similar situation a few years later when he wished to be relieved: 'I am kept here in ignorance of what is intended and of course cannot make arrangements necessary before quitting a command so extensive and so honourable, but of which I am tired.'[125] When Nelson commanded the Mediterranean Fleet in 1803–1805, he complained of the lack of direction from London and his reliance on French newspapers for news of the war. Instructions took three months to reach the fleet off Toulon in the autumn of 1803. Early the next year Nelson warned St Vincent of the difficulties resulting from delayed orders from the Admiralty which disrupted plans made with a more accurate knowledge of the disposition and condition of ships. He was relieved to receive a general statement of the Board's support for his decisions. The news of Spain entering the war in late 1804 took twenty-five days to arrive and even then there was ongoing uncertainty over the situation.[126] In the following year, Sir Robert Calder's lack of knowledge of the Board's strategy may have played a role in his failure to follow-up after an inconclusive action off Cape Finisterre, an error of judgement that ruined his career.[127] Collingwood was disconcerted by what he saw as the Admiralty's neglect but it was really a sign of its confidence in his judgement and vigour. He complained to Purvis that the only letters he received from Lord Mulgrave were lists of candidates for appointments and promotions.[128] When Home Popham's opportunistic anticipation of Britain's policy towards Spain's South American empire embroiled the Navy in operations in the River Plate, slow communications compounded by a rapid turnover of key ministerial figures in London, played a significant role in subsequent operations.[129]

In some circumstances distance might prove a blessing. Rainier exploited the communication gap to keep Lord Keith at bay when he was placed under his orders on the East Indian station in 1795. Later, however, when Rainier was left in the dark for long periods over the prospect of being relieved, he found his situation frustrating and unsettling.[130] During Sir Edward Pellew's command in the East Indies, he took advantage of distance to mitigate some of the personal and strategic effects of the disastrous decision to divide the command between him and Sir Thomas Troubridge. Pellew made full – in St Vincent's view dangerously excessive – advantage of a provision in his orders that permitted him to keep Troubridge under his command if circumstances warranted it. His increasingly disillusioned service patron warned Pellew that 'whether Lord Melville acted wisely in dividing the Indian Command is no affair of yours, and it is your indispensable duty to comply strictly with the spirit of his instructions'.[131] Cochrane's occasional embarrassment in divining the intentions of incoming first lords was offset by opportunities to promote the careers of officers whom he favoured.[132] Towards the end of the war when he held the North American command, Cochrane and his subordinate flag officer at Halifax, Rear Admiral Griffith, took advantage of a delay in sending plans for his official house to authorize work on a building of their own design. When the document finally arrived, construction was so far advanced that Griffith was able to report gleefully to his chief that '[i]t is now too late to build from it'.[133]

In addition to their public correspondence, flag officers might also send private letters to the first lord; these dealt with service matters but were not necessarily laid before the Board. Early in the wars Lord Spencer drew a sharp distinction between what he thought it proper for Lord Hood to say in private and public letters and removed him from the command of the Mediterranean Fleet when he criticized the Board through the latter.[134] Private correspondence with a first lord might be a source of support to a flag officer by setting him on a confidential footing with his political and ministerial chief. Spencer had extensive and mutually beneficial correspondence with both Duncan and St Vincent. However, when Lord Melville forwarded one of Sir John Orde's letters to Lord Barham's Board in mid-1805 – it was written while Melville was still first lord but arrived after he left office – Orde treated it as a breach of practice and trust because Lord Melville had encouraged the correspondence. Barham, however, dismissed the claim out of hand. He declared that he could never deal with the volume of correspondence that was addressed to him and routinely handed it over to the Board secretariat.[135] This was not the last time that the porous distinction between public and private letters caused controversy. When Thomas Grenville became first lord in the autumn of 1806 he wrote to Collingwood expressing high regard for his distinguished service and making a clear and open offer of a confidential correspondence: '[Y]our Lordship will find in me a real desire to endeavor to consult your wishes & to give to the execution of your present important public duties whatever assistance or accommodation it may be possible to furnish.'[136] Grenville's term lasted for scarcely more than six months, however, and, shortly after he left office, Lord Mulgrave, his successor, defended his own policy and embarrassed Grenville and his colleagues by tabling his private correspondence with Collingwood in parliament.[137]

Scrutiny and surveillance

It will be clear by now that to the extent that modes of communication allowed, admirals were the objects of a highly developed and relentless system of official scrutiny and surveillance. The demands of this system increased the pressure under which they worked and enhanced threats to their professional reputations and prospects if they failed to contend with them. Flag officers were also, however, subject to the scrutiny of other members of their profession, well-connected members of the public, the representatives of powerful interests and the more diffuse forces of 'public opinion'.[138] These sources generated impressions of performance that informed the judgements of ministries and the Board and increased the pressures under which flag officers worked.

Private correspondence between professional members of the Board and flag officers was one of many causes of friction between St Vincent and officers serving under him in the Mediterranean Fleet. In late July/early August of 1796 he accused Vice Admiral Waldegrave of informing on him to ministers at home and tried to control communications by insisting that they were dispatched through his flagship. Waldegrave rejected the claim and stressed his right of unhindered correspondence. He told Spencer that 'my only correspondents being (a few chance letters excepted) your lordship and the Under-Secretary of State, both very natural and convenient vehicles to the Cabinet, it must be granted'.[139] St Vincent would not have been assured by this explanation. When commander-in-chief of the Channel Fleet he complained to Spencer of the 'gossiping correspondence which is still carried on between officers of the squadron and puisine sea lords at the Board'.[140]

St Vincent was hardly in a position to object to this aspect of senior officers' conduct since he had provided critical commentary on his superiors to the Earl of Shelburne when a post captain. Later when serving as a commander-in-chief he maintained a private correspondence with the Admiralty secretary that was laced with sharp criticisms of the Board and its individual members.[141] The practice was, in any case, so widespread and so closely connected with the cultivation of interest there was no realistic chance of checking it. Lord Bridport corresponded with the Marquis of Buckingham and lobbied his friends in support of a long-running campaign to replace Lord Howe at the head of the Channel Fleet. When Cochrane was a captain serving under Bridport in the Channel Fleet, he conveyed critical comments on his commander-in-chief to Thomas Coutts, the banker. Coutts valued his frankness but warned of the dangers of indiscretion.[142] Cochrane continued his private correspondence with the first lord Melville after he had left office in 1805, and wrote privately to Melville's son before he became first lord in March 1812. The troublesome Sir Sidney Smith sent implicitly critical reflections on Keith's strategies as commander in the North Sea to his friends among the Pitt connection.[143] Keith also faced undermining challenges from his subordinate flag officer, Rear Admiral Montagu. St Vincent accused Montagu of intriguing with the Hoods and he was certainly in correspondence with the Earl of Sandwich and with ministers. The indignant first lord upbraided him sharply, noting that the burden of correspondence of which he complained was self-inflicted.[144] Nelson maintained a correspondence with the prime minister, Henry Addington, when St Vincent was first lord.[145] To Admiral Cornwallis's evident displeasure, Sir Robert Calder communicated directly with the Board from the Channel Fleet in early 1805. In the following year Sir John Duckworth corresponded with Rear Admiral Markham, a professional member of the Admiralty Board, when serving under Collingwood in the Mediterranean.[146] Long after his retirement from active service, Lord Hood (who had been notorious for his acerbic comments on his superiors) received reports on developments in the Baltic from his cousin Sir Samuel Hood, a junior flag officer in Saumarez's squadron. He included extracts from them in letters to his friend Lord Bruce, the politically unreliable member for Marlborough and heir to the Earl of Alesbury.[147] Both Duckworth and Pellew maintained an extensive correspondence with their patron the Duke of Northumberland in which they complained to him of the management of the Navy and he vented his grievances against the Army.[148]

On occasion, the Admiralty received unsolicited information and advice on matters bearing on flag officers' spheres of responsibility and brought them to their attention. Those serving off the English coast were particularly open to this sort of scrutiny. When Lord Keith commanded an extended North Sea station in 1803 the immediacy of the threat of invasion from France and the Admiralty's sensitivity to suggestions from local notables, military figures and other members of the service prompted unwelcome hints and a certain amount of detailed direction. Captain William Bligh (notorious for his role in the *Bounty* mutiny) forwarded his suggestions to St Vincent through his patron Sir Joseph Banks, MP. The first lord sent them on to Keith with the wry comment that 'the projects which are pouring in daily from all quarters exceed all imagination'.[149] One tip-off resulted in Keith being instructed to issue a general order reminding captains that officers were not to sleep out of their ships without leave, 'whereby the Coast is exposed & the King's Ships endangered'.[150] Even those employed in more distant waters were not always safe from oversight. In late July–early August 1803, Cornwallis was required to explain why one of his ships was off station. He sent a copy of the vessel's log and his orders to its captain as part of this explanation. The Admiralty's information came from a ship that 'spoke' the offending vessel in the straits of Gibraltar on its way home.[151]

Government and the Board were particularly sensitive to the demands of a range of trading interests, partly because of political and electoral influence, but also because they funded government loans. 'The protection of the trade' was a constant preoccupation of flag officers in the Channel and Mediterranean Fleets and a highly significant factor in operating strategies of blockade in the revolutionary and early Napoleonic wars. It was also a major preoccupation during the war with the United States in 1812–15.[152] During the course of his Channel command Cornwallis passed on many orders for cruising ships to 'afford every protection and assistance to the trade of his Majesty's subjects' and on one occasion warned his captains not to weaken the East India Company's ships' capacity for self-protection by stripping them of crews.[153] As we shall see, Sir John Laforey's failure to satisfy the demands of trading interests in the West Indies was a black mark against his second Leeward Islands command. Their complaints played a significant role in the downfall of Vice Admiral Charles Stirling towards the end of the wars. Duckworth was keen not to fall into this trap, writing anxiously to Lord Spencer on the lack of resources on his Jamaican command: 'I dread falling into dispute with the Islands for not giving them what they call proper Protection.' He overcame these difficulties so well that he left the command with a service of plate made up of 365 pieces gifted to him by the Assembly of Jamaica.[154] 'Protection of the trade' was also an issue in the North Sea command. Admiral Duncan assured the Board of his attention to British commerce at the beginning of his appointment on that station. He subsequently received a string of urgent requests for protection against French privateers from local representatives from Leith, Aberdeen, Edinburgh, Newcastle, Sunderland and Hull, the Baltic merchants and the Company of Adventurers of England Trading to Hudson Bay, and the merchants of Leith, Dunbar and Hull concerned in the Greenland and Davis Strait Fisheries. Trade protection was again important in the North Sea when Keith commanded there in 1806–1807.[155]

The complaints of trading interests posed a risk to the reputation and prospects of flag officers because these groups had strong connections in British politics and society, and could mobilize sections of the British press. First lords and other ministers had also to keep a weather eye on the indirect parliamentary implications of the praise and censure expressive of the 'feelings of the public'. These feelings were reflected in the rhetoric of politicians, the panegyrics and fulminations of leader writers in the newspapers and, occasionally, popular demonstrations of jubilation or condemnation. Late Georgian Britain was very far from being a democracy, but politicians, and the flag officers who depended on them, were acutely aware of what Edward Codrington termed the 'alehouse expectations of John Bull'.[156] These expectations tended to focus on the high and low points of naval performance, on splendidly seized and scandalously wasted opportunities. They played an enthusiastic role in celebrations that greeted victories and in the popular acclaim attached to Nelson but they also goaded Sir Robert Calder into a disastrous court martial, and stoked the outraged shock which followed early loses in the American War of 1812.[157] The Board responded to critical press reaction to these loses by placing Sir John Warren under great pressure. It authorized the purchase of suitable ships, but sheeted responsibility home to the commander-in-chief. He was reminded bluntly that any impediments to 'the greatest activity and exertion' had been removed: 'With the great force which will be under your orders, their Lordships are satisfied that you will have ample means for carrying on the war with that degree of Vigor and Effect which the honor of HM Arms, and the character and interest of the Country requires.'[158]

Conclusion

In the course of their rise through the ranks, flag officers had extensive opportunities to gain expertise in seamanship and in operational duties. They had been subject to the disciplinary requirements of the service and, as commanders of ships, assumed final responsibility for imposing discipline on others. They were also exposed to the administrative and logistical challenges of managing a ship at sea and might have assumed temporary command of a few ships. But while these duties were onerous, they did not compare with the range, intensity or sophistication of demands placed on flag officers, whether in independent commands or reporting to commanders-in-chief. The increasing pressures faced by flag officers undoubtedly owed much to the demands created by the Navy's critical role in a long and testing period of global conflict. While many of these pressures were likely to have arisen in earlier wars, it is significant that in the course of the French Wars flag officers' responsibilities for leading the response to them was increasingly emphasized. This tendency is clearly apparent when references to flag officers' duties in the pre-war edition of the *Regulations and Instructions* are compared with those of the new edition of 1806 which captured the emerging practice of the previous decade. In the earlier publication the focus is one flag officers' formal and procedural roles. By 1806 the account of their duties is more developed and stresses their responsibility for providing leadership in a service in which speed, 'zeal' and 'alacrity' have become requisite behavioral dispositions.[159]

In addition to the administrative and operational demands of their roles, flag officers had also to rise to the intellectual and cultural challenges entailed by their diplomatic and political responsibilities. Since most admirals lacked significant formal education or specialized training it is surprising how well they responded to these challenges. Only two wartime admirals attended English universities, and few had extended school educations or even attended the Royal Naval Academy in Portsmouth. This institution provided solid technical and practical training for aspiring sea officers but proposals to broaden its curriculum to include languages were not put into effect.[160] The Navy system for ship board schoolmasters has been described as 'chaotic' and while some of them were gifted scholars and teachers there were never enough schoolmasters to provide consistent non-technical education for 'young gentlemen across the service'.[161] In some cases, captains' and admirals' took a personal interest in the broader education of their midshipmen, and some more senior officers were sufficiently well motivated to continue their education through programmes of self-directed study. St Vincent, Nelson, Collingwood, Cochrane, Saumarez and Duckworth exhibited levels of literary flair in their correspondence that belied their limited formal education. Prolonged periods of half pay between wars provided sea officers with opportunities to travel in Europe to observe naval developments among likely future foes, and broaden their intellectual horizons. George Murray took advantage of the peace to spend two years in France continuing the studies of general literature that he began when a prisoner there a few years before. Both Duncan and St Vincent made frugal continental study tours. The latter stressed the importance of learning French, and gaining an understanding of the country that 'must ever be our rival in arms and trade'.[162] These forms of study, combined with the practice of writing innumerable letters and reports in the course of active service, doubtless helped to improve flag officers' literary ability and cultural understanding, and thereby augmented the nautical skills and commanding temperament required to meet the challenges of command.

2

Authority and Command

Obedience has ever been the maxim of my professional life – I regard obedience as the Pole Star of the Service.

—Earl St Vincent, to a captain considering questioning
an order from the Admiralty Board[1]

Flag officers stood at the apex of a hierarchical service in which subordinates were expected to yield unquestioning obedience to superiors' commands. Habitual obedience, and a corresponding habit of command, was ingrained in the minds of aspiring commissioned officers during the period of 'servitude' that preceded appointment as a lieutenant. As midshipmen (often in their early teens), future admirals learned to respond instantly and with due deference to the orders of commissioned officers. They also learned to expect outward respect and obedience from those subject to their authority. Most of those over whom they first exercised authority were older than they; many were skilled seaman with years of experience, hardened by the rigours of service at sea and in battle. The authority of embryonic sea officers was enforced by habits of deference embedded in the prevailing social hierarchy, by the force of their personalities and by the exemplary effect of their leadership under fire and in emergencies at sea. It was supported by the savage physical punishments available to the commanders of ships and, in the most serious cases, by courts martial empowered to pass sentences of death. While a majority of 'the people' were volunteers rather than pressed men, that did not necessarily reduce the challenge of managing them.[2]

As sea officers progressed through the ranks to become post captains, their power and responsibilities expanded. They commanded, however, within a general framework specified in the *Regulations and Instructions* and the Articles of War, and in response to the orders of their superior officers. In most cases the superior was a flag officer, either a commander-in-chief of a fleet, his subordinate flag officer or a port admiral. Commanders-in-chief took their orders from the Admiralty Board, either through direct written instruction from the first lord, or conveyed in writing by its secretary. Flag officers' attitude towards their authoritative roles, and the ways in which they exercised the powers vested in them, reflected shifting perceptions of the requirements of the service during the prolonged global conflict with France, generational shifts within the flag officer corps and the personal dispositions of those involved.

This chapter will examine the implications of the ethos of obedience for the evolving role of flag officers and consider how it was reflected in the careers of a number of admirals who saw significant service during the French Wars. St Vincent looms large in this discussion. His undoubted ability, reforming zeal and forceful personality were applied in the two major commands (the Mediterranean and the Channel) and at the head of the Admiralty Board. He was a particularly influential figure who has left an extensive record of his actions, views and interactions. He also gave considerable attention to specifying the qualities required of flag officers, relating these to what he saw as their key leadership responsibilities and sharing his views forcefully with first lords, members of the Board and his subordinates.

The ethos of command

During the French Wars there was increasingly overt stress on admirals' responsibilities for setting appropriate disciplinary standards. In these, as in other aspects of their duty, they were subject to the scrutiny and censor of both subordinates and superiors. When Collingwood was a recently employed post captain at the beginning of the war, he was highly critical of Lord Howe's dilatory handling of his fleet. Keith, a junior admiral in the Mediterranean Fleet, made a similar complaint against Lord Hood a few months later.[3] When Lord Bridport deputized for Howe in mid-1795 he came under pressure from Lord Spencer to get the fleet to sea as soon as possible. As commander-in-chief and as first lord, St Vincent chivvied his subordinates remorselessly and demanded vigourous action under all circumstances. St Vincent's imperatives prompted tenacious pursuit and uncompromising engagement with the enemy. When fleets were preparing for sea, admirals were increasingly expected to ensure a heightened general commitment to 'proceed without loss of time', repair and victual ships with the 'utmost dispatch'. Port admirals were enjoined 'to hasten ... by every means in your power' the departure of the vessels named.[4] One of St Vincent's early tasks as first lord was to urge Sir Hyde Parker to get the North Sea Fleet to sea as soon as possible.[5] St Vincent was not responsible for the new edition of *Regulations and Instructions* of 1806 but the sense of urgency that he brought to high command and to the Board was reflected in its newly framed strictures on the duties of commanders-in-chief and admirals.[6]

At various times St Vincent presented Collingwood and Keith as exemplary 'taut' flag officers. He praised Collingwood's efficiency in getting ships quickly back on their stations, repaired, watered and victualed, contrasting his admirable vigour with the dilatory practice of less effectual officers: 'Captain Tyler ... is the greatest skulker I ever met with, the Captains Stirling and Buller are of the same description, and I do entreat they may be all three sent about their business as soon as possible.'[7] Although the relationship between Keith and St Vincent was sometimes strained, St Vincent was in no doubt about his capabilities. When about to be relieved by Keith in the Mediterranean he told Lord Spencer that his successor would not 'I am sure ... disappoint the expectations of his most sanguine friends.'[8] While other flag officers did not necessarily adopt St Vincent's manner and style of command, his general outlook was common among his younger contemporaries.

The disciplinary ethos St Vincent promoted was underwritten by a particular habit of command that distinguished effective flag officers from their less successful, and less employable, colleagues. Throughout his career St Vincent fulminated on the very mixed quality of those on the list of flag officers. In 1780, for example, while still a post captain, he told his patron Lord Shelburne that disturbances in the fleet were due to the weak leadership of Vice Admiral Darby. 'Our poor, good humour'd Chief' was responsible for the 'entire dissolution of discipline & subordination in the Service.'[9] While commanding in the Mediterranean in the mid-1790s, St Vincent begged Lord Spencer to send him no more admirals, unless they were 'firm men'. Flag officers with these qualities were in depressingly short supply: 'Looking over the list of admirals with an impartial eye, I cannot find many men on it qualified to command ten line-of-battle ships on critical service.'[10] St Vincent was very hard to please but others shared his views. Sir Charles Cotton, whose disposition was far milder, provided his wife with a scathing caricature of Vice Admiral John Douglas, his superior officer in the Channel Fleet. When Cotton went on board Douglas's flagship, he found 'a gentlemanly stupid old man, shut up in his cabin, where he amuses himself. He has never been on deck but once before he came up to receive me. Stupid he may not be, but I heard no proof of sense, except his remaining shut up & not interfering where he might shew his ignorance.'[11] Douglas was, no doubt, an extreme case, but the correspondence of senior flag officers and first lords include numerous references to the limited pool of talent at their disposal. Vice Admiral William Young at the Board told his friend Sir Charles Pole that although the list of flag officers was now extensive, 'it is a sad thing to see how few there are of whom much is to be expected in service, or in whom much confidence can be placed'. Thomas Grenville and Lord Mulgrave, who presided at the Board from 1807 to 1810, echoed these views.[12]

If captains were to successfully transition from commanding ships to commanding fleets or squadrons, they needed to extend their skills and perspectives to meet the onerous demands of flag rank. This was not only a matter of seamanship and strategic sense; those fit for flag command also needed the resilience to cope with the psychological demands of fleet leadership. Over the course of his career St Vincent gave considerable thought to the disposition required for naval high command, boasting to one of Spencer's successors that '[f]ew men have had the opportunities of studying naval characters I have experienced from fifty-nine years' service, and mixing very much with them in society'.[13] He often identified a commanding disposition with 'firmness' but his most insightful characterization (which echoed his earlier judgement on Darby) occurred in his criticism of flag officers who demonstrated a deficiency of 'nerves under responsibility'.[14] This term referred to the temper of mind and spirit needed to shoulder the unrelenting burden of routine business faced by flag officers, and contend with the exceptional challenges of wartime service.

Successful fighting commanders were distinguished by confident aggression in action[15] but in order to be effective leaders of fleet, they had to direct their minds and energies towards a wide and diverse range of taxing and sustained responsibilities. Those who showed courage and spirit in the heat of battle were not necessarily suited to handling these demands. Lord Gardner is a case in point. Captain William Hotham praised Gardner's qualities as a fighting seaman but thought him indecisive at critical moments when commanding a squadron in the Leeward Isles at the beginning of the war: '[H]e seemed to shrink from responsibility, and was painfully nervous, the consequence which frequently happens of an honourable but overstrained effort to do right.'[16] Following his service in the Leeward Islands, Gardner was Lord Bridport's second-in command in the Channel Fleet. Although he had appropriate seniority he was not considered for the leading role on Bridport's retirement because it was said he did not wish to take a major command.[17] The king may have been genuinely misled on this point, but as Gardner had told the prime minister and a ministerial colleague that he wished to succeed Bridport, it seems likely that Spencer's views were coloured by doubts about his capabilities.[18] St Vincent later described him as one of those flag officers who while 'of greatest promise and acquired character' and 'brave as lions in the presence of an enemy' struggled under the pressure of flag officers' responsibilities.[19] Gardner's career lent credence to this judgement. He was ineffectual in dealing with mutineers in Bridport's fleet in 1797 and was physically and psychologically shattered when he stood in for him in 1799.[20] Gardner proved effective in the Irish command but when he temporarily relieved Admiral Cornwallis as commander of the Channel Fleet in 1805, the difficulties of an awkward arrangement, which smacked of divided command, induced him to ask Lord Barham's permission to go ashore to recover his equilibrium:

> the very unpleasant situation in which I have been placed … has occasioned a degree of anxiety and uneasiness in my mind not easily to be described, and which has affected my health and depressed my spirits so much, that I find myself unequal to the discharge of my duty in the manner I could wish; nor have I any hope of my being able to do so, until my mind is more at ease.[21]

Gardner took over the Channel command from St Vincent in April 1807 but held it for less than two years. When he died in 1809, aged sixty-six, he was said to look exceedingly old with a 'constitution quite worn out'.[22]

At the beginning of May 1798 St Vincent told Spencer how much he welcomed Nelson under his command. He then offered advice on his successor: 'The person to succeed me should possess both temper and good nerves, or he will be in continual hot water, and terrified at this anchorage, which appalls many a good fellow under my command.'[23] This specification ruled out Vice Admiral Sir Charles Thompson. He was a 'gallant Man' but 'the most timid Officer, as it relates to Rocks, Sands, Shores, and responsibility, imaginable'. St Vincent later raised questions about Sir Robert Calder's fortitude in the face of similar difficulties.[24] By contrast, St Vincent credited Lord Keith with showing 'great manhood and ability' when facing these hazards: '[H]is position having been very critical, exposed to a gale of wind, blowing directly on the shore. With an enemy of superior force to windward of him, and twenty two ships of the line in the Bay of Cadiz, ready to profit of any disaster, which might have befallen him.'[25] Flag officers' temperaments were subject to severe test when cruises were extended into winter and they were expected to maintain close blockades off hazardous coasts. Seamanship and navigation were essential technical skills but those who directed fleets in such conditions would only put them to good use if they were confident and psychologically robust.

Although subordinate flag officers acted under the orders of their commanders-in-chief, they were expected to demonstrate initiative and display appropriate self-assurance. As we shall see, the line between admirable self-direction, and ignoring, or willfully misconstruing, instructions was sometimes hard to draw. Cornwallis and Sir William Parker were brought to court martial for exercising their discretion, and Nelson (at the Battle of Copenhagen) and Duckworth before the action off San Domingo, took significant risks by taking matters into their own hands. On the other side of the equation, hard-pressed commanders-in-chief were understandably intolerant of subordinates' failures to assume proper responsibility. When St Vincent commanded in the Mediterranean, for example, he became so irritated by Vice Admiral Waldegrave's dependence that he asked Lord Spencer to recall him. A few years later, Lord Keith upbraided his second-in-command, Commodore Alexander Cochrane, for failing to act with appropriate autonomy during the landing of a British in Egypt.[26]

St Vincent's exercise of authority

In the early stages of the war St Vincent's self-image was forged by critical reference to Admiral Lord Bridport, his predecessor in the Channel Fleet. When commanding in the Mediterranean, where he had quite openly committed himself to reversing the dangerous laxity that had set in under Vice Admiral Sir William Hotham, he received an account of an incident said to have occurred when Bridport was entertaining his senior officers to dinner. He was told that a captain had proposed a toast that 'the discipline of the Mediterranean Fleet should never be adopted in the Channel'. This account was not wholly accurate, since, as Lord Spencer later told St Vincent, Bridport had made the remark and the company had not drunk to it.[27] The first lord's correction did not deter St Vincent. He told the story repeatedly, framing it in ways that combined contemptuous outrage and pride in equal measure. The original version provided scope for scandalized comment on Bridport's failure to correct his subordinates. In either form, however, it demonstrated what St Vincent saw as a telling example of a deplorably lax attitude towards discipline and a disregard of the exemplary role he expected flag officers to play.

In retelling this outrage, St Vincent wallowed in self-congratulatory approbation at having restored order and efficiency in the Mediterranean and anticipated with relish the challenge awaiting him in the Channel Fleet. He told his sister with grim complacency that he was welcomed to his new command by 'a few friends' on his flagship 'but not by other'.[28] There was a great deal of vanity and professional one-upmanship in all this, and an eagerness to take a shy at one of his enemies among the Hood faction. At the same time, however, St Vincent's reaction to Bridport's alleged shortcomings reflected a systematic approach to discipline, which he believed essential. This requirement applied at least as much to commanders-in-chief as it did to their subordinates. St Vincent's views on these matters long predated his attainment of flag rank. In 1780, for example, he told his patron Lord Shelbourne that mismanagement of the fleet at sea was due to the 'ignorance & dullness' of his commanding officer, 'the insufficiency of many of the Captains, and … the total annihilation of discipline and emulation'. He reasoned that since a fleet could only keep to the Channel in autumnal and winter gales if it maintained a very high state of discipline, these weaknesses limited strategic options.[29]

St Vincent held it as an article of faith that he was uniquely qualified to take the lead. After less than two years' experience as a commander-in-chief, the future Earl St Vincent presented himself to Lord Spencer as a model of the qualities required of (and so infrequently found in) flag officers: 'I see no difficulties which may not be surmounted, my mind always mounting to the situation I happen to be placed in.'[30] He took pride in identifying 'good men' and thought they were attracted to him because he did full justice to their merits and always distinguished them from 'malingerers.'[31] Later in his career, St Vincent's attitude towards discipline was expressed in terms of the recovery of an ideal of moral rectitude located in a golden age and fleetingly discernible in the contemporary service. Only he and a few admired subordinates now modelled true leadership, providing a bulwark against the swelling tide of self-indulgence and laxity that threatened the efficiency of the service and the safety of the public. St Vincent expected those who assumed positions of responsibility in the Navy to wage an ongoing struggle against the forces of darkness. In an odd but characteristic stroke of transference, he told Rear Admiral Duckworth that

> [t]he inroads and abuses which have crept into every department of the Navy, require a strong hand to crush.... . I am determined to support the Board ... in every strong measure which it is judged fit to take, whenever these evils present (which God knows happens frequently), and by that means lay a foundation for my successor to restore the Navy to its pristine vigour.[32]

This determination sparked an ill-timed wholesale assault on corruption and inefficiency in the royal dockyards during the Peace of Amiens that hampered the Navy's building and repair programme, preventing it stealing a march on the French when hostilities recommenced.[33] St Vincent's jaundiced eye rested on other naval institutions, including Greenwich Hospital and the Royal Naval Academy at Portsmouth, and looked beyond the service to a wider sea of corruption which included those 'sinks of inequity', the ancient universities.[34]

When St Vincent confronted attitudes and behaviour that fell short of his demanding standards, he invoked the idea of 'licentiousness'. This term referred to those who ignored, or circumvented, or failed to uphold, systems of necessary regulation. License was fatal to the well-being of the service and St Vincent was morally disgusted at the self-indulgence of those who undermined discipline through slack practice and poor example. His censorial vigilance also extended to the personal conduct of his officers. In the Mediterranean command he looked askance at young officers who ruined their health through sexual indulgence. Later, when he assumed command of the Channel Fleet, he claimed to have found the lieutenants in a state of 'continual intoxication ... which occasioned almost a total dereliction of discipline, and the most dangerously licentious conversation'.[35] He acted immediately to curb the abuse of alcohol in wardrooms, seemed to relish the resentment resulting from these measures, and encouraged Lord Spencer to extend the crusade to the whole of the Navy.[36]

St Vincent's obsessive determination to keep his ships at sea reflected a passionately held belief that the moral and disciplinary hazards of terra firma were far more threatening to the good of the service than reefs, shoals and lee shores. Ships in port were exposed both to the loss of men through desertion and the effects of debauchery. Crews were also liable to be unsettled in their obedience by pernicious influences emanating from centres of radical sedition, and exposed to the deplorable examples of lazy and corrupt dockyard workers. These considerations reinforced St Vincent's stridently promoted views on offshore victualing and reducing the reliance on shore-based maintenance to the minimum level compatible with the safety and efficiency of his ships. Significantly, his plans for the peacetime navy incorporated strictures on keeping crews away from Portsmouth, another 'sink of inequity'.[37] While wartime conditions prevailed, he insisted that if ships had to enter harbour, officers should actively superintend their crews and not prolong their absence from their station. To this end, he insisted (before this matter was addressed in the *Regulations and Instructions* of 1806) that all commissioned officers, including captains, sleep on board their ships, issuing measured but ominous warnings against those who transgressed: 'I submit to your judgment, and feelings', he told Captain Grindall, 'whether, after the very narrow escape you have had, of losing your well-earned reputation, you ought to hazard it a second time by sleeping out of the *Ramilles*.'[38]

It was common for officers' wives, sometimes with their children, to travel considerable distances to see their husbands when their ships were in port or within easy distance of the shore.[39] St Vincent's diktat undermined the benefit of these expensive and often exhausting journeys. In overturning a customary practice that had gone some way to mitigate family separations he aroused deep resentment among officers under his command and laid himself open to the abuse of members of their families. Markham's published papers include a copy of a letter to Admiral Gambier criticizing the application of this requirement to the officers of ships moored off the south west coast of England. The unknown writer, who was clearly a captain, complained of its impact on the domestic happiness of officers and also claimed that it was contrary to the good of the service. In a line of argument which challenged St Vincent head on, this order was presented as compromising the respect in which captains were held and thus prejudicing an important link in the fragile chain of authority that kept the potentially mutinous lower deck in check. It 'was issued in the common order book, for the amusement and ridicule of the lieutenants, warrant and petty officers, and foremast men, and the effect it has already had in lowering the consequences and degrading the situation of the captain is very visible'.[40]

Collingwood thought the management of the fleet improved markedly when Lord Spencer became established as first sea lord – 'our Ships are more at sea, and we have fuller possession of it, than when we moved in more parade' – but stressed that his 'vigilance' and 'industry' needed to be supported by effective executive action in the fleets.[41] St Vincent played this role admirably in the Mediterranean. Noting the lacklustre condition of the Channel Fleet under Lord Bridport, Collingwood gave St Vincent his preference to succeed him in that command. The determination to engage with the combined French and Spanish Fleets off Cape St Vincent was, Collingwood wrote, 'the highest compliment he could pay his fleet ... as it evinced his full and entire confidence in their ability and exertion in their country's service, and at the same time

the fullest proof of his undaunted spirit and resolution.[42] But if St Vincent's confidence, vigour and commitment could not be faulted, Collingwood discerned flaws in
his character that generated dysfunctional tensions in his relationship with his senior
officers, compromised the latter stages of his Mediterranean command and skewed his
judgement when first lord.

When Collingwood returned to England for a brief spell of leave in late 1798,
he was relieved to be removed from the 'disagreeable' atmosphere produced by St
Vincent's clashes with his subordinate flag officers, Vice Admiral Sir William Parker,
Vice Admiral Sir Charles Thompson and Vice Admiral Sir John Orde.[43] He referred
to the 'many violences and innovations which I witnessed' and to the commander-in-
chief's 'impetuous' conduct towards his officers. '[H]aving no very material service to
execute' St Vincent 'carried trifles with a high hand, took dislikes and prejudices most
capriciously'. Although Orde became notorious for challenging St Vincent to a duel,
Collingwood thought he had been subjected to 'indignities ... that were generally gross
enough for the roughest minds' and particularly hurtful to someone of Orde's sensibilities. He believed (and the Board's judgement supported this) that St Vincent was
guilty of an 'unwarrantable stretch of power' in ordering Orde home.[44] St Vincent did
not reserve rough handling for his most senior officers. Conflicts with them sometimes
drew in their captains and he was not above taking an ugly and crudely expressed
delight in imposing his will on them. As he boasted to Evan Nepean, a dressing-down
given to captains of the Mediterranean Fleet in August of 1798, 'if it did not bring them
to a stool, certainly made them piss and cry'.[45]

St Vincent and Keith fell out over the transition of command of the Mediterranean
Fleet in the autumn of 1799 when Keith suspected him of manoeuvring to maintain
the prize money, pay and allowances of a commander-in-chief. Collingwood did not

Plate 1: Admiral Viscount Keith (left) and Admiral Earl St Vincent enjoyed successful, sustained and very well-rewarded careers. St Vincent's active service career extended through
until 1807, while Keith held major commands until the end of the Napoleonic War in 1815.

stoop to accusations of venality but his comment on these flag officers' relationship was, if anything, more damaging. He attributed St Vincent's conduct to personal animosity and professional jealousy, and the Machiavellian deployment of his formidable mental powers in their service rather than that of the public:

> Lord St Vincent's sagacity and penetration I am sure saw this man failing in everything, without displeasure; he wou'd have ill brooked the laurels which presented themselves to us, being gathered by another hand under his nose as it were, and perhaps does not like him. To those in the fleet who only looked how best their country's interest might be supported, whose only object was the destruction of the enemy's fleet, it has been a continued series of vexations and disappointments.[46]

Although St Vincent relished the prospect of imposing his Mediterranean discipline in the Channel Fleet, the early stage of his command was marked by placatory gestures to a range of senior subordinates.[47] As time wore on, however, the strain of sustaining nerves under responsibility took its toll. Although never succumbing to nervous indecisiveness, St Vincent again demonstrated the vicious behavioural traits that Collingwood thought marred his Mediterranean command. Significantly, however, he justified his conduct by reference to internal discipline and operational effectiveness. Heightened fears – real or imagined – of serious disaffection on the lower deck and confirmation of his earlier jaundiced views of the quality of his captains and the depth of their commitment, combined to prompt bitter blanket condemnations of senior officers, his predecessor in the command, and the professional members of the Admiralty Board: 'I have worked miracles in this fleet without the smallest aid from the powers above, whence I receive nothing but little mean jealousy.'[48] At times Lord Spencer thought it necessary to attempt to moderate some of these harsh judgements. For example, by correcting St Vincent's understanding of the incident at Lord Bridport's table, he softened the general imputation against his captains implied in the original version.[49] Spencer also sought to make St Vincent see that the ravages of prolonged service in punishing conditions, rather than congenital moral weakness, might explain the lack of vigour and 'tautness' of some of his senior officers:

> Some allowance must be made for the impossibility of knowing accurately how far an officer's nerves have kept up to the mark who has been battered and worn in the service and to supersede a man who has many years of good service to cite as his claim merely because he is a little the worse for wear would be a harsher measure than could well be justified.[50]

St Vincent's appointment as first lord of the Admiralty provided an opportunity to stamp his conception of authority on the entire Navy. The cause of commitment, discipline and order was to the forefront of this agenda and began with the detailed management of his office. If people wished to see him on appointments, promotions and other essentially personal service business, the first lord insisted that they came between five and seven o'clock in the morning. This stipulation attracted ridicule from some members of the colony of unemployed flag officers and admirals' sea-widows who spent the winter months at Bath. Martha Saumarez passed on to her husband stories about 'the Premier's' demanding regime. Thus Vice Admiral Charles Chamberlayne, a 'great friend' of the first lord, was said to breakfast with him at the Admiralty every morning at six o'clock. Such assiduous attendance encouraged Chamberlayne's expectations that he would soon be given a command. Rear Admiral John Thomas was a far less enthusiastic dawn supplicant. He complained to his friends that if he wished for an audience with the first lord he was obliged to dress by candlelight.[51] As was to be expected, St Vincent's Board continued to exert the control over commanders-in-chief that had become increasingly apparent since the war began. In the early weeks of his term, the naval residents of Bath joked that it was he, and not Cornwallis, who really commanded the Channel Fleet. This comment was a little unfair since at this stage St Vincent's detailed knowledge of the situation in the Channel meant that he was able to give very precise directions to his successor.[52]

St Vincent could be courtly and even affable when he chose, but there was no doubting his determination to keep matters close in hand, and to adopt a tone of suave menace or open belligerence as circumstances required. Non-performing captains were skewed by his pen. He told one officer that 'your letter has taught me that desire and request are not synonymous, a classical refinement I was not before susceptible of, in future I shall strictly observe the distinction'. When he suspected another officer of resorting to sarcasm, he treated him to a sharp put-down framed, as was often the case, as an aggressive closing salutation: 'I hope this talent will not appear in your correspondence with Sir.

> Your humble serv.
> St Vincent'[53]

Sir Edward Pellew, who was at one time in St Vincent's camp, made an interesting observation on the dangers of taking him as a role model.[54] In mid-1807 after a bitter, long-running dispute with Rear Admiral Troubridge, Pellew described his antagonist as a 'Weak Man – entirely commanded by his passion; Who is every week dishonouring himself by striking some of his Midshipmen or anybody else who comes in his way'. Troubridge was St Vincent's particular protégé, praised for boldness and vigour, and favoured with a seat on the Admiralty Board during his patron's term as first lord. Pellew's singularly unattractive picture of Troubridge may have been coloured with personal animosity but is consistent with accounts of his violent interactions with victualing contractors in the Mediterranean and with Neopolitan officials.[55] Pellew's remark is particularly significant, however, because it related Troubridge's behaviour to the example of his patron: '[H]is good fortune (and Lord St Vincent's example of violence – who he attempts to follow without talents to bear him thro') have overset him for want of ballast.' St Vincent's other critics have not accused him of physical violence but it is easy to see how the menace emanating from his correspondence and conversation might take physical form. It is true that Troubridge and St Vincent worked under intense pressure but so too did colleagues whose conduct was more moderate and self-controlled.[56] Reflecting on Pellew's comment, Northcote Parkinson interestingly observed that while Nelson might be an inspiring model, those tempted to imitate St Vincent ran the risk of magnifying his vices.[57]

Nelson and flag authority

Nelson's conduct off Cape St Vincent and the Nile established his reputation as a spectacularly successful fighting flag officer. When he commanded the Mediterranean Fleet from May 1803 he rose to all the other challenges faced by commanders-in-chief on that demanding station.[58] As St Vincent had done before him, Nelson paid careful attention to the condition of his ships and to the need to organize their rotation and relief so as to keep as many of them on station as possible. He also grappled effectively with the challenges of victualing and watering when far removed from Britain. His attention to victualing was part of a wider concern with the health and fitness of his men. Throughout his Mediterranean command Nelson marvelled at the good health of the fleet and remarked with obvious pride on this achievement in official and private correspondence: 'We have literally not a real sick man in it.'[59] But if Nelson's attention to his men's welfare followed St Vincent's practice, it reflected an approach to the exercise of authority quite different from his.

Nelson's aggressive confidence as a fighting commander galvanized his officers and men and drew them to respond enthusiastically to his leadership in battle. It also encouraged them to endure the hardships of six weeks at action stations when pursuing the French Fleet in early 1805.[60] The real challenge, however, was to provide leadership that would sustain high levels of commitment and enthusiasm during the long periods of demanding, but largely routine, activity that marked the lives of members of the wartime service. Nelson met that challenge by pursuing a range of strategies that secured the confidence of his officers and men and attached them to him. These strategies, which focused on the welfare of his seamen and the quality of interactions with his officers, were underwritten by a style of engagement quite different from St Vincent's.

St Vincent's sustained attention to the physical welfare of his crews was of a piece with his restless exercise of close control over the flag officers and captains subjected to him. Both strategies were highly instrumental, with the humanitarian hue of the former contrasting sharply with the calculated verbal brutality of the latter. By contrast, Nelson's concern with the welfare of those for whom he was responsible was broad ranging and genuinely humane. It gave a distinctive quality to his exercise of authority and played a key role in his popularity in the service and among the people.[61] In addition to paying close attention to the food and medical necessaries provided for his crews, he applied himself to other aspects of their comfort and well-being. Nelson actively promoted the interests of wounded or seriously injured seamen by bringing them to the attention of the managers of Lloyds Patriotic Fund. Following a successful small-boat action against French vessels at La Vandour in early July 1804, he congratulated the officers involved, emphasized the link between their gallantry and that of their crew and reminded them of their obligations to ensure the welfare of the wounded:

> I never knew the superior Officers to lead well but that they were always bravely supported by the men under their orders. Wounds must be expected in fighting the Enemy. They are marks of honour, and our grateful Country is not unmindful

of the sufferings of her gallant defenders. A regular list will be sent to the Patriotic Fund … and the Captains are to give each man a certificate before he leaves the Ship, describing his wounds, signed by the Captain and surgeon. The wounded men to be sent to the three Flag-Ships, as they will probably find better accommodation than in a Frigate.[62]

In a prosaic but nevertheless important vein, he advised the secretary of the Board that changes to the routing of mail increased the cost to seamen and petty officers, and was a barrier to them uplifting their letters from home.[63] Nelson also went to some pains to scrutinize clothing supplied by the Navy Board and evaluating its quality and fitness for purpose. Thus while a shipment of Guernsey jackets was judged to be of excellent quality, he found the garments too narrow and short, with the result that they rode out of the trousers of men on yards exposing them thereby 'to great danger of taking cold in their loins'.[64] These interventions might be seen as reflecting a particularly far-sighted view of the preconditions of efficiency and sound morale, and there is no reason to suppose that Nelson was unaware of these advantages. At the same time, however, his consideration of such matters extended in ways that point beyond sophisticated instrumentalism to a broader sense of shared human feeling. Thus, in addition to petitioning the Board on matters having a direct bearing on the well-being, and hence the efficiency, of his crews, Nelson also approached it on the inadequacy of victuals authorized for troops being carried on his ships, and, more surprisingly, those of French prisoners of war. In the latter case, he drew the Board's attention to the hardship resulting from the proposed withdrawal of a wine allowance from those for whom this drink was a staple.[65]

Nelson exercised firm control over his subordinates but his relationship with them was not disfigured by the harsh reprimands and menacing undertones in which St Vincent specialized. For example, when the commander of a brig was brought to book for flogging the entire ship's company because he was unable to identify an offender, Nelson told him that 'I cannot approve of a measure so foreign to the rules of good discipline and the accustomed practice of his Majesty's Navy. And therefore caution you against a similar line of conduct'.[66] While St Vincent took the view that he commanded and everyone else obeyed, Nelson sought to establish a leadership culture incorporating a degree of consultation and delegation. This culture was reinforced by a lightness of touch in exercising authority in routine matters, by warm recognition of merit and the effective utilization of professional sociability such as dinners on the flag ship. These meetings facilitated delegation by solidifying confidence and clarifying understanding.[67] Although Nelson was prone to vanity and was sometime petulant, the genuine warmth and enthusiastic generosity of spirit that glows through his correspondence gave a distinctive quality to his engagement with his senior officers. By contrast, when St Vincent praised or signalled rewards, he did so from a position of lofty, patrician superiority that detracted from the collegial quality of these exchanges. Colin White notes that Nelson had the ability to bind men to him through 'simple friendliness and good fellowship' and illustrates this point from a personal note that Nelson sent to a subordinate flag officer who was suffering from poor health in the Baltic. Nelson fused sympathy and professional approbation with sentiments of gratitude so as to give his letter the warmth of a communication between men who were friends as well as colleagues:

> Be assured My Dear Admiral that no person in the Service has a Juster value for your Public Services than myself, nor any man breathing a more perfect esteem & regard for your private character. I have experienced all your Particularity towards Me for which I am grateful and I beg you to be assured I shall ever feel myself your most obliged & affectionate Friend.[68]

It has been suggested that Nelson's interactions with his senior officers were not always as intensive as the 'band of brothers' image suggests.[69] While this was true of the months immediately preceding Trafalgar, he had been continuously at sea for twenty-four months in 1803–1805, and earlier he promoted a close relationship with his captains when commanding the detached squadron that triumphed in Aboukir Bay. The quality of Nelson's interactions with his senior officers in his last command appear to have reinforced the sense of his leadership built up over his career as a flag officer, and generated a distinctive ethos within the fleet. This involved attempts to ensure that friends remained friends by smoothing over momentary difficulties between Rear Admiral George Murray, his first captain, and Captain Richard Keats.[70] Nelson continued to stress the extent to which the fleet's effectiveness was a team effort. In August 1804, for example, he wrote an upbraiding letter to the lord mayor of London (knowing it would be made public) over the Corporation's failure to acknowledge junior admirals and captains in a congratulatory resolution: '[I]t is impossible that I can ever allow myself to be separated in Thanks from such supporters'.[71] Nelson also attended to the claims of individual officers. Thus when the commander of a sloop was thought to have been unjustly treated by a court martial for the loss of his ship, Nelson wrote letters of support to the secretary of the Board and the first lord, Viscount Melville: 'You must my Lord, forgive the warmth I express for Captain Layman; but he is in adversity, and, therefore, has the more attention to my claim and regard'.[72] In the case of both officers and men, Nelson's approach to leadership helped to form bonds which generalized the spirit that he demonstrated in moments of critical combat, enhanced their sense of shared commitment and fostered a high level of mutual confidence.

Collingwood on command

Although Collingwood was critical of aspects of St Vincent's leadership style, he was, in his own way, an adherent of the Mediterranean discipline. In the early stages of the war, when still a post captain, he was highly critical of the preparations of the Channel Fleet: '[W]e do not manage our ships with that alacrity and promptness that used to distinguish our Navy: there is a tardiness everywhere in the preparation and a sluggishness in the execution that is quite new'.[73] He later made it clear that the lack of urgency originated with Lord Howe, the commander-in-chief: 'There is such a parade and ceremony in every-thing done here'.[74] Collingwood was equally critical of Lord Hood's 'gross mismanagement' of the preparations for evacuating Toulon and destroying the French ships and stores there, noting acerbically that the Admiral's 'ambition' far exceeded his 'abilities'.[75]

Collingwood's service under St Vincent in the Mediterranean marked a critical stage in his career, culminating in promotion to rear admiral in 1799 and early appointment as one of Bridport's subordinate flag officers in the Channel Fleet. Collingwood's judgement on his new commander-in-chief's fleet management was as critical as St Vincent's. It was expressed in a damning comparison between the Channel Fleet and the Spanish Navy: '[I]t is at present in a very relaxed state, so different from what I have been used to, that it often gives me pain to see with what indifference the service is done, such as you might expect from Spaniards, in the dog days'.[76] Collingwood's practice as a commander-in-chief brought a strong and unbending commitment to order and efficiency, and unremitting attention to the formidable range of duties for which flag officers were responsible.

Although Collingwood benefited from interest, his career demonstrated that success might rest as much on a reputation for superior professional competence as on family or political connections. As a captain and as a flag officer, he was a sharp critic of promotions and appointments where interest trumped capability and threatened the safety and efficiency of ships. In the early months of the war Collingwood reported a collision in the English Channel in which *Bellerophon* lost her foremast and had to put in to Plymouth to repair the damage. This accident, which interfered with the deployment of the fleet, he wholly attributed to the failings of her officers: 'This was not the fault of the ship or the weather, but must ever be the case when young men are made officers who have neither the skill nor attention, and there is scare a ship in the Navy that has not an instance that political interest is a better argument for promotion than any skill'.[77] Collingwood's reaction to this incident reflected a persistent concern with the quality of leadership in the Navy. Reporting on another serious mishap in the Channel Fleet in 1800, he commented that '[t]he truth is, in this great extensive navy, we find a great many indolent, half-qualified people, to which may be attributed most of the accidents that happen'.[78]

While Collingwood was as devoted to the cause of efficiency and order as any officer in the Navy, he did not believe that these objectives necessitated the verbal harshness St Vincent relished, or the physical brutality to which some other officers subjected their ship's companies. As we have seen, he was critical of St Vincent's rough handling of his immediate subordinates when they displeased him, and of his resort to deviousness and manipulation when he became jealous of them. Collingwood was also intolerant of subordinates who lacked the poise and leadership skills necessary to exercise authority effectively. In 1804 Captain Edward Rotheram was appointed Collingwood's flag captain and remained with him until after Trafalgar in late 1805. Although Rotheram was a protégé of Collingwood's old supporter Admiral Roddam, and a fellow Northumbrian, he was critical of his crude, ungentlemanly manners and blustering and overbearing language.[79] Neither St Vincent nor Rotheram's personal leadership realized Collingwood's ideal of discipline and order within the Navy. This ideal was reflected in his praise of the *Ocean*'s crew. Collingwood conjured up an image of patriarchal order grounded on willing deference and a sense of shared values very different from St Vincent's increasing reliance on surveillance and control, or

Rotheram's vulgar hectoring of his officers and crew: 'They have always preserved the order of a regulated family rather than of men merely kept in subjection by discipline, their duty seemed to be what most interested them.'[80] In the latter stages of his career Collingwood began to think that flogging was an ineffective means of ensuring compliance because it made the victim an object of sympathy among his messmates. He placed increasing reliance on punishment fatigues that lowered wrongdoers in the eyes of their fellows and on peer pressure from other members of the lower deck.[81]

Captain Edward Codrington was highly critical of Collingwood's management of the Mediterranean Fleet after Trafalgar, but allowed that he was genial in one-to-one interactions. He also acknowledged that his new commander-in-chief combined a strong commitment to efficiency with a willingness to recognize merit even in those with whom he disagreed.[82] Collingwood's dispatch after Trafalgar was widely regarded as a model of affectionate loyalty to Nelson's memory, surprising the Duke of Clarence by its eloquent statement of deep feeling. He showed considerate attention to the 'young gentlemen' for whom he assumed a paternal responsibility and since his practice of discipline corresponded with his theory, he was greatly respected on the lower deck of the ships which he commanded.[83] A man who served under Collingwood as a boy seaman recalled that 'a better friend to seamen ... never trod a quarterdeck.'[84] In this respect it is significant that when mutinous rumblings off Cadiz plagued St Vincent's fleet, Collingwood's *Excellence* was entirely free of them. But while he inspired affection in those who knew him well, in public settings his emotions seem to have been confined within a cool exterior that gave his leadership a detached and impersonal air. One benefit of this was the absence of overt and acute interpersonal conflict that punctuated the careers of a number of his fellow admirals. Sir Sidney Smith was a thorn in his side – 'he annoys me more than French or Spanish fleet'[85] – but Smith had that effect on most of those under whom he served. With this exception, Collingwood's communications with difficult or inadequate officers were generally cool and business like, relying on understated ridicule rather than loud rage. When the captain of a ship left for England without orders he calmly observed to Rear Admiral Purvis that he would have to 'account to the Admiralty' for his actions.[86] He put a blustering and woefully inadequate officer in his place by quietly telling him that 'I have been thinking whilst looking at you how strange it is that a man should *grow* so big and *know* so little.'[87] But while Collingwood's style of command avoided the destructive high drama that marked St Vincent's relationship with a number of his subordinates, it was open to other objections.

After more than three years' experience in command of the Mediterranean Fleet, Collingwood explained his approach to his sister: 'I leave nothing undone that I can devise for the public good. Where I fail it will be my misfortune, not my neglect. When there is a fault it will be all my own. In the plan, I involve no one, for I never ask for council, and this I do from principle, not pride.'[88] At the time he wrote this declaration, Collingwood was desperate to be recalled, worn out by the pressures of command and illness, and by the emotional toll of prolonged separation from his family. But while these considerations may account for the timing of his statement, it seemed to have reflected habitual practice. When Collingwood commanded a squadron of the Mediterranean Fleet in the months before the Battle of Trafalgar, Codrington commented critically on his failure to delegate, his penchant for doing 'everything himself with great attention to the minutiae'.[89]

It seems that Collingwood's sense of overwhelming personal responsibility mitigated against even the most limited ideas of consultation and tended to weaken the sense of collective engagement that Nelson fostered among his subordinates. The difference in approach was signalled in the two admirals' attitudes towards socializing with their captains at sea. Codrington complained to his wife that '[w]e have got into the clutches of another stay-on-board Admiral, who never communicates with anybody but upon service' and claimed that his view of Collingwood was shared widely among subordinate flag officers and captains.[90] He argued that Collingwood's unjustifiably censorious attitude towards ship visiting made it harder for commanding officers to build a sense of mutual confidence and *esprit de corps* among their captains.

Codrington acknowledged Collingwood's willingness to make great personal sacrifices, his commitment to duty and the leadership he had shown at Trafalgar. At the same time, however, he treated the failure to follow Nelson's lead in the matter of ship visiting as emblematic of a more general lack of consideration for other people's feelings. He claimed that the same myopia was reflected in Collingwood's failure to identify casualties among commissioned officers before sending his dispatch to the Admiralty after the battle.[91] This oversight left many wives and parents in painful suspense, knowing the extent of the action and the scale of casualties, while still awaiting news of the fate of husbands and sons. Collingwood was also criticized for refusing to allow Admiral Villeneuve to bring any members of his suite with him onto his flagship. The defeated French commander was left to find what comfort he could among total strangers. One of Collingwood captain's reported that '[t]he act in itself is so savage and unfeeling, independent of the impropriety of it …. [T]he people here don't fail to cry out at the cruelty of it'.[92] These examples suggest a tendency to construe immediate responsibilities in a way that displaced the sensibilities displayed in dealings with individuals. Nelson, by contrast, was able to integrate duty and personal sensibility to an unusual degree and in ways that had a profound effect on those under his command. His skills put other officers such as Collingwood at a distinct reputational disadvantage. It is telling that when the Duke of Clarence wrote congratulatory letters to Collingwood after Trafalgar, and letters of condolence to his widow when news of his death reached England, he framed his esteem for Collingwood in the glow of Nelson's personality, presenting his regard as in some way being a product of his standing as 'My dear Coll', Nelson's special friend.[93]

Evangelical religion and flag officers' authority

Robert Blake has aptly characterized St Vincent's appeals to religion as 'pragmatism devoid of piety', and contrasted them with those made by officers committed to evangelical expressions of Anglicanism. Other members of the service described these men collectively as 'Blue Lights', or more contemptuously, 'psalm singers'.[94] Blue Lights were markedly pious, strict in their religious observances and self-consciously upright in their personal conduct. They strongly depreciated the blasphemous language wide-spread among officers and men, and the drunkenness and sexual license that were a common feature of naval life, and used their power to curb such behaviour. They did so not only because it was contrary to the rules of the service, but because they thought they had a far more significant obligation to counteract sin, and to produce an environment in which the positive core of their programme – the conversion of men who were at most nominal Christians into committed believers and practical followers of Christ – might be pursued most effectively. Admiral Sir Charles Middleton (Lord Barham) represented this commitment in the upper echelons of naval administration until the conclusion of his term as first lord in 1806, while Lord Gambier and Sir James Saumarez were prominent among evangelically inclined flag officers who served at sea in the Revolutionary and Napoleonic Wars.[95] These officers' religious conviction gave a distinct stamp to their understanding of flag officers' roles and sometimes conditioned their subordinates' responses to their exercise of authority.

Gambier had been brought up in the Middleton family and his service career benefited from that connection and from his kinship with the Pitts. He served with Middleton on the Admiralty Board, supporting his work in revising the *Regulations and Instructions* to include rules governing religious observance on naval vessels.[96] William Dillon, one of his midshipman, wrote a not altogether sympathetic account of Gambier's determination to attend to the religious as well as the navigational educa-tion of his 'young gentleman', to curb blasphemous language, stamp out drunkenness by diluting the men's grog and eliminate ship-board vice by enforcing widely ignored Admiralty regulations prohibiting unmarried woman on warships.[97] More positively, Gambier hoped to advance the work of personal reformation by distributing tracts among his seamen and using the mandatory services, the efforts of his chaplain and his own example and influence as an officer.[98]

These efforts continued when Gambier served briefly as third-in-command of the Channel Fleet in 1801 and during terms as commander-in-chief at Newfoundland (1801–1804), in the Baltic in 1807, and the Channel from 1809 to 1811. He scrutinized marriage certificates of females who wished to come on board, and sought to curb sexual irregularity among commissioned officers. In late August 1808, for example, Gambier issued an instruction from the Admiralty Board, where he was the senior naval commissioner, that as it had been

> represented to me that common prostitutes have been brought on board & seated at the Table of the Wardroom of some of the Ships of the Channel Fleet, it cannot be necessary to make any remark upon the frequent breach of decency & deco-rum, as well as moral & religious principles, offensive to married officers, chap-lains & a charge on the provisions of the Wardroom paid for by brother officers.

He ordered first lieutenants to be accountable 'for all Women of low character being brought or entertained on Board by an officer of *any description*'. Gambier expected that conscientious officers would report offenders to their captains and that they would forward to the Admiral the names of any officer 'as may be found to transgress the rules of discipline & decency by a practice so base & immoral'.[99]

Most of the personal conduct that Gambier censured was prescribed by the *Regulations and Instructions*, but his evangelical commitments meant that he approached these aspects of discipline in a distinctive way and was more consistent in his condemnation of them than some other flag officers. As a captain and a flag officer, however, he suffered from accusations that his religious preoccupations compromised his professional leadership. Robert Blake has provided a robust defence of Gambier against these charges[100] and in any case, Saumarez's capacity to consistently meet St Vincent's highly exacting standards of 'nerves under responsibility', undermines the idea that there was any necessary connection between evangelical commitments and ineffectual fulfilment of flag officers' responsibilities. It is true that Gambier's career demonstrated an odd mixture of apparent indecisiveness and recklessness, but that probably had more to do with his character, and relative lack of experience, than with any fatal shortcomings arising from heightened sensibility towards the spiritual welfare of his subordinates.[101] Nevertheless, the way in which Gambier pursued his evangelical agenda posed a risk to how subordinates responded to his authority.

William Dillon claimed that Gambier's scrutiny of the marriage certificates of his ship's company encouraged some crew members to provide false documentation and commit bigamy. One can easily imagine that his strictures against the entertainment of women of easy virtue in wardrooms would generate resentment and tension between loose livers and the obedient and upright souls who were expected to inform on them.[102] These reactions were, however, far less serious than those arising from the tendency for Gambier's evangelical commitments to be used against him by those who had other grounds for impugning his authority. Gambier's Channel command was marred by two courts martial, the first on his senior subordinate, Vice Admiral Sir Eliab Harvey, the second requested by Gambier in response to Lord Cochrane's implied accusations of timidity in a planned attack on a French Fleet at Basque Roads. In the course of the first incident, Harvey claimed that Gambier was unfit to command the fleet and made abusive references to the commander-in-chief's religious views and to his alleged hypocrisy in favouring evangelical fellow travellers over worthy and highly competent officers like himself.[103] Harvey's conduct was widely regarded as outrageous, but it is significant that he saw Gambier's evangelicalism as a weapon to use in his bitter dispute with his commander-in-chief.

Even in the hands of far more stable figures like Captain Thomas Byam Martin, Gambier's 'methodism' could be invoked as an aggravating factor, making him a figure of ridicule. Martin resented having to give up the *Prince of Wales* when Gambier took up his Baltic Command in July 1807 and was stung by having to accede to the new command-in-chief's 'request' to let him use his furniture, crockery, cabin stores, steward and cook. Martin told his mother that while he felt regret at not venting his indignation publically, 'there is some satisfaction in knowing that I yield to the wishes of my friends, and in doing so, learn from them what Mr Gambier will never learn from a Methodist preacher, to return good for evil'.[104] Since Martin subsequently got on very well with Saumarez in the Baltic, it is unlikely that his reaction to Gambier's demands was influenced by his evangelical inclinations.[105] As with Harvey, however, these associations exacerbated other grounds of offence and gave rise to comment that compromised Gambier's professional reputation to some degree.

Although Saumarez was as devout as Gambier, he managed to avoid the anti-evangelical opprobrium sometimes visited on his senior colleague. He seems to have steered clear of the jealousy that Harvey displayed towards Gambier, and his record as a seaman, fighting captain and fleet commander was proof against claims of limited competence. Moreover, while he was sometimes prickly and self-righteous towards superiors when he thought his commitment and merits were not appreciated, there is no evidence of the tactless treatment of subordinates to which Gambier was prone.[106] Gambier's early forays into reforming the conduct of his officers and crew were sometimes marked by outbursts of angry and impetuous chastisement of blasphemers. There is no record of Saumarez behaving in this manner. To the contrary, his exercise of command reflected a disposition of calm, controlled assurance.[107] Consistent with his obligation to promote the conversion of the wayward, Saumarez at times assumed personal responsibility for reforming individual seamen under his command, and took a gentle and considered approach to this important duty. In this regard it is significant that his ship was entirely free of the mutinous tendencies that so exercised St Vincent when he commanded the Mediterranean Fleet off Cadiz in the second half of 1797. It is also worth noting Captain Ross's account of Saumarez's interactions with 'a hardened mutineer' who had been transferred into his ship from the *Royal George*, where capital sentences had been passed on several crew members. Saumarez did not, as was usually the case, order this man to witness the execution of his accomplices. Instead, he called him to the main cabin where he 'represented in the mildest and most feeling of terms the heinousness of the crime which he was known to have committed'. Ross's account of this conversation is infused with the language of religious repentance. He describes Sir James as having availed himself of 'this trying occasion to work out the man's entire conversion' and refers to the seaman, who later distinguished himself at the Battle of the Nile, as the 'penitent man'.[108] Saumarez's religious commitments underwrote a generally humane approach to the exercise of authority which produced a mild, paternal, order on his ships and within his fleets:

> The proper degree of discipline which was always maintained – the attention that was invariably paid to the wants and comforts of the crew, – the excellent regulations of the ship, which were subversive of every kind of vice and immorality, – his own unaffected piety, and lastly, the example he himself set before his officers and men, – established in his ship a feeling of respect for, and warm attachment to, the captain which could not be shaken by any artifice of the wicked; for every officer and man looked up habitually to their commander as their *best* friend and advisor.[109]

Conclusion

The authority of flag officers was highly personal in the sense that it involved endless vigilance on their part and open commitment to the strictest standards of discipline. These traits were most clearly apparent in St Vincent's forceful style of leadership, and in the practices he sought to enforce in the fleets that he commanded. However, in a more fundamental sense, this view of the authority of flag officers was mechanical and depersonalized. In place of what he saw as the dangerously casual attitude which he had witnessed as a captain and that lived on in the practice of Howe and Bridport, St Vincent sought to reduce fleet management to a system of rules and practices governing the deployment of ships, and the attitudes and behaviours of the officers and men who manned them. As first lord of the Admiralty, he extended this sense of system back into the dockyards and the administration of the Navy. The timing may have been unfortunate, but this programme was entirely consistent with those imposed on the Mediterranean and Channel Fleets.

St Vincent's disciplinary ideals were of long standing but his dominant role in the French Wars, his high status in the service and his willingness to proselytize forcefully on discipline and fleet management made him a powerful voice in reshaping the authoritative role of flag officers. The men who held the major commands in the early stages of the war – Howe, Hood and Bridport – were elderly and while this no doubt had an impact on the approach they took to their duties, it was equally clear that their ideas of what their commanding roles required differed from St Vincent's and from those of the succeeding generations of flag officers. Once the energetic Lord Spencer had replaced the lackadaisical Earl Chatham at the Board, the pressures of global war and the reforming zeal of St Vincent prompted a shift in the demands placed on admirals. His ethos of command brought a single-minded sense of professional commitment that became the measure of flag officers. Some admirals from the younger generation, however, managed to combine St Vincent's strictures on disciplinary efficiency with styles of personal leadership that avoided the rebarbative features of his approach.

3

Anxiety and Failure

God forbid, that a character which I have strove to support for so many years should be hurt by an unavoidable misfortune; but even that I must give way to, rather than my country should want those abilities, which I am sorry to say, I do not possess at present.
    —Rear Admiral Robert Man to Lord Spencer on requesting to be relieved of his command of a squadron under Sir John Jervis in the Mediterranean, June 1796[1]

While the quality of senior leadership in the late Georgian navy was generally solid and occasionally spectacular, there were times when even apparently competent admirals proved unequal to the intense demands of their wartime roles. This chapter will consider a number of cases which demonstrate how the unavoidable operational pressures of flag command were compounded by the perceived expectations of the Board and the impact of political considerations to which it was subject. These expectations had a direct bearing on the professional reputations of flag officers, their future prospects in the service and on their sense of personal pride and honour. Admirals' highly tuned awareness of the pressures to which they were subject is clearly apparent in regular appeals for the approbation of the Board and the first lord in their public and private communications, and in their more general sensitivity to working under the scrutiny of subordinates, peers and the wider public. As a result, the language of exculpation played a significant role in flag officers' correspondence, reflecting their awareness of a working environment that fulsomely celebrated triumphs and harshly condemned perceived failures of nerve, energy and professional judgement.

The cases considered here involve one instance of extreme anxiety, and four of outright, career-limiting failure. Rear Admiral George Murray's experience of flag command in 1806–1808 was psychologically fraught and may well explain why he never accepted another appointment. Other flag officers' careers were curtailed because of failures of nerve or judgement, or because they demonstrated insufficient vigour in critical situations. These lapses blasted their prospects of further active service and put an end to any aspirations for high public honours. After Rear Admiral Robert Man was so overwhelmed by prolonged and acute anxiety that he removed his squadron from St Vincent's Mediterranean Fleet, he never served at sea again. Two other officers failed under the indirect pressure of combat. In 1801 Sir Hyde Parker proved insufficiently active and vigorous at the Battle of Copenhagen and in its aftermath. Although this action was successful, he was removed from his command shortly afterwards and his career effectively came to an end. A similar fate awaited Sir Robert Calder in late 1805 when he was deemed to have exhibited poor judgement in deciding not to re-engage with the enemy after an initially successful action. The final section of the chapter looks at a failure of judgement that cut short Vice Admiral Charles Stirling's career.

Rear Admiral Murray's 'anxieties of mind'

Flag officers' correspondence with the Board invariably provided detailed explanations of their intentions and actions and in many cases openly sought confirmation that 'their lordships' approved of decisions they had taken and the way they had been executed. In some cases these bids for approval spoke of considerable anxiety and a painful search for personal and professional assurance. Anxiety is a matter of degree, of course, and temperaments vary. Lord Howe's nerves were said to be shaken severely when his fleet was exposed to extremely bad weather in Torbay in early 1795 and some junior officers gave him the sobriquet 'Lord Torbay'.[2] However, the incident did not result in his recall, damage his reputation or lower him in the king's favour. Lord Gardner's nerves sometimes became very frayed but they never let him down entirely; nor did these episodes blunt his taste for further service. Other highly experienced and resilient officers such as Duncan, Duckworth, Cochrane, Keith and Saumarez exhibited signs of stress from time to time but the experiences that induced it did not undermine their professional confidence or compromise their effectiveness. In Rear Admiral Murray's case, however, the experience of command at sea generated levels of anxiety that seem to have discouraged him from accepting further offers of employment.

Murray's career was built upon a record of strong performance and on interest arising from his personal and professional reputation within the service. He survived two shipwrecks, fought with distinction in bloody actions in North America and the East Indies, was present at Bridport's action off L'Orient and at the Battle of Cape St Vincent.[3] In 1791, during the crisis with Russia, Murray surveyed the approaches to Copenhagen and in early 1801 put this experience to good account when he led the line in Nelson's assault on the Danish Fleet. Murray's *Elgar* engaged closely with four Danish ships-of-the-line, suffering heavy casualties and great damage to its spars, rigging and sails. Nelson made Murray his first captain in the *Victory* in 1803 but he missed Trafalgar. He had taken leave on his father-in-law's death and was attached at that time to Duckworth's squadron, which was refitting in England. When St Vincent took the Channel command in early 1806, he was keen to secure Murray as his first captain, telling Rear Admiral Markham of the Board he was the best possible officer for the job.[4] Murray, however, was not keen to serve under St Vincent, probably thinking of the tensions that had occurred between him and his subordinate flag officers on earlier commands.[5]

In late 1806 when Murray was appointed to command a squadron escorting a convoy of troop and supply ships to Botany Bay via the Cape and then on to Chile, he became embroiled in the fiasco precipitated by Captain Sir Home Popham's unauthorized decision to seize Buenos Aires. Although Murray blamelessly carried out his orders and struck his flag in early 1808 without a shadow of disgrace being attached to his name, his private correspondence with Markham was riven with signs of oppressively high levels of anxiety. He wrote frequently, and in painstaking detail, to describe and explain his conduct, and secure Markham's and (indirectly) the Board's approval of it. Markham was given some inkling of what to expect at the outset when Murray reminded him 'this is the first command I have had since I have had a flag, therefore I shall be thankful for every instruction that may be necessary for my conduct'.[6] Murray's request for advanced permission to return home if the state of his health required it foreshadowed the weakening confidence that emerged over the coming months. He justified this request by noting ruefully that 'before an answer to an application comes I may be dead and buried'.[7]

In addition to contending with the usual inevitable frustrations over appointments, manning and provisioning his ships, Murray had also to convene a number of courts martial. Although a humane man, his thoughts were not with those undergoing trial: courts martial were 'sad things for a man who has so little time left before he sails'.[8] The aggravation of Murray's judicial duties was compounded by impediments to a pet project for ensuring the health and sobriety of his crews. The son of a wine merchant, and later the owner of a splendid cellar, Murray was, nevertheless, a great believer in cocoa and complained to Markham when the Victualing Office was unable to supply it: 'I had so set my heart on all the squadron having it that I am very much disappointed.'[9]

As it turned out, the squadron's departure was delayed by westerly winds so it did not finally get under way until the last day of the year. The delay made it possible to address the cocoa problem but introduced a range of new anxieties. Some of these concerns resulted from the difficulties in maintaining fresh supplies when men and livestock consumed those shipped for the voyage; others arose from separation from, and close proximity to, his family in Chichester. The delay gave Murray time to worry about the expenses of being at sea, and how his wife would manage ashore. He conjured up wry images of looming bankruptcy and debtors' prison: 'If we continue to live as we used to do, I must look out for a berth on the King's Bench on my return. My wife says she is frightened out of her wits for fear she should spend too much money in my absence. However I will trust her.'[10]

By December 1806 the growing impatience of the Admiralty compounded the frustrations and anxieties arising from delays and domestic worries. The poor sailing qualities of some of Murray's ships meant that if his squadron tried to get under way in marginal conditions he was unlikely to make progress down Channel and risked being swept further to the east. He thought his superiors gave insufficient weight to these considerations and was mortified upon receiving a hectoring letter from the Port Admiral (written at the prompting of the Board) reminding him that a single, very weatherly, ship had recently left St Helens and made progress down the Channel. Murray's attempts at philosophical resignation were swept away in a deluge of painful apprehension: 'Some one, or more, at the board must certainly have a very bad opinion of me as an officer to suppose I would not go to sea the moment I could; if really that is their opinion why was I employed?'[11] In response to the Board's pressure, Murray twice ignored his better judgement and attempted to put to sea in unfavourable conditions. On both occasions wind and tide carried his ships back to St Helens where they were fortunate to recover their recently vacated anchorages.

Murray's squadron finally sailed on 31 December 1806, making a fast passage south. At Port Praia in the Cape Verde Islands he received the news (withheld by Popham for six months) that the Spanish had retaken Buenos Aires. Murray handled this crisis well. He made arrangements for troops en route to South America to be warned to stay off shore, redeployed ships in response to this news and then pressed on to Cape Town to await orders. On arriving at the Cape, however, he found much to disturb his peace of mind. He was alarmed at the scale of unjustified expenditure being undertaken by reckless, and probably corrupt, officials. Murray was particularly concerned at the value of public bills drawn by subordinate officers and resolved to put a stop to this practice. Given the need to provide supplies for the 5,000 troops in his convoy, his resolution proved impossible to keep. Although he was able to assure Markham that he had driven down the price of supplies at the Cape, he emphasized how uncomfortable he felt in having to deal with 'money matters': '[O]f all things in the world, I wished to avoid the authorizing of purchase, and it will ease my mind very much to know if what I have done is approved of at home.'[12] Murray's concerns on this score were no doubt coloured by the knowledge that if the Navy Board refused to pass his accounts, he would bear personal responsibility for any payments it did not approve. The spectre of the King's Bench prison loomed even larger in Murray's imagination at the Cape than it had off St Helens. The effect of these worries was aggravated by growing alarm over the fate of his friend Rear Admiral Sir Thomas Troubridge, who was overdue from the East Indies.[13] Murray's concern for his friend's safety was compounded by his anxious wish for the forceful Troubridge to assume his command and set about putting 'things to rights'.[14]

When he was ordered to South America, Murray expressed grave (and as it turned out well-founded) reservations about the conditions the squadron would meet off the River Plate in winter weather. He reminded Markham of the advanced request to be relieved and was very frank about the increasing strain he felt: 'I find that anxiety of mind is making me nervous.'[15] As the squadron headed towards St Helena en route for South America, Murray sent the Board a 3,000-word statement of explanation and exculpation, going back to his departure from St Helens. It included detailed reference to why he had chosen his present route and an attempt to forestall criticism for having taken it: '[T]he more I think of it the more I am satisfied at being right in going there, and I hope your lordships will see it in the same light.'[16]

Off Buenos Aires Murray showed initiative in getting his ships into a position to support the attack by undertaking a risky passage across a stretch of shoals off the mouth of the River Plate. He then played an effective role in the evacuation of the British forces and took over the naval command from Rear Admiral Charles Stirling. As a result, Murray found it necessary to explain to Markham why he had agreed to put his name to the humiliating terms negotiated by the defeated military commanders: 'I cannot tell you how many uneasy hours it has and will cost me, but I hope I have done right, and that, placed in the situation I was, it was my duty to do so.'[17] To his evident relief, Murray was recalled to England, ordered to strike his flag and go ashore. He returned to his home in Chichester and never went to sea again.

During his service as a commander-in-chief Murray never faced the prospect of a fleet action or, indeed, the watching, covering and chasing that sometimes preceded them. In other respects, however, his remarkably unguarded correspondence with Markham demonstrates an important range of the challenges faced by flag officers on active service. While preparing to depart from St Helens, Murray contended with the logistical complexities that were inseparable from the role, and with the concerns over domestic arrangements that must have been felt by all those embarking on a service expected to extend to several years. He also experienced Admiralty pressure for fleets and convoys to put to sea at the earliest possible time. The unreasonableness of these demands did nothing to blunt their imperative force. In Murray's case, the sense of frustration and perceived injustice generated by the imputation of timidity and insufficient vigour increased the psychological burden that he already carried. Once at sea, delayed and ill-sequenced communications forced him to second-guess the Admiralty's wishes when circumstances changed. In common with officers similarly placed, he did so in the knowledge that mistakes in divining the Board's intentions might well count against his reputation and future prospects in the service. Finally, Murray's uncomfortable experience as senior officer at the Cape included exposure to the financial risks that commanders-in-chief faced if they could not justify expenditure made on their stations.

But while Murray's correspondence with Markham laid these anxieties bare, he did not succumb to them, and they did not damage his reputation. Markham was a professional member of the Board, but he was also a close friend who could be relied upon not to take unfair advantage of their correspondence. Murray did not expose his anxieties in public reports to the Board, and the tone of his official journal has been described as 'laconic'.[18] Some of Murray's letters were passed on to Thomas Grenville after he relinquished the first lordship but his reaction was acute and sympathetic: '[T]hey bear strong evidence of an anxious and active mind. It is no light service to be sailing round the world with generals, troops and transports.' Grenville had expected Murray to remain as commander-in-chief off the coast of America.[19] Although he never served at sea again, Lord Mulgrave offered Murray the important post of second-in-command of the Channel Fleet early in 1808 and he was widely tipped for the Halifax and Newfoundland Stations in late 1810.[20]

Rear Admiral Robert Man's 'imaginary ills'

Man, the son of a captain killed in the Seven Years War, had fought with distinction as a frigate captain during the American War and had sufficient interest to command a ship-of-the-line through most of the peace that followed it. Following Man's appointment as subordinate flag officer in the Mediterranean Fleet, St Vincent had enough confidence to give him command of a detached squadron, operating initially under orders that came from Sir Hyde Parker, his second-in-command. In light of subsequent developments it is significant, however, that Man was reluctant to take on this responsibility and wrote to Spencer in apprehensive tones about it.[21] In the first half of 1796 Man suffered what appears to have been a nervous breakdown. Signs of mental stress were apparent early in the year as the squadron patrolled off Cadiz, charged with keeping watch on the Spanish ships in that port while St Vincent and the rest of the fleet supported a landing on Corsica. Man asked to be relieved of his command and became increasingly anxious as he awaited news of the outcome of his request. He told the first lord that he felt 'in the most embarrassed state a man can be placed in … I want to do what is right, though feel excessive difficulties arise in the wished for performance, but I strive to act in the best manner for his Majesty's service, and in the hope of it proving so, I must rest.'[22] When Spencer encouraged Man to stay in his post, he replied that 'the anxiety I have suffered since on this service has reduced me to the necessity of making my case known. I have already done my duty to the utmost of my abilities, but am now so much reduced as to make a change absolutely necessary.'[23] St Vincent, who was aware of Man's condition and its impact on what he described as the 'vigour of his command', nevertheless treated it as a chimera: 'Poor Admiral Man has been afflicted with such a distempered mind, during the last few months, that imaginary ills and difficulties have been continually brooding in it, when in fact he has never had a real one.'[24] Man's already extreme state of anxiety was increased by concerns about the impact of the early termination of his appointment on his professional reputation and career prospects. He made a plea for Spencer's sympathetic understanding, hoped he would intercede with the king on his behalf and looked forward, on his recovery, to 'prove my duty to the best of sovereigns'. A few days later Man reiterated these sentiments in pained, apologetic terms.[25] By the time his squadron was ordered to rejoin the rest of the fleet off Corsica two months later, however, Spencer hoped Man had recovered his nerve. He wrote encouragingly and also began to take steps to replace him. Before Man received news of his impending relief, however, his anxiety overwhelmed him entirely.[26]

When Man failed to replenish his supplies at Gibraltar on his way to rejoin the fleet off Corsica, St Vincent ordered him to return there to do so. During the passage down the Mediterranean, his squadron encountered the Spanish Fleet and was chased into Gibraltar. From there he wrote to Spencer in utterly demoralized terms, talking up the strength of the forces facing the British Navy in the Mediterranean and bewailing his inability to offer help to St Vincent. Most importantly, however, Man announced that he had consulted his captains and decided that the best course of action was to take his squadron home.[27] He arrived at Spithead in early January 1797, sent Spencer a long and painful letter of explanation on his extraordinary conduct and struck his flag.[28]

Although St Vincent had shown some unsympathetic insight into Man's state of mind, he claimed to have found his decision to return home 'incomprehensible'. Characteristically, given some of his other disciplinary preoccupations, St Vincent dwelt on the role played by Man's captains, all of whom 'wanted to get to England'.[29] His exasperation at Man's conduct was heightened by the belief that it compromised his attempts to find the Spanish Fleet and bring it to action. Despite these considerations, however, Man was not ordered to face a court martial and, although never appointed to serve at sea again, he was not disgraced publically. To the contrary, he retained sufficient professional standing and interest to be appointed to the Admiralty Board.

When Man arrived at Spithead, Spencer wrote to express disappointment at the step he had taken but also made it clear that he regarded it as a discretionary response to changed circumstances rather than direct disobedience. He agreed with Man's claim that his orders from Hyde Parker had been overtaken by events and while observing that new orders from St Vincent would have made it clear that he should rejoin the fleet at all costs, he noted that these had not been received and that Man had therefore to act on what he understood was for the good of the service. Although Man saw Spencer's regret at his failure to anticipate St Vincent's orders as a partial rebuke, he nevertheless treated the other principal points of his letter as exculpatory prompts from the first lord and retailed them in justification of his conduct.[30] Given that Man's mental state made it highly unlikely that he could have acted in any other way than he did, the undelivered dispatches from St Vincent provided a providential escape. Man's case was thus one of those occasions when poor communications worked to a flag officer's benefit. They also saved Spencer from having to order a court martial on a senior officer when the war in the Mediterranean seemed to be going very badly. In these circumstances, a public trial of Man might have been a source of acute political embarrassment and would have drawn a number of other presumably well-connected officers into a net of official and public disapprobation. Finally, the significance of Man's desertion of his commander-in-chief may well have been cast safely into the shadows by the glow of triumphant celebration sparked by the victory off Cape St Vincent, which occurred within six weeks of his arrival at Spithead.

Sir Hyde Parker's eclipse

If victory shielded Man's failures of command, it highlighted those of Vice Admiral Sir Hyde Parker. After a successful career as a captain and continuous service at flag rank, including a highly lucrative spell commanding at Jamaica, Parker was a notable early victim of St Vincent's determination that flag officers should model the virtues of activism, commitment and vigour which he had extolled as a commander-in-chief.[31] Parker was triply unfortunate to be appointed to a major command when his personal powers and enthusiasm were waning, St Vincent was first lord and Nelson his second-in-command.

In late 1800 Lord Spencer had appointed the 61-year-old Parker to the senior role in the North Sea Fleet, with Nelson as his second. Parker's previous experience during the 'Russian Armament' of 1791, a crisis of Anglo-Russian relations that seemed likely to lead to war, was one of the considerations in his favour.[32] He had very strong connections in the service – his father was an admiral with sufficient interest to have made him lieutenant at 16 and ensure ongoing employment thereafter – and it was a measure of Parker's general effectiveness as a flag officer that he had held commands at sea throughout the Revolutionary War. His appointment to the North Sea command was endorsed by St Vincent, under whom he was serving in the Channel Fleet. In light of subsequent developments, however, it is significant that Parker had not been enthusiastic about serving as St Vincent's deputy while he lived ashore. He only took the role because he understood Lord Spencer to say that he would be given the command if St Vincent's health failed. When Hyde Parker deputized for his commander-in-chief in late November 1800 the painful thought that St Vincent continued to get the lion's share of any prize money, and the harrowing conditions at sea prompted him to tell his brother that he was of a mind to give up the command: 'I feel the responsibility so heavy while the Chief is enjoying himself at Torr Abbey, that I do not think I can possibly support it.' Sir Harry Parker, no doubt mindful of Lord Spencer's views, counselled his younger brother that if he resigned he would never be asked to serve again.[33] Hyde Parker was certainly unenthusiastic about taking up the Baltic command. Shortly after leaving England he told his wife that he would much rather be at home with her and that the service was the 'most displeasing' he had ever been on. This unease was due in large part to the quite understandable sense that St Vincent was placing him under great pressure. Hyde Parker felt that if he succeeded it would be taken for granted, and if he failed he would 'receive nothing but abuse and Blame'.[34]

By the time Hyde Parker was readying his squadron for sea at Yarmouth, St Vincent was at the head of the Admiralty Board. Initially, the new first lord wrote to his recent colleague in the most cordial terms: 'That all honour and glory may attend you is the fervent wish of your steady friend.'[35] Following a tip-off that he was tarrying, however, St Vincent sought to hasten the fulfilment of this wish by ensuring that the fleet put to sea as soon as possible. St Vincent's moral appetite for censuring unwarranted delays was sharpened by the knowledge that Parker had very recently married the young daughter of Vice Admiral Onslow, and the suspicion that the social demands of this attachment were encouraging him to linger at Yarmouth. Lady Parker had actually left Yarmouth before St Vincent made his move but her presence there had been seen by members of the fleet as an impediment. As Captain Thomas Freemantle put it, '[U]ntil my Lady goes away I don't think we shall make very great progress. They get up too late and all business in consequence is much delayed.'[36] St Vincent told Parker that his advice was 'sent by a messenger purposely to convey to you my opinion, as a private friend, that any delay in your sailing would do you irreparable injury'. The first lord expected that Parker would appreciate that 'I could not give you a stronger proof of my friendship than by conveying this opinion in the way I have done'. Significantly, and unusually, St Vincent timed his message as well as dating it.[37]

Once Parker was on station off the coast of Denmark, St Vincent made it clear that he was expected to play an aggressive and vigorous role and to bring his fleet to action. He was told that his objective was to destroy or capture the Danish ships moored off Copenhagen and force the Danes to come to terms.[38] Shortly thereafter, ships under Parker's command inflicted a crushing defeat on the Danish Fleet at the Battle of Copenhagen. It soon became apparent, however, that this triumph of arms was due to Nelson's determination rather than his commander-in-chief's. Parker's approach to the action was exceedingly slow and once it was under way he made a recall signal which would have aborted the attack, had Nelson obeyed it. Since none of these details appeared in Parker's report to the Admiralty, the first lord sent him a 'hearty' congratulation and plaudits on his 'bold design' and 'daring execution'. St Vincent also wrote a glowing letter to the lord mayor of London on the importance of the victory in protecting the Baltic trade, and passed on congratulatory addresses voted by both houses of parliament.[39]

In the aftermath of the battle Parker predicted that he would receive 'little merit' from the victory since he was not 'in it'.[40] As further questions emerged about the leniency of the convention Parker agreed with the Danes, this gloomy judgement proved unduly sanguine. Once St Vincent was informed of Parker's questionable role in the action, he ordered his recall. He thus endowed the connection he had made earlier between 'steady friendship' and performance with a sinister prescience. Parker did not even have time to bask undisturbed in the approbation of the City and Parliament. By a cruel coincidence, the congratulatory messages came into his hands at the same time as the notice of recall.[41] The fact that Parker was given the option of going home in a humble sloop, a ship unfit for a post captain, or limping back in a badly damaged first-rate ship compounded the public ignominy of his recall. He chose the battered *Blanche* as the lesser of two evils. The ship was holed below the water line, had poorly set-up rigging and sailed very badly. Its performance was further impaired when it took the ground off the Danish coast and lost its false keel. *Blanche's* captain commented on the sudden and unexpected timing of the recall and the fact that Parker had to come home in such a slow and un-handy ship. He noted that neither of the other two flag officers on the station (Nelson and Graves) were fit, and Nelson was widely thought to want to go home.[42] This reaction signalled that Hyde Parker's humiliating treatment was noted by other members of the service and would therefore be felt even more sharply by him.

Although St Vincent exposed Parker to a galling combination of open disgrace and official disregard, the vice admiral had some sympathizers in the service and friendly questions were asked in the House of Commons about his recall. Initially, he seemed resigned to take comfort from these signs of professional regard and let the matter rest. However, Sir Harry Parker, a country gentleman and a prominent prize agent who saw family and professional pride at stake, reacted angrily to this stance and urged his brother to seek public vindication of his conduct.[43] When Hyde Parker subsequently wrote to Evan Nepean requesting a court of inquiry, a process designed to uncover facts, rather than try a particular person, he received one of the Board's standard, opaque rebuffs: 'I have their Lordships commands to acquaint you, that, on a due consideration of the circumstances, they do not think it proper to institute an inquiry into your conduct in the manner you have pointed out.' All that was left for Hyde Parker to do was to print the correspondence and circulate it to his friends, this 'being the only method by which, he is of opinion, that any unfavourable impression, which may have arisen, relative to his conduct, can be effectually removed'.[44] Shortly thereafter, a barrister of the Inner Temple published a pamphlet on the recent international politics of the Baltic which included a vindication of Hyde Parker's agreement with the Danes.[45] In early 1803 Parker made an enquiry to the Board about cases where other officers had been peremptorily recalled from their commands but does not appear to have pursued the matter further.[46]

The Board made much of Hyde Parker's statement that its instructions were difficult to fulfill and seems also to have raised the question of the leniency of the Convention. These matters were presented as a concern of the Board and the Cabinet. However, both Hyde Parker and his brother thought that St Vincent was the prime mover. Although Nelson had played a role in alerting St Vincent to Parker's performance off Copenhagen, he retained some personal sympathy for him in adversity, backhandedly ascribing his chief's lacklustre conduct to 'idleness', not to a lack of courage.[47] Even if this judgement was unduly harsh, it seems clear that Hyde Parker did not take an enthusiastic approach to the challenges that faced him in the Baltic, and, in the climate of prevailing expectations, his lack of vigour left him seriously exposed. During the action Parker's judgement was probably affected by physical exhaustion and anxiety (he had not slept for five days and had expressed frequent concerns about the hazards of the undertaking) and by inaccurate information.[48] Nelson's assessment was vindicated to some degree by Parker's subsequent conduct. He did not show significantly renewed vigour in the weeks that followed, failing to press home the advantage by pursuing the Russian Fleet, or to respond to peace overtures from the emperor.[49] Arguably, however, Nelson's role in Parker's eclipse was more critical than that of a mere informant. Service pedigree and past effectiveness notwithstanding, Parker had the misfortune to have his leadership exposed to comparisons with Nelson and other admirals of the younger generation, at a time when age, weariness and rich living blunted his appetite for action and sapped his vigour. With St Vincent continuing to preside at the Board until well into the next stage of the war, his fate was sealed.[50]

Sir Robert Calder's dilemma

Parker's personal and professional pride was no doubt wounded severely when St Vincent recalled him without a charge and without the chance to vindicate himself before a court of inquiry. But if he was deprived of the hope of public exoneration, Parker was spared the indignity of prolonged public disgrace and professional annihilation that would have followed an unfavourable court martial verdict. Lord Radstock offered a cruelly dismissive and ill-informed judgement of Miss Onslow's prospects of happiness as Hyde Parker's wife – 'She will be as happy as Jewels & fine clothes can make her, & this, in my opinion, is all the happiness she deserves' – but he had made it clear that he had lost his taste for service and was eager to be at home. After Copenhagen he was free to enjoy with her the fruits of a prize-rich career without any risk of being tempted back into active service.[51] Sir Robert Calder's situation was altogether different. He was six years younger than Parker and had a record and connections that seemed likely to lead to a major command. He was employed continually as a flag officer at sea until two ill-judged acts in the second half of 1805 ended any hopes of further advancement.[52]

In early July 1805 Cornwallis ordered Calder's squadron to cruise off Cape Finisterre to intercept a combined French and Spanish Fleet that was reported to be heading west from Antigua. On 22 July, in the course of a confused engagement with the combined fleets in banks of thick fog, the squadron captured four ships-of-the-line and inflicted heavy damage on other enemy ships. However, two of Calder's ships-of-the line were mauled so badly that they could not be restored to fighting condition at sea; others suffered significant damage. The enemy ships remained in sight for the next two days but Calder did not re-engage with them. He was concerned with the condition of his fleet and its prizes and not prepared to risk an unsuccessful action that would leave British shipping and the coast of England exposed. It is significant that Calder was unaware that the Admiralty had decided it was necessary to inflict as much damage on the enemy as possible in order to discourage further excursions from port.[53] Nevertheless, initial official reactions to Calder's action seemed reassuring and in mid-August he acknowledged a letter signalling the Board's approbation of his conduct. Even at this stage, however, he was aware of critical comments on his performance in 'the papers' and in London gossip, which he attributed to the Board not having published his public letter in full. While accepting stoically that he had to 'put up with' a 'great deal of nonsense', Calder appealed for Lord Barham's support and repeated his earlier explanation: 'I pledge myself to your lordship that everything was done that was possible with the combined squadrons; and my situation was critical in the extreme from the Ferrol and Rochefort squadrons, after the action, with the wind then easterly.'[54]

By the time this letter reached the Admiralty, the first lord had received a translation of an account of the action by the Spanish admiral Frederico Gravina, published in Madrid earlier in August. Gravina claimed that after the initial battle the combined fleet pursued Calder's squadron for two days but was unable to bring it to action. He assumed that this was due to the damage Calder's ships had sustained: 'I consider the English squadron having avoided a second attack to have been caused by the damage they received in the action, since the forces of the two fleets were equalised by the quality of the ships – we having, on our side, no 3 deckers and two small ships of 64 guns.'[55] From Gravina's point of view, this narrative salvaged something from what might be seen as an unqualified, if limited, reverse. In the hands of critical British observers, however, it prompted the question whether the damage sustained by Calder's ship was severe enough to justify avoiding further action.

If Calder had stuck to his original determination to weather the 'John Bull sentiments' of the press, the Board may well have let this questionable prelude to Nelson's victory at Trafalgar slip below the horizon. As time went on, however, he became increasingly concerned at the effect of hostile commentary and gossipy society speculation on his 'character as an officer or as man'. In late August the government-inclined *Morning Post* was sceptical of French accounts of the action but claimed that in light of them 'Sir Richard Calder must now feel it doubly incumbent upon him, most satisfactorily to clear up all doubts and mysteries'.[56] Consequently, and despite an expectation that courts martial never had a favourable impact on public opinion, Calder, following Nelson's advice, sought to preserve his professional reputation through that means. He felt that while he could withstand short-lived notice in the press or even in parliament, the doubts of friends and members of the service made his position untenable.[57] As Calder told the court, 'The consciousness of having done my Duty, would … have induced me to treat these Aspersions with Contempt, had they not become so general that I was apprehensive that silence on my part would be construed into Acknowledgement of their Truth, and an Admission of my own Misconduct.'[58] In making this call, he may have been influenced by the extent to which press criticism was conditioned by the uncertainty on the facts of the case, and by the hope that a court martial would resolve these in his favour.

Calder left the fleet shortly before Trafalgar to face a court martial at Portsmouth over the Christmas of 1805. He was charged with 'not having done his utmost to renew the engagement' after the battle. In his defence, Calder acknowledged that it would have been possible to bring the enemy to action but insisted that his decision was 'not only *justifiable* but the most proper and prudent course, under all the Circumstances to be adopted'. Forcing a renewal of the action risked his prizes, his fleet and, as the Ferrol and Rochefort squadrons were thought to be out, the safety of the country. He referred to the strength of the enemy squadron, the poor condition of his own, his lack of frigates and to the fact that both his commander-in-chief and the Admiralty had approved of his action. As in an earlier trial of Cornwallis, Calder appealed to the discretion that must be allowed to a flag officer, 'to be exercised according to the best of his Judgement, and subject to the *Responsibility which attaches to all Persons* in *Situations of Command*'.[59] He advanced decisions made by Howe and St Vincent in the wake of their victories as precedents.

Calder's arguments had some impact on the court but did not secure his exoneration. His honour was spared by its ruling that he had not been motivated by 'Cowardice or Disaffection', but his professional standing was seriously compromised by its determination that his judgement was found wanting. His failure to re-engage 'had arisen solely from Error in Judgement'. It was thus 'highly censurable', and warranted a severe reprimand.[60] In a highly competitive environment the verdict effectively put an end to any expectation of a major command to which he aspired.

Although Nelson advised Calder to seek a court martial, he also urged him to delay his return to England because a major action seemed likely and it would be to his advantage to serve as second-in-command in it.[61] Calder and Nelson had been rivals in the past, but the latter generously, if vaingloriously, anticipated that the 'huzzas and illuminations for a glorious Victory' under his command would sink Calder's 'great difficulties'.[62] The loss of an opportunity that might have been Calder's salvation probably sealed his fate. Like Hyde Parker before him, Calder found himself judged against the exalted public and professional expectations that arose from Nelson's achievements. As has been often noted, the cumulative effect of Nelson's successive victories set new and demanding standards of bold persistence in chases and engagement.[63] In addition, however, it was almost certainly a mistake for Calder to seek to justify his actions by references to the aftermaths of the Glorious First of June and the Battle of Cape St Vincent. These engagements occurred in a very different climate and had been incorporated in the Parthenon of great victories at sea that were celebrated by the people of London and numerous flag officers in late 1797.[64] To claim them as precedents was implausible and only likely to antagonize powerful admirers of Howe and St Vincent.

Contemporary views of Calder's personality differed. St Vincent became increasingly contemptuous of his former flag captain but other colleagues were more forgiving. Edward Codrington spoke warmly of his social engagement with captains under his command, and while Thomas Freemantle thought he was 'not wise' he went on to say that Calder was 'so fair to serve with and so accommodating, that I am much interested in him getting off with credit'.[65] The shortcomings in judgement he demonstrated in the battle and its aftermath accord with Rear Admiral Thomas Byam Martin's assessment of Calder as 'a wrong-headed, and consequently often a wrong judging man' but it seems likely that it was the context that was critical in determining his fate not his popularity in the service.[66]

The impact of the court martial verdict on Calder's subsequent career was exacerbated by another poor judgement. Thomas Grenville briefly considered him for a subordinate role in the Channel Fleet in 1806 but found informed opinion (probably including St Vincent's) against it: if Calder did not lack courage his 'indecisiveness' was 'almost as bad for command as downright fear'.[67] In 1807 Calder told the Board that he was willing to serve but when offered a subordinate role declined it as being insufficiently important for an officer of his rank and experience. This was to be his last chance for a role at sea and he should have recognized it as such. When Charles Yorke offered him the port command at Plymouth in 1810 because he had reservations about his treatment in 1805, Calder accepted it with concealed reservations. In the spring of 1811, after a criticism of his condemnation was published in the *Naval Chronicle*, he told the first lord that he had only accepted this command (which he found 'obscure and laborious') in the expectation that he would subsequently be offered more 'honourably profitable' and generally congenial 'employment in the great line of the Service to which I had always been accustomed'. In reply to this ungracious epistle, Yorke made it clear that he had viewed the Plymouth appointment as a gesture of rectification, an 'act of justice', not as a stepping stone to greater things. He was happy to provide Calder with an opportunity to hoist his flag again, but showed not the slightest inclination to satisfy his wishes for a command at sea.[68]

Calder was relieved of the unrewarding trials of the Plymouth command in 1812. Having benefited from a succession of wartime promotions, he rose to Admiral of the White on the half-pay list, and when a military division of the Order of the Bath was established in 1815 his earlier service was recognized by inclusion in its second echelon. St Vincent looked down his nose at being made a Grand Cross of that order, so Calder's undistinguished place within it can hardly have been a source of much gratification.[69] It was a far cry from ambitions he no doubt harboured as commander of a large squadron in a critical theatre of war, and those reflected in his fruitless anticipation of a return to 'the great line of the Service' in 1811.

Vice Admiral Charles Stirling's misadventures in Jamaica

On 9 May 1814 a court martial at Portsmouth ruled that Vice Admiral Charles Stirling was guilty 'in part' of charges arising from a freight transaction he entered into when commanding at Jamaica.[70] Up until this point, Stirling had enjoyed a solidly successful career. He had fought with distinction in the American War, was promoted to post captain in 1783, regularly employed at sea in the French Wars and had seen action under Saumarez at Algeciras in 1801, and with Calder off Cape Finisterre in 1805. He was promoted rear admiral in the large promotion that followed Trafalgar, served in the Channel Fleet and within a year had been appointed to command a convoy taking troops to the River Plate to invest Montevideo. This appointment was followed by a commander-in-chief's role at the Cape of Good Hope and a command at Jamaica, a station where he had been naval commissioner between the wars. In late 1812, however, the Jamaica squadron was incorporated into an enlarged North American command and Stirling became subject to Sir John Warren's authority. He lost his independent power of nomination to vacancies and his entitlement to a commander-in-chief's share of prize and freight money.[71]

In late February 1813, Warren received a letter from Naval Commissioner Wolley at Jamaica accusing Stirling of receiving a payment under the guise of freight money for arranging convey protection for two merchant vessels sailing from Jamaica to the Spanish Main and returning to the island. Wolley claimed that these transactions were common and that Stirling had long been implicated in them. Warren received further information of this transaction in June 1813 when Captain Hayes O'Grady of the sloop *Sappho* informed him that he, Stirling and the admiral's secretary received their payments before the convoy left Kingston, and that the freight was not on board his ship when he sailed. O'Grady repaid his share of the freight shortly before reporting these transactions to Warren. Although Wolley named a flotilla of officers who could provide witness to his claims, O'Grady was the only officer called by the court. Wolley's testimony was given in an affidavit.

Stirling was superseded before the Admiralty heard of Wolley's claims and was only ordered to face a court martial on his return to England. The trial opened on 7 February 1814 before a fourteen-man court that included eight flag officers. Stirling made an unsuccessful attempt to exclude Wolley's statement on the grounds that he was unable to cross-question this accuser. He made it clear that his relationship with Wolley had long been a very difficult one. In his evidence, and in response to cross-questioning, O'Grady gave an account of Stirling's offer and of a visit to his agent's house in Kingston at which the details were arranged. Although he made much of the fact that Stirling had asked him not to discuss the matter with other captains on the station, and insisted that it was highly unusual to receive freight payments in advance of a voyage, O'Grady carefully avoided openly accusing Stirling of corruption.

In his statement of defence, Stirling admitted to authorizing the convoy but swore that he was not a party to discussions between his secretary and O'Grady on prepayment. He claimed that he regarded these payments as improper and had sought to suppress them during his time at Jamaica. However, he justified the convoy on the grounds that it protected a trade that provided a market for British goods in the Spanish colonies, and generated much needed species for Britain's West Indian islands. Stirling pointed out that all the arrangements involving O'Grady and his representatives, the admiral's secretary and other agents in Kingston had been completely open, and claimed that this testified to his sense of their propriety. He had asked O'Grady not to discuss the arrangement with other captains to avoid stirring up jealousy among them, not because the transaction was underhand. Stirling also pointed out that the pecuniary incentive for corrupt conduct in this case was ludicrously slight. As the sole beneficiary of a flag officer's share of the freight he would have received a little over £160. In reality, however, as there were five junior flag officers on the station and Stirling was under Warren's command, his share would have amounted to only £16, equivalent to a few days' pay.

As was only to be expected when responding to a charge of dishonesty, Stirling claimed that his reputation in the service was spotless. Certainly, from what is known of his earlier career, there is no indication that he had the money-getting avidity for which Lord Keith was notorious. On being promoted to flag rank Stirling's ambition was to be comptroller of the Navy so that he could live at home among his family, a preference that indicated a taste for comfortable domesticity rather than for the riches that could be acquired through prizes and freights.[72] Far from being grasping, Stirling had once given up his share of a vessel that was taken within sight of Stirling's flag-ship after a two-day chase by Captain Phillip Brooke.[73] In his post-trial statements of vindication, Stirling dwelt at length on his record as an economizing reformer and the unpopularity he had courted in curbing the self-serving practices of captains on his station. He also pointed to instances off South America and in the West Indies when he eschewed the pursuit of booty and prizes, and produced accounts to show that as commander-in chief at Jamaica his share of prize and freight was a modest £4,000.[74]

Stirling's court martial has been seen as a straightforward trial for corruption sparked by the Admiralty's concern about widespread abuses on the Jamaica station.[75] While these considerations may have played a role in Stirling being brought to trial, the court did not seem to think there was sufficient evidence to convict him of corruption. It determined that Stirling was 'guilty in part' and the sentence passed on him – that he never be employed again, or be advanced in rank – seems inconsistent with a find-ing of corruption. The evidence on that score was certainly not compelling. Stirling testified under oath that he had known nothing of the prepayment arrangement, and O'Grady was only able to swear that he was standing close by when he discussed it with the vice admiral's secretary.[76] Similarly, although the court refused to exclude Wolley's statement, Stirling's responses to its claims were not refuted in the trial and the court knew it came from a hostile source. Moreover, it would be surprising if reports of Stirling's criticism of the commissioner and his Jamaican friends were not known to some members of the court, or that they did not appreciate that their lucrative 'trade in money' at the expense of the Crown would be threatened by the flow of gold from Spanish colonies.[77] When Warren first told Stirling of Wolley's charges, he responded that he could not 'conceive it possible for enmity to be carried to such an extent as it has been by Commissioner Wolley'.[78] The commissioner was in England when the trial took place and an unsuccessful request to recover 'lodging' costs from the Board over the winter of 1813–14 suggests that it had considered calling Wolley as a witness, but then thought better of it.[79] If the court had thought that a case of corruption had been made, it is hard to see how Stirling could have escaped an unqualified verdict and a sentence of instant dismissal.

In the context, the 'guilty in part' verdict suggests that Stirling's authorization of convoy protection was seen as a very serious professional misjudgement rather than a corrupt practice. In early 1813 the Admiralty had received letters from trading interests in Jamaica complaining about the lack of convoy protection for ships sailing north of the island and the serious threat posed to the trade by American vessels.[80] There had, in fact, been no losses, and these complaints may well have arisen from interests in Jamaica who resented Stirling's attempt to curb their money trade, and possibly also his commitment to economizing. Understandably, however, the Board was highly sen-sitive to the claims of well-connected trading lobbies and at a time when resources on the North American command were stretched, it would not tolerate misapplication of them. As a consequence, it demanded an explanation from Stirling. Although he rejected the charge, pointed out that no ships had actually been captured and dismissed the complaints as a product of 'private pique', it seems likely that they played a role in the Board's decision to bring him to trial.[81] If that is so, then the 'guilty in part' verdict can be explained as an adverse judgement on Stirling's fulfilment of his duty. The sentence demonstrated the seriousness of this error in prevailing conditions, and the need to send a strong signal to other flag officers. Convoying neutral vessels to the Spanish Main exposed the Jamaica trade and left the government and the Navy open to politically embarrassing claims that it was failing to protect important British interests. In this respect, it is significant that the order recalling Stirling was dated a few days after the Board had received the letter of complaint about convoy protection and before it had received Warren's communication on Wolley's claims.[82]

Conclusion

The episodes considered in this chapter illustrate the impact of the challenges of command on the careers of a number of admirals. In one way or another, the events described here all concluded with the effective termination of officers' careers in active service at sea, and hence also of any ambitions they might have had of scaling the heights reached by St Vincent, Duncan, Keith, Nelson, Collingwood or Pellew. These cases show how the immense practical challenges of command were compounded by perceptions of intra-service, official and public expectations that increased the psychological burdens of active service in war time. Admirals were powerful figures but they occupied exposed positions. When they conducted successful and timely operations, they were praised by the Board and those who commanded successful actions were lionized by the public.[83] When flag officers were seen to fail in their duty, however, they were liable to face censure by the Board, vilification by members of parliament and sections of the press, and loss of face among at least some of their colleagues.

Murray's anxieties reflected his awareness of the implications of failing to satisfy professional and public expectations and so too did Man's. Man was desperate to return to England but acutely aware of the reputational impact of unilaterally abandoning his commander-in-chief. Man's failure played a role in two insiders' responses to his appointment to the Admiralty Board in the autumn of 1798. Rear Admiral William Young had backed his friend Sir Charles Pole to join him as a naval commissioner but reported that the appointment had been offered to Man following discussions between Spencer and William Pitt. The content of these discussions is not known, but Young's comments throw interesting light on them. He told Pole that the new commissioner was a 'sensible man, and knows as well as any man what may be expected of ships, and is, I believe, a man of method and business'. Young's even-handed assessment of Man's technical and administrative accomplishments implied that the 'nerves under responsibility' that had failed so badly in the Mediterranean were not necessary on the Board and that Man could thus be expected to play an effective, if limited, role there. He would, Young concluded patronizingly, be a 'very useful assistant to us'.[84]

Hyde Parker's approach to his last command may have been affected by the impact of age and prosperity on his motivation, but as in Calder's case, the career-terminating consequences of failures of judgement were due to shifts in the Board's expectations and those of the wider public to which it responded. These officers were judged by standards that would have seen well-rewarded officers like Lords Bridport and Hotham retire from active service under a cloud and might not have left Lord Howe untouched. Sharpening public expectations played an overt role in Calder's downfall and these were, no doubt, fanned by the official expectations brought into play by St Vincent in determining Hyde Parker's fate. Thus while opportunities for fleet actions were rare and sought after, they were freighted with reputational risk. As Edward Codrington put it in his reflection on Calder's fate: 'How few there are who even at the close of a long life of hard service have had during that life an opportunity of distinguishing themselves; and how few of those have been favored with an opportunity and done their utmost have escaped public reprehension.'[85]

It was noted in an earlier chapter that flag officers faced consistent pressure from the Board to protect British trade on their stations and were often the targets of letters of complaints from disgruntled trading interests. Just as the timing of Hyde Parker's and Calder's alleged shortcomings was critical in explaining the Board's response to them, so too was Stirling's ill-judged deployment of Captain O'Grady's ship. It compromised operational requirements and threatened the interests of a significant lobby in British politics at a time when the Board was leaning heavily on his commander-in-chief to stem a tide of American naval successes that posed an alarming threat to British trade.[86]

The fate of Hyde Parker, Calder and Stirling exemplify the role that public and political expectations played in shaping the environment in which flag officers worked. These expectations added to the unremitting psychological pressures generated by the challenging operational requirements of high naval command. All officers on active service faced these pressures but very few succumbed to them. They were, however, often very frank in acknowledging the impact they exerted on their personal and professional confidence, and sense of emotional well-being. In doing so, they signalled an awareness that their professional lives required the ongoing management of tensions between ambition, duty and the desire for relief from the heavy burdens of command.

Authority and Dissent: Flag Officers and Their Subordinates

I shall at all times be ready to account for my Conduct either to the Admiralty or any other court competent to judge thereupon.
>—Captain the Honourable Alexander Cochrane to Vice Admiral Lord Keith
>during their dispute in the Mediterranean, 1801[1]

Flag officers' professional lives were sometimes punctuated by open and bitter disputes with their superiors and immediate subordinates. Most flag officers on active service had been accomplished captains and carried their generally well-merited self-regard through into the next stage of their careers. Successful participation in the competition for flag appointments tended to enhance these officers' sense of self-worth and of the importance of the rights and dignities of their high office. At the same time, however, the responsibilities of command produced stresses that prompted some flag officers to react sharply to the perceived failings of immediate subordinates. The officers subject to these criticisms were often working under extreme pressures and highly sensitive to comments or behaviour that might impugn their professional reputation or personal honour. Rear Admiral Sir Richard Strachan, who was regarded as basically affable but well known for his unbridled language, thought that subordinate flag officers were in a highly vulnerable position. After a passing dispute with the irascible Vice Admiral Sir George Berkeley on the North American station, Strachan told a friend at the Board that 'a junior flag officer may be subjected to many unpleasant things on his falling in with or going on the station of superior officers, and is much worse off than the captain of any ship, or even his own captain, who cannot be turned out without giving him another ship'.[2]

Since the *Regulations and Instructions* and the ethos of the service enjoined the due subordination of officers and men to their superiors, any dissenting behaviour by senior officers was seen to pose dangerously contagious threats to the good of the Service. Captain the Honourable Thomas Pakenham, who had suppressed a mutiny on board the *Culloden* in December 1794, made the connection very clear in a letter to Lord Spencer. Writing in condemnation of a protest of captains at Portsmouth in late 1795 against regulations that undermined their right to punish soldiers on-board naval vessels, Pakenham claimed that 'such combination or round robin ... being ... as great an outrage against naval discipline and the plain intention and obvious construction of the articles of war, as if it had happened among any inferior officers or men in his Majesty's navy'.[3]

This chapter will examine a number of particularly sharp clashes between commanders-in-chief and their subordinate flag officers, and flag officers and their captains. These episodes differed in magnitude, duration and intensity from the short-lived clashes that occurred on countless occasions and were part of the culture of the late Georgian navy.[4] Some disputes involved a concerted challenge to a superior's authority, most extended over a period of time and all came to the attention of the Board. In one case, the Board considered a flag officer's behaviour to be in clear breach of the Articles of War or *Regulations and Instructions* and ordered him to face a court martial. Another officer seems to have avoided court martial because his antagonist died. Like a number of other combatants (ignoring St Vincent's warning that 'the sound of a Court Martial, has the same pestilential effect, as a suspicion of female chastity'[5]) this officer appealed loudly but unsuccessfully to have his day in court. St Vincent's personality, status in the service and emphatic view of subordination made him a central figure in a number of these disputes. More generally, however, these clashes disrupted the relationships of authority and obedience between flag officers and their subordinates in ways that laid the latter open to the charge that Pakenham had made against the protesting captains at Portsmouth.

Feuding in the West Indies: Vice Admiral Sir John Laforey and Rear Admiral Charles Thompson, 1795–96

In 1795 Vice Admiral Sir John Laforey was the commander-in-chief in the Leeward Islands. Up to this point, he had had a long and generally successful career at sea, although like some other officers he compensated for limited opportunities for active service in the mid-1780s by accepting an appointment as naval commissioner at Antigua. Laforey had commanded on the Leeward Islands station from 1787 to 1793 and resumed the command in mid-1795.

Rear Admiral Charles Thompson, Laforey's second-in-command, had clashed with him at Antigua by challenging the legality of Admiralty Instructions authorizing the commissioner to assume command of naval vessels in the vicinity of the port when no senior sea officer was present.[6] At the time, this dispute was highly embarrassing for Laforey but by 1795 he appears to have forgotten Thompson's role in it.[7] His initial communications with his second-in-command were certainly professional and courteous. As Thompson set off on a cruise in mid-June, Laforey told him that 'I most heartily wish you health and success and remain with great regard'.[8] Within a month, however, as they lay off St Pierre's, Martinique, ships' boats shuttled between Thompson's and Laforey's flagships carrying a series of increasingly acrimonious communications. On 7 July, in a letter opening with the cold formality of 'Sir' and concluding with 'I am Sir, Your most obedient humble Servant', Laforey asked Thompson to explain why he had ignored his orders and cruised off Antigua rather than St Kitts. Without any hint of apology, Thompson sought to vindicate his actions by referring to intelligence he had received on the movement of enemy ships. He claimed that cruising between these islands best ensured the defence of St Kitts.[9]

Without waiting for Laforey's response to this explanation, Thompson went on the offensive. He pointed to St Pierre's pestilential climate and its attractions as a refuge of deserters and offered a gratuitous critique of his commander-in-chief's strategy: 'I must own it appears to me a very extraordinary measure assembling all your forces at St Pierre's and leaving our Trade open to the enemy.' He concluded with an insolently patronizing and patently insincere acknowledgement of Laforey's right to run such a risk: 'I dare say you have sufficient reasons for your present measures.'[10] This letter would have particularly offended Laforey because he was under pressure from local trading interests over the deployment of his ships to deter attacks by French privateers based at Guadeloupe and was attracting criticism from Lord Spencer for his lack of activity.[11] Even before he had received Thompson's second letter, however, Laforey penned a sharp response to his subordinate's original attempt to vindicate his conduct: 'I am very sorry that I cannot dispense with declaring my entire disapprobation of a measure that if adopted, tends to frustrate any plan and arrangement made in the distribution of the Squadron to promote the Public Service.'[12] Thompson's rejoinder was immediate and intemperate. He claimed that the commander-in-chief's letter

> both astonished and surprised me, being so different from any letter I ever received, or I believe was ever written under the same circumstances to a person of the rank that I have the honour to hold, it has however, pointed out to me the line of Conduct I am to follow while under your Command.[13]

Laforey reacted sharply to what he rightly described as Thompson's presumption in 'calling me to account for my conduct', and announced that he would lay the correspondence before the Admiralty Board. A day later, probably in response to Thompson's most recent outburst, Laforey told him that he would be sent back to England with the next convoy.[14] Laforey later found out that Thompson had been criticizing him around the squadron and to his secretary, James Dick. Dick reported sardonically that Thompson received him 'with his usual civility', and asserted to him that the commander-in-chief was obliged to receive advice from his subordinate flag officers and act upon it. Laforey forwarded Dick's letter to Sir Charles Middleton at the Board. He told him that Thompson had treated his predecessor, Vice Admiral Benjamin Caldwell, in a similar manner but that he 'sat much quieter under it than I am disposed to do'.[15]

Thompson appears to have arrived home ahead of Laforey's report to the Admiralty, or at least before the Board had decided how to act on it. In any case, he was not exposed to immediate disadvantage as a consequence of his strained relationship with Laforey, being almost immediately appointed to command a detached squadron off Brest, under Lord Howe. This appointment, however, was short-lived. Thompson was ordered to strike his flag on 6 November 1795. Subsequent correspondence with the Admiralty suggests that this order was related to a decision to hold a court martial on his behaviour towards Laforey. Early in the following year a misdirected letter from the Board acknowledging a request for employment brought the irascible Thompson on to the front foot:

There must be a mistake somewhere as I never wrote such a letter. I should certainly prefer being employed to remaining idle in the height of war but could not think of asking for employment after having been ordered to strike my flag and given to understand I was to be tried by Court Martial so soon as Adml Sir John Laforey returned.[16]

While Thompson harassed the Board in London, Lord Spencer decided, for reasons that were not connected overtly with Laforey's relationship with his second-in-command, to recall him. He left Martinique towards the end of April 1796 and died at sea, on 11 June, two days away from England.[17] News of this event probably prompted Thompson to write again to the Board on 3 July demanding to know when the court martial would take place and what the charges would be.[18] The Board responded by saying it would seek further information from a captain who had been on the station and from Laforey's secretary. After establishing that Laforey had not intended to lay further charges against Thompson, it told him that in light of the admiral's death 'their Lordships have no motive for reviving the subject, by instigating a public investigation of your conduct'.[19] Thompson responded by providing a long justification of his behaviour and open criticism of Laforey. He demanded a court martial, and concluded with a characteristic assertion that 'I don't feel myself in the smallest degree culpable'.[20] The Board rejected this demand, saying the 'original cause' did not make it 'expedient', which might have meant that it regarded Thompson's initial action as falling within reasonable discretion in relation to Laforey's orders and the situation he faced. At the same time, however, the Board rapped him across the knuckles over the manner in which he had responded to Laforey: 'they are of opinion your correspondence with Sir John Laforey as your commanding officer, has been carried on in a style which they must always feel a disposition to discourage.' Three days later, Thompson wrote seeking employment and was shortly after appointed to a subordinate role in the Mediterranean Fleet.[21] Since Thompson's aggressively uncompromising style was unlikely to have appealed to members of a court martial, he was most fortunate to avoid being brought to trial. He does not seem to have learned from this experience, however, and was soon at loggerheads with his new commander-in-chief, the far more formidable Sir John Jervis.

St Vincent and 'fractious discontent' among flag officers in the Mediterranean and Channel Commands, 1796–1801

During the French Wars St Vincent became embroiled in a series of bitter disputes with his subordinate flag officers in the Mediterranean and Channel commands. These conflicts, which undoubtedly owed something to the strain under which he and his colleagues worked, increased noticeably in scale and intensity as time wore on. When St Vincent's openly declared sense of personal and professional invincibility was infused with an element of paranoia, it gave rise to an idea of absolute authority that militated against the smallest degree of tolerance or accommodation. His domineering personality, openly displayed taste for manipulation, and an increasingly marked propensity to show public disrespect to those with whom he differed, exacerbated tensions that might otherwise have been contained within the bounds of cold, professional civility. At the same time, however, it seems significant that these disputes arose after the fleet mutinies at Spithead and the Nore in the spring of 1797 and were thus part of a disciplinary context in which Pakenham's views on insubordination in the upper echelons of the service assumed heightened significance.

The first major dispute was with the incorrigible Vice Admiral Sir Charles Thompson, Sir John Leforey's *bête noir* in the West Indies.[22] Thompson's service under St Vincent on the Leeward Islands station in 1794–95 had passed without any apparent difficulties and he was seen as a welcome addition to the Mediterranean Fleet when he joined it as a junior flag officer in 1797. Thompson led a division of the fleet in the action off Cape St Vincent and received the thanks of both houses of parliament and a hereditary knighthood for his contribution to the victory. The relationship between the two men deteriorated sharply, however, when St Vincent became aware that Thompson's failure to undertake a manoeuvre and respond to a signal had momentarily compromised his battle plan and exposed his commander-in-chief's flagship to heavy fire.[23] His angry reaction to this discovery was probably fuelled by embarrassment at having initially commended Thompson's role in the battle to the Admiralty Board, and by that officer's ungracious response to the offer of a baronetcy.[24]

When Sir Charles placed his own head on the block by protesting sharply against St Vincent's decision to execute two mutineers off Cadiz on a Sunday, St Vincent seized the opportunity. Having already told Spencer of Thompson's failure to obey orders in the battle and given what he later described as 'a pretty broad hint' that his removal would be 'very desirable', St Vincent used Thompson's Sabbatarian remonstrance as an excuse to reframe his hint as an ultimatum: 'I am now to request that it may take place immediately, or that I may be relieved.'[25] At this stage St Vincent had not received a letter in which the First Lord had indicated delicately that he was 'much too well aware of your title to have such persons under you as will make your command pleasant not to be very desirous to take any hint on this subject, whenever it may be in my power to act upon it.'[26] Spencer was as good as his word, and in September it was confirmed that Thompson was to be recalled.

The first lord's 'new arrangements' included the appointment of Vice Admiral Sir John Orde as second-in-command off Cadiz. Orde had had a distinguished career, with notable service in the American War and as governor of St Dominica.[27] More recently, he had presided over the courts martial of the Nore mutineers and received a letter of approbation for his role from his future commander-in-chief.[28] St Vincent welcomed Orde to his fleet and praised his performance in maintaining the blockade at Cadiz.[29] Within six months, however, he was savagely disappointed by Orde's behaviour and alarmed at its impact on the discipline of the fleet. Orde undoubtedly faced a severe trial at St Vincent's hands, one that was exacerbated by the commander-in-chief's harsh and contemptuous treatment. At the same, however, his vanity and pomposity contributed to the escalation and prolongation of the dispute. Orde's subsequent history indicated that these traits, and the failures of judgement that resulted from them, were not wholly due to St Vincent's goading.

St Vincent's dispute with Orde originated with an instruction that small boats deployed to attack guard boats, cut out ships moored in enemy harbours and on other 'special duties', should be treated as if they belonged to the commander-in-chief's flagship and placed under the direct control of his staff. Orde believed that this instruction, which arose from a misadventure involving boats from his flagship, was an adverse reflection on him and his officers.[30] What Orde saw as further encroachments on his dignity followed, when Sir Roger Curtis replaced him as second-in-command off Cadiz and Nelson was appointed to command a detached squadron.[31] From this stage, the dispute escalated into more or less open warfare, with St Vincent accusing Orde of fermenting a conspiracy against his authority with the other flag officers and their captains. Although at times there were signs of a *rapprochement*, these episodes probably owed as much to St Vincent's penchant for playing cat and mouse with his subordinates as to any spirit of reconciliation on his part.[32] Thus when he offered Orde an apology for accusing him of writing a letter that was now acknowledged to have come from another officer, it was framed in an abrupt and uncompromising way that seemed designed to prolong the insult. Orde subsequently wrote and circulated a pamphlet on their disputes that St Vincent described as being composed of 'misrepresentations, partial statements, and gross falsehoods'. It was, he thundered, an exercise in character assassination: '[H]e has taken down every conversation he hears, and uses, it, as an Italian does a stiletto.'[33]

Collingwood told a correspondent that St Vincent indulged in savage oral attacks on Orde, and he certainly crowed over his bullying behaviour towards captains in the fleet.[34] He declined to open some of Orde's letters, refused to answer others and did not conceal these acts of discourtesy. Orde's formal letter of remonstrance to Spencer was treated with sardonic contempt: 'The letter ... expresses precisely what I should have done under similar circumstances, for I never was blest with *prudence* and *forbearance*.' A series of increasingly acrimonious exchanges concluded with Orde demanding that St Vincent face a court martial, and St Vincent describing Orde's communications as being 'expressed in terms of insubordination, that even in these times I did not conceive could have come from an officer of your rank'. He then took the extreme, unilateral and unauthorized step of instructing Orde to return to England.[35] Once he left the fleet, St Vincent continued to attempt to undermine Orde's credibility by questioning his qualities as a seaman and belittling his achievements as governor.[36]

From Orde's perspective, the key issue was St Vincent's usurpation of the rights of subordinate flag officers and the slights to himself and his colleagues entailed by this. When he protested that St Vincent was undermining the position of subordinate flag officers and the captains who served under them, his commander-in-chief told him bluntly that he had an unquestionable right to issue commands without considering the views of any of his subordinates. St Vincent viewed the powers conferred on him by the Articles of War and the *Regulations and Instructions* through a lens borrowed from a notoriously high-handed contemporary in the Spanish Navy: 'I must enter my protest against explanations and discussions, which I never will admit, for I subscribe to Don Juan de Langara's creed, that the whole system of discipline is comprised in one word – *obedienza*.'[37]

There were two sequels to Orde's departure in September 1798. Having failed to secure exoneration through a court martial, he treated the dispute as a matter of personal honour and challenged St Vincent to a duel when he returned to England in late 1799. He and his second laid psychological siege to St Vincent from an inn a few miles from his home in south Essex, waiting impatiently until he was well enough to answer the challenge. Orde's search for satisfaction was frustrated by St Vincent's ongoing refusal to meet him. He claimed that his health precluded it, and insisted that in any case he was not personally responsible for public measures. In the event, the issue was taken out of the admirals' hands. They were bound over to keep the peace by magistrates and the king finally ended the matter by ordering St Vincent not to accept a challenge and Orde to desist from pressing it.[38]

While St Vincent was feuding with Orde, he also came to verbal blows with another subordinate flag officer, Rear Admiral Sir William Parker. Parker, like Orde, claimed that his position had been undermined by Nelson's appointment to command a detached squadron and by the commander-in-chief's favouritism towards Sir Richard Curtis. As in Orde's case, Parker's pursuit of these grievances escalated into what St Vincent saw as a serious challenge to his authority. In his initial protest to Spencer, Parker asserted that his professional *amour-propre* was compromised by being passed over for an officer who was his junior in age and rank:

> I have been, my Lord, many years in the service, and in employ, and met general approbation, therefore but little prepared to expect an injury of this kind .... I was happy to be employed, my Lord, in any situation, holding it my duty to be so while the nation was engaged in war; but could not thereby expect to be subject to the degradation I suffer indeed, after so many years' service with a reputation unexceptionable, to be stripped of it as I am in the instance of this appointment, my feelings are more hurt than I can describe, or any event likely to occur can bring me to recover or reconsider.[39]

Although St Vincent appears not to have been receptive to Parker's complaints, there is no indication of open antagonism between the two officers at this stage. Parker did not ask to be removed from St Vincent's command and wrote to Spencer on St Vincent's suggestion. As in his interactions with Orde, however, St Vincent assumed the role of a large and vindictive cat playing with an increasingly frantic mouse.

Over the following months, it became increasingly clear that personal relations between the two men had broken down utterly and that their professional relationship was seriously compromised. Parker told Spencer that hitherto consideration for the good of the service had prevented him openly challenging St Vincent's mistreatment, but that 'conduct hurtful to my feelings' had increased to such an extent that he would find it hard to exercise such constraint in future.[40] Spencer evidently sent a copy of this letter to St Vincent who responded angrily that it 'bore no mark of the character of an officer or a gentleman'.[41] Parker continued to complain to Spencer of the reputational damage he suffered from being overlooked. Spencer's decision was, he claimed, 'very prejudicial to my reputation as an officer, and to my feelings as a man'.[42]

St Vincent believed that Orde – a character 'fraught with the most malignant policy' – had 'worked on' Parker, a 'very weak man', using courts martial over which he presided to spread criticisms of orders that Marines should be berthed apart from the rest of the crew.[43] St Vincent may initially have regarded Parker as Orde's dupe, but as the dispute escalated, Parker's responses to St Vincent's rough handling aggravated their personal interactions. St Vincent treated Parker's protests as intolerable challenges to his authority and was soon demanding that he be ordered home, noting truculently that he had learned the unreasonable lesson read to him when he had dismissed Orde: 'I shall not again, subject myself to reproof for sending a Flag Officer to England, without … authority.'[44] Spencer's view of Parker's conduct and standing clearly differed from St Vincent's and he found him new employment as commander-in-chief of the North American station. Nevertheless, St Vincent could not resist a final fling against this vexatious subordinate. He forwarded a letter which he had withheld while Parker remained under his command, noting in the aggressive closing salutation that 'I am no longer bound to conceal the opinion I formed of your conduct towards Sir, your obedient humble servant, St Vincent'.[45]

In the following year when St Vincent was first lord, an opportunity occurred to act upon this opinion.[46] During the winter months, when the North American squadron sailed south to the Caribbean, *America*, one of Parker's few ships-of-the-line, took the ground on the eastern coast of Jamaica and was seriously damaged. Parker sent the Board a report on this disaster, along with a copy of his instructions to *America*'s captain. He wrote in strong exoneration of the captain and crew of the wrecked ship: 'nothing that human prudence … could have been foreseen to guard against'.[47] The Board considered this matter on 25 April 1801 when it formed the view that Parker demonstrated 'great indiscretion' in sending a ship-of-the-line to carry out a task – the landing of soldiers at Martinique – that could easily have been performed by a frigate. More damaging still, it suspected that the real reason for the deployment was to provide *America* (and the flag officer under whom she served) with the benefit of an 'advantageous cruise' on another station. The Board noted that Parker had more recently sent his only remaining ship-of-the-line to cruise off Barbados with the same end in view. It condemned these 'extraordinary proceedings', made 'more reprehensible' by an earlier order reiterating the unacceptability of an unauthorized and indefensible practice, and recommended his recall.[48] St Vincent was not present when the Board considered the wreck of the *America*, but he attended on the days on either side of that meeting, suggesting that he may have sought to avoid the appearance of the vindictive pursuit of Parker by relying on the agency of two strong service allies on the Board, Captain John Markham and Captain Sir Thomas Troubridge.[49]

If there was such a plot, it did not work out in quite the way St Vincent intended. Parker was recalled but not ordered to face a court martial, perhaps because, as in the case of his namesake Sir Hyde Parker, Vincent used recall without court martial as a weapon of silent humiliation. Unlike Sir Hyde, however, Sir William had enough credit and interest to secure a court martial. In evidence at his trial at Portsmouth on 13–14 November 1801, before a court of five flag officers, he claimed that the terms and manner of his recall was 'so injuriously degrading to my reputation and distressing to me under all the Circumstances of my Situation, I was led upon my arrival in England to desire that my Conduct might be investigated … at a Court Martial …

I conceived I owed it to my own Reputation and necessarily to be expected of me to retain my Credit in the Service'.[50] Parker's gamble of risking public disgrace rather than face the certainty of private contempt paid off. He defended himself by claiming that the deployment of the *America* was justified by the requirements of the service and was not motivated by a lust for prize money. The court accepted this argument, and while noting that he had been 'indiscrete' in providing too detailed orders about the route his ships should take back to Halifax, declared that his character precluded 'the Idea that he had been guided by any motive unconnected with the Good of His Majesty's Service'.[51] Despite this largely favourable verdict, St Vincent's animosity would probably have been enough to keep Parker out of employment as long as he headed the Board. That point was never put to the test, however. The vice admiral had often shown signs of being overwrought and on the last day of 1802 he succumbed to a fatal apoplexy.

St Vincent did not leave difficult flag officers behind when he took command of the Channel Fleet in 1800. To the contrary, he immediately became embroiled in a dispute with Admiral Sir Alan Gardner, his second-in-command. The initial difficulty arose, as with Parker, in an appointment made by Lord Spencer. In this case, however, St Vincent himself was the direct beneficiary. When Spencer appointed St Vincent to replace Bridport, he claimed that it was widely known among other flag officers that Gardner did not wish to have the command. Since Gardner had written to the prime minister and the Earl of Chatham two months earlier expressing his desire to succeed Bridport and hoping they would use their 'good offices' with the king to secure it, it is understandable that he reacted angrily to the decision and to the grounds on which it was supposedly made.[52] Like Parker, he stressed the effect Spencer's preference would have on his professional reputation.

> I say, my Lord, I will loudly complain of the harsh, unusual, and severe treatment I have received, and I do not know what reparation I have received, and I do not know what reparation your Lordship can make to me for the disgrace you have loaded me with, and the injury done to my character. I have stated, but with reserve, my feelings to Lord St Vincent, and even his Lordship is candid enough to declare that I have been harshly used and that I have strong ground for complaint.

Gardner presented himself as Lord Bridport's 'lawful and natural successor' and proclaimed his right to protest 'as an Englishman' using 'the plain and honest language of a seaman, and of an officer who had vainly flattered himself that his long and faithful services merited a different treatment'.[53]

Gardner's view of 'reserve' was clearly different from St Vincent, who reported to Spencer that he could not describe the 'disgust manifest' by Gardner at a recent meeting.[54] But while his temper may have been threadbare, Gardner was sufficiently collected to suspect that his new commander-in-chief was playing with him. Thus when told that St Vincent had not sought the appointment and that 'it came suddenly and unexpectedly upon him, and that he was dragged out of a sick room with swelled legs and laboring under other infirmities', he treated this statement, and St Vincent's assurance that he would not have taken the command if he knew Gardner wished for it, with scepticism. Gardner pointedly declined to 'make any observations' upon these claims.[55] If Keith's report that St Vincent was scheming for the Channel command was true, Gardner had good grounds for taking this stance.[56]

To judge from St Vincent's account, Gardner was far less reticent in their personal interactions. He told Spencer that Gardner's conduct towards him 'has been and still continues outrageous' and thought it was only explicable on the assumption that Gardner was part of a plot: he had been 'worked up by a party which considers my elevation as an obstacle to the further aggrandisement of them. I mean the Hoods who have shown hostility to me ever since the court martial on Admiral Keppel'.[57] Within a few weeks, St Vincent was so overwrought that he told Nepean that either he or Gardner should go.[58] This ultimatum seems to have galvanized Spencer into action. He wrote to Gardner in especially smooth terms remarking that he understood fully that continuing service under St Vincent 'could not be perfectly agreeable to you' and offering him the chief command on the Irish station.[59] To his credit, Gardner immediately accepted this offer, excusing the manner of his reaction to St Vincent's appointment by reference to mental strain: '[M]y mind has not been at ease for some time past, and my sensations were such on the late very unexpected appointment of Lord St Vincent that I could not help expressing my disappointment … in strong terms.' The king was appreciative of Gardner's gracious acceptance of the command offered to him: 'I am certain there are few Admirals that have more merit in the profession, and as private men none can exceed him in the goodness of his heart. The manner in which he received the offer of the appointment to the Irish Station is a strong proof of the latter.'[60]

St Vincent's domineering personality had a significant impact on the way his disputes with subordinate flag officers unfolded, and Thompson's high-handed arrogance, Orde's overweening self-importance and Parker's and Gardner's sense of offended entitlement played a role in pushing their personal and professional relationships beyond the point of no return. Whatever the initial cause of these disagreements, however, or the contributions of the participants to exacerbating them, St Vincent's increasingly savage engagement with his adversaries was framed in terms of a general disciplinary agenda that had been given a new sense of urgency by the mutinies at Spithead and the Nore. St Vincent saw fleet discipline as a system that embraced all members of the service. It relied upon them taking their place within this system and performing their role within it. For those in positions of authority, these roles necessitated the close and consistent control of subordinates and exemplary obedience to superiors. While these heated exchanges were thus coloured by the personalities of the officers involved and affected by the pressures under which they all operated, they also reflected competing conceptions of the implications of the disciplinary requirements of the service for flag officers.

Lord Keith's difficult subordinates: the non-combatant trials of the Egyptian expedition of 1801

The caballing spirit that had been condemned by Laforey, Pakenham and St Vincent was a source of significant difficulty to Lord Keith when he took over the Mediterranean command from St Vincent in 1799. The major naval operation of this command – supporting the landing that secured the defeat of Napoleon's army stranded in Egypt after the Battle of the Nile – was a great success. Keith's role in this operation helped him to secure the English peerage that he had coveted for some time and marked the high point of his career up to this date. During the course of it, however, he faced a serious challenge to his authority and to his personal honour from Captain the Honourable Alexander Cochrane, who held the temporary flag appointment of commodore during the landing. These officers shared family connections in the Scottish nobility and were both clients of Henry Dundas. Cochrane had a good record of service and Keith's faith in him was vindicated by his management of the landing. He planned and marshalled an armada of 300 boats and worked effectively with the army to secure a firm foothold in the face of heavy, sustained and accurate fire from the French defenders. No sooner had the landing taken place, however, than Keith found cause for doubting Cochrane's temper and judgement. Over the course of the next few months he assailed Keith in a series of increasingly vituperative letters, and encouraged other captains to question his leadership.

Keith, who was given to bouts of irascibility, appears to have precipitated the breach by a lapse in civility. Showing the strain of his responsibilities in a complex and risky undertaking, he gave a sharp response to an understandably anxious enquiry from Cochrane on the day after the landing: 'Sir, When I gave out in orders that you were to superintend the Army supplies, and to execute the duties of a flag officer in the squadron until further orders, I certainly meant that you should make use of that authority without sending to me, who am eight miles distant, in a gale of wind.'[61] Other occasions for offence followed. Cochrane complained how 'hurt' he was that his 'birthright' as senior captain had been extinguished when he was not appointed to lead the battle line of the fleet. He appealed to Keith to be given his 'due', trusting that he did not 'deviate from that respect which I shall ever pay to those under whose orders I may serve.'[62] Such respect notwithstanding, Cochrane soon identified another cause for harrying Keith and enlisted his fellow captains in it.

Far removed from his main sources of supply, and lacking significant material support from his Turkish allies, Keith found himself hard-pressed to provision his ships and secure fresh food for the sick. He had expressed concern on these matters to Lord Spencer long before the landing commenced but the difficulties of the situation were exacerbated when the army ashore was still engaged against the French.[63] Sometime in April, Keith received reports on the pressing needs of the sick from Rear Admiral Sir Richard Bickerton, his junior flag officer. These reports, originating in concerns raised by the surgeon of Cochrane's ship, do not appear to have been the source of any immediate ill feeling.[64] Keith responded by taking steps to acquire what he termed 'necessaries for the use of the sick' and authorizing £8,000–£10,000 for this purpose. Moreover, when the matter came up in conversation between the two men, Keith sent Cochrane an accommodating progress report: '[A] proportion of these articles are now on their way, if they have not already arrived; and if you will point out other articles of that description … that can be purchased here, I will forthwith order them to be procured.'[65]

Two days earlier, however, Cochrane had been the first of three signatories of a not yet delivered letter sent on behalf of thirteen captains who discussed the matter at a court martial on *Swiftsure*. The captains' delegates letter was respectful enough in tone, but partly because it went beyond reporting an ill to prescribing the cure (we 'would request you would be pleased to direct such steps to be taken as your Lordship may think proper for causing supplies to be brought'[66]) and also because Keith had already moved to address the issue and had told Cochrane so, he was highly irritated by it. He wrote immediately to rebuke the three officers concerned: 'Gentlemen, I have received your letter … and am of opinion that the interference is highly improper on your parts.'[67] In response to a letter from the captains questioning this rebuke, Keith repeated his reprimand and advised that he would send the correspondence to the Admiralty.

Cochrane, however, continued on the offensive. He took umbrage at Keith's manner in refusing him the use of a small sailing vessel to run ashore to pick up fresh provisions. Keith had told him in the presence of other officers that 'indeed you shall have no such thing'. Cochrane made an ineffectual attempt to deflect Keith's sharp reminder that he had been advised on the steps taken to secure provisions for the sick before the matter had been raised among the captains. He questioned a detail of their earlier discussion while grudgingly conceding that Keith's substantive claim was true.[68] There were further exchanges in mid-May when boats plied to and fro between the *Ajax* and Keith's flagship *Foudroyant*, with testy letters about firewood for the *Ajax*. While Cochrane hinted at hard and unreasonable treatment, Keith insinuated inefficiency and extravagance. In the month following, Cochrane wrote to Keith in the third person raising grievances about the supply of paint and oil to his ship.[69] More significantly, he complained that his services at the landing had not been recognized as they deserved, and warned Keith that the absence of any mention of his role in a parliamentary votes of thanks would be noted by other members of the fleet: 'What must be the opinions of the Officers and Seamen of the ships then present, when they observe the Thanks of the British Legislature given where none were due and for Services performed by others?'[70] Cochrane also claimed that Keith had taken vindictive advantage of a collision (of which *Ajax* was a victim) to subject her captain to the unjust indignity of a court martial to be presided over by Keith's flag captain.[71] In terms of the history of the dispute, however, these were merely parting shots.

The main action took the form of an extraordinary letter from Cochrane to his commander-in-chief following a heated discussion of the former's wish to return to England. Cochrane presented himself as a wounded and disappointed friend of Keith and claimed to be acting on that basis:

> As your Lordship has expressed your sentiments so unequivocally with respect to our intercourse by saying that less intimacy should subsist in the future, I shall therefore take my leave by the last act of friendship in my power to perform, but which I conceive myself bound in duty to do from the long intimacy that has subsisted between our families.

As Cochrane's accusations unfolded – always presented indirectly as things that were being said *of* Lord Keith *by others* – his spiteful narrative was larded with pained protestations of the obligations of friendship, and implausible attempts at justification by reference to the real kindness of complete disclosure:

Another point remains to be mentioned of a much more delicate nature, but as it is in such current circulation your Lordship ought to know it, but how to express myself in a manner the least hurtful to your Lordship's feelings I know not. It would however be the height of cruelty to allow you to remain in ignorance any longer.

Cochrane made a range of specific charges against Nicholas Brown, Keith's secretary, and James Meek, Brown's assistant. He referred to the damage done to Keith's reputation by Brown's and Meek's alleged profiteering in the supply of slops – in this case, shoes purchased in Palermo – and in the rates of exchange applied to payments made to, and on behalf of, officers and men in local currencies. More directly, Keith was reported to be favouring Brown as a prize agent and conniving at self-interested delays in the payment of prize monies. Even more damaging than these specific charges, however, were those touching on Keith's standing among his fellow sea officers:

> As an officer you were spoken of with slight. You was said to be hasty without method, and allowing your passions to carry you beyond those rules which the dignity of your situation required you to adhere to; that you made much ado about trifles while the great objects were neglected … Painful as it is to me to relate it, I must now acquaint you that a due confidence is not given to your Lordships assertions.[72]

Cochrane professed to be surprised when Keith declined to accept this missive as friendly advice and was offended that his commander-in-chief's conduct towards him seemed to have changed after he had received it. He later told Keith that he was going to make a 'public representation' to the Admiralty about his mistreatment and that he would send it to Keith for his 'perusal'. Keith responded by rejecting Cochrane's claims of ill treatment and advising him not to send him the report as he would not read it.[73]

Although the other captains submitted to Keith's rebuke over their protest, he had an ongoing exchange with Captain Benjamin Hallowell of *Swiftsure*. He claimed that his men were being overcharged for shoes purchased at Palermo, and declined 'in justice' to authorize their issue. Hallowell requested that 'your Lordship will be pleased to order some enquiry into the statement I have made and if found correct that the additional charge … may be taken off'. Keith does not appear to have resented this letter and wrote to Hallowell the following day to assure him that he had looked into the matter some time ago and was 'perfectly satisfied that the transaction was honourable and correct'.[74] Unfortunately, Hallowell did not accept this assurance and Keith came to believe that he and Cochrane had been acting in concert.[75] In addition, however, the condition of Hallowell's ship soon became a further source of contention. This dispute drew in Vice Admiral Bickerton, and as with the matter of the overpriced shoes, resulted in an appeal to the Admiralty. Keith had known of the very poor condition of the *Swiftsure* since at least November of 1800 when he received reports from dockyards at Gibraltar and Port Mahon.[76] In May 1801 a decision was made to send the ship back to England with a convoy, a step that provided Keith with an opportunity to rid himself of a troublesome captain. Hallowell made a series of representations to Keith on the state of his ship, warning of the dangers of slowing its passage to England and compromising the safety of its convoy. He advised Keith that he would warn the masters of the ship under convoy, and their owners' insurance undertakers, of *Swiftsure*'s condition 'that no responsibility may be attached to me if I am obliged to abandon the ships placed under my protection'.[77] In the event, *Swiftsure*, which was stripped of eighty seamen and loaded with large numbers of sick and wounded from the fleet, had the misfortune to fall in with a superior French force and after a spirited action Hallowell and his shipmates were taken prisoners.[78]

Keith's letter to the Admiralty on the protesting captains was couched in terms likely to appeal to a body presided over by a first lord who had long associated mutiny on the lower deck with the disciplinary failings of those who paced the quarter deck. The captains' conduct was, Keith claimed, 'unprecedented, disrespectful and subversive of that subordination and discipline which it is the peculiar duty of those in high rank to observe'.[79] The Board agreed and signalled its approbation of the line that Keith had taken. The initial response, however, came in a private letter from St Vincent, written four months to the day after the captains had met at the court martial on *Swiftsure*. The first lord assured Keith that he was 'extremely concerned to learn that there is any ill humour among the Captains under your command; anything like combination has a most dangerous tendency'. Having endorsed Keith's reaction by reference to matters of general principle, St Vincent then encouraged him to take a more considered view of the individuals involved. Observing that all but one of the captains were well known to him, and all were highly regarded in the service, the first lord commented that he 'could not conceive it possible that anything intentionally wrong was in the minds of any of them'.[80]

This moderation was a far cry from the intransigent attitude exhibited by St Vincent towards his captains in the Mediterranean Fleet. Even given his newfound sense of detachment, however, it is very unlikely that St Vincent would have been as sanguine if he had seen Cochrane's diatribe. The most damaging claims made in this letter did not come to his notice until more than a year later, when Keith was back in London. At that stage St Vincent sought to placate him by general expressions of approbation: 'considering the length of our acquaintance, and the habits of friendship in which we have always lived, your Lordship may readily believe that I am not at all disposed to listen to representations to your prejudice'.[81] Whatever he thought of these assurances, Keith was not prepared to let the matter drop and harried the Admiralty and Navy Boards for another two years.

In February 1802 the Admiralty received a report from the Navy Board but delayed a decision until Hallowell returned from captivity. When Keith responded with blistering accusations of procrastination and a plot to 'protect' Hallowell, the Board rebuked him for 'the very improper style in which your Lordship has thought fit to address it'.[82] A conclusive statement on the fairness of the price charged for the Palermo shoes was not forthcoming until November when the Board endorsed Keith's censure of Hallowell for not accepting his earlier assurances on this issue. The resolution of other factual claims of financial impropriety was far more protracted and not settled until 1808.[83] Keith had to come to terms with what was at best a draw on the court martial. The Admiralty did not accept Cochrane's claims about the motivation prompting Keith to order him to stand trial, but it advised Keith that the appointment of his flag captain, Captain Elphinstone, as president of the court would be improper. This advice did not amount to a censure of Keith since he had reconsidered the matter at the time, withdrawn his order for Elphinstone to preside at the trial and given that role to Bickerton.

Cochrane was careful not to disobey Keith's orders but he had questioned his judgement, encouraged other officers to do the same and, more seriously, sought to undermine the commander-in-chief's authority by impugning his honesty, honour and reputation. This line of attack was so closely aligned with Cochrane's grievances over recognition for his role in the landing and his status in the fleet that it seemed to be motivated by personal considerations. Perhaps mindful of St Vincent's view of the reputational risks of taking disputes between senior officers to a court martial, Keith does not seem to have demanded that Cochrane face one.

There was a bizarre, distant coda to these transactions. In 1815 Hallowell was flying his flag in *Tonnant* as a junior admiral when Keith commanded the Channel Fleet following Napoleon's defeat at Waterloo. Keith was responsible for the former emperor (now reduced to plain 'General Bonaparte') while the government finalized arrangements for his exile at St Helena. When doubts were raised in some quarters about the legality of this plan, Keith was concerned that a writ of habeas corpus would delay his charge's departure. He was utterly sick of Napoleon by this stage and feared that he would continue to play a celebrity role in a man-of-war off Plymouth for many months. The risk of legal interference seemed to have materialized when a document-bearing gentleman pursued Keith from his house. He spent the rest of the day ducking round the fleet to avoid this person and at one stage went aboard *Tonnant*. Keith's resentment against Hallowell still lingered and he told his daughter that he had declined an introduction to the rear admiral. It later became apparent that Keith's pursuer was not trying to serve a writ of habeas corpus but a subpoena requiring Napoleon to appear as a defence witness in a libel case. The plaintiff was another old antagonist from the Mediterranean Command, now enjoying the dignity of flag rank and baronetcy as Vice Admiral Sir Alexander Cochrane.[84]

Admiral Lord Gambier, Rear Admiral Harvey and the dispute off Basque Roads, April 1809

Following a long term at the Admiralty Board and success at the second Battle of Copenhagen in 1807, Admiral Lord Gambier was appointed to command the Channel Fleet in early 1809. His subordinate flag officers included Rear Admiral Sir Eliab Harvey, a member of a prominent family of Tory gentry from Essex, who had commanded the *Téméraire* at Trafalgar. This ship had been at the centre of the battle and suffered a significant number of casualties. Harvey was promoted to flag rank immediately after Trafalgar and gained St Vincent's approval when serving under his command in the Channel Fleet in 1806–1807. In the late spring of 1809 discussions took place between Gambier and some of his senior officers about using fire ships to attack a French Fleet moored in the Isle of Aix. Gambier raised the matter with the first lord, who authorized the attempt but directed Captain Lord Cochrane to lead the attack.

Although Cochrane had considerable experience of unconventional operations, this decision caused resentment among Gambier's captains and sparked a blazing, one-sided row between him and Harvey. The dispute took place over a couple of days, but it lived on and gained wide exposure when Gambier successfully applied to have his second-in-command tried by court martial. This was the only occasion during the wars when a flag officer faced trial on charges arising from failure to show due subordination to, and respect for, a superior officer.

Harvey's trial focused on events that had occurred at Basque Roads in early April 1809. He was charged with using 'vehement and insulting' language to his commander-in-chief, having 'otherwise shewed great disrespect to him' in that role and conveyed this disrespect to other officers in a way that gave wider publicity to these demonstrations. Most of the alleged offences had taken place on Gambier's flagship *Caledonia* on the 2 and 3 April, when Harvey had gone on board and held very heated discussions with Gambier and several of his officers. On the first occasion, Harvey told *Caledonia*'s commanding officer, Captain Bell, to inform Gambier that he was keen to lead the attack on the French. He then complained bitterly in the presence of several officers of delays in putting the plan into action. Bell told the court that Harvey 'seemed excessively angry'. The next day Harvey came on board again and spoke with Gambier in his cabin. Having declared his willingness to lead the attack, he was told that the first lord had instructed Gambier to give the role to Lord Cochrane. After expostulating violently to Gambier, Harvey continued his rant in the cabin of the captain of the fleet, Sir Harry Neale, in the presence of Lord Cochrane. He then went with these officers on to the quarterdeck of the *Caledonia* where he again exposed Captain Bell to extreme and contemptuous statements on Lord Gambier's conduct and capabilities.

The evidence of Harvey's disrespectful conduct to Lord Gambier was overwhelming. Gambier referred to Harvey's 'high tone and disrespectful' and 'vehement and insulting' manner. Although the other witnesses claimed not to have heard these transactions, their references to Harvey's 'great vehemence and rapidity of expression' and his 'warmth' when addressing them testify to his lack of self-control and to the grossly disrespectful manner showed towards his commander-in-chief. The substance of Harvey's super-heated declamations aggravated the offence to decency and discipline. He berated Gambier for the 'neglect' he had suffered at his hands when he sat on the Admiralty Board, and extended this line of criticism to include the Board in general. He also told Gambier that he was not fit to command the fleet and announced that he would be demanding an enquiry on his shortcomings in due course. These charges were repeated before the other witnesses from the *Caledonia* and were also aired at Harvey's table and on the quarterdeck of his flagship. Harvey had denigrated Gambier's character to his flag captain in terms that were, given their shared religious views, particularly unwise: he spoke of Gambier's 'methodistical, Jesuitical conduct, and of his vindictive temper'. Harvey also made what Lord Cochrane construed as an allusion to the commander-in-chief's blue light affiliations when he expostulated that he was 'no hypocrite, no canting Methodist, and no psalm-singer. I do not cheat old women out of their estates by hypocrisy and canting'.[85]

Harvey's brief statement of defence made no attempt to question the evidence of Gambier and the other witnesses, but he did claim that his remarks had been heard only by a few officers not by other members of the ship's company. Nor did Harvey deny that his language towards Gambier and the other officers was most improper: 'I should ... not act a fair or candid part, were I to deny that a conduct which I cannot justify has been proved against me; and for this I now offer my most humble apologies to the Court.'[86] But while admitting his conduct was indefensible, Harvey tried to argue that the evidence did not prove the charges made against him. The defence rested on two claims. He sought to justify his 'intemperate expressions' by referring to the irritation provoked by the lack of response to his plan for attacking the French, suggesting other officers might have reacted similarly in the circumstances. He implied that he was understandably provoked by Gambier's dilatory leadership: 'An excess of zeal, and an impatience of constraint, when an opportunity for enterprise presents itself, although faults, are such from which the most eminent Naval Commanders have not been free.' If this part of Harvey's defence seemed designed to emphasize his criticism of Gambier's vigour, his second claim initially seemed more promising. Harvey denied any intention to 'thwart' a superior officer and declared his lifelong commitment to the Navy's doctrine of obedience. Unfortunately, however, he coupled this claim with an appeal to the court members' knowledge of his character. This was not a compelling line of defence. When one of Harvey's colleagues heard of the case, he claimed that he could deduce the name of the offender from an account of the offence. If this view was widespread, it seems unlikely that members of the court would have regarded Harvey's reference to his character in the service as a consideration mitigating his offending.[87] The court's verdict was that Harvey was guilty of all charges and that he be dismissed immediately from the Service.

Although the expressions of dissent discussed in this chapter would have been seen as gross insubordination if uttered by junior officers and men from the lower deck, only Harvey suffered career-terminating consequences for openly challenging his superior officer. There were a number of reasons for this. In the first place, it seems that his attack on Gambier was so intemperate and so open that it could not be ignored. Moreover, Harvey's imputations of Gambier's favouritism towards fellow blue lighters impugned his honour and no doubt offended the sensibilities of like-minded officers. His abuse of Gambier on these lines was publicized before the trial in the *Naval Chronical*.[88] Finally, Harvey chose to tackle his commander-in-chief at a time when his star was in the ascendant. Gambier had been elevated to the English peerage after distinguished service in the Baltic in 1807, was a naval commissioner from 1807 to 1808 and had just been given the prime command in the Royal Navy. Finally, the reaction to Gambier's acquittal in a subsequent court martial provoked by Lord Cochrane showed that he had many friends. After receiving the thanks of both houses of parliament following an attack on Basque Roads, William Wilberforce, the prominent MP and anti-slavery campaigner, sent congratulations 'animated with a grateful sense of the Goodness of Him who has established your righteous cause'.[89]

Conclusion

The cases discussed in this chapter are among the best-documented examples of serious and sustained personal and professional conflicts that occurred between flag officers and their subordinates during the course of the French Wars. These conflicts were personal in the sense that they were usually exacerbated by the personalities of those involved and also because they were often fuelled by the participants' belief that their honour had been impugned. The professional dimension of these conflicts arose because the disciplinary ethos of the Navy made the boundary between stated disagreement with the views and orders of a superior and dangerous insubordination difficult to draw.

Some dissident officers thought there was safety in numbers and appealed to the idea that superior officers were under an obligation to consult with their senior colleagues. Thompson invoked this idea when he tried to substitute his judgement for that of Laforey; Cochrane operated in the spirit of it when he tried to force Keith to accept his captains' collective views on the important question of supplies for the sick. Keith was not offended when the captains identified a need but would not accept that they had a right to dictate a solution to him and to imply thereby that he was neglecting his duty. As it had done earlier during St Vincent's dispute with Orde, concerted action compounded the offence against the prerogatives of a commander-in-chief and by inference, the discipline of the service.

After the Spithead and Nore mutinies, St Vincent became absorbed with the challenge of maintaining discipline. His ideal of fleet discipline as a system and his commitment to consistent subordination and exemplary leadership made him increasingly intolerant of any sign of questioning or dissent on the part of his subordinate flag officers, and hardened his determination to stamp his authority on them. They were skewered with his pen, lashed with his tongue and he savagely and publically repelled any pretensions to independent action and judgement. St Vincent's incessant drilling of his fleet paid a handsome dividend in a successful fleet action, and maintaining rigorous blockades thereafter, but his harsh and high-handed treatment of Orde, Parker and Gardner soured collegial relationships within his commands and made officers like Collingwood thankful to be relieved of the oppressive atmosphere that resulted from it. But while these bitter disputes were disruptive in some ways and had a marked impact on the professional lives of those involved, they did not produce significant operational dysfunction.

Orde's and Parker's stormy passages with St Vincent had an adverse impact on their careers but any long-term damage was a consequence of intervening factors. Lord Spencer's Board did not employ Sir John Orde again, though this was because he declined a subsequent appointment, not because of his extreme reaction to St Vincent's rough handling. But while Orde seems to have overplayed his hand on this occasion and would continue to pay the cost of alienating St Vincent, interest is always relative to circumstances and times change. Orde's distinguished service in the American War had earned him the notice of the prime minister's brother and the king.[90] Moreover, his older half-brother was a wealthy peer who had worked closely with Pitt and Henry Dundas when he was chief secretary of Ireland in the 1780s. These connections no doubt played a role in Melville's decision to appoint Orde to command a squadron off Cadiz. He enhanced the value of this appointment by ensuring that Orde's orders put him in the way of capturing Spanish ships freighted with large amounts of bullion from South America. No sooner had Orde secured the bullion ships, however, than he set about questioning the Board's orders for Nelson's prize agent to take responsibility for their cargo, and to extend the range of his responsibilities to include the protection of convoys passing through the Straits of Gibraltar and on to England. In a private letter of complaint to Lord Melville which he passed on to Barham's Board, Orde rashly offered his resignation. Barham promptly accepted this offer and Orde was never employed again.[91] Like Spencer, Barham had no doubt come to the view that the weight of Orde's professional merits and his interest had again been outbalanced by his refusal to sit quiet under the authority of his superiors. Sir William Parker's career was also disrupted by St Vincent but had he not been struck down by 'apoplexy', he would probably have secured further employment when St Vincent left the Board. Harvey received the severest punishment for his insubordination but its effect was short-lived. Although he was never employed again, in 1810 his service record provided the ground for reinstatement.

A number of considerations explain why these officers' more or less direct challenges to their superiors did them so little damage. First, where the disputes in which they were involved gave rise to more or less open insubordination, grossly disrespectful communications and challenges to the letter and spirit of instructions from superiors, they stopped just short of direct disobedience. Second, it is significant that Lord Spencer, a key figure in a number of these disputes, was keenly aware that they arose in a context where the leading protagonists were working under immense pressure. His soothing responses to Gardner's and Parker's cries of hurt outrage, and his deft handling of St Vincent's rapier thrusts and broadsword slashes, suggest that his reaction to extreme ill temper and difficult and disrespectful behaviour was tempered by a sympathetic understanding of the taxing conditions under which flag officers served, and a keen awareness of the difficulty of finding men who consistently demonstrated 'nerves under responsibility'. St Vincent talked slightingly of Thompson's seamanship after they had fallen out, but this view was not shared by Spencer or Rear Admiral Young at the Board. On hearing of Thompson's death in March 1799 Young described him as a 'zealous, determined officer such as is much wanted in the service these days'. He told Sir Charles Pole that it had been Spencer's intention to recall Thompson from his subordinate role in the Channel Fleet to take up a commander-in-chief's appointment.[92]

It seems likely that official responses to flag officers' disputes with their superiors may also have been influenced by the tendency for offended (and offending) officers to frame them in terms of personal honour, and the indignity of being 'degraded' unjustly in the eyes of their fellows. These sentiments were conveyed through their frequent resort to terms such as 'hurt', 'wounded', 'mortified'. It is not surprising that those who had invested emotional capital in images of themselves as men of honour would react sharply to slights that compromised that perception. More prosaically, questions of honour and the symbols of reputation were important professionally and might have a bearing on flag officers' prospects of future appointments and rewards.

Even St Vincent's devious responses to Parker and Gardner paid lip service to these sensitivities.

Of course, subordinate flag officers who behaved badly ran the risk of forfeiting future favour, but that was in the hands of the Admiralty, not their offended superior. St Vincent had to put up with Vice Admiral Parker's misbehaviour in the Mediterranean Fleet but probably acted against him when he presided over the Board. In other circumstances, the materialization of the risk depended on a range of factors that overlay relations of formal authority and responsibility. Appointments invariably resulted from the delicate interplay of interest, clientage and perceived merit, and serious challenges to them threatened the basis of this system. While Spencer's good sense and delicacy tempered tendencies to overreact, he would also have been aware of the constraints imposed by the role of interest within the Navy.

Sir Charles Thompson was probably shielded from the most painful consequences of his indiscriminately querulous disposition by interest arising from his natural father's connections to the Dukes of Beaufort, and a relationship with the king that went back to the early years of his reign.[93] The other flag officers considered here were all well connected. At the time that Cochrane was embroiled with Keith, he was MP for Stirling Burghs and had a long-standing connection with the powerful Dundas family, who supported his subsequent career as a flag officer. Hallowell, an intimate of Collingwood and Nelson, had been the first lord's flag captain at the Battle of Cape St Vincent and was highly respected by him. Harvey's family's political interest in Essex may perhaps have played a role in securing his speedy restoration to the admirals' list a year after he was struck from it. The *Naval Chronicle*'s report of Harvey's brave and dignified demeanour as he walked from the court martial to his house in Portsmouth suggests that there was some sympathy for him among his colleagues. It noted regretfully the exemplary importance of the verdict in demonstrating the impartiality of discipline in the service. When Lord Mulgrave sought the king's leave to have Harvey's appeal considered by the Privy Council, he referred to his heroic role at Trafalgar and the Board's judgement that his forgiveness would not compromise discipline in the service. Mulgrave also told the king that Lord Gambier, the personal victim of Harvey's abusive behaviour, begged him to consider the request favourably.[94]

Authority and Dissent: Admirals and the Admiralty Board

[T]hese great Cabinet Warriors *do not like to have their schemes even doubted, but I think it at least the part of an honest man, altho' perhaps not a* prudent *one, to tell the Truth, especially when the blame is thrown on them who are ordered to carry the plans into effect.*
  —Vice Admiral Honourable George Berkeley to Sir Charles Pole, 1799[1]

When St Vincent was a commander-in-chief, he insisted that admirals who reported to him owed the strictest obedience to his orders. Anything that fell short of unquestioning acceptance of instructions was increasingly seen as destructive of necessary authority and detrimental to the discipline of the wider service. This approach bore the marks of St Vincent's supreme self-confidence and domineering personality. But it also reflected, in an exaggerated and sometimes ugly form, the unquestionable supremacy of commanders-in-chiefs over their fleets. While these officers reigned supreme at sea, however, they were subject to the ultimate authority of the Cabinet channelled through the Admiralty Board. The Board's authority was constantly expressed through streams of written orders from its office in London to senior flag officers around the globe. Commanders-in-chief were subject formally to the Board collectively, and received many directions from its secretary on behalf of 'their lordships'. Lord Spencer and his successors as first lord, however, increasingly assumed a dominant role in appointments, strategy and in directing the commanders of the fleets under the Board's authority.[2]

While commanders-in-chief and senior flag officers grumbled in private and occasionally let their disenchantment be known to the Board or the first lord, they usually obeyed without question. This behaviour reflected the impact of the habit of obedience central to the disciplinary ethos of the Navy, and a keen appreciation of the fate that awaited those who challenged the first lord's authority. When Spencer removed Lord Hood from his command in 1795 for trying to apply political pressure on the Board over the deployment of ships to his Mediterranean command, his career was over, and he seemed quickly resigned to not serving again.[3] At this stage Hood's active service career did not have long to run and he had sufficient reputation and interest to ensure that he was well provided for in his retirement.[4] Other officers, at more critical periods in their careers, might not be so fortunate. They risked permanent, premature relegation to the ranks of 'admirals unemployed', and the termination of any prospect of military glory, honours and further prize money. Understandably, most flag officers showed little inclination to court this fate and dutiful obedience to first lords was the norm during the Napoleonic War. Prior to that, however, Lord Spencer had experienced highly challenging passages with a number of senior admirals. These clashes resulted from the interplay of powerful and well-connected personalities in an unusual combination of circumstances. Early in his term Spencer clashed with the senior flag officer on the Admiralty Board and forced his resignation. Subsequently, he also faced challenges from three senior flag commanders, Vice Admiral William Cornwallis, Lord Bridport and Earl St Vincent.

Feuding at the Admiralty Board: Lord Spencer, Admiral Sir Charles Middleton and the supersession of Vice Admiral Sir John Laforey

The first dispute discussed here involved a battle of wills between the first lord and Sir Charles Middleton, the future Lord Barham, a senior and highly capable naval commissioner on the Admiralty Board. Middleton's dispute with Spencer was fuelled by his exalted sense of self-worth and the new first lord's determination to be master in his own house. It took place at a time when the government was under great pressure to respond effectively to reversals in the West Indies and develop a strategy to respond to them. When Spencer took his seat at the head of the Board in mid-December 1794 he immediately assumed responsibility for the naval aspects of this strategy. Initially, the war was seen as providing opportunities to snap up French territories in the region and great things were expected of the first expedition led by Sir John Jervis and General Sir George Grey. As the politician and diplomat Granville Leveson Gower noted in the autumn of 1793: 'People ... imagine that early in spring we shall hear of all their West Indian islands being in our possession.'[5] By mid-1795, however, the early tide of Jervis's and Grey's initially triumphal endeavours was in danger of being reversed.[6]

At about the time that Sir John Laforey and Rear Admiral Thompson were coming to blows in the heat of the West Indies, Lord Spencer and the Cabinet were considering Britain's next move in that theatre of war. In August a decision was made to send a new expedition to reinforce land and sea forces ravaged by disease, and facing increasingly effective resistance by movements of recently liberated slaves. The expedition, which was to be led by Lieutenant General Sir Ralph Abercromby and Rear Admiral Hugh Christian, was delayed by bad weather. It suffered a disastrous false start in mid-November 1795 when a storm drove part of the fleet up the Channel and several hundred lives were lost in wrecks on the English coast. Even before this tragedy, however, the expedition claimed two casualties from the admirals' list: Laforey and Middleton.

Rear Admiral Hugh Christian had been appointed to the expedition because of expertise acquired as chair of the Transport Board, and with the expectation that he would be able to work effectively with the Army. Having only been promoted to flag rank in mid-1795, however, he was considered too junior to assume a commander-in-chief's position when the expedition reached its destination. Spencer thus faced the question of whether Laforey should play that role, and, if not, to whom it should fall. Vice Admiral Cornwallis later observed that the command of the Leeward Islands was difficult because of the number of islands and the 'jarring interests' among them.[7] This was a strictly political rather than a geographical point. Each colony had its own interests and elite, and its friends in official circles in London. Asides by Henry Dundas, the secretary for war, indicated that he was aware that Laforey had already alienated some of these interests. It also seems likely that his acrimonious exchanges with Thompson had raised questions in Dundas's and Spencer's minds about Laforey's fitness for handling the interservice challenges that were about to unfold on his station. Spencer had already written to express 'much dissatisfaction' at the inactivity of his forces.[8] Dundas discussed Laforey's temperament and unpopularity, and probably also his age, in a meeting with Spencer and repeated his views in a letter sent on the following day.[9] His comments were prompted by Spencer's suggestion that since Laforey was too senior to recall without cause – he would be 'unprecedently and unjustly degraded in the eyes of the whole service' – he proposed to leave him in place but instruct him not to interfere with plans and instructions that had already been agreed with Abercromby and Christian.[10]

Although Dundas clearly believed that this arrangement would be unworkable, and that it risked the success of the expedition for what he dismissed as the 'etiquette of rank', Spencer's compromise seemed to prevail by default. That is, while it was not supported by Dundas or Abercromby, Spencer failed to tell them that he intended to persist with it.[11] When this determination came to Abercromby's attention, however, it was subject to a strident and cogent challenge. In a letter to Dundas, Abercromby raised the risks of divided command and also questioned the efficacy of Spencer's uncharacteristically clumsy attempt to spare Laforey's feelings and preserve his reputation: 'Will an oblique mode of supersession be less liable to reprehension, less productive of discontent in the navy, and less injurious to Sir John Laforey, than a direct one?'[12] Dundas forwarded this letter to Spencer, told him that it echoed objections made by the prime minister, and quashed a suggestion that the matter be put to cabinet.[13] Under this pressure, and in the knowledge that Abercromby's emphatically stated preference was to continue to work with Christian, Spencer beat a retreat. In a letter exuding embarrassment, he argued that as Abercromby's apprehensions were likely to prompt the dire consequences he predicted, he would revert to what was presented as his initially preferred position. Laforey was to be recalled, Christian would take the expedition to the West Indies and launch it and a more senior flag officer would be sent out as commander-in-chief.[14]

Significantly, Spencer told Dundas that he had abandoned this original plan 'from knowing how very strong an impression was made on the professional feelings and opinions of all the professional members of this Board by the proposition of recalling Sir John Leforey in this manner'.[15] An earlier remark by Spencer, and subsequent developments arising from Laforey's supersession, suggest that Middleton was the professional member uppermost in the first lord's mind. He would no doubt have been supported by Rear Admiral James Gambier, a nephew who had been brought up in his house. Middleton held decided opinions on a wide range of service subjects, including West Indian strategy. Although he was Dundas's cousin, the secretary of war warned Spencer of his Board colleague's determination to have his own way, and of the indiscrete conversations and correspondence he had had with him.[16] True to form, Middleton forcefully advised Spencer of the fundamental unsoundness of the proposed expedition, declaring that the West Indies should either be given up or left entirely to the protection of the Navy. He strongly depreciated amphibious adventures aimed at extending Britain's colonial possessions: 'It is this system of unlimited conquest that cripples us everywhere, and diverts the fleet from its natural use. It is like a farmer wishing to occupy a large farm without money to manage it … [H]e begins a beggar and ends a ruined man.'[17]

It is unclear if Middleton thought that Laforey shared his views on this question, but the two men had a long-standing relationship, corresponding as 'My Dear Friend' from the early 1780s.[18] Middleton was certainly a resolute supporter of Laforey's claim to retain his command. He described his friend's supersession as 'unprecedented', extolled his virtues and reputation in the service and begged to be excused from taking an active role in the business. Middleton also asked Spencer to consider whether 'under every circumstances of this unusual measure it would not be proper to screen the Admiralty from the injustice that will be imputed to it, by desiring a letter from the Secretary of State on which to ground their order'.[19] Both these ploys failed. On being told by Spencer that he must sign the minute or resign, Middleton, one of the 'blue light' evangelical faction in the Navy, tendered his resignation and set Spencer's authority in its proper, subordinate context: 'No Consideration will induce me to concur in what I think an unjust measure, however recommended, because I know myself amenable to a much higher tribunal than any on earth.'[20]

Middleton's attempt to distance himself from the decision to recall Laforey allowed Spencer to invoke the idea of collective responsibility that Lord Sandwich had introduced when he was first lord as a bulwark against the disruption of business through politically driven service factionalism.[21] In Spencer's formulation, this idea was given a distinctly top-down bearing in that the first lord assumed a position of preeminent independence and expected other members of the Board to support him: 'in every measure determined upon and officially proposed to the board by the first lord, every member of the board is considered as ready to take an active part by his signature; and though the responsibility unquestionably rests on the first lord, the other members are always understood to concur in his measures.'[22] There had been a lingering history of disagreement between Spencer and Middleton on what the latter saw as the first lord's willingness to allow another naval commissioner, Captain Lord Hugh Seymour, to continue to serve at sea and to act as a conduit for measures promoted in the fleet that were claimed to favour senior officers at the public's expense.[23] It also seems likely that Spencer would have resented Middleton's high-handed assumption of a privileged status in Board business that was demonstrated most sharply in 'advice' about its proceedings that he sent to the first lord when he assumed office.[24]

While Laforey's recall precipitated Middleton's resignation, his letters to Spencer and Dundas presented the first lord's insistence that he fall into line and endorse the decision, as the real cause of it. Middleton told Dundas that without this provocation he would have been prepared to sit quiet at the Board and do what he could to limit the impact of Spencer's errant administration.[25] He claimed that the first lord had been running the Board through an 'inner cabinet' and had tolerated his demeaning situation while he could still be of some service to the country. In private correspondence, Middleton told Dundas that his idea of service to his country encompassed an intention to work to 'modify' a measure of which he disapproved in the course of putting it into effect.[26] When Spencer insisted on directive collective responsibility, however, it became clear that his position was untenable:

> [I]t was [a measure] impossible for me, as an admiral, high in rank, and not ill-informed perhaps in my professional duties, to receive with implicit consent. I did not, till then, understand, that I was to dwindle into the wretched insignificance of sitting as a numerical member of a naval board, to receive a salary for signing my name to whatever might be put before me; to concur in all measures, without question of hesitation, whether dictated by ignorance or pride, and to undergo the humiliation of obsequious attentions, without difficulty or delay. I was not prepared for all this, and therefore was compelled to seek a refuge in retirement.

As was common when flag officers fell out with their superiors, Middleton accompanied the confirmation of his resignation with a declaration that he was willing to serve if the 'honour and advantage' of his country required it.[27] Middleton assumed that he, Dundas and Pitt belonged to a circle of mutual approbation from which Spencer, who was their cabinet colleague, was excluded. He 'flattered himself' that his 'withdrawal' would be met by 'the candid approval both of you [Dundas] and Mr Pitt, whether concealed or expressed'.[28]

Middleton's disinclination to subordinate his views to the first lord's was reinforced by a belief that Spencer's 'doctrine' compromised his standing in the service and failed to pay him due respect. It was Spencer's intention to ignore his rank, experience and expertise and to degrade him to a mere cipher in the hands of a civilian first lord. This interpretation reflected Middleton's personal and professional pride, his sense of honour and repulsion against the idea that he would receive a salary for being a mere placeholder.[29] It was also, however, a consequence of the dominant role that Middleton had become accustomed to play in naval administration for the past two decades and of the strength of his interest. Ironically, while Middleton was the most notable victim of a growing concentration of independent power in the hands of the first lord, he later provided the earliest formal articulation of this system when he (as Lord Barham) headed the Board from 1805 to 1806.[30]

Obedience and discretion: Vice Admiral Cornwallis's court martial, 1796

In late 1795, as the West Indian expedition was being assembled off Portsmouth, Army-Navy relations reached a nadir. The incident that precipitated this crisis was the refusal of a junior army officer, Lt Gerald Fitzgerald, to plead before a naval court martial on charges of insulting the captain of the ship on which he was serving with a detachment of soldiers. Fitzgerald's commanding officer supported his stand but although the king had confirmed the sentence of dismissal handed down by the court, legal difficulties left both the particular matter, and the issue of general principal, unresolved. Senior sea officers were gravely alarmed by these events, seeing them as a threat to their disciplinary power when transporting troops, or when soldiers were embarked to cover shortfalls in complements of marines. When the Duke of York, as field marshal of the Army, sought to regularize the situation by issuing instructions to his commanders, he merely aggravated naval opinion.

The duke's instructions, and the developments that made them seem necessary, provoked a protest from flag officers at Portsmouth. Rear Admiral Christian and Vice Admiral Waldegrave, the port admiral, reported the protest to Spencer, the latter conveying his sense of the seriousness of the situation and his sympathy with his colleagues: 'I think it proper to acquaint your lordship that hitherto I have not met two opinions on the subject in question, as we all feel convinced of the impossibility of carrying on the discipline of the service under the new regulations.'[31] Sir Ralph Abercromby sought to forge a compromise by not putting the instructions into force in his command. While this moderation, combined with a concerted attempt to replace soldiers with marines, calmed the situation to some degree, it did not address the fundamental question of the authority of commanders of ships over army personnel. This issue played a role in Spencer's next set of West Indian difficulties, which involved Vice Admiral William Cornwallis, one of the most widely respected and best-connected officers in the Navy.

Cornwallis (a party to the flag officers' protest) told Spencer in November 1795 that the dispute over disciplinary powers was of such importance that it might result in an officer declining to serve. When he was appointed commander-in-chief in the Leeward Islands in late January 1796, he again raised the question. Cornwallis noted that Abercromby's accommodation relied on the disposition of the parties involved, and might not survive a change of key personnel. He made it clear to Spencer that he would not have accepted the command if he had known of the situation, and expressed a 'sincere desire' to be relieved. Spencer sidestepped this request by stressing the Board's confidence in Cornwallis.[32] Since the Board's strategy from early November was to avoid provoking resistance in the senior echelons of the Army that might delay the dispatch of the expedition, and squelch any tendency for the Navy to be seen triumphing over the Army, Spencer's statement of confidence must have been somewhat strained, and conditional upon the needs of the expedition. In private correspondence, Seymour explained the Board's approach to his close friend Waldegrave. He was sympathetic to the admirals' position but thought the protest at Portsmouth had got out of hand and that its 'violence' threatened larger strategic objectives.[33] These considerations very likely played a role in how Cornwallis's subsequent relationship with Spencer and the Board evolved.

Cornwallis's reservations on the army discipline question, and other concerns over the quality of some of the ships and captains placed under his command, must have tried the first lord's patience, especially as they were raised at the same time that he was fending off challenges to the appointment from Abercromby and Christian. Spencer told the prime minister that Cornwallis's appointment was really none of Abercromby's business. Although he doubted whether Christian ought to go to the West Indies after he raised difficulties about serving as second-in-command, Spencer determined that

Plate 2: Admiral Sir William Cornwallis served with distinction in the East Indies and as commander-in-chief of the Channel Fleet. In 1796 he defended himself against charges that he had disregarded the Admiralty's instructions when commanding a convoy bound for the Leeward Islands.

he take up the appointment. 'This', he told the prime minister, with an elegant under-statement of his forceful role, 'is a motive which cannot be allowed to be attributed to an officer, and in a very long conversation with [Christian] the other morning I explained myself so fully on the subject that he no longer persisted in making any objection to serving in the West Indies'.[34]

The expedition finally cleared St Helens on the last day of February but immediately encountered rough weather and Cornwallis's flagship, the *Royal Sovereign*, was badly damaged in a collision. The commander-in-chief continued to convoy the troopships until they were clear of the Channel, and then, having handed over to Sir Charles Cotton who was commanding a squadron under Admiralty orders, returned to Spithead for repairs. On his arrival there in mid-March, Cornwallis was informed of his appointment as vice admiral of England. In a separate communication, however, he was told that the Board believed that he should have carried on to the West Indies, if necessary shifting his flag into Cotton's *Minatour*. He was ordered to sail immediately in a frigate, *Astraea*. When Cornwallis told Spencer that he was 'not able' to sail in a frigate, he was reminded that this was tantamount to indicating that he would relinquish his appointment. In that case, he could not be employed in future 'without giving … a very dangerous example to the service, and entirely subverting every idea of the discipline so necessary to be maintained in it'.[35] Having initially instructed Cornwallis to continue flying his flag in the *Royal Sovereign*, the Board then ordered him to appear before a court martial at Portsmouth. The trial was held on 4 April before a court made up, according to Evan Nepean, secretary of the Admiralty Board, of the largest number of flag officers who had ever heard a case against a flag officer.[36] Lord Howe was its president.

The charges were that Cornwallis had returned to Spithead when not authorized to do so, that he had failed to shift his flag into another ship when his was seriously damaged and that he had not obeyed orders to sail for the West Indies in *Astraea*. Although the court found that 'misconduct was imputable to the Vice Admiral' for not continuing to the West Indies in another ship, it issued no further reprimand on this charge and found him not guilty of the others.[37] Cornwallis was defended by Thomas Erskine, who, after a brief career in the Navy, made his name in the early 1790s by successfully defending a number of prominent political radicals. While the distinguished counsel may have been responsible for framing some of the more subtle arguments in Cornwallis's statement of defence, there is no reason to suppose that the views contained in it were Erskine's rather than his client's. If that is so, the document provides an interesting insight into a senior flag officer's perception of the complexities of command and the difficulties of navigating the shifting sands that separated admirable initiative from insubordination.[38]

Cornwallis presented a range of detailed arguments to demonstrate that he had not refused to obey direct orders issued by the Board. More interestingly, however, he also offered some general observations on the discretionary rights and responsibilities of flag officers and how these related to the ethos of subordination on which the service was thought to depend. Thus when discussing whether he should have shifted his flag to one of Cotton's ships, Cornwallis argued that since he was not facing a critical situation, 'and being invested with that discretion which must belong to every officer invested with a superior command, I had a right to judge what was best, and I formed and exercised a different judgment'.[39] In a line of argument that no doubt appealed to the splendid array of flag officers on the court, Cornwallis stated that 'for the honour and advantage of the service, I feel an interest beyond myself in claiming for a Flag Officer, charged with a high command, the exercise of a reasonable discretion in service, if to your justice it shall appear that I acted to the best of an honest judgment'. Such judgements may, particularly with the benefit of hindsight, differ and, Cornwallis argued,

> I confess it appears to me, that if without any standard but the infinitely divided opinion of men in official situations, the characters of officers were subject to be shaken by trials, without any previous complaint, or antecedent judgment of the profession on their conduct, it might be attended with the most serious consequences to the dignity and independence of the Navy.[40]

Cornwallis contrasted the 'simple' 'distinct' orders to obey that were issued to captains, with the responsibilities of an admiral:

> [H]e has many judgments to form, which must be formed upon the sudden, and which must proceed upon his own views and opinions. If upon small occasions, where the public service has sustained no stateable loss or inconvenience, and without the charge or complaint of any officers witnesses to his proceedings, the conduct of such an officer were subject to be hung in the wavering scales of opinion, instead of being subjected to the plain and ordinary principles of criminal justice, there would be a speedy end of all that firmness and confidence which is so essentially necessary to high command.[41]

Cornwallis had not openly rejected Spencer's or the Board's orders, but he had, at critical junctures, followed his own judgement in taking steps that departed from them. It is significant that in his defence, Cornwallis dwelt at length upon the distinctive challenges of superior command and the need for flag officers to act with 'firmness and confidence' if they were to succeed on active service. Shortly before the trial Cornwallis told his elder brother that he had been made a scapegoat of the 'violent' intentions the Board harboured towards the 'elder admirals' who had been prominent in the protest. He saw the trial as being for the good of the service and the country because it would ascertain 'the stretch' to which 'an officer in my situation is liable to be degraded and insulted'.[42] Seen in this light, a successful defence relying on appropriate discretion upheld Cornwallis's personal honour and the professional practice necessary for the effective exercise of a flag officer's power.

Lord Spencer's role in this affair is not entirely clear. He did not think it necessary to lay before the court a letter in which Cornwallis had asked to be relieved of his command and when he wrote to the Earl Cornwallis (a ministerial colleague) to tell him of the outcome of the trial, expressed satisfaction with the verdict and stressed the role that his sense of 'public duty' played in bringing the matter to court martial.[43] Vice Admiral Cornwallis was said to have initially absolved Spencer of any 'hostile motives' and blamed other members of the Board for bringing him to trial, but in the months that followed his view changed. Having given up the command after the trial, he subsequently came under pressure from his brother for failing to make a 'general offer of service'. In the strained passages that followed, he laid the blame firmly at Spencer's door. He described his proceedings as 'most violent and arbitrary', a 'cruel persecution' and an 'unmerited attack ... commenced against me'.[44] This episode had a lasting impact on Cornwallis's availability for active service. Despite his widely recognized skills and family connections he remained on half pay until St Vincent took the first lordship in early 1801 and appointed him to command the Channel Fleet.

Admiral Lord Howe, Admiral Lord Bridport and disputes in the Channel Command, 1794–99

While Spencer grappled with tensions produced by developments in the West Indies, he had also to contend with difficulties in the upper echelons of the Channel Command. The prime mover here was Alexander Hood, Admiral Lord Bridport. The initial object of contention was Spencer's determination to retain Lord Howe as commander-in-chief of the Channel Fleet when his physical infirmities prevented him serving at sea. Howe was appointed to the Channel command at the beginning of the war because of his vast experience and distinguished performance, his high standing in the service and the strong support, and indeed friendship, of the king. The Ministry thought the appointment would boost public confidence and the king (who told Howe that he regarded him not just as *an* admiral by as '*my* admiral') regarded his presence at the head of the fleet as absolutely essential.[45]

These considerations overrode reservations concerning Howe's age – he was in his sixty-seventh year when the war began – and the fragile state of his health. It was agreed, however, that if his health made it necessary, he might command the fleet from ashore during the winter months, with operational responsibilities being entrusted to his second-in-command, Lord Bridport. He too was elderly (having been born in the same year as Howe), plagued by gout and known to be demanding. He had, however, showed great vigour and personal courage on the Glorious First of June 1794 and a year later when he commanded a smaller scale action off L'Orient.[46] These recent contributions, the strength of Bridport's connections (which included relatives among the Pitts) and the limited options open to the Board meant that it was prepared to put up with a certain amount of the diva-like behaviour expected from a Hood. The same considerations explained why Bridport's elder brother, Samuel, Lord Hood, was given the Mediterranean Command. The background to Bridport's appointment was not auspicious, as he and Howe had clashed in the past over Greenwich Hospital business. When Bridport was Treasurer he was said to have been deeply offended by an instruction from Lord Howe (then first lord) which implied impropriety in his handling of the hospital's funds.[47]

Howe's last command was a mixed success. In some circles he was dubbed 'Lord Torbay' because he so often took his fleet into that haven. Younger up and coming officers such as Collingwood and Keith were irritated by his leisurely and ceremonial approach to getting his fleet to sea. These very demanding officers nevertheless agreed that he had showed admirable leadership in bringing the French Fleet to action on the Glorious First of June 1794.[48] By the end of that year, when the weather was particularly inclement, Howe wrote to Spencer from Bath to renew an earlier request to be relieved of his command, pleading 'an increased deafness, added to many constitutional infirmities'.[49] Elsewhere in Bath, Howe's second-in-command, also recovering his health, sought permission from the Board to prolong his recuperative stay on shore.[50] The Admiralty granted this request but told Bridport that as the Channel Fleet was nearly ready to put to sea, he should be prepared to join it at short notice. Bridport, who was probably aware of Howe's state of health, told the Admiralty that he would go immediately to London 'where I shall hold myself in readiness to receive their Lordships' orders'.[51] It seems that in addition to awaiting his orders, Bridport complained to his well-connected friends of having to serve under Howe and deputize for him. This campaign did not have the effect he intended. The king intervened to encourage Howe not to resign his command, telling Spencer in early January 1795 that if Bridport declined to serve, his 'conduct will be highly absurd … and I confess, however I may think in general well of his nautical abilities, I do not look on them as superior to those of Vice Admiral Cornwallis'.[52] Within a month of rejoining the fleet in late January 1795, however, and having faced unnervingly difficult conditions in Torbay in early February, Howe secured permission to go ashore. But while he told Bridport that henceforth he would exercise 'charge and government' of the fleet, Howe had not given up the command and did not do so until April 1797.[53] In the intervening years Bridport gave an ample demonstration of how far a senior subordinate flag officer might go in actively and passively resisting the wishes of his superiors.

Bridport chaffed constantly and openly under an arrangement that failed to recognize his claims to supreme command. He was indignant at the thought that Howe and his flag captain continued to share in prizes taken by ships of the Channel Fleet while living snug ashore. Bridport was particularly aggrieved that Howe received the lion's share of the flag officer' prize money for the French ships captured off L'Orient in mid-1795. He told Rear Admiral Lord Seymour that 'the six thousand [pounds] received by Lord Howe, I shall ever feel the loss of being unhandsomely taken from me'.[54] Bridport retaliated against these perceived injustices by failing to acknowledge instructions from Howe to report to him on the state of the ships under his command. When Howe's reminder caught up with him, Bridport's response was inaccurate, bad tempered and insubordinate. Referring to Howe's formal instruction that he should report to the secretary of the Admiralty Board, Bridport claimed that these instructions 'manifested to my weak understanding that your Lordship did not expect to be troubled with business in your retirement'.[55] Bridport's friends in London continued to press his case for an independent command in place of Howe, and the Marquis of Buckingham went to the length of securing confidential information on the ailing commander-in-chief's health. Buckingham told Bridport the general view was that Howe would not go to sea again and that 'the opinion is very strong against his retaining his command by his fireside'.[56]

When the king got wind of Bridport's disrespectful behaviour and suggested that the Board remove him to the North Sea command and bring Sir John Jervis into the Channel Fleet, Spencer demurred. He was probably and rightly concerned at how Jervis would respond to the frustrating anomalies of the situation, but the declared reason for declining the king's suggestion was sensitivity to Bridport's seniority and service record. He (and no doubt his friends) would consider his replacement at this stage as 'entirely cutting him off from any chance of ever commanding the Channel Fleet'. As an alternative, Spencer proposed another uneasy compromise, which involved Bridport's appointment as a commander-in-chief of a 'squadron employed on a particular service'. He thought this arrangement would satisfy Bridport's claims while avoiding giving the impression that Howe's retirement was permanent.[57] In the event, Bridport complained bitterly to Buckingham, wrote an ungracious reply to Spencer and offered some gratuitous criticism of the first lord's direction of the fleet.[58]

Spencer usually showed considerable patience when dealing with touchy flag officers but his response on this occasion was short and blunt. He told Bridport that he had done all he could to explain the circumstances of his command, that he did not think it necessary to say anything more on the subject and would lay his letter before the king 'for his information'.[59] Bridport's letter prompted the king to comment on the Hood family's overblown sense of entitlement – 'it appears too plain that in his family self-value is so predominant that all other objects are not sufficiently attended to' – and to 'more eagerly wish' for the recovery of Lord Howe's health.[60] When Seymour congratulated Spencer on the arrangement, he took a sharp cut at his commander-in-chief: 'Lord Bridport *should* be as much satisfied with the compliment you have paid him as he is sure to be with the advantages and emoluments which he will derive from his new commission.'[61] Although Bridport was grudging in acknowledgement of this compliment, he was predictably outraged when the special command came to an end in October 1795. Having told Spencer that he was 'obliged' for his communication of the news, he launched a diatribe against the financial disadvantages of a return to the status quo and offered a transparently insincere comment on Lord Howe's resumption of his command: 'I am glad His Majesty is likely to have his Lordship's services in this time of public warfare which calls for the experience and abilities of meritorious officers of every rank.'[62]

On one particularly vexed matter, Bridport seemed determined to follow his elder brother's unfortunate example. In the spring of 1795 Lord Hood had been effectively removed from the Mediterranean command after a spell of leave in England. This unusual move followed a public expression of resentment at the size of the fleet assigned to him, during which he warned the Board that an officer serving on these terms risked becoming 'the instrument of disgrace to the nation'.[63] Spencer told the king that it was necessary to remove Hood because 'the discipline and subordination so necessary to be maintained between the Board of Admiralty and the officers entrusted … with the conduct of your Majesty's naval forces would be entirely at an end, if public and official representations of this kind were allowed to pass unnoticed'. The king agreed.[64] Nelson and other of Hood's friends in the service were stunned and disappointed at his dismissal but other officers thought he had gone too far.[65] Seymour (an ally of Jervis and thus no friend to the Hoods) told Spencer that 'the Navy in general will be pleased at [Hood's] being taught that there are bounds to the authority of all officers which he had appeared to have lost sight of'.[66] Andrew Lambert has suggested that Hood was the innocent scapegoat for the Ministry's inadequate logistical planning but this judgement ignores the fact that Hood put his head in the noose by public grandstanding intended to embarrass Spencer and his colleagues. His letters to Bridport suggest that he was well aware of the risk he was running.[67] In any case, Bridport did not appear to have benefitted from his brother's experience. He made a stream of intemperate demands on Spencer and the Board for more ships, and came dangerously close at times to ignoring Admiralty instructions in trying to secure them. He was particularly resentful of restrictions on the deployment of squadrons of frigates commanded by Sir John Warren and Sir Edward Pellew. In early August 1797, in flat contradiction of the Admiralty's stipulation that Pellew's squadron should be based in Falmouth 'in readiness', Bridport ordered it to join the fleet off Brest. After the event, he reported the matter to the Admiralty, asserting, in flagrant disregard of his instructions, that 'I conclude when ships are put under my orders I am authorized to direct their proceedings to the best of my judgment, for the services committed to my charge as long as they shall remain part of my squadron'.[68] Bridport continued to push the boundaries whenever he could and was duly chastised by the Board. When questioned on why one of his ships was off station, and reminded of the general requirement that vessels should be deployed in conformity with the Board's instructions, Bridport replied (in clear and truculent contradiction of the evidence) that he and the Board were in 'perfect agreement' on the matter.[69]

Bridport's service in the Channel Fleet provides numerous examples of a senior flag officer pushing the boundaries of due subordination by pressing on the judgement and authority of a relatively inexperienced civil first lord. First lords' responses to these incremental challenges were conditioned to some considerable degree by a perceived shortage of talent. As a result, they felt constrained in their choice of commanders-in-chief on the most demanding stations and showed a corresponding reluctance to make changes unless they were absolutely necessary. These constraints made it difficult for first lords to respond to extremely forceful senior flag officers who questioned their instructions and showed open reluctance to accept their decisions, especially when their high sense of self-regard was fortified by the self-affirming protection of well-placed friends.

Having ridden out the squalls generated by Middleton, Cornwallis and Bridport, Spencer faced ongoing challenges from St Vincent, who showed himself a past master of the questioning reaction to superior authority. This was ironic given his uncompromising view of his own authority, and steely determination to maintain it in the face of what he saw as improper, discipline-sapping reactions from senior officers under his command.

The authoritarian dissenter: St Vincent's challenges to the first lord, 1797–1801

Although St Vincent insisted on unquestioning obedience from his subordinates, he did not always live by this rule himself. Thus in his feud with Sir John Orde formal compliance with the instructions of the first lord was sometimes accompanied by a barrage of affronted remonstration. Although open disobedience did not follow these protests, by the standards that St Vincent imposed on Orde and other flag officers in the Mediterranean Fleet, they bore all the hallmarks of clear insubordination. He boasted to one of his subordinate flag officers of his triumph over Lord Spencer in securing Sir Alan Gardner's removal from the Channel Fleet in mid-1800 and pulled no punches in emphasizing his necessary power on such questions: 'I should have deserved insult from every officer under my command, had I *permitted* him to return ... upon which I put my absolute veto.'[70] This is a very partial account of the affair but it illustrates St Vincent's aspirations about the balance of power between a first lord and a senior officer such as himself. When he did not get his way, he reacted angrily to what he saw as the indignity of being rebuked by the Admiralty Board. He thus deeply resented its response to his unauthorized termination of Orde's appointment, insisting that the least he deserved was '*silent approbation*'. Orde's attempt to get up 'cabals' to pull down his commander-in-chief left him with 'no other card to play but to get rid of him'.[71] In a letter to Evan Nepean, St Vincent launched a vituperative attack on their mutual masters:

Formed as your Board is, I am not surprised at the letter you were ordered to write, which I would not endure for one moment, but for the critical state of naval operations in these seas.... But I confess myself not Christian enough either to forget or forgive those who have most unjustly condemned me, unheard. Much fitter would it have been to put me on my trial.[72]

Given St Vincent's tactic of denying his antagonists the satisfaction of a court martial, the last part of this outburst is particularly ironic. On this occasion he presented himself as being victimized for maintaining discipline within his fleet, and was sharply critical of the Board's failure to suppress Orde's printed account of their exchanges: 'you will give a *coup mortel* to subordination, of which there is very little left.'[73]

In addition to these spectacular one-off episodes, there was a continual undertow of grumbling complaint and grudging acquiescence over appointments and promotions that were not made, or of which St Vincent disapproved because they were unmerited, or because they crowded out his influence and undermined his standing.[74] He made his objections on these matters known to Lord Spencer and in his clandestine correspondence with Evan Nepean indulged in trenchant, unbridled criticism of the Board. St Vincent particularly resented the pretensions of professional members of the Board and what he viewed as their unwarranted interference in the affairs of *his* fleet. In May 1797 he launched a stinging attack on Sir Charles Middleton who though no longer a member of the Board was still treated by some of its members as a key authority on Navy business. In common with other 'blue lights' such as his nephew Gambier, who now sat on the Board, Middleton believed he had a duty to encourage those under his command to seek salvation through godly living.[75] These aspirations were not shared by St Vincent. While nominally an Anglican, and fully prepared to use religion as what Robert Blake has aptly termed 'an engine of compulsion', his attitude towards Christianity was infused with a strong dose of Enlightenment scepticism.[76] In a letter to Nepean, St Vincent accused Middleton of hypocrisy and venality, scorned his piety and dismissed his pretensions to professional eminence:

[A]fter making more money by the sale of offices at the Navy Board, than any of his predecessors, [Middleton] comes to the Admiralty with his cant, imposture, loads of precedents and scraps of stay tape and buckram and makes you all believe, that he is the only man capable of regulating your proceedings ... [H]e neither possesses a mind to direct great ventures, nor was ever in a situation as an officer to gain knowledge or experience, the utmost extent of his abilities having gone no further than forming a swaddling system of morality for his ship's company.[77]

St Vincent was equally scathing on Vice Admiral William Young, who had been brought to the Board by Spencer when Middleton resigned and enjoyed a long spell as the senior naval commissioner. As a protégé of Keppel's protagonist Sir Hugh Palliser, Young was naturally suspect. However, the way St Vincent aired his criticisms necessarily reflected unfavourably on Lord Spencer's judgement, and he made them to the secretary of the Board over which he presided: 'It will very soon come to pass, that I shall tell Lord Spencer bluntly, if Admiral Young continues on the Admlty Board

I will cease to command the Channel Fleet.' St Vincent questioned the need for more than one seaman to sit on the Board, ridiculing the current members (Young and the unfortunate Vice Admiral Robert Man) by saying that Lord Spencer and Evan Nepean were better informed than either of them: 'I should pay you a very ill compliment if I compared them to you in any point of nautical or geographical knowledge.'[78] In praising Spencer and Nepean, St Vincent was arguably most unfair towards both Young and Man. Young's letters from the Board suggest that he was a thoughtful administrator and he subsequently served with distinction in command of a squadron off the Texel at a critical time in the Napoleonic War.[79] As we have seen, Young thought Man brought a range of valuable nautical knowledge to the Board. The significant point, however, is St Vincent's willingness to question Spencer's judgement. He continued in the same vein when commenting on the first lord's support of Sir Richard Bickerton – 'he is vain, ignorant, obstinate and presumptuous' – and renewed his attack on Young, blaming him for the acid tone of the Board's communications and again threatening to resign his command. St Vincent warned Nepean that 'if Vice-Admiral Young is permitted to mix so much gall in your ink, every officer of Spirit and distinction will be driven out of the Service ... [T]he next impertinence I receive, will make room for Sir Hyde Parker.'[80] Such language would not have been tolerated by St Vincent's disciplinary hero Admiral Langara, whether in command of a fleet, or in his role of Spanish minister of marine. Nor, as we have seen, did St Vincent put up with it from his subordinate flag officers.

Conclusion

When Sir Edward Pellew was inclined to quarrel with the second Lord Melville in 1812, he was advised by his patron, the politically troublesome Duke of Northumberland, not to resign his command: 'Men in high situations, like yourself, must pretend not to see many disagreeable circumstances which happen to them; attributing always to accident, what perhaps however they know was done by design.' Pellew held his tongue on this occasion and duly received the recognition he sought. As we have seen, not all of his distinguished colleagues showed such politic constraint.[81] But while Sir John Orde behaved in a way that made Lord Barham very willing to accept his offer of resignation, and Sir John Duckworth and Sir Alexander Cochrane continued to wrangle with first lords about appointments, the accession of St Vincent to the head of the Board in early 1801 was something of a watershed. Given his unbending attitude towards his subordinates when he commanded at sea, and his resentment against those who crossed him, it is perhaps not surprising that flag officers were reluctant to challenge decisions coming from St Vincent's Board. His brutally forceful style and overwhelming self-confidence meant that he was not tempted to seek the compromises which were a source of difficulty in Spencer's early transactions with flag officers. When St Vincent returned to active service in command of the Channel Fleet in 1806, he was forthright to the point of being domineering in his correspondence with Rear Admiral Markham, who remained on the Board. He made a point, however, of minimizing his role in appointments and refrained from engaging in the disrespectful sniping he had directed at Lord Spencer. Other officers for whom employment was less certain were even more circumspect. In mid-1808 when Sir Richard King was serving as Lord Gambier's subordinate in the Channel, he complained bitterly to Cornwallis of Lord Mulgrave's board's favouritism in approving leave to other senior officers. At the same time, however, King noted that his wife persuaded him against sending a formal letter of complaint to the Board: as there were as 'many admiral as ships' such a step would be 'imprudent'.[82]

Mulgrave was reported to have been exhausted by his prolonged tenure of the first lordship, but neither he nor his successors had to contend with quite the challenging personalities that Lord Spencer faced. His considerable resources of ingenuity and tact were taxed heavily as he attempted to balance the demands of well-placed and assertive senior officers against the claims of their colleagues, the pull of interest and the operational and strategic requirements of the service. During the early stages of the Napoleonic Wars, most of these elderly men were no longer fit for active service and were replaced by a slightly younger generation with a less assertive sense of entitlement. It is instructive to compare Nelson's correspondence with Lord Barham with the combative tone of many of Bridport's and St Vincent's written engagements with Lord Spencer. The contrast with Sir John Warren's correspondence with the second Lord Melville towards the end of the wars is even more striking. When Warren was being 'micro-managed' by the second Lord Melville during the early stages of the American War, he sat quietly under a stream of blunt rebukes and implied criticism that would have provoked Bridport and St Vincent to near mutiny.[83] It is ironic that after St Vincent passed from the scene, the relationship between first lords and flag officers came to reflect more nearly the ethos of obedience that he had sought to impose on his subordinates. It was as if his commanding and intolerant disposition towards his superiors was the last flicker of a culture he condemned in practice. His first lordship ushered in a future where the grievances of flag officers were muted, and any inclination to challenge the instructions of first lords was suppressed.

Admirals and Mutineers

*[B]y persuasion urged through the medium of all the most esteemed and credited
naval characters and by force kept in reserve to second the effects of persuasion.*
—Edmund Burke's deathbed prescription for dealing with the Spithead mutiny,
conveyed to Lord Spencer by William Wyndham, the secretary for war[1]

The formidable hardships that seamen faced in the usual course of service were exacerbated when ships went into action, struck particularly foul weather or faced emergencies such as groundings and collisions. Even everyday tasks such as loading munitions and supplies, and working ships' boats, involved back-breaking work.[2] Tight discipline and instantaneous responses to orders were essential if large numbers of men, some utterly lacking in experience or seamanship skills when swept up into the Navy, were to be trained to endure these hardships and contribute to complex ship-handling and fighting tasks. An important part of this training was directed towards establishing and maintaining a disciplinary order through which a few commissioned and non-commissioned officers exercised control over large numbers of seamen. In a first-rate ship-of-the-line, fourteen commissioned and warrant officers and a couple of dozen midshipmen were responsible for ensuring the disciplined efficiency of crews of more than 800 men.[3] Although a large majority of these men were volunteers, the lack of shore leave, the unavoidable hardships of the service and vulnerability to harsh treatment by some officers meant that some of them were prepared to risk capital punishment by refusing to obey orders and making themselves liable to charges of mutiny.[4] Individual acts of contempt or disobedience came within the compass of 'mutiny' but collective acts posed a far more immediate threat to the discipline and efficiency of the service.

The first concerted mutiny of the French Wars seems to have occurred on the *Windsor Castle* in the Mediterranean Fleet in June 1794. There was another instance on the *Culloden* in the Channel six months later. Admiral Hotham played a weak part in the first incident and Admiral Bridport, Rear Admirals Cornwallis and Colpoys failed to bring the *Cullodens* to obedience. Captain Thomas Pakenham achieved that by seizing ten ringleaders, half of whom were subsequently executed.[5] In the first half of 1797 large-scale mutinies broke out at Spithead, the Nore, Plymouth and off Yarmouth, and further episodes occurred on a more restricted scale on the North American station in 1797–98, at the Cape of Good Hope towards the end of 1797 and in the Mediterranean. A foiled mutiny led by United Irishmen on *Caesar* in the North Sea Fleet in August 1798 resulted in six sentences of death.[6] Mutinies on the Irish station in the early days of the Peace in 1801 were sparked by extreme resentment at the prospect of being sent to the West Indies.

In a few cases, mutineers aimed to seize control of their ship, hand it over to the enemy or destroy it and liberate the crew from the service. The first such incident in the French Wars occurred in December 1795 when the *Shark*, a small four-gun vessel under the command of a lieutenant, was taken into La Houge by her crew. In September 1797 some of the crew of the *Hermione*, a thirty-two-gun frigate, murdered their captain and eight other commissioned and non-commissioned officers, and handed the ship over to enemy authorities at La Guaira in the Spanish West Indies. Two months later the commander of *Marie Antoinette*, a ten-gun schooner, was killed by the crew, who then took their ship into a French port in the West Indies. The frigate *Dänae* suffered the same fate off Brest in March 1800 but her captain and officers were unharmed. Far from gaining their liberty, the crew members found themselves incarcerated by the French. In November 1800 mutineers on the *Albanaise*, a sixteen-gun bomb vessel, took their ship into Malaga. Mutinies of this type were far less common in the Napoleonic War when only one British vessel was passed directly into enemy hands: the six-gun cutter *Dominica* was handed over to the French at Guadeloupe in late May 1806 but retaken a few days later.[7] As Britain prepared to launch an attack on French possessions in the Indian Ocean in 1809, members of a prize crew of a captured brig killed their commanding officer and handed their vessel over to the French at the Isle de France.[8] While the instances of mutinous crews handing their ships over to the enemy were thus rare, this was alleged to be the object of plots exposed in the Mediterranean Fleet under St Vincent, and was at least threatened by some mutineers at the Nore in 1797. In June of that year the *Pompée* was taken back to Portsmouth and six of her crew court martialled for hatching a plot to take their ship into Brest. Seaman with United Irish sympathies made similar plans in the Channel Fleet under Admiral Cornwallis in 1804 and three of them were sentenced to death.[9]

Mutiny was dealt with explicitly in the nineteenth Article of War in terms of 'mutinous assembly', uttering 'words of sedition and mutiny' and 'showing contempt for superior officers'. There was some overlap with article twenty-two, which dealt with striking a superior officer and disobedience, and article eleven, which addressed disobedience in battle. These regulations made mutiny a capital offence; article twenty left it to courts martial to determine the punishment of those who concealed 'mutinous words spoken by any' or failed to resist 'any mutiny or sedition'. In the eighteenth century concerted disobedience was often a form of quasi-industrial action designed to address particular grievances rather than a final rejection of authority, but from the 1790s some historians have discerned the influence of popular radicalism and Irish republicans in framing these incidents.[10] Whatever their underlying or immediate causes, however, mutinies on any scale imperilled the efficient operation of affected vessels and in some circumstances compromised national security. They also posed a fundamental challenge to the system of discipline that flag officers were responsible for upholding, threatened their authoritative confidence and dealt sharp blows to their professional pride and to preconceptions about their relationship with the men under their command.

The late Georgian Navy's approach to upholding the authority of admirals and captains has been aptly characterized as a system of 'selective terror' in which mutinous outbreaks were followed by punishments designed to deter disobedience by swift responses and severe but targeted punishments.[11] The system was selective in that it directed punitive force at 'ringleaders', rather than all the seamen involved. Thus while thousands of men took part in the Nore mutiny, 412 faced courts martial. Of these, 345 were pardoned, and 59 sentenced to death. Of these sentences, 29 were carried out and the remainder commuted to floggings or terms of imprisonment.[12] Even after the *Hermione* mutiny, not all of the recaptured men and boys were condemned to death.[13]

Selective terror was consistent with the widely held view that poor leadership lay behind systemic ill-discipline, and that mutiny occurred when basically good men were led astray by a few desperate individuals. It also provided a deterrent that was consistent with the Navy's pressing need to retain the services of as many fit and healthy seamen as possible. Mass punishments that killed or even temporarily incapacitated dozens of highly skilled men were clearly not in the interests of the service. At the same time, however, the practical operation of this approach might involve difficulties. The final deterrent of death could only arise from a court martial authorized by a commander-in-chief, or the Admiralty on home stations. Where an appeal for mercy was issued by the court it had to be considered by the king.[14] These processes took time, so unless there was a commanding flag officer close by, the benefits of swift retribution were compromised. Summary punishments by captains avoided these difficulties but the limitations on what sanctions they could authorize (up to fifty lashes) reduced the gap between the penalties suffered for mutiny and for lesser offences such as drunkenness and theft. There were sixty-eight summary punishments for mutinous behaviour on the North American and West Indian stations during the war of 1812 and only nine courts martial, none of which resulted in executions.[15] Since summary punishments also meant that the facts of a case were not aired before a court, there was a significant risk that resort to them provided a relatively safe option for captains and admirals who had reason to conceal the general state of discipline on their ships.

This chapter considers a range of concerted mutinies in which flag officers were directly involved. It focuses on the ways in which they reacted to these unsettling events, how their responses related to perceptions of their overarching disciplinary responsibilities and how effective they were in dealing with these critical challenges to their authority and the system of subordination upon which the efficiency of the service was thought to depend. The mutinies at Spithead, the Nore and off Yarmouth were atypical in that they involved fleets rather than single ships,[16] but for that reason admirals responded directly to them. St Vincent and Vice Admiral Waldegrave dealt subsequently with mutinies in ships under their command on the Mediterranean and Newfoundland commands, while Vice Admiral Sir Hyde Parker and Rear Admiral Richard Bligh were involved in the trials of crew members of the *Hermione* on the Jamaica station in 1798.

Admirals in the Spithead mutinies: Bridport, Gardner, Colpoys, Howe and Curtis

A number of admirals faced particularly challenging tests in the spring of 1797 when there were concerted breakdowns in discipline in ships at Spithead. These vessels were either part of the Channel Fleet, or under the command of Admiral Sir Peter Parker, the port admiral at Portsmouth. Mutiny was precipitated by the Admiralty's failure to respond to respectfully worded petitions from seamen for increases in pay to match those recently provided for soldiers in the army and commissioned officers in their own service. Well-grounded complaints were also made about the use of short measures by ship's pursers and failures to grant shore leave. Anonymous statements of these claims had been sent to Lord Howe, but Bridport and Parker advised him that they were the work of an ill-disposed individual and did not represent widespread unhappiness in the fleet, so he took no further action.[17] When the Admiralty finally got wind of these difficulties, it hoped that they would blow over if the fleet put to sea immediately.[18] As a result, the authorities were taken by surprise when ships' companies refused obedience, seized control of their vessels, rigged nooses on the yard arms as a warning to those who might be inclined to resist them, elected delegates to provide leadership and coordinate their activities and detained unpopular officers or sent them unceremoniously on shore.

Within a week Lord Spencer, Vice Admiral William Young and civilian members of the Board travelled to Portsmouth to meet the mutineers' representatives. They agreed to address the men's grievances over pay and victuals and to secure a general pardon from the king.[19] When there were delays in furnishing a copy of this document under the king's signature and seal, and uncertainty arose in the men's minds over parliamentary approval of the funds required to meet the other claims, they became suspicious and unsettled. Much to the offended surprise of senior officers and Admiralty officials, the men's distrust precipitated a second round of mass disobedience on four ships at Spithead and the rest of the fleet that had been moved to St Helens off the north-east corner of the Isle of Wight.

Lord Bridport, who had taken command of the fleet just prior to the outbreak, counselled moderation, kept on good terms with the men and actively addressed their claims to be given their full weight of rations. He also advised the Admiralty of the risks that officers ran if the ships were hurried to sea before a settlement was made.[20] However, Bridport's active role in securing a return to obedience was constrained by his belief that the men had the whip hand and would resume their regular duties only if their demands were to some degree satisfied. Interestingly, when Bridport met the Board during the course of its visit to Portsmouth, he portrayed the admirals as the victims of mutinies. He claimed they were placed in a 'disgraceful situation' and would only be able to recover their authority if the men's demands were satisfied.[21] The second outbreak was a particularly severe blow to Bridport's confidence and sense of authority. He told Lord Spencer that 'I cannot command the fleet, as all authority is taken from me.... My mind is too deeply wounded by all these proceedings, and I am so unwell that I can scarcely hold my pen'.[22]

From time to time Bridport had the assistance of other flag officers but their interventions were not particularly effective. When Vice Admiral Gardner, Bridport's second-in-command, Vice Admiral Sir John Colpoys, a subordinate flag officer, and Rear Admiral Sir Charles Pole, his captain of the fleet, tried to persuade the *Queen Charlottes* of the validity of the pardon offered by Spencer and his colleagues, Gardner's high-handedness inflamed their suspicions. Gardner told Lord Bridport that my 'admonition and friendly advice was rejected in a manner which has hurt my feelings exceedingly', and acknowledged that his interventions had exacerbated the situation on his flagship (the *Royal Sovereign*). He closed his report by expressing 'great concern … that the whole of this ship's company is in a state of mutiny and that their temper and disposition is materially changed for the worse since yesterday'.[23] The delegates told Bridport that they believed that Gardner was attempting to 'sow division and mistrust in the fleet and in fact to separate our interests'.[24] When mutiny flared up again, Gardner attributed his crew's 'mutinous disposition' to parliamentary speeches made by the Duke of Bedford and other opposition figures who questioned the Ministry's good faith once the mutiny had ended and the men had obeyed orders to take their ships to sea.[25]

Gardner experienced ongoing difficulties with the crew of the *Royal Sovereign* that terminated in them sending him ashore. He told Bridport that he had 'been removed from my command in the Fleet, in so very indecent & ignominious a manner' that he could not resume it and he begged to be allowed to resign his command. When the crew changed its mind the next day and sent their admiral a deferential invitation to return on board, he declared that he had no intention of putting himself in a position where he could be insulted further.[26] Gardner agreed to go back on board the *Royal Sovereign* a few days later with very bad grace, aggrieved with the Admiralty Board for not allowing him leave to recover his health. The crew had written to Bridport seeking his support for Gardner's return and expressing deep regret for its 'impulsive' and 'misguided' dismissal of their admiral. The vice admiral was not won over by these placatory sentiments, complaining bitterly of the crew's failure to remove the 'yard ropes' and expressing regret at having agreed to return to his flagship: 'I … lament my having *again* put myself into so degrading and humiliating a situation, from which I see no probability at present of my being soon released'.[27] As with Bridport, Gardner's reaction to the mutinies showed the toll they had taken on his nerve and confidence.

Just as the second wave of mutiny broke over the heads of Bridport and his colleagues, the Board sent an order emphasizing that commanding officers were not to tolerate further outbreaks of disobedience and instructing them to take all necessary steps to put them down if they occurred. The Board had already ordered that gun ports and portholes should be closed to prevent crews talking with men from other ships.[28] Sir John Colpoys received this order the day before the second outbreak occurred, as he took command of four ships that were held at Spithead because of doubts over the crews' willingness to obey orders. With unrest continuing on these ships, Colpoys ordered the crew of his flagship (*London*) below decks, closed the gun ports and secured the hatches. When the men attempted to surge up on to the main deck and deploy one of the guns against the officers and Marines, he ordered them to open fire. Most of the Marines dropped their arms, but other members of Colpoys's party shot and mortally wounded at least three mutineers. As soon as it was clear that further resistance would cause extensive bloodshed, Colpoys ordered his colleagues to cease fire. The crew threatened to hang Lieutenant Beaver, the junior officer who had fired the first telling shot, but Colpoys claimed personal responsibility for the causalities and he and the other officers were eventually confined to their quarters. In explaining his conduct to the crew members, Colpoys emphasized his determination to carry out the

Admiralty's order and to seek to maintain his authority in the face of their attempt to take it from him. At the same time, however, he tried to assure the men that by returning to obedience they would become his responsibility and would thus avoid getting in 'any Disgrace with your bretheren in the Fleet'.[29]

Colpoys's letters to Bridport make it clear that he expected to be tried by the mutineers, since he referred to his captives as 'the poor misguided men who are to be my judges'.[30] The delegates began to take steps to hold a mutineers' court martial and the possibility was widely discussed in London. Colpoys assured the Board (and the mutineers through whose hands his letters passed) that his action 'did not proceed from Hasty or Tyrannical motives but its only guide has been the fulfilling of my Duty as a servant of my King and Country'.[31] Colpoys was clearly worried that he would be blamed for making the men more intransigent. He also seemed to have had misgivings on how the Board would view his decision to save Beaver's life by offering himself in his place and agreeing to be placed in confinement.

After being held for three days, Colpoys and the other officers were sent ashore to answer to the civil power. Although the coroner's jury returned a verdict of 'justifiable homicide', Colpoys was determined to resign his command because he thought the deaths made his position untenable with the men. In a final gesture of leadership he subscribed a hundred guineas for the relief of the families of the seamen killed in the incident.[32] Colpoys did not command at sea again but served on the Admiralty Board from 1804 to 1805 and then took up a well- remunerated life appointment as treasurer of Greenwich Hospital. His firmness in the face of the mutinous *Londons* earned him the plaudits of Lord Spencer and Vice Admiral Young, and the warm and lasting admiration of St Vincent.

Colpoys was the only flag officer during the wars to personally lead armed resistance to mutineers but his uncompromising attitude became common in the upper echelons of the service. In the short term, however, his action may have hardened the men's determination. In the face of these escalating difficulties, and Bridport's professed inability to influence the men, Spencer called in Earl Howe to reassure the mutineers of the honesty of government's intentions, stress its determination to get the fleet to sea and to conclude the negotiations.[33] He was chosen for this role because he had the trust of the king and the Admiralty Board, and, perhaps more importantly, a reputation for trustworthiness and fair dealing with the men that had survived initial criticism over his earlier apparent inaction.[34] Howe is reported to have met with most of the cabinet at Lord Spencer's apartments in the Admiralty before travelling to Portsmouth.[35] Spencer explained to Bridport that he and the Board thought it better if someone who was not the men's commander-in-chief took on this role. As the crews at St Helens had already refused his order to go to sea and Bridport had asked to relinquish his command, Spencer might also have thought that he lacked the confidence, temper and spirit for the task at hand.[36] Gardner, who was now distrusted by the crews and did not seem to be able to act tactfully when he was under pressure, could not have acted effectively for Bridport. Given Howe's and Bridport's history of difficulties, however, it is not surprising that the latter expressed hurt surprise at the role given to his former commander-in-chief. In recognition of the awkward position in which Bridport had been placed, the Ministry went to some lengths to give Howe's role a distinctive, non-service, status. It was not a conventional naval appointment, being established under the 'Sign Manual', an order issued over the king's signature that was used, among other purposes, to authorize a negotiator to treat with a foreign power.[37] This face-saving form was accompanied by private expressions of professional regard. Bridport thus received what he described as an 'obliging and affectionate' letter from William Pitt on Howe's appointment and responded in kind to his kinsman and most well-placed backer.[38] Nevertheless, and entirely predictably, the temporarily displaced commander-in-chief made it clear that he thought he had been ill-used and studiously ignored Howe's negotiations when he visited London.[39]

Since the flag officers at Portsmouth seemed to have been immobilized psychologically by their loss of authority, it was highly significant that Howe's first steps were designed to restore the men's sense of subordination. He reasserted the authority of senior officers by insisting that the men acknowledge they had acted wrongly and begged him to secure the 'King's pardon for their transgression'. He also, however, invited them to name the officers who they wished to see removed.[40] Over the next four days Howe, who was aged 71, was rowed round the ships at Spithead and St Helens in an open boat, hauling himself up the towering sides of men-of-war, addressing crews and talking with their delegates, listening to grievances, appealing to shared experiences and a commitment to duty, and encouraging assurance of a speedy return to obedience and duty. Howe's mission concluded with a reading of the proclamation containing the king's pardon on the deck of Bridport's flagship and a maritime procession in which Lady Howe took part. This event symbolized the restoration of unity within the fleet and dissolved the earlier disagreements in the enthusiastic atmosphere of a fête. When Howe landed at the Sally Port to make his way to a feast held at the military governor's house in Portsmouth, he was so exhausted that he had to be carried on the delegates' shoulders.[41]

Rear Admiral Sir Roger Curtis's reaction to the Admiralty's order to tolerate no further disobedience was very different to Colpoys's. In early May he was commanding a squadron moored at Torbay that was about to be ordered to sea. When his men got wind of the fresh developments at Spithead, however, they told Curtis that they had determined to join the rest of the fleet. Curtis reported to Bridport that he had tried without success to dissuade them from taking this course of action, but he also advised his commander-in-chief that it would be very unwise to put the Board's uncompromising order into effect. By the middle of the month when Lord Howe's intervention had helped the men under Curtis's command settle down, Curtis defended his placatory approach: '[F]rom the universality of the combination to shake off all obedience, resistance would not possibly be attended with any good consequences, my whole aim was the prevention of still greater, and more dangerous enormities.'[42] In a context where the rest of Bridport's fleet were returning to obedience, Curtis's strategy proved effective. But while it seemed to do him no damage in the eyes of the first lord, it lowered him in the esteem of the officer who was to succeed Spencer at the head of the Admiralty Board. When Spencer ordered Curtis to join the Channel Fleet a couple of years later, St Vincent sent him a scornful commentary on his protégé's disciplinary capacities. He 'heartily' hoped that Curtis 'will not have a seditious squadron, for he has no fortiter in re, although he abounds in the suavitier. I never in my life, saw a man, who shrank from the audacity of United Irishmen like him, or who sacrifices discipline to the popularity of the moment'. He later complained that Curtis's 'pusillanity of character and love of popularity' meant that many 'delinquents' got off completely or were punished too lightly.[43]

Flag officers were not slow to assign responsibility for the Spithead mutinies to the failings of their colleagues. St Vincent attributed insubordination in the fleet to Bridport's slack disciplinary practices, while Collingwood thought that Howe's initial inaction played a significant role in precipitating the mutiny itself.[44] If Barrow was well informed, however, responsibility at that stage appeared to rest with Bridport and Parker who had discounted the seriousness of the threat when Howe had consulted them.[45] Howe's decision to support the men's demand for unpopular officers to be sent ashore was criticized by St Vincent and Collingwood on grounds of disciplinary principle, and by those like Captain Richard Keats who suffered as a result of it.[46] At one stage Bridport condoned this measure but then changed his mind.[47] Although Young had reservations about the strategy, he told Rear Admiral Lord Hugh Seymour that it was authorized by the Board as a means of ensuring a speedy settlement that would ensure the fleet put to sea.[48]

By mid-May 1797 the Admiralty seemed confident that when crews elsewhere received news of the Spithead settlement, any inclination to disobedience would dissipate. It thus regarded signs of disturbance in Admiral Duncan's North Sea Fleet off Yarmouth, among ships under Vice Admiral Charles Buckner at the Nore, and Vice Admiral Sir Richard King at Plymouth, as terminal flickers of the spirit that had prevailed at Spithead and St Helens. As the King put it, 'I trust the disturbance at the Nore, as it seems ungrounded, when it is known that the fleet has sailed, will cease.'[49] These expectations proved wildly sanguine and over the coming weeks several flag officers faced serious challenges to their authority.

Admirals and mutineers at the Nore, in the North Sea and Plymouth: Buckner, Duncan and Keith

From his base at Sheerness the elderly Buckner was responsible for vessels undergoing refits, or waiting to be assigned to a squadron from a string of anchorages in the Thames estuary. When the crews of ships under Buckner's command refused obedience and organized themselves on the Spithead model, the Board made it clear that no more concessions would be made, and rejected the men's demand for it to come to Sheerness and treat with them. Spencer and some of his colleagues finally travelled there to reiterate that they would not negotiate, and make it clear that all that was on offer was the promise of a pardon to those (other than ringleaders) who returned to duty. In spite of the Board's determination, however, the mutineers seemed to have the upper hand for the first couple of weeks. They blockaded the Thames, detained a large fleet of merchant ships and won support from most of Admiral Duncan's fleet off Yarmouth. Thereafter, however, the authorities managed to isolate the mutinous crews from the shore and threaten them with a concentration of well-led land forces and artillery. These measures impeded communications and provisioning, and the removal of navigational aids made escape down the Thames a very risky option. These difficulties and increasing internal dissension among the mutinous crews eroded solidarity and prompted a series of capitulations to the authorities.

In the early stages of the mutiny Admiral Buckner adopted a wait-and-see approach that was consistent with the expectation that the mutiny would fizzle out. When the Board began to take a more active, but still largely defensive, role, Buckner did not demonstrate any notable leadership. He reported assiduously, managed the resources that remained under his control, liaised with Sir Charles Grey, the very active commander of the land forces, acted conscientiously on the Board's instructions and made a useful suggestion about the placement of a shore battery. When it became necessary for a flag officer to go on board a couple of the more intransigent ships and talk their crews into submission, Vice Admiral Lord Keith, who was Buckner's temporary second-in-command, undertook the role. Since the Admiralty was determined not to negotiate with the mutineers there was no need to involve someone like Howe who was outside the command structure. Buckner was a far less prominent and well-connected figure than Bridport, so the Board did not seem to have any qualms about him being put in Keith's shade. He appears to have been treated with open disregard by mutineers ashore and by the crew of his flagship, who told him that he had no authority over them.[50] Keith, by contrast, demonstrated the active, energetic and effective managerial spirit that the occasion required. He also possessed the ability to impose his will without prompting the counterproductive reactions that met some of Gardner's attempted interventions.

Keith approached his role with cool determination, intelligence and tact. He consulted Grey on plans to use the army against the mutineers if that became necessary, and it was his idea to disable the navigation marks in the Thames estuary. Initially, Keith's credibility with the men was called into question by claims over his handling of prize money in the East Indies, but once this matter was resolved, he dealt most effectively with dangerously disaffected crews. He encouraged the mutineers to resist what he presented as the self-interested manipulations of ringleaders, and asserted his own case for leadership by appealing to them as fellow seamen with a sense of common identity and a shared commitment to the service. 'For God's sake', he wrote in an open letter to crews at the Nore,

> reflect on the happy times in which we served together, and on the advantages we brought to our country. Be not too long misled by designing men; but return to your old friends, who, like myself, have spent their days among you, and who can defy the world to say they ever did you an injury … I would add much more, but there is reason to believe that truth is kept from you, therefore having said this much in my justification, I bid you farewell, until we can meet as before, like men and friends, when you will find me, with true affection, your &c.[51]

Keith succeeded in confirming the underlying loyalty of most of the crew of the *Repulse* and *Ardent*, and persuaded them to identify ringleaders to face court martial. He had to exercise great tact in dealing with his commanding officers, and a mixture of tact and firmness in engaging with the crews. He made clear to them the folly of their recent proceedings without provoking antagonism through contemptuous high-handedness. In carrying out his duties Keith was not weighed down by the psychological burden carried by flag officers who felt they had lost their authority and been let down by their men.

When the crews at the Nore had returned to obedience, Keith and other flag officers assigned to the station were involved in an extensive mopping-up operation. Admiral Sir Skeffington Lutwidge replaced Buckner as commander-in-chief in mid-May 1797. He combined the regular duties of a port admiral with the extraordinary ones arising from the mutiny. With the assistance of Keith and Vice Admiral Sir Thomas Pasley, Lutwidge went on board ships at the Nore, testing where necessary the loyalty of the crews, reading the king's pardon and arresting those who were excluded from it. Occasionally, with the help of captains, they identified men who had been excluded unjustly from the pardon and brought them to the attention of the Board.[52] In due time, Lutwidge reported to the Board that twenty-nine confirmed death sentences were carried out.

Having completed his work at the Nore, Keith moved onto Plymouth as Vice Admiral King's second. In the wake of the mutiny King took a very hard line approach to mutineers. He stressed the salutary effect of swiftly imposed capital punishments, reporting with evident approval the death sentences passed on eight ringleaders from *Saturn* after Keith had brought that ship back to order.[53] However, Keith's appointment to his command suggests that the Board thought that King lacked the skills to engage effectively with the men to bring them back to obedience. Keith faced some testing moments at Plymouth. When he went on board *Saturn* and found an atmosphere of marked 'gloom and taciturnity' he decided that a bold display of personal courage was called for:

> After setting forth the enormities they had been guilty of in the strongest terms I was able, I told them their ringleaders must be delivered up and I trusted the well behaved men of the ship would bring them forth to save the lives of others, for if I was obliged to select men for trial I might be led into error.

During Keith's transactions with the *Saturns*, he sensed 'an inclination' to physical resistance among those who jostled round him on the tightly packed deck. In one report of this incident, Keith met the prospect of being 'crowded' with a threat to 'run the first man through who stirred'.[54] The account he sent to his sister was less dramatic but still conveyed a sense of a formidable physical challenge and the need to confront this with a courageous show of determination: 'At a moment I thought there would have been resistance but a good face had its effects and it went off.'[55]

Keith's earlier investigations at the Nore concentrated on a number of ships taken by their crews from Duncan's fleet at Yarmouth. The management of this fleet was always difficult because ships were constantly being taken from and added to it. As a result, Duncan had only limited opportunities for impressing his powerful personality on crews in his command.[56] Despite this disadvantage, he thought he had dealt successfully with initial outbreaks of insubordination and sent sanguine reports to Lord Spencer. Over the days that followed he tested the people's resolve to disobedience by issuing many orders and working them hard. He reported to Spencer that 'I will answer for it there will be no more of it in the North Sea fleet.... For my own part have ever thought it impossible for a ship's company to get the better of their officers, and in my time have seen a stop put to mutinies more than once or twice by proper exertion'.[57] True to the spirit of this injunction, Duncan gave his flagship's crew a 'few lectures on their late behaviour' and a warning that '[i]n all my service I have maintained my authority; which I will not easily part with'. In demonstration of this determination he put to the *Venerables* the question whether they would go to sea if ordered, and received unanimous confirmation. He believed these strictures had been effective: 'I never saw them more alert or do their duty better'.[58]

Unfortunately, the 'late behaviour' of the *Venerables* unsettled some other crews and bad weather prevented Duncan going on board to read his lectures to them.[59] In early May, however, he gave a powerful address to the crew of the *Vanguard*, telling them that '[t]he regard we owe our country and our families' should

[a]nimate us to exert ourselves in a particular manner and not flinch at the appearance of danger. You see me, grown grey with fifty-one years' service. In every ship I had the honour to command I have endeavoured to do justice both to the public and the men I commanded, and have often been flattered with particular marks of their regard; and I still hope, in spite of all that has happened, this ship's company have not lost their confidence in me. Both my officers and me are always ready to redress any supposed grievances when asked in a proper manner.[60]

When *Adamant* proved particularly troublesome, Duncan ordered Vice Admiral Sir Richard Onslow, one of his subordinate flag officers, to go on board and bring the crew to discipline. Onslow lacked Duncan's touch in these matters so he had to go on board to secure the crew's assurance that it would do its duty.[61]

Duncan continued to play a highly active role in monitoring the temper of the crews under his command, going on board ships in the fleet to make his presence felt, and to literally and symbolically uphold his authority. His courageous air and imposing stature – he was six foot four inches tall and large enough, as Lady Spencer jokingly put it, 'to make many reasonable-sized men' – would have been of considerable assistance.[62] Like Keith, Duncan sought to capitalize on his reputation with members of the lower deck and to invoke a sense of shared identity and commitment. He also appealed to the men's patriotic and professional pride by reminding them of the fleet's long anticipated engagement with the Dutch. He set these obligations within the context of divine governance by chiding his men for the profanity of their language and reminding them of the respect they owed to God.[63]

Although Duncan appeared to have settled a new bout of unrest that surfaced in other ships and received assurances of loyalty from their crews, his earlier confidence was shaken: 'I have known the time when the name of an enemy would have raised a ship's company to every exertion, and put aside every grievance through zeal to get to them. I fear those days are past.'[64] This fear proved well founded. By early June when eight ships that had been with him off Yarmouth (including the *Vanguard*) joined the mutineers at the Nore, Duncan found himself trying to contain the Dutch Fleet with a greatly diminished force. He drew some comfort from his success in securing the ongoing loyalty of the *Adamants* to offset his angry disappointment with the crews of the other ships: '[I]t would give me double pleasure to give the Dutch a thrashing without the aid of those scoundrels that have so shamefully deserted me. Particularly after the promises they gave.' Characteristically, Duncan did not permit his own disappointment to blind him to the impact of these events on Lord Spencer: 'I really feel much for your lordship in all this distress.'[65]

Duncan was reported to have been criticized by St Vincent for pardoning those responsible for the initial disturbance on *Venerable* and in other respects he had only limited success in dealing with mutinous crews in his fleet.[66] The first lord, however, thought he had done very well. In mid-June 1797 Spencer sent Duncan an enthusiastic report of a recent Trinity House dinner that he had attended: '[Y]our Health was drunk with Universal Applause. Your firmness on this occasion has indeed most deservedly earned you the Appreciation of the Country.'[67] This appreciation was soon to be expressed in the offer of an Irish peerage.

Vice Admiral William Waldegrave and the mutinous *Latonians*

While Keith's and Duncan's handling of mutineers enhanced their professional standing, other flag officers exposed weaknesses in their exercise of authority. Vice Admiral Waldegrave is a case in point. He was caught up in the later stages of the disturbances at Spithead while preparing to take up the naval command and governorship of Newfoundland in the spring of 1797.[68] Some of the crew of his flagship, *Latonia*, became unsettled when it was moored in Torbay and broke out into open mutiny when their ship arrived at Spithead. They sent their admiral, the captain and commissioned officers ashore. When Waldegrave came back on board he was anxious to get to sea in order to forestall further trouble. He told Evan Nepean that 'the men seem to be in that state where the sight of an inflammatory Newspaper or any verbal account (no matter from whom) of the Seditious proceedings at Sheerness wou'd render them again wholly ungovernable.'[69]

Waldegrave referred to these events in bitter terms when castigating the *Latonians* for their behaviour in Newfoundland. Further difficulties had occurred during a brief stop at St Michael's Roads in the Azores, but these seemed to have been settled when a promise was extracted from the crew 'to ever behave themselves with obedience to their Officers.'[70] This promise was not kept. Indeed, when the ship was at St John's in August 1797 the level and scale of disobedience increased significantly. On 3 August the fore-top-men refused to go aloft and challenged their officers to put them in irons. On the days that followed there were outbreaks of extremely unruly behaviour on shore (which alarmed the locals) and further incidents of mutinous conduct on board. The extent and character of this disorder may be gauged by the bitter satirical link that Waldegrave made between the situation on his command and that which now prevailed at Spithead:

> Now that the King's Officers are once again restored to Command, you seem to think that all discipline should be at an end, and that you may get drunk, fly in

the face of your Officers, disobey their Commands, stay on shore as long as you please, abuse and plunder the Inhabitants, and in short commit every enormity that merits the Gallows.[71]

Grievances over victuals, and a shortage of specie that left the crew open to exploitation by local traders, played a part in prompting these disturbances. Waldegrave took steps to address these matters but, while commending the petty officers and marines and seamen who remained actively obedient, he simultaneously cajoled, shamed and threatened the rest of *Latonians*:

> If the greater number of you are against your Officers and refuse to obey their lawful commands, I have a right to say that you are traitors to your King and Country; if there are only a few bad men among you, which you pretend to be the case, I maintain that you are a set of dastardly Cowards for suffering yourselves to be bullied by a few villains, who wish nothing better than to see us become the Slaves of France.[72]

He told the crew that this was not the conduct to be expected of 'true born Englishmen' or noble 'British Seamen'. Heavy moral suasion was accompanied by threats to hang ringleaders and to turn the artillery batteries of St John's on to the *Latona* if the mutiny continued. When some members of the crew sought to affirm their loyalty, Waldegrave would not accept these protestations unless the ringleaders were handed over. He warned the crew that their officers would have no confidence in them, that they would enjoy few comforts in this world and could expect short shrift in the next: 'Suspicious of each other, your guilty consciences will torment you day and night, till an untimely end shall relieve you from the Miseries of this world, to face that awful Tribunal, the justice of which neither the Monarch or the Beggar can escape.'[73]

As the commander-in-chief at St John's, Waldegrave had overall responsibility for punishing misconduct. Given the level and nature of the disruptions that he reported to London, the formal retribution suffered by *Latonians* was remarkably light. No courts martial were held and six ringleaders were punished summarily with floggings of between half and three dozen lashes each.[74] Not surprisingly, neither the threats nor these punishments proved effective and when the *Latonians* continued to be seriously unsettled, Waldegrave removed their insidious influence from his station by ordering the ship on a long cruise to Madeira and Lisbon to pick up a convoy bound for England.

Waldegrave's handling of mutiny on his flagship seemed unlikely to placate or overawe agitated members of the lower deck, or to impress the Board. The addresses that he made to the *Latonians* were strong on shame and threats of human and divine punishment, but lacked the appeals to manly fellow-feeling, comradeship and shared experience, which distinguished those made by Duncan and Keith in similar circumstances. Waldegrave was aloof and distant with his brother officers so it not surprising that he lacked the human skills necessary to deal effectively with aggrieved members of the lower deck. Moreover, unlike Duncan or Keith, he won no plaudits from his superiors for the way he had handled the mutinous events on *Latonia*. He was inconsistent in reporting the seriousness of the challenges involved, and the sus-piciously sudden return of order and calm – he announced a condition of 'perfect tranquility' five days after threatening the *Latonians* with death and damnation, and a month before packing them off to Madeira – did not reassure the Admiralty Board. Waldegrave was criticized overtly for sending the *Latonia* away without orders and implicitly, though unmistakably, for not addressing the long train of ill-discipline that he thought made this step necessary. The Board told him that it was concerned that 'such a disposition should have shown itself'.[75] When Waldegrave had served under St Vincent in the Mediterranean earlier in the war he irritated him by displaying a marked lack of confidence in his own judgement and an undue reliance on that of his commander-in-chief. His performance at Newfoundland suggests that he had not overcome these weaknesses.[76]

St Vincent's Mediterranean discipline and mutineers from the lower deck

St Vincent held that it was the responsibility of flag officers to model and enforce strict and consistent discipline, and to ensure that those under their command maintained it. If worse came to worst, and mutiny showed its loathsome visage, admirals who were worthy of employment would swiftly gauge the extent of the threat and act decisively against it. However, they relied on captains for the day-to-day management of ships' companies. When commanding in the Mediterranean Fleet, St Vincent dealt swiftly and ruthlessly with those he thought were not up to the disciplinary aspects of the job. Even before the Spithead mutiny sent shock waves through the upper ranks of the Royal Navy, he told Lord Spencer that he had arranged Captain Sir Charles Knowles's transfer out of the *Britannia*. Sir Charles had a distinguished record at sea and was well known for his interest in proposing innovative, scientifically based solutions to a range of ship design and handing issues.[77] St Vincent, however, found him singularly lacking as a dis-ciplinarian. Although his treatment of Knowles may have been tainted by past animos-ity, his correspondence with the first lord was framed in terms of general disciplinary ideals.[78] He told Spencer that 'the ship's company took the command from' Knowles when he went on board, 'and have been in a state of licentiousness ever since'. St Vincent presented this incident as a seaman's saturnalia rather than a concerted mutiny and laid the blame squarely and damningly at Knowles's door. They were 'nothing like a mutiny, having proceeded from the notorious imbecility of Sir Charles Knowles'. St Vincent hinted darkly 'there are many such in the command of line-of-battle ships' and went on to describe Sir Charles as 'feeble'.[79] Once an effective commanding officer was installed in their ship the *Britannias* recoiled from their state of sybaritic anarchy, practically reaffirmed their obedience and returned to a condition of due subordination and decent order. Several months later mutinous outbreaks in the *Theseus* were attributed to the inadequacies of her officers, particularly her captain, John Aylmer. He was reputed to be a weak man who was afraid of his crew and sought to keep them in awe through exces-sive floggings. St Vincent ordered Nelson to hoist his flag on *Theseus* and to bring with him his flag captain Ralph Millar, six lieutenants, seven midshipmen and twenty-nine prime seamen. These officers and men provided the nucleus of a new regime which restored order among what was considered to be a basically sound crew whose sense of discipline had been undermined by poor leadership and weak exemplars.[80]

St Vincent dealt with a range of mutinous outbreaks during his Mediterranean command but his general perspective is perhaps best illustrated by his response to an early episode on the *Kingfisher*, during which Captain Maitland killed a ringleader. In one of those equivocal pound-each-way verdicts that were not uncommon when senior officers stood trial, Maitland was acquitted of any definite charge but warned to exercise more constraint in future. At a dinner to which he invited the court, St Vincent raised a toast to 'Maitland's radical cure', thereby showing his true colours and upbraiding the court for its qualified verdict.[81] St Vincent thought the mutinies on home stations in the spring of 1797 had not been dealt with effectively and that those in positions of authority had not given sufficiently strong signals to members of the lower deck who were tempted to disobedience. He was determined not to repeat these mistakes in his Mediterranean and Channel commands.

Shortly after the mutiny at the Nore had been put down, St Vincent confirmed sentences of death on two members of the crew of the *St George* who were alleged to have been ringleaders of an attempt to free men charged with sodomy and a more extensive plot to seize a number of ships and hand them over to the Spanish at Cadiz. He refused the prisoners' request for five days to prepare themselves – 'in which', he fumed, 'they would have hatched five hundred treasons' – and ordered the sentences to be carried out the day after the court martial.[82] The day in question was a Sunday but the Sabbatarian qualms of a subordinate flag officer were brushed aside on the grounds that the fleet should be purged of contagion at the earliest possible opportunity. St Vincent was a whole-hearted believer in the salutary effect of speedy executions. As he later told Evan Nepean, 'Prompt execution for mutiny being in my judgment of greater effect than the punishment itself.'[83]

As soon as the hangings had taken place, captains were ordered to hold divine service. St Vincent then sent the men into action against encroaching Spanish gunboats that had slipped out of Cadiz under cover of the grim theatre being played out on the *St George*.[84] The sequencing of these activities was of a piece with St Vincent's commitment to the deterrent value of executions for mutiny. All the men in every ship in the fleet would know that the hangings were taking place and some of their shipmates would witness them at close hand. The physical and psychological lessons of the punishments were underlined by the men's immediate exposure to a liturgy that was rich in the language and imagery of authority, obedience and punishment. Finally, the call to action was both a reminder of duty and an exemplification of St Vincent's faith in the beneficial effects of keeping his crews fully occupied.

During the remainder of his service at sea, St Vincent acted vigorously to crush incipient mutiny and eliminate any disposition to respond to mutinous overtures. Where he thought it necessary, he broke up the crews of ships who seemed to have acquired a taste for mutiny and employed 'firm' officers in ships where their presence seemed particularly necessary. St Vincent's system of fleet management reflected a belief that the devil would find work for idle hands, and that the men should be insulated from precipitators of unrest on shore.[85] He also insisted on separating the seamen from the marines on board his ships to guard against cross-contamination and weaken any sense of shared identity. Even so, he was alarmed at what he saw as the tenacity of the spirit of mutiny, warning in mid-1800 that this 'disposition … has never been extinguished'.[86]

In common with some of his colleagues, St Vincent was particularly suspicious of seamen from Ireland who were thought to have volunteered in order to extend their revolutionary struggle to the Royal Navy. In July 1798 he reported a plot orchestrated by United Irishmen in the *Princes Royal* in terms that recalled the *Hermione* mutiny of the previous year: 'I was to have been hung, with the other admirals, captains and officers'.[87] He later warned Sir Thomas Pasley, who was serving under him in the Channel, that there was an imminent threat of mutiny by Irish seaman. Consistent with his view of discipline as a universal system, St Vincent told Pasley that the scandalous example of staterooms and wardrooms of the fleet was a cause of ongoing concern: 'The licentious conversation of the wardroom officers, and, in some instances at the tables of officers of high rank … has occasioned infinite mischief, for it soon circulates through the Fleet'.[88]

Just as St Vincent was about to give up the Channel Fleet to preside over the Admiralty Board, his informants revealed another plot in which the 'Irish' were reputed to be prominent. They reported many seditious utterances and a plan to set fire to the fleet anchored in Torbay.[89] When St Vincent reported these matters to Evan Nepean, the secretary of the Admiralty Board, he improved on the occasion to provide characteristic abuse of his colleagues at sea and on the Board: 'The Irish in the fleet who are to a man incorrigible villains, have been continually at work to bring about another mutiny and to make it a bloody one; and the conduct observed by my predecessors & two or your puissant Lords, has certainly encouraged it a very great deal'.[90] St Vincent went further, claiming that flag officers' resistance to the spirit of mutiny was impeded by the Admiralty. For example, he complained that in the Channel and North Sea they were always under the watchful eye of the Board and were liable to suffer for taking actions that were not specified clearly in their commissions. Even when commanding in the Mediterranean, St Vincent was hindered by 'hair-splitters' who made procedural objections to the arrangements for securing sworn statements from Roman Catholic witnesses.[91] He railed against the consideration shown to those involved in earlier mutinies off the English coast, complaining to Evan Nepean that the Admiralty sent him ex-delegates as petty officers – 'a reward for the distinguished share they had in the Mutinies at home' – and drawing attention to his unusual fortitude in the face of such weakness: '[Y]ou will see that I stand almost alone to combat the infernal spirit, which still pervades His Majesties Fleet'.[92]

Vice Admiral Sir Hyde Parker, Rear Admiral Richard Bligh and the mutinous *Hermiones*

Sir Hyde Parker shared St Vincent's frustrations when he was responsible for dealing with the aftermath of the *Hermione* mutiny. The first *Hermione* court martial, which took place on the Jamaica station in early May 1798, resulted in capital sentences on three members of the crew. At a trial in late May 1798, however, the court returned a not-guilty verdict on a crew member and his son. Rear Admiral Richard Bligh, Parker's second-in-command, presided at the trial. The boy was 12 when the mutiny took place, and he and his father had handed themselves in at the first opportunity. The evidence presented at the trial showed them to have been bystanders, and while they did not actively resist their homicidal shipmates, they had not engaged in mutinous conduct. Parker, however, was so incensed by this verdict that he wrote to the Admiralty Board demanding Bligh's recall, and threatened to resign his command if it declined to do so. Parker accused Bligh of 'lacking the Energy for Enforcing Discipline by the terror of Exemplary Punishment in this melancholy crisis'. He attributed the not-guilty verdicts to Bligh's 'supineness' as president.[93]

Collingwood, who admittedly had no respect for Parker and retailed accounts of his alleged financial and sexual irregularities at Jamaica, attributed his mistreatment of Bligh to personal antagonism. He conjectured that 'no man could be more disliked by the people of Jamaica' than Parker, and 'Bligh being a cheerful good humoured man was perhaps more in their esteem, and attentions to him created jealousy'.[94] It is perhaps significant that Parker did not provide a detailed critique of Bligh's handling of the trial in his reports to the Board, basing his conclusion about Bligh's role on its outcome. He thus pointed out that since Bligh was the only member of the court who had not sat on the previous trial, the differing verdicts must have been due to his malign influence in the second court martial.[95] Lord Spencer ignored these specious claims, and Hyde Parker's resignation threat, and told him that he depreciated his treatment of Bligh.[96] The fact that the King endorsed the court's recommendation of mercy for the one prisoner who had been condemned to death, indicated support of its verdicts and implicitly at least of Bligh's conduct of the trial.[97] Bligh presided at subsequent trials which returned guilty verdicts on some *Hermiones* but also acquitted a man who was too ill to have taken part in the mutiny or resist the mutineers.[98] Far from neglecting his duties as president of the court, Bligh seems to have had a well-informed understanding of his role. By contrast, Parker's eagerness to ignore the evidence presented to the court and his forceful insistence on exemplary punishments that flew in the face of it ran contrary to the well-established legal conventions which required courts to base their judgements on the evidence presented to them.[99]

Conclusion

It is hard to comprehend the impact of mass mutiny on the morale and professional self-confidence of those who sat at the head of a service imbued with an ethos of habitual obedience. Flag officers in this situation faced the galling prospect of remaining nominally in command even though their authority had been set aside. Bridport and Gardner seemed at times to be almost overwhelmed by the affront that the Spithead mutineers posed to their professional pride and personal leadership. However, the feelings they experienced were apparent also in Duncan's occasional expressions of despondency, and in the angry and strongly punitive response of officers such as St Vincent, King and Hyde Parker. The threat and reality of concerted mutiny, as opposed to isolated incidents of mutinous behaviour, provided a test of flag officers' 'nerves under responsibility' that was as challenging in its way as those they faced in fleet actions, commanding a fleet on blockade duty or in interservice expeditions.

Having once referred quite narrowly to matters to do with working and fighting a ship, discipline came to mean 'the steady enforcement of its own law on all ranks, the working of an institution above and independent of the character of particular men and the maintenance of a standard of conduct in daily life'.[100] These requirements, which overlapped with operational imperatives for tight refitting and victualing schedules, placed a premium on a 'taut' officer corps, on the vigilant commitment of commanding officers and on the exemplary oversight of flag officers. They became the key element in a system of fleet discipline of which St Vincent was an early and persistent advocate. The Spithead mutinies proved highly salutary for Lord Spencer in that respect. He told Bridport that his wish to make the service 'as agreeable as possible to all those engaged in it' may have 'misled' him into giving 'a little more indulgence than could in strictness be justified'.[101]

After obedience had been restored in these commands, Spencer and his successors certainly kept a close eye on disciplinary matters. The Board subjected logs, journals, musters and punishment books to close and speedy scrutiny, and made further enquiries of flag officers when the documentation indicated cause for concern.[102] Its interest extended beyond ensuring that punishments were within the regulations to a consideration of what reports revealed about the underlying state of discipline in the vessels under a flag officer's command. Vice Admiral Sir Alexander Cochrane's alarm at the extent of punishments authorized by his newly promoted son is a telling example of a flag officers' awareness of the Board's expectations. He feared that the Admiralty would raise questions about the disciplinary condition of a ship that made such punishments necessary.[103]

Captain Cochrane and his father escaped Board censure on the state of discipline in their commands but Admiral Sir John Warren did not. During the war with the United States he was called to account for not keeping a strict eye on the disciplinary practices of eight of his captains. The Board noted the levels and frequency of summary sentences recorded in their punishment books and became concerned that if punishment on this scale was justified, the ships under Warren's command must be very ill-disciplined. It rebuked him for not commenting on what it regarded as aberrant and unsatisfactory returns and clearly believed that the general unrest indicated by levels of punishment across a range of ships pointed to more widespread disciplinary weaknesses.[104] The risk materialized when the crew of the *Epervier* (whose captain was one of Warren's favourites) fought the ship with such intentional inefficiency that she was captured by the Americans.[105]

Flag officers' responses to mutinous outbreaks depended on their personalities, their professional confidence and on the situations they faced. St Vincent would no doubt have regarded Bridport's lapses into fatalistic impotence as reflective of his general lack of commanding vigour, and his placatory reaction to the men's demands as entirely consistent with the weak disciplinary ethos of the Channel Fleet. By contrast, St Vincent's praise of Colpoys reflected his standing as a model of disciplinary rectitude. In other cases, admirals' handling of mutineers reflected more general limitations of their leadership skills. Both Gardner and Waldegrave demonstrated tendencies towards indecisiveness at moments of stress that were reflected in their agitated, threatening but largely ineffectual interactions with mutinous crews. The shortcomings of Gardner's and Waldegrave's leadership contrast sharply with the personal skills demonstrated by both Duncan and Keith. Duncan was unable to prevent a large-scale defection from his fleet but he was highly successful in dealing with the crews of particular ships. So too was Keith, although his skills were only brought into play when the tide of mutiny in the fleet had begun to turn.

St Vincent's and Parker's verbal responses to mutiny were more extreme than their colleagues, but flag officers generally shared a belief in the efficacy of selective terror. Duncan did not shy from seeing capital punishment as the best way of dealing with ringleaders: 'I shall be glad to hear my scoundrels are come to their senses again ... am sure it will give me much satisfaction to hear some of them are hanged, as they deserve.' In August 1798 six mutinous United Irishmen from a ship in Duncan's Fleet were condemned to death.[106] Nelson supported St Vincent in the face of claims that the execution off Cadiz profaned the Sabbath, claiming that 'had it been Christmas Day, instead of Sunday, I would have executed them. We know not what might have been hatched by a Sunday's grog; *now* your discipline is safe'.[107] Collingwood expressed some private sympathy for the crew of the *Dänae* because of their captain's violent disciplinary practices – 'There may exist a degree of violence when severity is substituted for discipline that is insupportable'[108] – but that did not mean that he was any less committed publically to selective terror when the need arose.

In the wake of the Spithead mutiny, Vice Admiral Young, the senior naval commissioner and Rear Admiral Pole of the Channel Fleet discussed the desirability of 'steady regular discipline without violence'. The two men also considered the preconditions of such a regime. In the first place, it required eternal vigilance on the part of those officers who dealt directly with the crew. They would have to pay close attention to 'every movement, almost to every look of the men'. The second condition was that officers would have to model 'regular discipline' and avoid doing or saying anything in front of the men that compromised the fabric of authority upon which obedience depended. Young was particularly concerned at the risk posed by officers' 'private words' since they could not be concealed from the men and had 'infinitely more effect than is generally believed' on their disposition to obey.[109] Like St Vincent and their other contemporaries, Young and Pole believed that discipline must become systematic and that it was flag officers' responsibility to identify and maintain it.

Admirals and the Georgian Patronage Network

It will afford me much pleasure receiving your Lordships further commands and be assured that the earliest attention will be paid to your recommendations.
—Sir Alexander Cochrane responding to Lord Melville, who was first lord and the Vice Admiral's patron[1]

The Royal Navy was a major agency of the late Georgian state, endowed with very significant resources and much prestige, and bound inextricably to the complex web of patronage relationships through which offices, incomes and honours were allocated. Ministers of the crown were the focal point of networks of patron-client relationships that helped the king's first minister maintain a workable majority in the House of Commons. In the absence of strong party groupings, majorities were constructed by aggregating single votes and small blocks at the disposal of those with significant electoral influence in a number of constituencies. This system came under pressure in the late Georgian period but the direct and indirect use of offices, pensions, and honours and titles for political purposes, continued to be a significant feature of the social, political and military landscapes.[2] As we shall see, the language and practice of patronage were all-pervasive within the upper echelons of the Navy. Patrons responded to appeals for 'attention', 'consideration', 'notice' or 'protection' for, or on behalf of, 'friends', bringing their 'interest' to bear on those who directly or indirectly influenced the allocation of offices and honours. Interest – a circularly defined quality known by its efficacy – derived from family connections, political and electoral influence, social and professional status and office holding.

The Navy's place in the patronage network depended on the scale of its activities and hence the extent of the opportunities it furnished for employment, advancement and other rewards. Although its fleets multiplied hugely during the French Wars, the burgeoning lists of lieutenants, masters and commanders and post captains generated by successive general promotions and one-off appointments outstripped rapidly growing opportunities for employment at sea. The imbalance has been attributed to the increased opportunities for displaying bravery in a long war, and Lord Spencer's profligate use of his prerogatives as First Lord.[3] Consideration should be given, however, to the significant increase in the numbers of flag officers over the course of the wars. After the promotion of February 1793 there were 64 admirals on the active list whose relatives, friends, protégés and followers relied on their good offices. By the last big promotion of the wars in November 1814, the system was subject to the variable interest of 223 flag officers. Because naval patronage was part of a far more extensive network, increases in the number of participants in influential positions introduced new lines of interest deriving from their familial, political and professional connections.

Patronage was not always a sufficient condition of advancement in the service, and, as we shall see in the next chapter, promotions and appointments were subject to distinctive intra-service obligations and expectations. It was, nevertheless, a powerful and widely canvassed determinant of naval career prospects. Interest flowed through two discrete but sometimes mingled channels. The first was fed by the imperatives of parliamentary politics and the highly variable electoral practices that determined the membership of the House of Commons. The second channel arose out of familial, local and personal relationships, and reflected the economic, social and political significance of landed wealth and the concentration of wealth in the hands of male heads of families.

Some flag officers sat in the House of Commons and others aspired to do so. They lent their own and their families' support to parliamentary candidates and, like other members of the professional and landed classes, engaged in complex exchanges of interest and obligation that derived from familial and personal connections. Through these means they might acquire interest that could be deployed across the patronage network. If they wished to direct it towards securing benefits which were under the control of the Navy, however, they had to gain the sympathetic attention of those within government and the service who played a determining role in allocating these benefits. Flag officers serving in subordinate and chief commands, as members of the Admiralty Board and, above all, in the office of first lord were particularly well-placed with respect to naval patronage. But while office-holding in the service was an important patronage asset, particular appointment decisions were likely to be subject to a range of expressions of interest within the Navy and in the more extensive extra-service network in which it sat.[4]

Patronage relationships were based on principles of reciprocity that extended more generally in polite society.[5] Flag officers and those who approached them couched their requests in terms of grateful anticipation and responded warmly to concrete expressions of support from patrons and officeholders. When serving away from home, admirals might demonstrate their respect for key decision-makers by judicious gift-giving. Thus Admiral Duncan provided the first lord and his lady with homely treats from the North Sea: herrings for Lord Spencer, and a painting of a Dutch pilot for Lady Spencer. Rear Admiral John Duckworth's offerings were much more exotic. He supplied Lord Spencer with turtles and French liqueur from the West Indies while Lady Spencer was favoured with pots of ginger. When Vice Admiral Berkeley was commanding at Lisbon in 1811 he offered presents of gold chains, mats, ornamental summer furniture and wines to Lord Grenville for his wife. He also sent her specimens of an unusual wild lily that grew in sand on the coast.[6] On occasion, flag officers' pursuit of the ultimate gift misfired. Vice Admiral Sir Edward Pellew obtained a 'white tyger' for his patron the Duke of Northumberland but by the time the animal arrived in England it had grown too large to be a safe pet. Northumberland described it as 'noble and most curious' but told Pellew that 'having no proper Place for receiving so terrible & unruly a Personage' he was going to offer him to the king. George III seems to have declined the offer so the duke thought he would try Lord Mulgrave, the first lord: 'I am told he is very vain, & loves flattery; such a mark of attention will I trust have its due weight with him.'[7] Other officers paid their respect to patrons by naming their children after them, or by asking them to be their sons' godfathers. Two of Admiral Lord Duncan's children had 'Dundas' as a second name; the Admiral's wife was a niece of the great Scottish borough-monger and Westminster powerbroker. Vice Admiral George Murray's only son (who never went to sea) carried his father's name and that of three distinguished colleagues: St Vincent, Nelson and Thomas (after Troubridge). St Vincent, though apparently sceptical of the spiritual role of godparents, seems to have nevertheless expected that his senior officers would ask him to stand sponsor to their sons.[8] These civilities, which were characteristic of familial and neighbourly interactions, marked a confluence of the personal and official channels of the patronage network.

Electoral interest in naval patronage

Admirals participated directly in parliamentary politics as members of the House of Commons, or in a few cases, of the House of Lords. They also helped their friends and allies secure seats and rallied support for them in elections. The Commons was more important than the Lords because ministers needed to control that house if they were to conduct the government's business and retain the support of the king. Ninety-eight flag officers filled 156 seats in the lower house during the six parliaments of the war years, with some of them occupying the same seat in successive parliaments. The numbers fluctuated from a low point of 18 in 1796 to a peak of 30 in the 1806–1807 and 1807–12 parliaments. As the number of admirals more than doubled over the course of the war, the proportion of flag officers who held seats in the House of Commons declined from about 25 per cent to 12 per cent. Eighteen of these men sat for counties and seventy-five for boroughs. Of the latter, thirty-four were returned with the support of aristocratic landholders and another two dozen owed their seats to the influence of their families; seventeen relied to some extent on the support of government, including those who sat for seaport boroughs where the economic presence and patronage of the Admiralty was significant.

Few flag officers spoke to much effect in parliament.[9] Berkeley, Pole, Markham, Orde, Pellew and Warren were among the exceptions in the House of Commons and St Vincent in the Lords. However, even silent support of the government strengthened flag officers' interest and if the stakes were high, intervention in parliament might yield significant benefits. Thus in mid-March 1804 when Sir Edward Pellew was still a senior captain, he made a spirited defence of St Vincent's naval administration in the face of a sharp attack by the former prime minister William Pitt.[10] His son was immediately made a commander and shortly afterwards Pellew was promoted to rear admiral and appointed to the East Indian command. He was able to avoid forfeiting that appointment when Pitt came into office by agreeing to vacate his seat in favour of one of the prime minister's friends and by utilizing the support of his patron, the Duke

Plate 3: At one stage in the 1806 election in the Westminster borough, Sir Samuel Hood faced the unwelcome prospect of sharing expenses with the notoriously profligate Richard Sheridan. Hood is shown here with the empty uniform jacket sleeve he wore after losing an arm in action.

of Northumberland.[11] He told the duke that he wished to express 'in the strongest language my mind could form, the lively and deep impressions your goodness has rested in my breast.'[12] Pellew reciprocated by promoting the career of Northumberland's son, Algernon Percy, sending glowing reports on his character and developing professional capabilities. The circle of mutual regard was completed when Pellew received the plaudits of Percy's grateful father: 'Nothing can be so advantageous to him as learning his Profession under such an Admiral.'[13]

While Pellew was in the East Indies he used his powers of appointment as a commander-in-chief to further the electoral interests of Captain (later Rear Admiral) John Markham, a friend who sat on the Board and was an MP for Portsmouth. In the 1780s the Admiralty's grip on the representation of Portsmouth was broken by the concerted action of a powerful group of Protestant dissenters who were suspicious of the corrupting power of established churches and government ministries. This group's aversion to government candidates was weakened by the radical turn taken by some dissenting colleagues in the mid- 1790s. In 1796 its leader, Sir John Carter, agreed to countenance the return of a popular navy candidate, the first of whom was Rear Admiral Lord Hugh Seymour. On Seymour's death in September 1801, St Vincent used his position as first lord to secure Carter's local interest for John Markham.[14] Markham garnered additional support from the Harts, an influential Portsmouth family, by advancing the naval career of one of its sons. In this case, the golden chain of interest stretched from the Solent to the Bay of Bengal. Pellew was the critical link. He promoted Hart to a commander's vacancy, confident that Markham would arrange for the appointment to be confirmed: 'Hart's friends I know are your supporters at Portsmouth, and with that view I embraced the means offered.'[15] Markham was also consulted by Admiral Rowley, commanding at Sheerness. Rowley told him that Sir Sidney Smith was unpopular with the freemen of Rochester but if Lord Howick would back him, Rowley was confident of winning the seat. He had lived in Rochester for a number of years and was 'well acquainted with many of the leading people.' Howick did not take up this offer but Rowley was right about Smith who finished bottom of the poll in November 1806.[16]

By assisting the electoral prospects of their colleagues, flag officers repaid past favours and laid the groundwork for subsequent claims. In September 1794 Admiral Sir Richard King forwarded a request for a senior post in the dockyard at Chatham to the Board. The basis for consideration was made crystal clear: 'Having served your Hon[r] at the late Election I write relying on your Hon[rs] friendship to apply to the Earl of Chatham.'[17] At the beginning of the next war, Rear Admiral Sir Alexander Cochrane appealed to Markham to appoint a political ally into his ship: 'Lieutenant George Steel, who has been very attentive to my interest during the late election, and in whose favour much interest was used at the time of the last promotion, has lately wrote to be employed.'[18] The reference to Steel's interest alerted Markham to influential figures who would be gratified by his support of this officer. Cochrane's friendship with Markham, and his status as an MP, lent weight to his attempt to secure an appointment for his troublesome nephew, Captain Lord Cochrane.[19] When Pellew, as the newly ennobled Lord Exmouth, sought a favour from the second Lord Melville in early 1815, he appealed to the first lord's political interest and that of his own son. The person in question came from a family that was a 'strong supporter of Government and Constituents of my son'. Captain Pownall Bastard Pellew, MP for Launceston, held this seat through the Duke of Northumberland's interest. The duke's original intention (arising in response to Sir Edward's advancement of his son's naval career) had been that Pownall would be merely a placeholder until the father returned from service in the Mediterranean. When the elder Pellew took a seat the House of Lords, however, Northumberland continued to lend his electoral interest to his son.[20]

As first lord, St Vincent had a dual motive for supporting naval officers' bids to win and retain seats in the House of Commons. He wished to maintain parliamentary support for the ministry to which he belonged, and, as a flag officer, had an interest in deploying and acquiring assets in naval patronage. St Vincent was assisted in the pursuit of these objectives by having direct access to the electoral influence which government wielded in some seaport boroughs. He corresponded with Sir John Carter and John Godwin, his successor in the mayoralty, to assure him of the Prime Minister's attention to his wishes over the patronage of Portsmouth borough. His letter to Godwin was a masterpiece of graciously concealed direction: 'Without the most distant idea of availing myself of the official situation His Majesty has been graciously pleased to advance me to, I beg leave to name Captain Markham to you and the Body Corporate of Portsmouth.' St Vincent also rallied support for the candidature of his protégé Captain Thomas Troubridge, and his nephew, in his former constituency of Yarmouth, the homeport of the North Seas Fleet. The 1802 contest proved to be particularly difficult and gave St Vincent some anxious moments. At one stage, after the First Lord's friends in the borough showed signs of getting out of control, he sent their leader a characteristic letter, congratulating them on their good sense in abandoning 'all Party Politics', underlining what they had to lose, and issuing a direct threat in the event of any backsliding: 'Be assured that a long perseverance in the system they were pursuing would have terminated in utter disappointment, vexation and total loss of the benefits which by a more moderate conduct will be lastingly secured to them.' A postscript warned that 'the whole weight of Government in every form and shape must have come against you had not temperance succeeded passion.'[21] St Vincent was also active, though to a far lesser extent, in elections for the County of Essex (where he had an estate) in support of Rear Admiral Sir Eliab Harvey, Stirling Burghs on Cochrane's behalf, in Queensborough, Bridport and Barnstaple where other naval connections were candidates, in Kent, Plymouth, and in Queen's County, Ireland, where Admiral Crosby had some electoral influence.

The influence of a first lord could spoil as well as assist, and it did not always favour naval candidates. In a sharp letter to Lady Calder, St Vincent headed-off a bid for one of the Plymouth seats from her husband, Rear Admiral Sir Richard Calder.[22] He later warned two senior officers against putting themselves forward there because the sitting members had the support of the Prince of Wales. In the contest for the borough of Stafford in his native county, St Vincent supported the sitting members against Admiral Cornwallis' close friend, Captain John Whitby.[23] St Vincent's forceful involvement in naval electoral politics did not cease when he left the Admiralty Board. In 1806, when commanding in the Channel, he worked hard through his friend Lord Howick, the first lord, to secure the return of Vice Admiral Pole for Plymouth. The defeated sitting member, who had had the temerity to criticise St Vincent's measures to reform Plymouth dockyard, claimed that he used Dr Andrew Baird, the physician to the fleet, to threaten Plymouth shopkeepers' access to naval contracts if they did not support Pole.[24]

When Henry Dundas, the first Lord Melville, died in May 1811, Captain Thomas Cochrane passed the news to his father in the West Indies. He accurately described Melville as 'our best and warmest friend.'[25] Melville was the leader of a powerful family faction in Scottish politics that wielded formidable electoral interest. He had also been a key member of Pitt's administrations and was a former first lord. The elder Cochrane had benefited from the Dundas' support to secure his return as MP for Stirling Burghs, and was appointed to command in the Leeward Islands when Melville presided at the Admiralty Board. As we shall see, Cochrane reciprocated by paying careful attention to Lord Melville's recommendations for appointments on that station, risking the displeasure of his successor as he did so. Within a year of his father's death, the second Lord Melville, Robert Dundas, embarked upon a prolonged spell as First Lord. He quickly reminded the Cochranes of their obligations to his family. In October 1812 he ignored the precarious state of the younger Lady Cochrane's health, and put great pressure on her husband to travel to Edinburgh so he could take an active part in what was expected to be a very closely fought election. Having faced a serious challenge to its position in

1811, the Dundas family was determined to ensure that the 33 voters supported Lord Melville's nephew (a member of the Admiralty Board) at the general election of August 1812.[26] By this time Sir Alexander's obligations to Melville had deepened by his son's knighthood and appointment to command the *Surprise*.

Family connections and naval patronage

Family attachments often overlapped with political and territorial sources of interest and identity. In late eighteenth-century politics the terms 'whig' and 'tory' referred to shared ideological tendencies and political loyalties, rather than to organized parties that structured parliamentary politics. Political alliances formed around powerful aristocratic figures such as Lord Rockingham and the Duke of Portland, office holders such as William Pitt who enjoyed the king's support, and rivals for office like Charles James Fox who did not. Family attachments were particularly important in forging connections between politicians and mobilizing support for them. Some flag officers owed their seats in the Commons to familial and local connections. For example, Admiral Cornwallis's family had extensive estates in north Suffolk, centred on the market town of Eye. Eye was a pocket borough of the family and William Cornwallis was one of the borough's two members for a total of twenty five years. Vice Admiral Sir Charles Thompson represented the borough of Monmouth for three years through the interest of the Duke of Beaufort, head of the family to which his putative father belonged. Cochrane's six year term as member for Stirling Burghs was made possible by Dundas's support, but his family also had interest in two of the notoriously venal burghs that made up the seat.[27]

These aristocratic and gentry connections contrasted with Vice Admiral Peter Rainier's position at Sandwich in Kent. He was a native of the town and probably benefited early in his career from his family's interest as freemen of the borough, and substantial local merchants.[28] The ministers (who exercised some influence arising from the borough's status as a Cinque port) declined to support his bid but Rainier defied them. He rallied his local interest and made use of his considerable wealth to win one of the seats as an independent. He came in for his fair share of political criticism for spreading some of his prize money among the 700 voters of Sandwich. Rainier also had to support his constituents' sons' naval ambitions. He told Sir Alexander Cochrane that these calls had all but exhausted his service interest.[29]

Collingwood entered the Navy with the support of Captains Richard Braithwaite and Robert Roddam. These men, who both became admirals, were part of a nexus of Northumbrian interest that incorporated familial, geographical and professional loyalties and identities.[30] Roddam, a relation of Collingwood's wife, worked hard to secure his protégé a post command at the beginning of the wars.[31] As Collingwood became an increasingly respected and influential figure in the service, he applied his interest to aid the careers of fellow Northumbrians. In common with other senior officers, he often received requests from local connections and family members to take midshipman into his flagship or to arrange for them to be given berths on ships under his command. If the friendship was close, flag officers might assume a duty of care towards those for whom they provided midshipmen's berths. Collingwood was particularly attentive to the progress of those placed under his protection at the request of members of his family. His charges included the weakly, ill-educated son of Walter Stanhope MP, a cousin who had assisted him to his first command of the war. His initial report on the boy was sympathetic but not hopeful: he was 'the poorest, puny thing I am told that ever was seen, and excites the pity of everybody, for the child has been ruptured three years.... It is not astonishing that people should be so inattentive to the circumstances of their children?'[32] Collingwood's sense of decency and duty led him to worry about Stanhope's prospects, take steps to redress the deficiencies of his upbringing, and monitor his progress. After an unpromising start, he was able to report that the boy was 'very well and much grown'. Collingwood enlisted 'Little Stanhope' on a scheme that would help his education and assist another boy who was almost blind: 'Young Crespigny is one of the best boys in the world, sensible and well behaved but, poor thing, he has no health for this life. His eyes are weak to the greatest degree .... What I have devised for his relief is that Stanhope and he read by turns, Stanhope a long lesson and he a short one.'[33] Claude de Crespigny, the younger son of the heir to a baronetcy and a grandchild of the Earl of Plymouth, was recommended to Collingwood by his sister; the boy's mother had been kind to Collingwood's daughters. He liked the boy for himself and persevered with him for eighteen months before sending him home. Crespigny was keen to stay but Collingwood thought him 'totally unfit for the sea and ... would not encourage his parents to expect any thing from me.'[34] When Sir John Duckworth was made rear admiral Lady Cremone took immediate advantage of the occasion. She sent Duckworth a letter of congratulation on his promotion and then entered a plea on behalf of a family connection. She assured Duckworth that her family would be 'obliged to you for whatever kind care & protection you shew him that I hope he will do everything you wish him to do, well knowing it will be for his real good.'[35]

To modern eyes some of the claims of family connections might appear highly tenuous. For example, Lady Nelson became a target for what she described as 'very extraordinary applications' when her husband's star was in the ascendant immediately after the Battle of the Nile.[36] St Vincent's niece sought to secure her uncle's interest on behalf of the son of a medical attendant who had seen her safely through a crisis in her health.[37] This appeal was unsuccessful but that had more to do with prioritization and opportunity than propriety. The case was rather different when Duckworth asked St Vincent to make John Trelawney, his daughter's fiancé's brother, a commander. The First Lord responded by entering 'very feelingly into the description you give touching Miss Duckworth's early passion, and lament exceedingly that there is a stain in the reputation of Lieutenant Trelawney that will undoubtedly operate against the desire I feel to co-operate with you in promoting, by any justifiable manner, the happiness of your daughter.'[38] The Lieutenant was dismissed from the service shortly afterwards for sodomy.

Flag officers often received appeals from female friends and relatives of those seeking advancement. St Vincent was usually ponderously gallant, even when not accommodating, but was sometimes goaded into archness by these requests. For example, he responded to what he described as the 'witty sarcasms you have judged fit to exercise on me' by referring to the favours bestowed on the woman's grandson, 'which I should have thought, might have exempted me from the reproach of overlooking old friends and a charge of it proceeding from too rapid a flow of honours on Madam, Your obedt. &c'.[39] When supplication or sarcasm failed, well-placed women might resort to raillery which tweaked a flag officer's dignity. Thus in mid-1812 Lady Caroline Warren play-fully upbraided Sir Edward Pellew for neglecting one of her protégés: 'you are a very naughty admiral indeed.'[40]

Well-placed family interest was not forgotten in the press of urgent public busi-ness. In the midst of the extreme anxiety surrounding the dispatch of an expedition-ary force to the West Indies in late 1795, for example, Spencer unabashedly promoted the claims of friends of his family, recommending Captain Richard Fellowes to Rear Admiral Christian for a post captain's appointment in his new command. He was a 'very promising young man and a very near relation of Lady Spencer's.'[41] Fellowes, the son of the physician-in-ordinary to the Prince of Wales, presumably enjoyed the prince's support as well. He was promoted to post rank a few weeks after Spencer drew him to Christian's attention, gaining a place on the captains' list in time to secure flag rank in the last promotion of the French Wars. Similarly, St Vincent thought it entirely proper to give priority to his kin and assumed that his colleagues shared this view. In mid-1800 when still a commander-in-chief, he traded on his professional friendship with Lord Hugh Seymour to secure his nephew William Parker's appointment to a post captain's vacancy in the West Indies. When St Vincent was First Lord, and mak-ing much of the constraints he faced, he sent 'Captain Fane … a near relation of mine' to Halifax to be promoted post captain.[42] He responded to Vice Admiral Sir Charles Pole's enquiry about the vacant post of Receiver of the Commissioners of Greenwich Hospital in May 1803, by saying it was reserved for Lady St Vincent's nephew.[43] St Vincent's open determination to provide for his family was demonstrated particularly sharply by an elaborate series of manoeuvres he conducted over the disposal of the lucrative Treasurer-ship of Greenwich Hospital.

In 1799 Lord Spencer had given this valuable post (worth £500 pa) to Vice Admiral John Payne, a close friend of the Prince of Wales who had pressed his case with William Pitt.[44] By mid-November 1803, however, Payne was so seriously unwell that his service colleagues started to show an interest in the future disposal of the office. When Admiral Lord Radstock (William Waldegrave) made a preemptive bid for the post, St Vincent professed surprise at his report of Payne's imminent death, expressing the optimistic view that 'the great medical skill he has resorted to, will succeed in prolonging his days.' He then squelched lingering expectations by telling Radstock that Spencer had broken with convention in giving an admiral the position and that he, having never approved of this step, would revert to the practice of appointing the Treasurer from the captains' list.[45] The officer he had in mind was Captain Jervis, his nephew and heir. A day later he wrote to the Honourable Captain Grey in response to his query about the anticipated vacancy. This letter, much franker than the one to Lord Radstock, appealed to Grey's sympathetic understanding of St Vincent's obligations to his relations:

It is very natural and becoming in you to seek situations for the laudable purpose expressed in your letter of yesterday; but when you consider that my Nephew and presumptive Heir is without a shilling more than his Pay, and that Lord Northesk, who married my niece, has a very slender fortune, I am sure you will agree with me in opinion that I should do great injustice to them if I let slip such an occasion as that you allude to providing for one of them.[46]

St Vincent assumed that Grey would agree that the financial needs of *his* family members should be given priority over any claims arising from the First Lord's friendship with Grey's father, his own merits, or the 'laudable purpose' he had in mind. The keen interest shown in the Treasurer-ship prompted St Vincent to act quickly when it became clear that his hopes for Payne's recovery had been unduly sanguine. The Vice Admiral died on 17 November and on the twentieth of that month the pretensions of Admiral George Montagu were dismissed with the announcement that 'the moment the death of Vice Admiral Payne was reported at this Office, a Patent was prepared appointing my Nephew Captain Jervis'. In fact, as St Vincent's response to another disappointed Admiral shows, the patent was still a work in progress a few days later.[47]

While the formalities were being concluded, St Vincent consoled Lord Northesk with the thought that if it were not for the embarrassed state of Captain Jervis's financial affairs, he would have been given the post. The first lord undertook to 'serve him' when an opportunity arose.[48] Northesk, at this time a captain in the Mediterranean Fleet, did not have to wait long. He was promoted to rear admiral on 23 April 1804 in the middle of a long list, which suggests that there was not much for St Vincent to do. However, Northesk's employment shortly afterwards as a junior flag officer in the Channel Fleet was directly due to the interest of his distinguished and powerful relative. Sir Edward Pellew was not impressed with Northesk's professional capacity, and he subsequently cut a poor figure at Trafalgar, but the warm support of a first lord helped compensate for any professional shortcomings.[49]

St Vincent's handling of non-familial contenders for the treasurer's post may have been devious, but nothing in his open advancement of Parker's, Jervis's or Northesk's careers would have disconcerted his senior service colleagues. Thus in early 1802 he told Admiral Dickson, who was commanding in the North Sea, that '[a]s I naturally conclude you had rather see your nephew ... a Post Captain than the 1st Lieutenant of the *Blenheim* a Commander, I have arranged it so'. This was by way of being part of a family compensation package because Dickson was about to be relieved of his command, at which point he was rewarded directly with a baronetcy.[50] A few years later, Nelson's younger colleagues, Troubridge and Pellew, both of whom had been patronized by St Vincent, seized opportunities to provide for their sons when they commanded in the East Indies. Indeed, it has been suggested that Troubridge may well have accepted his appointment as a way of ensuring his son's promotion at a time when he could expect few favours from the government.[51] Following a successful action with a Dutch frigate, Edward Troubridge's father wrote to Markham requesting his son's confirmation as a post captain in the captured vessel. A few days earlier Pellew had sought Markham's support in confirming the rapid promotion of a 19-year-old son through the rank of commander to post captain, claiming that he was 'uncommonly well informed and capable'.[52]

Where interest played a major role in appointments, there was always the risk that it would threaten the efficiency of the service by elevating those unfit to perform their duties. Sometimes this risk arose from misapplied patronage of senior officials. In the early stages of the wars Lord Howe complained of the Board's appointment of officers who 'never before commanded a ship of the line, and who, residing in town in discontinuance of all professional duties for ten or twelve years, were never afloat, unless upon a sea of politics in a parliamentary character'.[53] Collingwood and St Vincent were sharply critical of the role played by Sir Philip Stephens, an MP, and a senior official in the Admiralty who ended his career as a civil commissioner. When Collingwood hoisted his flag in the *Triumph* in late 1799, he faced the unwelcome prospect of having Stephens's nephew as his flag captain. He regarded this officer as a threat to the physical and disciplinary safety of the ship: 'I have a Captain here, a very novice in the conduct of fleets or ships. When I joined her I found she had been twice ashore, and once on fire, in the three months he had commanded her, and they were *expecting* that the ship's company should mutiny every day'.[54] Stephens remained a threat to men and ships until 1813 when he became a rear admiral. He was never employed as a flag officer and gained no marks of distinction. Nevertheless, his early promotion to post captain helped him rise to admiral of the Red before his death in 1846.

Senior officials did not have a monopoly on inappropriate favouritism. St Vincent had supported the rapid advancement of Captain Lord Proby whose excessively harsh discipline was thought by Collingwood to have provoked the crew of the frigate *Dänae* to mutiny off Brest in April 1800.[55] St Vincent was also a party to the rise of Nelson's stepson. With his help, Josiah Nesbitt became a post captain, even though both men had reservations about his ability, commitment and temperament. Nesbitt's brief career in command of a frigate was marred by bullying, drunkenness and inefficiency, and public exposure in an embarrassing court martial he demanded on a subordinate.[56] Collingwood's regard for Admiral Roddam resulted in him supporting the promotion of an officer against his better judgement, while Pellew was singularly one-eyed where his sons were involved. He sang the praises of his younger son, Israel, whose inclination for excessively harsh discipline provoked two mutinies when he was a post captain and resulted in the ignominious termination of his only command as a flag officer.[57]

Even where fundamental competence was at issue, unacceptably rapid promotion might blight an officer's prospects and damage the standing of his patron by showing flagrant disregard of the need for young men to demonstrate competence in the ranks through which they passed. These consideration lay behind St Vincent's reaction to a request to make the Earl of Westmoreland's nephew a commander and post captain on the same day. Despite this officer's merits and his connections (including the first lord's wife) St Vincent insisted he should command a sloop before making the next step. He told Westmoreland that it was 'morally impossible' to accede to his request: '[T]here is a line of conduct which cannot be departed from without being exposed to just reproaches and every species of inconvenience'.[58]

Sir Alexander Cochrane was aware of these risks when he pushed his 17-year-old son Thomas through the ranks of lieutenant and commander to post captain between June 1805 and April 1806. The fact that such a rapid ascent was prohibited by the revised *Regulations and Instructions* increased the elder Cochrane's anxiety. He worried whether Thomas had the necessary experience and maturity and alerted him to the delicacy of his position. He was warned that the Admiralty Board had a 'loathing' of employing officers who had been '*prematurely promoted*'. Thomas's correspondence with his father was not reassuring: 'I was hurt at your letter – it vexed me to see that you could not embrace my advice in the double light of Your Parent and Admiral, – take great care how you write to other commanding officers.' Captain Cochrane weathered this storm of parental disapprobation and as his professional competence developed, his relationship with his father improved. By 1809 he was arranging for Thomas to share in an exceedingly valuable freight from the West Indies to Cadiz, telling him gleefully that 'our share will be from £18-£20,000 – Lucky Day'.[59]

Decision-makers: admirals, commissioners and first lords

A few highly placed and well-connected veterans such as Howe and St Vincent almost certainly retained a strong capacity to aid their friends when they were on half pay. In the latter's case, this was seen by Henry Addington, the prime minister, as a useful way of curtailing acrimony arising from St Vincent's resignation from the first lordship.[60] Generally, however, since half-pay admirals lacked powers of appointment, they had to give effect to their interest through the agency of service friends who held active commissions or key offices.

Although the Admiralty established a pathway for aspiring sea officers that was under its control in 1794, this never met the demand and most appointments as midshipmen were made by captains.[61] These officers balanced the appeals of more or less distant relatives, the well-connected friends of applicants, including those with the ear of members of the Admiralty Board, their friends in the service, and the recommendations of admirals ashore and afloat. When the interest of a flag officer secured a berth on a ship for the young son of their friends, the captain concerned had an opportunity to enhance his interest. For example, Captain Charles Paget responded to an enquiry from Admiral Duncan by writing, '[I]f your Lordship thinks proper to send your young friend to me you may depend on the greatest care & attention being paid him.' When Paget described the request as 'flattering conduct towards me', he was not indulging in an empty show of deference. Rather, he was acknowledging that he was being presented with an opportunity to assist a young man with powerful friends and could expect to reap benefit from that.[62]

Subordinate flag officers serving at a distance from their commander-in-chief were able to make acting appointments and provide those holding them with opportunities to shine in their temporary rank. These appointments, which might follow a recommendation from a captain, were essentially nominations. When vacancies were created by death, or dismissal following court martial, the power of recommendation vested in commanders-in-chief was significant but their nominations were subject to confirmation by the Board. Commanders-in-chief on foreign stations could issue a commission subject to confirmation by the Board but those on home stations could only make acting appointments to vacant posts, with the issue of commissions being dependent on the Board.[63] New appointments were the prerogative of the Board, and as we shall see, first lords pre-empted other vacancies by sending lists of favoured candidates to flag officers. In some instances they arranged for their protégés to travel to the station

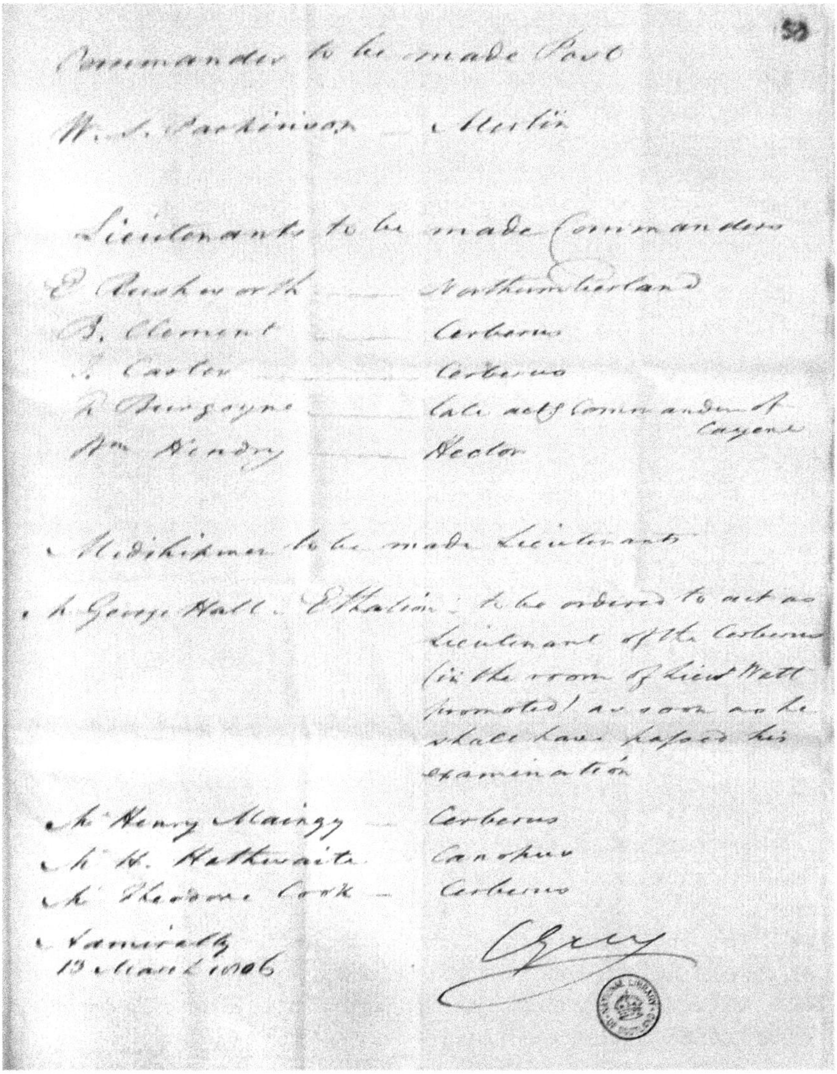

Commander to be made Post

W. J. Parkinson — Merlin

Lieutenants to be made Commanders

E. Rushworth — Northumberland

B. Clement — Cerberus

J. Carter — Cerberus

R. Burgoyne — Late actg Commander of Cayenne

Wm Hendry — Hector

Midshipmen to be made Lieutenants

Mr George Hall – Ethalion: to be ordered to act as Lieutenant of the Cerberus (in the room of Lieut Watt promoted) as soon as he shall have passed his examination

Mr Henry Mainguy — Cerberus

Mr H. Hathwaite — Canopus

Mr Theodore Cook — Cerberus

Admiralty
13 March 1806

Grey

Plate 4: Promotion lists were valuable bills of exchange in the Georgian patronage network. This list details Charles Grey's 'requests' for clients of the first lord to be appointed into vacancies on the Leeward Islands Station in March 1806.

concerned so they would be on hand when vacancies occurred. This practice was particularly common in the East and West Indies where health hazards were a fruitful source of 'death vacancies'.

People occupying key points in the patronage system maintained lists of candidates to whom they were willing to lend their interest. These lists were hierarchically ordered staging posts which marked the distance between various list holders (ministers and the first lord, royal dukes, commanders-in-chief, subordinate flag officers, private patrons) and those making final decisions on the allocation of benefits. Lists were both a way of organizing claims for favour and a means of signalling priorities. During the course of the wars first lords played an increasingly assertive individual role in a wide range of appointments, and this was reflected in the significance placed upon their lists.[64] Spencer and St Vincent were both powerful personalities and their combined tenure of almost a decade established first lords as the dominant players in naval patronage. During Lord Barham's first lordship in 1805–1806, the management of appointments up to the level of post captain was systemized, with the senior naval commissioner being given this responsibility.[65] St Vincent later encouraged Sir John Duckworth to attribute his disappointments over promotions and appointments after his victory off San Domingo to an enemy on the Board.[66] It is significant, however, that Barham specified that the senior naval commissioner was to 'check all promotions' not authorize them. Other commissioners would expect to receive a sympathetic hearing for their friends but their requests required the support of the senior naval commissioner and the concurrence of the first lord. This matter aside, the relationship between first lords' official and personal priorities and those of commanders-in-chief was a critical issue in naval patronage. In the 1750s and 1760s these officers raised principled objections to being directed in appointments and promotions on their stations by civilian first lords,[67] but these constraints seem to have fallen away by the French Wars.

Lord Spencer's correspondence with St Vincent was freighted with 'requests' to further the careers of those under the first lord's protection, and even in a moment of supreme professional triumph, the first lord's list came into play. Thus in reporting vacancies created during the action off Cape St Vincent in early 1797, the victorious commander-in-chief told the first lord that he had managed to provide for all but one of the officers on Lord Spencer's 'very long list'. In this case, as in others, St Vincent recognized (sometimes with bad grace) that Spencer's protégés had priority and acceded to his requests for their advancement. Even when St Vincent seemed inclined to get his own way, he made a bow to the first lord's claims, smoothly attempting to pass off a proposal to usurp the Admiralty's patronage by presenting it as a compliment to Lady Spencer.[68] For his part, Spencer emphasized how ready he was to accommodate St Vincent's recommendations when opportunities arose.[69] He later reassured St Vincent that his recommendations 'shall not be lost upon me, though from the present state of the numerous engagements I have been obliged to contract, and the vacancies which offer for them, I am not always able to forward them as fast as I should wish to do so'.[70]

Where personal relationships were especially cordial, senior flag officers might gain a ready hearing for their clients. In these cases, leverage arising directly from the political, social and familial currencies of the patronage network was augmented by respect for flag officers' professional capabilities and personal character. Lord Duncan's interactions with Lord Spencer are a case in point. He was related by marriage to Henry Dundas, Spencer's cabinet colleague, and had been the protégé of Admiral Keppel. These powerful pillars of current and residual interest were bolstered by Duncan's close professional and personal relationship with the first lord. This relationship, which provoked claims of extreme partiality from the politician William Windham, seems to have been the product of spontaneous regard rather than the fruit of cultivation.[71]

Mutual respect glows through their correspondence and the bond created by it was strengthened by Lady Spencer's warm and open admiration of Duncan's character. When writing on the anniversary of the Battle of Camperdown, she saluted Duncan as 'My dear and good Lord'.[72] The character and basis of the relationship was reflected in the tone Spencer used in responding to Duncan's recommendations as well as in his willingness to adopt them. In late 1795, shortly after he had taken up his North Sea command, Spencer assured Duncan that he would pay 'all attention' to a recommendation 'when there is a proper opportunity for it'; this officer was promoted in the middle of the next year.[73] Spencer promoted Duncan's son in late May 1797 and the Admiral's friends continued to be favoured by the first lord throughout his command.[74] Significantly, the occasional resentments at overreaching demands from first lords that crop up in the correspondence of St Vincent, Nelson, Cochrane, Duckworth, Rainier and Warren are absent from that of Duncan and Spencer.

The importance of the personal dimension of the Duncan-Spencer relationship is very apparent in an episode which risked compromising it. In late November 1799 Spencer began a private letter to Duncan by referring to the 'friendly and confidential footing' on which they had acted since the admiral's appointment. He then proceeded, however, to express hurt protestations (worthy of a flag officer) that Duncan had undermined their relationship by writing publically to the Board in support of a candidate for promotion. Spencer claimed that this approach, which would be seen as a 'slap in the face' to him as first lord, was entirely unnecessary since he had always shown himself 'as ready to pay attention as I believe any one situated as I am ever was'. Duncan seems to have written to the Board because he thought the injustice suffered by his candidate, and the 'indignity' suffered by him as a consequence, was due to its action not to Spencer's. The first lord was reassured and relieved by this explanation and the relationship continued on the same happy footing.[75]

While there was scope for gestures of mutual goodwill and forbearance, first lords' disposal of patronage could be a source of tension and disappointment. In mid-1796 St Vincent complained that Spencer's instructions disturbed his conscience when he thought of the merits of junior officers under his protection. On another occasion, he grudgingly concurred with a request to promote an officer whose father was a courtier with connections to the earls of Pembroke, despite his complete lack of experience and 'an utter dislike and inattention to the service ... as he stands on your lordship's list'. The rebuke inadequately concealed beneath a nod of deference occasionally gave way to open defiance. At a time when his temper and judgement was frayed by bitter struggles with recalcitrant captains and flag officers in the Mediterranean Fleet, St Vincent issued an ultimatum to the first lord on a question of patronage: '[U]nless I have the power to promote the lieutenants of the *Ville de Paris*, who have served with me during the last twelve months, I cannot serve an hour longer with honour to myself or advantage to my country'. Though St Vincent did not persist with this threat the fate of these officers still rankled with him two years later.[76] His extreme irritation sprang in part from the common expectation that officers gaining appointments in flagships would receive priority when vacancies occurred in the fleet. Consequently, it was assumed that an admiral's standing in the service was compromised when these officers' claims were ignored by the Board.[77] He also ran the risk of offending the officers' friends and lost the opportunity to increase his own interest by putting them under an obligation to him.

Occasionally, St Vincent was so persistent that he had to be put in his place. He was particularly exercised over a case involving Lieutenant Frances Austen in early 1799. On being instructed to appoint Austen to command the *Petrel* sloop, St Vincent wrote an angry letter to Rear Admiral Sir James Gambier, a professional member of the Board who shared evangelical sympathies with the Austens and was related to them by marriage.[78] The Reverend Charles Austen had sought Gambier's support for his son's promotion and when news of it arrived the lieutenant's sisters eagerly anticipated 'the Earl's' receipt of the Board's letter authorizing the appointment. Their pleasure in the family's good fortune seems never to have been tainted by knowledge of St Vincent's incandescent reaction to Gambier's interference.[79] He told him that the Board had done 'unheard of and unmerited injustice' to the officer to whom he had given an act-ing commander's commission, and subjected his service patron to an 'outrage'. While St Vincent felt personally affronted (and no doubt embarrassed on account of his obli-gations to the other officer's friends) he also claimed that such acts undermined the authority of commanders-in-chief. In response to a rebuking letter he grudgingly told Spencer that he would not renew the issue but insisted on reminding him that 'it has wounded me more than I can express'.[80] When he commanded the Channel Fleet, St Vincent complained that the scope for the effective exercise of his interest had virtually disappeared. He told Rear Admiral Payne, who wrote on behalf of the Prince of Wales, that he was unable to 'make a lieutenant': 'it would astonish you to hear a recital of the lessons of humility I have been subjected to since I was invested in this command.' The impact of what he shortly afterwards described as Lord Spencer's 'lust of patronage' was compounded by the malign influence of Vice Admiral William Young. St Vincent accused Young of doing 'all he can to frustrate every application I make'.[81]

St Vincent's reaction to these setbacks was marked by the aggressive tone he invari-ably assumed when his wishes were thwarted. The underlying issues were, however, an inescapable aspect of naval patronage. Indeed, when St Vincent became first lord, the disposal of patronage caused difficulties in his relationship with Nelson. His refer-ence to his predecessor's 'lust for patronage' was largely rhetorical, suggesting stand-ards of propriety that were never spelt out and were, by the very nature of things, very much in the eye of the beholder. When St Vincent took over from Lord Spencer at the Admiralty Board, he told Nelson of the weight of responsibility he felt with respect to 'a just disposition of the Patronage' of the office. He announced that he was under obliga-tions to no one and that he would dispense patronage with scrupulous impartiality.[82] As we shall see, St Vincent's idea of 'just disposition' included recognition of merit and sometimes he gave priority to it. His idea of impartiality meant that he adopted prin-ciples of allocation that reflected service considerations rather than political partisan-ship. Nevertheless, his handling of appointments at the Admiralty was never entirely insulated from the claims of interest.

As first lord, St Vincent showed no signs of weakening the allocative role his prede-cessors had assumed and had no compunction in forcing the hands of commanders-in-chief. Rear Admiral Duckworth, commanding at Jamaica, received ten sets of appointment instructions from St Vincent between May and October of 1802.[83]

Towards the end of that year Vice Admiral Rainier commanding in the East Indies had the mortification of being told by the first lord that 'appointments from hence have interfered very much with those you have made in India ... [A]ll acting orders ... are very doubtful in their effect under the most favourable appearance'.[84] Where he thought it necessary, the first lord emphasized the imperatives that lay behind his 'requests' by signalling the connections of the officers concerned. Thus when he informed Duckworth that 'three midshipmen will ... make their bow to you – Mr Lake, son to the General, a Protégé of the Prince of Wales; Mr Shirreff, son to the General of the name; and Mr à Court, son of Sir Wm Ashe à Court, in all whose fortunes I am deeply interested', the rear admiral would have been in no doubt how he should fill lieutenants' vacancies in his squadron.[85]

Forceful introductions by a first lord necessarily constrained commanders-in-chiefs' disposal of vacancies. The West Indian environment was extremely unhealthy for British crews and for that very reason provided plenty of opportunities for those who did not succumb to it.[86] In the Mediterranean the situation was different. In late 1803 Nelson complained to Admiral Sir Thomas Pasley of the Admiralty's monopolization of promotions in his fleet, noting that the climate on the station was so healthy that only two captains had died of natural causes in the course of the wars. Nelson made much the same point to his friend Vice Admiral Bligh who wrote on behalf of his son: 'You are sure of my regard, but I cannot kill people; and, I am more likely to go off myself than anyone about me.'[87] He cautioned St Vincent that by constricting the patronage of flag officers, the Board risked undermining their capacity to motivate their officers, and compromised discipline by lowering their reputation in the eyes of both officers and men. In making these points Nelson appealed to St Vincent's principles and practice. In a case that paralleled that of Frances Austen's, he objected to an Admiralty nominee being favoured at the cost of one of his own: '[H]aving appointed a very gallant and meritorious Officer, who had in a most particular manner distinguished himself on board the *Isis* at Copenhagen, it would have lowered me in the fleet, that my follower, who had performed gallant services under my eye, should be displaced.'[88] This appeal was successful and the officer's appointment as commander was confirmed.

Duckworth, in one of the rare bursts of open resentment that punctuated his plaintive relationship with St Vincent, complained bitterly in mid-1801 that his officers had failed to gain appropriate recognition following a joint action with the army in the West Indies. He faced similar frustrations in his dealings with Lord Barham and his immediate successor after his victory off San Domingo in early 1806. Although four out of the six acting appointments he had made in February 1806 were confirmed, Duckworth's failure to secure promotions for officers from his flagship became the subject of letters of sharp grievance addressed to successive first lords, and canvassed with his patron the Duke of Northumberland. Duckworth argued that his concerns were disinterested because these officers were unknown to him, insisting that the Admiralty should have recognized his claims as the officer in command 'for the *good of the service*'.[89]

When Barham declined requests for Admiralty patronage, he took the usual line of referring to the constraining effect of the deplorable open-handedness of his predecessors. His practice reflected a dual determination to exercise his patronage prerogative as first lord and to curb the pretensions of commanders-in-chief. As soon as he was settled in the first lord's seat, Barham issued a series of pre-emptory notices on appointments and promotions to Rear Admiral Dacres, who had succeeded Duckworth in the Jamaica command. He sent four sets of requests in the second half of 1805: all referred to the officers' connections and were silent on their merits.[90] He was vigorous in ensuring that commanders-in-chief did not attempt to usurp 'the Board's' (primarily the first lord's) role in appointments and promotions.[91] Shortly after Collingwood took command of the Mediterranean Fleet, Barham accepted his recommendations but reminded him that while commanders-in-chief might make acting lieutenants' appointments into vacancies created by courts martial or death, they were subject to confirmation by the Admiralty, and that should not be taken for granted. The neglect of this rule had 'created much disappointment to individuals as well as to families and occasioned great trouble in this office'.[92] The sense of disappointment was compounded if those in unconfirmed appointments had laid out money on expensive uniforms and equipment in anticipation of being confirmed in the rank. Collingwood was said to have been irritated by Barham's instructions and was certainly criticized for adhering to them by at least one of his senior captains.[93]

The management of patronage during Sir Alexander Cochrane's term as commander-in-chief of the Leeward Islands (1805–10) was particularly challenging. Difficulties arose (as they had for Rainier in the East Indies) from lags in communication and the consistently high death rates on that station which made it a favourite target of patrons at home. In addition, however, the early years of Cochrane's command coincided with an unusually rapid turnover of first lords. Four men held the office in the three years following Melville's resignation in early May 1805: Barham, Howick, Grenville and Mulgrave. This combination of circumstances often left Cochrane in the dark about incoming first lords' intentions, and unsure of the status of the residual claims of their predecessors. It also seems, however, to have provided opportunities for him to benefit from the general uncertainty.

In mid-September 1805, having not yet received instructions from the new first lord, Cochrane told him that he assumed it was his intention that Admiralty vacancies should be filled from his predecessor's list. On the same day he wrote to assure Melville on this point, declaring that he would 'always be happy in complying with your Lordship's wishes'.[94] Cochrane's assumption on this occasion had more to do with his attachment to Melville than his desire to anticipate his successor's wishes. Early in the following year, Cochrane advised Barham that he would appoint his nominee to the first available vacancy but he also told him that he had found a place for officers recommended by Melville and 'his much regretted friend Lord Nelson'. On the same day he sent a reassuringly triumphant note to Lord Melville: 'I have had it in my power to promote all the gentlemen recommended in the first list.'[95]

Charles Grey – soon to become Viscount Howick – was very quick off the mark. His first letter to Cochrane on succeeding Barham included a ranked list of one commander, five lieutenants and four midshipmen to be appointed into Admiralty vacancies. Grey kept the pressure on by recommending a further six officers a few months later.[96] Cochrane responded fulsomely to the first list and assured Howick after his term had finished that in gratitude for the favours he had received (which included the promotion of his son) he would 'ever feel pleasure in obeying your commands'. At the same time, however, he grumbled about the difficulties caused by the Admiralty's frequent recourse to the West Indies as a focus of its patronage. Cochrane pointed to the injustice done to acting commanders with significant experience of the hardships of the West Indies when officers who had just arrived from England displaced them. This practice was unfair on the officers concerned and placed the commanders-in-chief in an invidious position. New arrivals were often unable to stand the conditions, and if they were refused leave to return home Cochrane might be seen to be creating death vacancies for the benefit of those who were able to cope with it. If he relieved afflicted unseasoned officers, however, he further extended the uncertainty imposed on those who were able to act effectively in West Indian conditions.[97]

Shortly after Thomas Grenville became first lord in September 1806, Cochrane placed an officer from Howick's list into a vacancy and asked the new first lord to confirm it. Several months later, when Cochrane began to address Grenville's list he attempted simultaneously to secure the first lord's confirmation of his own appointments.[98] Under Lord Mulgrave, Grenville's successor, tenure of the first lordship was more settled so there was less scope for Cochrane to take advantage of transitional periods. However, the timing and sequencing of Mulgrave's instructions sometimes resulted in confusion that worked to the advantage of the commander-in-chief's nominees. Cochrane emphasized his conscientious attempts to juggle out-of-sequence lists (one of which mistakenly included a candidate for promotion to commander among the midshipmen), death vacancies, and promotions and appointments already made, or frustrated by the failure of the intended beneficiaries to arrive on his station. Despite these efforts at self-justification, however, Mulgrave upbraided Cochrane when the juggle collapsed.[99]

Perhaps in anticipation of this rebuke, or in an attempt to gain some moral high ground from which to protect his own appointments, Cochrane had already gone on the offensive. At this stage he presented his case as a general one and carefully avoided criticizing Mulgrave directly:

> The patronage now left with Admirals on foreign stations, can but ill admit of being curtailed – until Lord Spencer came to the Admiralty, they gave away all ships taken from the Enemy – but the hand of power wrested this from them – and they are now left with the sad prospect of only serving their friends by the deaths of those they held equally dear – or the dismission [sic] of the unfortunate from the Service.[100]

Having made a virtue of not attempting to press his candidates on the Admiralty following the conquest of Martinique in February 1809, Cochrane launched an attack on Mulgrave for refusing him a death vacancy because the officer who held it had died a few days before his appointment was confirmed. He then accused the first lord of following Spencer's practice of overloading commanders-in-chief with demands, claiming that there were so many officers on Mulgrave's latest list that they would have to take up quarters ashore.[101] Cochrane retained the Leeward Islands command in the early stages of Charles Yorke's first lordship. When he grudgingly left the command in late 1810 he and his successor, Rear Admiral Sir Francis Laforey, wrangled over Mulgrave's and Yorke's residual claims. In this, and in other commands, the new first lord showed himself just as committed to exercising patronage from afar as his successors had been. Significantly, Laforey arrived on the station with a list that Yorke had given him in London.[102]

Cochrane's final wartime command was on the North American Station when Robert Dundas, the second Viscount Melville, was first lord. Cochrane, long a client of the Dundas's, maintained an extensive private correspondence with Melville throughout 1814 and mid-1815, and paid close attention to his patronage requests. The new first lord provided Cochrane with his list before he left England to take up his command, and when he arrived at Bermuda he checked the names on it against those who were actually present on the station in an attempt to mitigate the confusion that had arisen earlier on his Leeward Islands command. Once Cochrane had taken over his new command in early 1814 he began to give effect to Melville's wishes and also to press his own claims. Thus having cleared the first lord's list of midshipmen for promotion to lieutenant, Cochrane brought forward a relative for confirmation in that rank.[103] Cochrane's handling of the patronage requests of a series of first lords demonstrates the importance of personal relationships in smoothing interactions that could be a source of tension in their professional relationships with flag offices. It is noticeable that the open frustrations that marked his interactions with Lord Mulgrave did not occur when Lord Melville and his son presided at the Admiralty Board.

Considerations of what was due to first lords, and to commanders-in-chief, explain a series of carefully balanced transactions involving Charles Yorke and Vice Admiral Sir James Saumarez, then commander-in-chief in the Baltic. In late June 1810 Yorke's plan to promote Commander Matthew Bradby to post rank seemed to conflict with Saumarez's wish to make Commander Thomas White a post captain and Lieutenant Daniel Ross a commander. Yorke wrote to tell Saumarez that he regretted that he could not give 'complete effect to the arrangements you proposed' but suggested a solution to the problem. Bradby was to be promoted only 'for rank', that is, to gain a place on the captains' list. In order to secure this objective he would need to be posted into an appropriate ship but would be quickly superseded by a more senior post captain whose ship would be given to White. White's current command, a sloop, would then be available to facilitate Lieutenant Ross's promotion to commander. Though these appointments were 'acting', Yorke assured Saumarez of his intention of confirming them in due course.[104] This arrangement meant that Yorke's protégé would stand above Saumarez's on the post captains' list but given the prerogatives of a first lord that was to be expected. Saumarez responded with fitting gratitude: 'I beg to return you my sincere thanks for the arrangements you have been pleased to make for the promotion of Captain White and Lieutenant Ross who I have long been solicitous to get advanced in the service.' In seeking indicative endorsement of the promotion of 'several deserving characters in the *Victory*', Saumarez undertook to pay 'due attention to those who you may be desirous to have advanced in preference'. It is significant that throughout these transactions Saumarez gave no hint that he thought that Yorke was abusing the prerogatives of a civilian first lord.[105]

The strong prospect of hostilities with the United States in the early summer of 1812 did not distract Lord Melville from considering the disposal of patronage on Admiral Sir John Warren's enlarged command. In addition to receiving briefings from Lord Castlereagh on how he should approach the initial diplomatic part of his mission, Warren had discussions with Melville about consolidating and re-prioritizing the lists which had already been sent to the flag officers whose stations were to be subsumed in Warren's command. He was given a list with the names of seven commanders, twenty-eight lieutenants and thirty-four midshipmen, immediately followed by a supplementary one of two more commanders, thirteen lieutenants and nineteen midshipmen. Within six months further lists naming another eleven commanders, eighteen lieutenants and thirty-two midshipmen followed Warren across the Atlantic. After throwing him a bone in the form of appointments on his flagship and a single Admiralty vacancy, Melville almost always found reasons for not accommodating the commander-in-chief's requests.[106] On one occasion he offered Warren a vacuous half apology framed in terms of the justice of the claims of those who, by virtue of their place on his list, deserved 'the attention of the Admiralty'.[107]

Conclusion

While the decisive influence of first lords in allocating appointments and other benefits was sometimes a source of tension between these officials and flag officers, this was as likely to occur when first lords were admirals as when they were civilians. Given the ubiquity of interest, and the limited range of objects to which it was directed, such tensions were inescapable. By the same token, however, the widespread understanding of the implications of the principle of reciprocity which underwrote the patronage system meant that even when such a forceful personality as St Vincent was involved, tensions were manageable and did not produce dysfunction within the upper echelons of the service. In some cases, the working of patronage resulted in appointments that were detrimental to the good of the service, and it must inevitably have meant that many able officers were neglected by their superiors or failed to gain the effective support of flag officers. To some degree, however, the dysfunctional effects of interest arising from political and family connections were mitigated by the impact of distinctive forms of intra-service interest.[108] These transactions will be considered in the next chapter.

Service Interest: Followers, 'Sons of the Service' and the Claims of Merit

There is a charming brig ... at Chatham, if you wish her for one of your followers.
—Admiral Rowley, port admiral at Sheerness, to Rear Admiral Markham,
Admiralty Board, July 1806[1]

In addition to participating in the patronage system, flag officers also had a key role as 'service patrons' engaging in exchanges of 'service interest'.[2] This form of interest arose from the distinct conditions and needs of the Service and was not found elsewhere in the patronage network. It was available only to those connected to the service and was used exclusively for their benefit. It might, however, feed back into the patronage network, drawing upon other forms of interest and producing obligations that were repaid through benefits and favours beyond the reach of the service. This chapter will consider three expressions of service interest: the attention paid to 'followers', obligations to 'sons of the service' and the promotion of the careers of officers on the grounds of merit.

Admirals and followers

'Followers' were commissioned and warrant officers and seamen who were attached to a senior officer and looked to him to support claims for promotion, appointment and assistance. Connections between service patrons and their followers were recognized officially when senior officers were authorized to bring their followers with them when they moved from ship to ship. When unemployed admirals sought the Board's support for their service clients, their correspondence was sometimes annotated with the word 'follower' by the Admiralty clerks. Some attachments between followers and service patrons originated in local associations. Sir James Saumarez, for example, drew on his fellow Channel Islanders to provide the nuclei of his crews, and while William Dillon probably exaggerated when he described Sir Thomas Pakenham's crew at the Battle of Cape St Vincent as 'all Irish', the captain's countrymen were undoubtedly a significant presence among the *Invincibles*.[3] Collingwood's local following was smaller and less compact but he kept a weather eye out for men from Newcastle who had volunteered to serve with him.[4] In many cases, shared experience, admiration, mutual regard and a good record of securing prize money encouraged men to look up to a superior and seek his protection. Followers expected their service patron to respond to requests to advance their careers and to pleas from their dependents in the event of death or disablement. While opportunities opened up for a flag officer's followers when their service patron was ordered to hoist his flag, the careers of others were liable to disruption. Thus when Rear Admiral Sir William Parker arrived on the *Blenheim* in late March 1797 with a mass of followers, the existing officers were turned out of their places to take their chance in a highly competitive job market.[5]

When admirals went on half pay, their followers risked being stranded and sometimes there was no time for any advanced planning. Thus when Admiral George Bowyer lost his leg on the Glorious First of June and went ashore, Collingwood told his friends that he and the other officers were 'adrift and separated, [and] have, as it were, the world to begin anew'.[6] Lord Hood worried about his followers' fate when he was summarily removal from the Mediterranean command in May 1795 and did not expect to ever hoist his flag again.[7] When a command appeared to be coming to an end, admirals' followers became anxious if their service patron failed to provide for their ongoing employment. John Whitby, Cornwallis's favoured flag captain, faced this difficulty in late 1805 when it became clear that his chief was about to be superseded. Cornwallis's failure to secure Whitby another appointment momentarily soured a very close personal and professional relationship.[8] In other cases, the end of a command could be anticipated and the interests of followers considered. Thus when Lord Bridport was on the verge of retiring from the Channel Fleet, he reminded Lord Spencer of the merits of Captain Domett and sought a new appointment for him. In some cases, first lords gave early notice of their intention to relieve a flag officer. Charles Yorke was particularly punctilious about this matter. He advised flag officers of their impending supersession so they might make provision for their followers and expressed a general desire to 'consult your convenience as much as possible'.[9]

Where there was no preexisting attachment, well-managed personal contacts could foster valuable and long-lasting follower/service patron relationships. Early in the wars Midshipman Dillon was despondent upon being turned over to Captain James Gambier's *Defence*, being unsure how his new captain would receive him. While Dillon was at home before joining his ship, his father went to work to secure 'strong letters of recommendation' from those known to Gambier, including William Wilberforce MP, a fellow evangelical. Dillon presented these letters to Gambier at the first opportunity and was assured of the captain's protection. Although he never became an unqualified admirer of Gambier and did not share his religious views, Dillon looked to him for ongoing support, described him as 'my friend' and corresponded with him throughout his career.[10]

Because officers on flagships were directly under the eye of an admiral, they expected preferential consideration when opportunities arose and, as we have seen, flag officers believed that their reputations would be damaged if the competing demands on first lords prevented them providing for their followers. On one occasion St Vincent was accused of extending a vendetta against a subordinate flag officer (Sir John Orde) by taking steps to ensure that his followers would leave his flagship with their patron to face the prospect of uncertain employment.[11] Even where no malice was involved, arrangements might cut across flag officers' relationship with followers. Thus when Sir William Parker was offered the North American command in the spring of 1799 he bridled at the suggestion that he should go directly from the Mediterranean. He complained to Spencer that this requirement would prevent him dealing with necessary personal business in England and also deprive him of the opportunity to gather up his followers there: 'those officers and gentlemen who have long served and attached themselves to me, and which they are entitled to expect in a situation to receive the advantages the service may give'.[12] Flag officers were as alive to their obligations to warrant and petty officers as they were to those who held, or were seeking, commissions. Saumarez was able to capitalize on his reputation as a commanding officer and his standing among his neighbours in Guernsey to recruit large numbers of prime local seamen. Press gangs did not operate there, but subscriptions were raised to provide bounties for volunteers. Many seamen flocked to Saumarez's flag and volunteered to follow him from ship to ship.[13] When he commanded the *Crescent* at the beginning of the war more than half the ship's company were volunteers from Guernsey.[14] This vessel was a frigate, service on which was often thought the most likely route to prize money. When their captain was appointed to command a ship-of-the-line, however, the entire crew of the *Crescent* volunteered to follow him.[15] Given his reliance on these followers and sense of obligation to them, it is not surprising that Saumarez was incensed when he lost the command of a squadron in the Mediterranean in late 1801 and his recommendations in favour of a number of warrant officers were set aside. He told Sir Thomas Troubridge that he was 'truly grieved' and would feel this injustice 'as long as I live'.[16] Duckworth faced similar problems. He was especially aggrieved that Lord Howick showed little inclination to reward his followers after the victory off San Domingo in early 1806, and referred plaintively to the Board's neglect of a boatswain and a gunner.[17] Sir Edward Pellew mourned the 'woeful prospects' of his followers when his East Indian command was divided in mid-1805.[18]

When senior captains promoted to rear admiral did not immediately secure an appointment at sea, their followers might be seriously disadvantaged. An interesting example occurred after the Battle of Trafalgar when the badly damaged *Téméraire* was put out of commission and her crew dispersed to other ships. In mid-January 1806 her former captain, now Rear Admiral Sir Eliab Harvey, forwarded a letter to the Admiralty Board on behalf of ten of her ship's company. These men, senior able seamen, carpenters' and gunners' mates and a quartermaster, had been drafted into inferior positions in the *Audacious*. They told Harvey that 'since your Honour has parted from us we have been oftime Neglected as not being Befriended by your family'. They appealed for his help, making reference to the 'Memorial Day', off Cape Trafalgar and pleading to Harvey not to 'forget the regard we acknowledge your Honour'. The rear admiral's covering letter to the Board offered strong support for the men's claim: '[T]he Names of these men are well known to me to be amongst the very best of the *Téméraire*'s Ship's Company and deserving their former ratings'.[19] These men were drafted into Harvey's flagship when he took up a subordinate command a couple of months later.[20]

The Board often accommodated admirals' appeals on behalf of their followers when they struck their flags. Thereafter, they had to compete for attention from among the ranks of the admirals unemployed, utilizing where possible the good offices of friends. Popular officers with strong service networks were likely to be more useful to their followers than less well-connected unemployed admirals. When Rear Admiral George Murray retired to Chichester in 1808, he remained closely engaged in service matters and received many appeals for support. One request came from Robert Brereton, who had served as a midshipman under him in the *London* in 1801. His father was a captain who was superannuated in 1787. Over the course of 1809–10, Brereton wrote to Murray from the Isle de France in the Indian Ocean where he was a prisoner of war, waiting to be exchanged. His career had not flourished since he served under Murray and he was worried that captivity would damage his prospects of finally securing a lieutenant's commission. Murray wrote on Brereton's behalf to Commodore Rowley who was commanding the squadron blockading the Isle de France, and rallied support from Rear Admiral William Drury on the East Indies station. Drury told Murray that 'your recommend'n shall meet my ... notice and attention', noting that 'the Father I perfectly recollect'. These efforts were successful and on his release Brereton was made a lieutenant. He wrote to Murray thanking him for his help, addressing him as 'My dear and Sincere Friend'.[21]

Flag officers' sense of obligation towards followers extended beyond those who were still on active service. They petitioned the Board to provide places at Greenwich Hospital and asked for pensions for those who had been seriously injured in the line of duty. Some of these obligations went back a long way and some had occurred in unusual circumstances. In mid-winter 1806–1807, for example, Vice Admiral Sampson Edwards approached the Board on behalf of a seaman with whom he had served fifty years ago. The man, aged 97, was in want of proper clothes for the winter and needed extra nourishment to sustain him at that time of the year.[22] Vice Admiral Thornbrough wrote to the Board in 1802 at the request of an American pilot's wife. This man was captain of a merchant ship during the American War that had rescued Thornbrough's shipwrecked crew from a remote island off the coast of Nova Scotia. On his return to Boston, he was vilified by his neighbours for this humanitarian gesture and imprisoned briefly before fleeing to Halifax where he found work as a pilot. He was now blind and without any means of supporting himself or his family.[23]

Admirals and 'sons of the service'

The claims of family, friends and followers sometimes overlapped with those advanced on behalf of 'sons of the service'. This category included grandsons and nephews of commissioned officers, as well as their sons. Appeals on these grounds, however, differed from the straightforward direct advancement of sons by their fathers and other close relations because they were invoked by friends in the service, as well as by those who were related to them. They thus involved the exercise of professional rather than familial interest.[24] As was to be expected, relationships with flag officers tended to carry most weight, particularly when they were friends of significant dispensers of patronage. The principle, however, was also applied in varying degrees to the relations of more junior officers although they relied on others to bring their cases forward.

Shortly after St Vincent succeeded Spencer as first lord, he recommended Peter Parker to Lord Keith, then commander-in-chief in the Mediterranean. He reminded Keith that Parker was the son and grandson of admirals and issued him with this injunction: '[I]nsure him protection and promotion when you shall judge him fit for it.' Young Parker did not have long to wait. St Vincent's letter was dated from mid-May 1801 and by October of that year he was promoted to lieutenant. He was a post captain within three years.[25] When St Vincent responded to an appeal from the father of a boy with close connections in the baronetcy and aristocracy, he referred to his 'great satisfaction in facilitating the views of your Son, not only out of respect to the memory of his Great-Uncle and Godfather [Admiral Hon. Samuel Barrington] but attention to you'.[26]

With Spencer's help and presumably with Henry Dundas's blessing, Lord Duncan secured his son Henry's promotion to lieutenant while his father commanded the North Sea Fleet. A year later, however, Duncan had lost Spencer's direct support at the Admiralty Board and was no longer in employment. Henry Duncan's interest now relied on his father's professional reputation and standing in the service, his noble status and connections with the Dundas's and St Vincent. By this stage in his career, however, young Duncan had also had opportunities to demonstrate his ability and courage to his commanding officer, Captain Ross Donnelly, who drew the young man's merits to the first lord's attention when they dined together in late 1803.[27] While preparing the way in London, Donnelly also ensured that Henry Duncan's virtues were known to Nelson, the commander-in-chief of the fleet in which he was serving. Lord Duncan had written to Nelson several months earlier but by the time the letter arrived Donnelly had already brought Henry to his commander-in-chief's notice. Nelson told Duncan that 'I had desired to be introduced to your son whose character stands very high with Captain Donnelley' and invited the young man to dinner. Death vacancies were in short supply in the Mediterranean Fleet so Nelson encouraged Lord Duncan to use his interest in London to secure an Admiralty vacancy into which Nelson would then appoint his son. St Vincent agreed to this arrangement but it was left to his successor, Lord Melville, to give effect to it. As Robert Dundas told Duncan, with 'so near a friend at the Head of the Admiralty, the young sailor, independent of his own claims, is in a fair way of getting everything you think good for him'.[28]

After Lord Hugh Seymour's death in 1801, St Vincent recommended his son George to Nelson who found him a lieutenant's vacancy in the Mediterranean Fleet.[29] He had assured Seymour's uncle, the Marquis of Hertford, that the 'thirst for glory in my young friend Seymour after a very hard knock, proves him to be of the true breed and the worthy son of his much lamented Father. Your Lordship may rely on his receiving from me every mark of kindness and attention in my power'. George Seymour was promoted commander in January 1806 and with St Vincent's ongoing support was made post captain at the end of July.[30] In early 1810 when Seymour was commanding a ship in Sir George Berkeley's squadron off Lisbon, the Vice Admiral wrote enthusiastically to his neighbour George Murray to say how pleased he was to have an officer who was 'almost one of his children' serving with him.[31] Later that year Murray helped Captain James Bowen secure the command of a frigate. Bowen's father, also called James, was a distinguished senior captain and an old service friend of Murray.[32]

Even where distinction was lacking, however, the claim of a 'son of the service' might be effective. As St Vincent told Lord Spencer when recommending an officer from the Mediterranean Fleet, '[H]e is a child of the service, being the son of an old captain, and brother-in-law of Commissioner Hartwell; and though neither of these persons had much public character in the profession, I feel it a duty to take care of the offspring and near connections of my brother officers'.[33] This preference applied to the sons of junior officers without any other interest as well as to those with more helpful connections. Thus in late October 1814, for example, Rear Admiral Hotham, who was serving under Sir Alexander Cochrane on the North American station, appealed to his commander-in-chief to take a midshipman, Thomas Coleman, onto his flagship. Coleman, the son of an old lieutenant 'having no friends to assist him, has applied to me, and I know no better way' of helping him. Cochrane gave Mr Coleman a berth and he was appointed lieutenant in February of the year following.[34] The timing was most fortunate since it at least ensured that Coleman would receive half pay when peace came.

Claims made on behalf of those who were related to officers who had been killed on active service gained strength from their sacrifice. After Hyde Parker's father was lost in a shipwreck in 1781 his son's career continued to benefit from residual interest and from a sense that the honourable fate of the father should not disadvantage the son. Sir James Saumarez's father was a doctor in the Channel Islands but two of his uncles were distinguished sea officers killed in the line of duty; these connections were important in securing his appointment as a midshipman.[35] Captain Edward Brenton, St Vincent's first biographer, and his brother Jael, who attained flag rank, both benefited from being the sons of an officer and enjoyed the additional advantage of being brothers of an officer who had died on active service.[36] Nelson was on good terms with Lord Radstock but he told him that the claims of his son would have to wait until another young man had been promoted. He assumed that Radstock would endorse his prioritization: 'Granville [Waldegrave] will be promoted next but one, and that *one* is Mr Faddy, who was a child in the Vanguard when his father was killed. I have protected him ever since, and he served his time and passed last October. Your excellent heart will, I am sure, accord in this respect with mine'.[37] Vice Admiral Chambalayne appealed to service genealogy and sacrifice in early 1805 to secure the confirmation of a son, Edwin, as a commander. His letter to the Board referred to two sons who had already died in the service and to 'your Lordships' kind attention to the sons of old officers'. Chambalayne's appeal was acted on immediately.[38]

Obligations arising from service connections might be sufficiently strong to override other considerations. Lord Rodney's overreaching behaviour ruined his son John's career but Nelson (at one time Rodney's protégé) thought that his younger brother's status as a 'son of the service' was good grounds for taking him under his protection.[39] Although the recall of Sir Hyde Parker after the Battle of Copenhagen meant that his career ended under a cloud, and St Vincent's bitter dispute with Sir John Orde terminated in the issue of a challenge, he nevertheless advanced the careers of these officers' sons.[40] In other cases, however, lurking personal animosity and perhaps also a lack of professional regard overrode obligations to 'sons of the service'. Admiral Isaac Prescott's attempt to secure St Vincent's support on behalf of his son, Lieutenant Henry Prescott, was declined on the grounds that he had already over-recommended. It seems clear, however, that Prescott's request irritated St Vincent because he told him, 'I cannot account for a passage in your letter insinuating that I may have taken a dislike to you, for I have always observed the civility due from one Flag Officer to another in the intercourse I have occasionally had with you.' St Vincent emphasized how cool this civility was by addressing Prescott as 'Sir', rather than as 'My dear Admiral', a salutation reserved for more welcome correspondents.[41] Prescott had been promoted to flag rank in 1795 but was never employed and gained no other distinctions.

Lieutenant Prescott had to wait almost two years for promotion to commander and although he eventually obtained flag rank his career was hindered by a lack of interest.[42] His case is similar to that of the sons of Admiral Peter Aplin in that it demonstrates the accumulative disadvantage experienced by those with limited interest and a lack of professional standing. Aplin made numerous unsuccessful appeals for employment and had to rely on well-placed friends in the Service to advance the careers of his sons. Thus in early February 1808 he wrote to the Board seeking the confirmation of lieutenants' appointments made by Sir Edward Pellew in the East Indies:

> Not having been so fortunate as to have been called into service since I have become a Flag Officer ... I have placed them with such of my Friends on foreign Commands who might have it in their power to promote them if their conduct should merit their attention – being the sons of an old officer who has passed his whole life in the service.

Although this appeal was successful, his sons' careers did not flourish. Alpin was told in December 1812 that his son John was on Lord Melville's list but that it was a very long one and early promotion should not be expected.[43] Lieutenant Alpin was promoted commander in March 1814 but he had to wait until 1826 to be made post captain. He retired in that rank twenty years later. His brother Christopher died a lieutenant in 1820.

The requirements of the service and the claims of merit

Although promotions were subject to the influence of interest, the operation of the patronage system in the Navy was conditioned to some degree by the needs of the service. These requirements reflected the practical demands of command at sea, and the Royal Navy's status as an agent of governments whose survival depended on accommodating a range of powerful interests, and avoiding the censure of public opinion. The Navy's key role in protecting trade, and the influence of trading interests in politics and public finance, gave a sharp practical edge to considerations of effectiveness and meritorious performance. Although patronage may have become more prominent in the French Wars,[44] references to potential and performance nevertheless played a significant role in the discourses of promotion and appointment, and had a discernible impact on some of the decisions arising from them. As a result, the challenge of integrating interest and merit played an important role in the complex processes of recommending, recognizing and rewarding which occupied so much of admirals' time.

Wartime service was extremely demanding, even without the hazards of battle. Because the Navy was always at sea and operated on a global scale it was particularly vulnerable to the elements. As a result, while almost all (about 98 per cent) of the losses of France and her allies resulted from enemy action, a disproportionately large number of the Royal Navy's losses (about 60 per cent in each war) resulted from foundering on the high seas, or shipwrecks off the coasts of Europe, the Americas and the East and West Indies.[45] In these circumstances, it is not surprising that many of those responsible for training, appointing and promoting sea officers placed a premium on seamanship. Collingwood, for all his solicitude towards conscientious midshipmen, was sharply intolerant of incompetence in prospective sea officers. His comments on a young man who was being sent back to his family made the issue crystal clear: 'Perhaps he might make an apothecary. If he did poison a patient now and then, better that than lose a whole ship's company.'[46] But while it was widely recognized that those advanced in the service should be competent seamen, some attention was also paid to merit. This principle invoked considerations of the relative worth of those being considered, and privileged those who had demonstrated superior professional character and performance.

The dominant members of the flag officers' corp in the French Wars had been distinguished post captains who continued to show high levels of commitment, determination and skill when commanding fleets, squadrons and ports. Furthermore, whether as first lords, commanders-in-chief or subordinate flag officers, admirals had a vested interest in employing the active and meritorious and shunning the incompetent, the timorous and the idle. The bravery and skill of sea officers was a major factor determining the fighting qualities of the ships under admirals' commands, and hence their potential to engage successfully in fleet actions and to undertake less spectacular but highly demanding wartime duties. From a purely personal perspective, admirals relied on the efficiency of their subordinates to maintain the standing necessary for future employment, and to ensure a steady flow of prize money. These official, professional and personal motivations came together with the requirements of the service to ensure that considerations of performance were brought to bear on a system where the usual tokens of patronage – ties of blood and friendship, political allegiance, deference to rank and status and ideas of reciprocity – also exerted a powerful influence. These considerations applied to key port appointments as well as to service at sea. As St Vincent put it to Admiral George Montagu when he was appointing a flag captain at Portsmouth, '[A] head of arrangement and unceasing zeal are requisite in the person who is to carry into execution the details of the Port, and in making the selection favour, friendship and patronage should be put totally out of the question.'[47]

Merit-based recommendations often arose from senior officers' reports of actions they commanded. These occasions also provided an opportunity for more general notice that built up reputational stock that might yield future benefits. For that reason, official reports of battles and single ship actions and armed landings were scrutinized closely, and those who thought their contributions had been ignored or underplayed complained to their friends of the partiality or ingratitude of their superior officers. They did so to relieve their hurt feeling and in the hope that the harmful impact of omissions and errors would be mitigated to some degree. Collingwood and a number of other officers were outraged by what they saw as Lord Howe's shabby treatment of them in the report on the 'Glorious' First of June, written on his behalf by his flag captain, Sir Roger Curtis.[48] Collingwood launched a furious attack on Curtis and made it clear that dissatisfaction was widespread among Howe's captains:

> That extraordinary production of Sir Roger's pen threw the fleet into the utmost consternation and astonishment. There was not a cool heart among us ... and though the situation of the ships in so large a fleet must necessarily be very different on such a day, there was not, I believe, a suspicion in the mind of any man that all had not done their duty well. The appearance of that letter had nearly broke my heart.[49]

Howe's reticence on this occasion was only one of a number of less extreme instances. There were hurt feelings after the Battle of Cape St Vincent too, but Nelson, with the help of Colonel John Drinkwater, a witness of the battle, and Captain Sir James Saumarez, made sure that his spectacular capture of two major Spanish prizes received the attention at home. Nelson's carefully orchestrated public appearances when he finally returned to England in late 1800 were designed to press home the advantage.[50] In light of Saumarez's disinterested contribution to Nelson's post Cape St Vincent campaign, it is not surprising that he deeply resented not receiving timely public credit for his role as second-in-command at the Battle of the Nile.[51] Saumarez was not named in his commanding officer's post-action dispatch, although his contribution was recognized later in Nelson's maiden speech in the House of Lords. Two years later, Captain Alexander Cochrane's resentment at Lord Keith's miserly recognition of his contribution to the Egyptian expedition helped prompt a vendetta against his commander-in-chief.[52] Collingwood was widely praised for the dignified eloquence of his dispatch after the Battle of Trafalgar, but his peroration on Nelson's greatness did not comfort a captain whom he had failed to name in his second and fuller dispatch. A few years later, Captain Sir Richard Keats's warm relationship with Saumarez was disturbed momentarily by what he saw as his commander-in-chief's failure to report adequately on his role in an attack on the Russia fleet in the Baltic.[53] Resentment against those who failed to give their subordinates due recognition might linger for decades. In 1826 Vice Admiral Charles Stirling continued to dwell on Saumarez's failure to mention his role in the action off Algerciras in 1801 and Sir Robert Calder's neglect of his contribution to that off Cape Finistere in 1805.[54]

Officers looked closely at how their contributions were reported in official dispatches because merit had to be brought to the attention of those with the power to reward superior performance and the wider circle that influenced them. Merit and interest overlapped when the meritorious built up stocks of professional support reflecting senior officers' and officials' personal admiration and appreciation of an officer's future value to them and the service. Nelson was a strong backer of Collingwood, Murray and Keats, and Saumarez lent his support to Keats and to Byam Martin when he commanded in the Baltic. St Vincent's professional interest assisted all these flag officers. He also played a key role in Thomas Troubridge's career. Troubridge's forceful and effective commanding style and his commitment to radical reform of naval dockyards no doubt appealed to St Vincent. After the Battle of the Nile Troubridge's role in warning off other ships and saving his own after it was grounded was presented as a triumph surpassing those of the officers who actually fought in the action. St Vincent, driven to outrageous hyperbole in promoting his protégés' career, assured Lord Spencer that Troubridge was 'the greatest man in his walk that the English navy ever produced'.[55]

Sea officers were often highly critical of one another but their inclination to cast a scathing eye over the failings of weaker brethren was matched by a willingness to openly and pointedly praise those they thought worthy of it. Such professional generosity reflected favourably on the character and judgement of those who demonstrated it, and gave them a role in a rising officer's career that might deepen their interest. In late August 1795, for example, Admiral Duncan praised acting Lieutenant James Oswald's role in capturing two French national brigs. He repeated these comments in a later letter and placed subtle pressure on the Admiralty by reporting widespread admiration of Oswald's performance: 'I cannot sufficiently express my satisfaction of Mr Oswald's conduct ... which was noticed by all the Squadron, & in my opinion merits every Promotion their Lordships may please to bestow on him.'[56] Their lordships responded immediately, confirming Oswald's appointment as commander two days later and positioning him for promotion to post captain before the century closed. Duncan's professional generosity embraced the achievements of fellow admirals as well as junior officers. On the anniversary of Camperdown, Lady Spencer praised him warmly for his enthusiastic recognition of Nelson's victory in Aboukir Bay: 'You are my great Hero, and what say you to my little hero? ... it is beyond expression animating to hear the applause of a great & splendid deed given by one whose own illustrious life exhibits an equally glorious one.'[57]

Since professional interest depended on merit being recognized and promoted, chance might play an important role in an officer's advancement. The pre-war career of a now obscure Irish officer, Vice Admiral Moriarty, is a case in point. Sylverius Moriarty, born in 1735 in County Kerry, was destined originally for the priesthood. He studied under the Jesuits at St Omer, but having decided not to enter the church, set out for home in 1756 in a French ship. When a warship commanded by Captain Peter Parker captured this vessel, Moriarty and the other passengers were taken prisoner. Parker, who was Anglo-Irish, recognized Moriarty among the captives, and, mindful of his superior education, employed him as a tutor and music master to his family in Portsmouth. He subsequently joined the Navy, subscribed to the Thirty Nine Articles of the Church of England and was commissioned lieutenant in 1775 at the relatively advanced age of forty. Thereafter the Parker connection (he became a rear admiral in 1777), reinforced by Lord Howe's attention, and underwritten by distinguished service at the taking of Quebec and in the American War, secured Moriarty's promotion to master and commander in November 1780 and to post captain six months later. Having gained this critical step by the age of 46, he was able to work his way up the captains' list during the peace while holding shore-based appointments in Ireland. As a result, Moriarty was well positioned to benefit from the numerous flag promotions that occurred during the 1790s. Since he had commanded a ship of the line in the American War, had a clean record (he was exonerated by a court martial on the loss of *Ramilles* in exceptionally severe weather in 1782) and demonstrated a willingness to serve, there were no impediments to flag promotion in 1801. Moriarty died a vice admiral in 1809, having enjoyed a career in which a happy coincidence of ability, augmented by superior education and fortunate timing, overcame the disadvantages of limited means, obscurity and a very late start.[58]

When claims of merit were part of an overt bid for favour, they were frequently advanced to support cases that rested to some degree on interest. St Vincent's recommendations to Lord Spencer often included a reference to the capabilities of the officers concerned as well as to their connections, and as first lord he drew merit to the attention of admirals when he recommended worthy candidates for their protection. For example, writing to Lord Keith in the Mediterranean command, the first lord reminded him of the double claims of Admiral Sir Thomas Pasley's nephew: 'very deserving of the rank of post-captain, and everything is due to the uncle'.[59] The same point might be made when the relationship between a patron and client was very close. Thus when Sir Edward Pellew recommended his son's promotion to Rear Admiral Markham at the Admiralty Board, he claimed without a hint of embarrassment that he was 'uncommonly well-informed and capable'.[60] A little later Rear Admiral Philip d'Auverque, Prince D'Bouillon, covered a range of bases when appealing with Gallic insouciance on his brother's behalf: 'I feel a sort of Claim from my own great length of services & those of every individual of our family, the loss of my property by the spoliation of the rapacious Napoleon in France, but much more as an Act of Liberal Justice, to the personal merits of an Officer, whose further Services I know it will emulate.'[61]

William Waldegrave (Lord Radstock) worked his considerable interest to advance both his career and that of his son George. Waldegrave sought to impress on his son the importance of acquiring a deserved reputation for conduct that advanced his professional standing. He warned him that it was particularly important to avoid giving other members of the service the impression that he was being promoted only because his father was an admiral. He told George that his 'first ambition after that of meriting the esteem of the World must be that of shining in your profession'.[62]

Flag officers with strong interest were able to advance the claims of worthy officers whose careers demonstrated a distinct lack of it. In early October 1797 Duncan appealed to Spencer on behalf of one such officer: 'I hope I shall not be thought importunate in begging the rank of Commander for Lieutenant Cleland, my own First, who is an old and faithful servant, and a worthy man.'[63] John Cleland, who had been a lieutenant since 1782, was promoted almost immediately and in eighteen months was made post captain. Spencer's willingness to listen to this claim reflected his respect for Duncan's professional judgement, their warm mutual personal regard and his readiness to gratify a senior officer whose own merit had just been recognized by the offer of an Irish peerage. In early 1799 Vice Admiral Rainier approached the Board on behalf of worthy commissioned and warrant officers who had been waiting three years to have their acting appointments on the East Indian station confirmed. He justified this approach by noting that other officers had already received full commissions through 'the interest of … friends at home' and asked that he be permitted to correct what he clearly saw as an injustice by confirming the warrants and commissions of those who had been serving so long in an acting capacity.[64] In other cases, appeals to first lords' sensitivity to the claims of merit might play a role in framing an application for favour.

Thus when Duckworth recommended an officer to Spencer in early 1801 he made encouraging references to 'your Lordship's general attention to Men of Merit'.[65]

St Vincent was as alive to the claims of interest as anyone, yet when he became first lord early in 1801, he made a point of emphasizing his commitment to rewarding the meritorious.[66] On assuming office, he enunciated a policy that gave preference to unemployed captains and commanders who had been willing to serve on any station and in any capacity. Having declared proudly that he brought 'no prejudices into office, and as few partialities as any man who ever filled the post', St Vincent told Lord Duncan that 'no person existing has a claim upon me, except those which arise from meritorious service'.[67] In correspondence with Sir James Saumarez and Admiral William Dickson, St Vincent signalled his commitment to merit by announcing his intention to give priority for post captains' appointments to the officers promoted to commander after the Battle of the Nile. These men (who had been under St Vincent's ultimate command at the time) had been languishing on half pay ever since, presumably because they lacked the interest necessary to achieve the next step. St Vincent's commitment to merit gave him a degree of independence in exercising the patronage prerogatives of first lord that justified his refusal to act on some recommendations from other admirals, members of the aristocracy and even the king's sons. He told Lord Minto that a recent decision to promote two officers 'of long standing and uncommon merit' meant that his son would have to wait for his appointment to be confirmed. 'They are personally unknown to me, but the whole Board are interested in their favour from the meritorious services they have performed.' These officers may have had influential friends but the important point is that St Vincent explained his preference for them wholly in terms of their professional merits.[68]

When war broke out again in early 1803 and there was an upsurge in the demand for appointment to ships, St Vincent favoured those who had been willing to serve during the peace, and warded off claims of those who had not. As was often the case when he was evading unwelcome applications, St Vincent's language assumed a shared appreciation of the priority of the principle being evoked. Thus in response to a recommendation of Viscount Falmouth, the head of a family with strong service roots, St Vincent told him that '[a] number of officers who offered themselves for service in any clime some months ago have a just claim to an early attention, in which I am confident that Your Lordship will agree, and that those who have preferred living at their ease ashore should not take precedent of them'.[69] In demonstration of his determined impartiality, St Vincent assured a female correspondent with great suavity and gallantry that his nephew, Commander William Parker, still held the same rank as before his appointment as first lord. This was true at the time, but Parker was a post captain within six months.[70] St Vincent's preference for officers who had been prepared to take peacetime commands favoured those who were largely or wholly dependent on their pay, and for whom peacetime employment at sea, even without the prospect of prize money or glory, was preferable to subsistence on half pay ashore. Since these officers usually lacked significant private means, it was likely that their interest was limited and that career advancement would rely to a significant degree on merit.

St Vincent remained sensitive to the claims of merit when he returned for his second spell in command of the Channel Fleet in 1806–1807. As he put it in acknowledging the Admiralty Board's endorsement of one such recommendation, 'In the character of a protector of friendless merit, I thank you kindly for the promotion of Captain Langford.'[71] The triumphant flourish is indicative of the relative rarity of these cases but also demonstrates the exemplary value St Vincent placed upon them. Recommendations framed solely in terms of emphatic professional approbation were not confined to commissioned officers. During his last appointment St Vincent described a 'master' as 'by far the ablest seaman and navigator I have ever met with in that character, and a perfect gentleman', and a master shipwright as endowed with 'powerful ability, integrity & manhood.'[72]

When Sir Alexander Cochrane commanded the Leeward Islands station he drew Lord Barham's attention to St Vincent's failure to reward those (including himself) who had served with distinction on the Egyptian expedition of 1800. Given St Vincent's and Barham's antagonism, this comment was well designed to attract the latter's favourable attention now that he was in the ascendant. Cochrane brought this matter forward so as to give Barham the opportunity to correct his predecessor's injustice towards a meritorious commander by confirming his appointment as a post captain. The officer concerned was John Morrison. He had been a commander since 1797 after serving seven years as a lieutenant, and appears to have had only his talents to recommend him. Cochrane praised his service in defending Diamond Rock in June 1805 and in a subsequent letter to Lord Barham stressed that it was from 'his merit alone that I feel interested in Captain Morrison's favor – he is no follower of mine, nor did I know him until we met upon service.'[73] Cochrane's appeal was successful and Morrison's post rank was confirmed in March 1806.

For those with a personal commitment to merit-based promotions, the overbearing exercise of interest might be a source of private embarrassment. In February 1793 at the very beginning of the Revolutionary Wars, Thomas Byam Martin, then a lieutenant with only three years of peacetime service as a commissioned officer, played a significant role in *Juno*'s capture of the French armed ship *L'Entreprenant*. Even before news of this action reached England, however, his father had taken steps to secure his promotion.

> On arriving at Spithead I had the happiness to learn by a letter from my father, who then held the office of comptroller of the navy, that an arrangement was under consideration for promoting me to the rank of commander, not on account of the capture of the Enterprise, or any other account than the good name, interest and services of my father.

Martin privately resolved to strive especially hard to vindicate 'such an early advancement.'[74] If Martin was a little embarrassed by the exercise of interest on this occasion, others with less self-confidence might be positively alarmed by the responsibility thrust on them. When an inexperienced midshipman in the Collingwood's Mediterranean Fleet was told his friends in England had secured his promotion, he was 'quite shocked at the idea of his being a Lieut … he did not feel fit for it.'[75]

Collingwood was attentive to the representation of his family and friends but also alive to the risk posed by the powerful pull of interest. Early in his career he had noted its disruptive effect on discipline when interest was invoked to move officers from ship to ship in order to obtain more promising berths.[76] Later, Collingwood agonized over the advancement of a young man recommended by his old patron Admiral Roddam. He was mortified to have his misgivings confirmed: 'My conscience reproved me when I promoted him, which I made two or three efforts to do before I could bring myself to do it ... and now Capt. Lechmere tells me he is so entirely useless that he is afraid he must try him by court martial to get rid of him.' The historian Michael Lewis made much of Collingwood's knowledge of irregularities in this officer's service record and the fact that he finally promoted him. But if Collingwood's judgement on this occasion was swayed by his attachment to the venerable Northumbrian, he did not repeat the mistake. Roddam's protégé had to wait until long after Collingwood's death before he made the step from lieutenant to commander.[77] By the end of his career, Collingwood thought he had acquired an eccentric reputation for giving precedence to merit. He told his sister-in-law that he was 'reckoned rather queer in the promotion of young men. I advance a great many who have not a friend to speak for them, while those I respect most in the world sometimes plead in vain'.[78]

Saumarez followed St Vincent's and Collingwood's practice of keeping a weather-eye out for officers whose careers were built largely on meritorious performance. Two recommendations that Charles Yorke approved in mid-1810 seem to have rested on that basis.[79] The correspondence is silent on interest or powerful friends, other than Saumarez himself, and the career trajectories of both Commanders White and Ross suggest that any interest at their disposal had never been significant. Thomas White served eight years as a lieutenant and twelve as a commander; Daniel Ross was a lieutenant for eleven years before being promoted commander and served a further six years before achieving post rank. Two years after these officers were promoted, Saumarez endorsed Rear Admiral Martin's appointment of an acting post captain on the grounds of merit. He hoped Lord Melville would confirm the appointment, even though the man concerned was not at the top of the first lord's list.[80] A few years later Melville received a similar appeal from Sir Edward Pellew, now Lord Exmouth. He had unashamedly promoted the interests of his son but was also prepared to expend interest on those he deemed professionally worthy. Exmouth asked Melville to assign two ships to his station so he could give his protection to their commanding officers, 'having no other Friends, both good officers'.[81]

If merit sometimes served as an unalloyed ground for favourable attention from an admiral at sea, or on the Board, its clear absence might inhibit promotion or appointment. As first lord, St Vincent was in a position to actively prevent or delay promotions and appointments of those who were professionally inferior to other contenders. He was not shy in exercising this prerogative and in making his reasons clear. Thus he told a correspondent that while the Earl of Kingston's son was 'brave and enterprising ... like the rest of the Aristocracy, thinks he has *from that* circumstance a right to promotion in prejudice to men of better services and superior merit, which I will never submit to'.[82] He held the same line when rejecting an appeal from a well-regarded senior captain. Making a bow to the claims of 'sons of my brother officers' he nevertheless insisted that 'it cannot be expected that I should attempt to break through a system to serve them at the expense of a very large number of meritorious officers who have highly distinguished themselves during the late War'.[83]

In these cases, St Vincent calibrated merit to prioritize claims for advancement and to offset influence derived from patronage or professional interest. Where he thought candidates were incompetent he dismissed their claims out of hand. He did not scruple to remind the Duke of Clarence of the professional failings of one of his nominees and was adamant in refusing the Duke of Kent's recommendation for a civil office in the Navy: '[I]t was not a seemly thing to place a gentleman who has contrived to get rid of a handsome fortune and who, it may reasonably by supposed, is not a man of business, to execute the duties of the office, with advantage to the public'.[84] In his last command he warned the first lord against an appointment arising from family interest on the grounds that the officer in question was the 'merest sailor in the Service'.[85]

Conclusion

The advantages enjoyed by admirals' followers and sons of the service meant that they had enhanced opportunities for employment in positions where their merits could be recognized and brought to the attention of others. The sons and nephews of officers also enjoyed the advantage of being brought up in the service by fathers, uncles or their friends who could superintend their professional education and manage their early careers. The various aspects of service interest were mutually reinforcing, and in the context of the war time, the requirements of the service tended to reinforce the professional commitments and personal interests of flag officers. St Vincent was characteristically emphatic in endorsing that commitment, and it was consistent with his reformist zeal, with his strong reservations about the competence of post captains and concern at the thin field of viable candidates for major flag commands. As we have seen, a range of his younger colleagues also regarded merit as sufficient grounds for favourable attention. Even when they advanced the careers of those whose claims were supported by powerful messages conveyed through the patronage network, they often made reference to how deserving their clients were. Lord Spencer sometimes made reference to the worthiness of those for whom he wished to find appointments but neither he nor his civilian successors matched St Vincent's declarations about the claims of merit.[86] Their approach points to the intractable presence of the political, social and familial relationships of the patronage network in late Georgian Britain and the need for participants in it to take account of them. Even in St Vincent's case, however, the practical and ideological attractions of meritocracy within the Service were moderated by considerations that flowed from the network of patronage relationships in which it was located. We have seen in an earlier chapter that he was an unabashed supporter of members of his own family, and continued to respond positively to the appeals of well-placed friends of aspirants for promotion. Sir John Duckworth does not seem to have been far from the mark when he told St Vincent that he realized he had a 'predisposition to award merit whenever consistent with your engagements'.[87] The good of the service was far more sharply delineated in war than in peace, but a commitment to it did not obviate the need to balance merit with other considerations. Flag officers had constantly to determine when the claims of merit should override the political, familial and personal obligations that clung to those who held high office. Even meritorious conduct in battle needed to attract the receptive notice of a patron and decision-maker and this could not be taken for granted. When Captain Byam Martin confidently proposed one of his officers for promotion, St Vincent challenged his presumption and was met with a riposte worthy of himself. Martin told him that he was 'not aware of the impropriety of addressing the First Lord … in behalf of a deserving officer'.[88]

Admirals' Ambitions: Promotion and Employment

I certainly feel my own consequence ... and I may without vanity say, there is no one above me so capable of serving as myself.
　　　　　　　—Vice Admiral Sir Hyde Parker to the first lord of the Admiralty seeking
　　　　　　　to succeed St Vincent in the Channel command[1]

Promotion to flag rank was heavily influenced by seniority and having achieved this status admirals advanced through the ranks as a matter of course when general promotions took place. Their employment on active service, however, depended on an appointment authorized by the Admiralty Board, but in practice resulting from a decision by the first lord made in consultation with the prime minister and the king. Since the numbers of those on the admirals' list heavily outweighed the number of active service appointments, competition for them was intense. As a result, questions of timing, the varying weight of interest and perceptions of professional capacity and reputation meant that the services of a relatively restrictive cadre of admirals were in strong demand and a significant numbers of flag officers never held active service appointments, or enjoyed only fleeting periods of employment.

This chapter examines the system of flag promotion in the late Georgian navy, its outcomes over the course of the war years and how captains who were passed over responded to this blow to their lifelong ambitions. It then considers competition for flag appointments and the Admiralty Board's responses to bids for employment. It concludes by contrasting the careers of flag officers who dominated the major commands over the course of the wars with those of two officers who were regularly employed but whose ambitions for prime appointments were largely frustrated.

Flag promotions

When the Board had the option of diversion to the 'Yellow Squadron', or consigning lacklustre admirals to permanent unemployment, questions of competence rarely played a decisive punitive role in flag promotions. Indeed, in some circumstances, the advancement of undistinguished senior captains might be seen as a benefit to the Service. While commanding the Mediterranean Fleet, for example, St Vincent welcomed a recent flag promotion because it removed ineffectual (and presumably well-connected) senior captains from their commands. He told his sister that he looked forward to ongoing improvements in the discipline, efficiency and resilience of the fleet 'now we have, by the late promotion, got rid of a great deal of Trash'.[2]

Although most officers were keen to avoid terminating their careers in the Yellow Squadron, appointment as a superannuated rear admiral was an object of ambition to a few aged, and often infirm, officers. The rate of pay – 17sh 6d *per diem* until 1803 and £1 2sh 6d thereafter – was markedly superior to the 10sh paid to superannuated captains. Moreover, the title 'admiral' presumably had some cachet among the uninitiated.[3] Rather than initiating superannuated rear admirals' appointments, the Board passed some officers over for promotion to rear admiral and then considered appeals on a case-by-case basis. Following a large flag promotion in 1793, the first since 1790, the Board made it clear that appointment as a superannuated rear admiral was not an entitlement. In March 1793 three petitions for superannuated rear admirals' commissions were declined because the officers concerned had not served in the last war.[4] Subsequent petitioners were more fortunate. Captain Duddington appealed successfully for a place in the Yellow Squadron following the general promotion in late 1794, as did seven captains who were initially passed over in the promotion of early January 1799. One of these officers, Captain David Graves, wrote a long, anguished letter to the Board listing his service and saying how devastated he felt when 'your Lordships' protection was withdrawn from me'. Graves assured the Board that he had never dabbled in politics and feared he had been 'secretly undone' by his enemies.[5] These anxieties proved unfounded and Graves joined the ranks of superannuated rear admirals. The test applied in these cases was whether an officer had commanded a post ship in the last war and was 'free of stigma'. When St Vincent was first lord, he also considered the 'professional character' of those wishing to be made superannuated rear admirals. An Order in Council of 19 December 1804 added another eligibility condition: only those who had sought employment would be eligible for superannuation as a rear admiral. During the Napoleonic War eligibility for promotion to rear admiral on the active list depended on having commanded a ship-of-the-line since the outbreak of war in 1803.[6] Captain Edward Griffith told Thomas Byam Martin that he was keen to remain afloat to avoid the risk of superannuation but this was a strategy to cope with possible changes to the rules, rather than a reflection of prevailing practice.[7]

The big promotion that took place in June 1814 produced a flurry of appeals from disappointed post captains. Captain Simon Miller, a prisoner in France since the beginning of the Napoleonic War, was placed on the superannuated captains' list on his release. When he sought promotion to rear admiral of the blue and cited precedents from the army, the Admiralty denied that these were relevant and refused to promote him. It did, however, grant his subsequent appeal for a superannuated rear admiral's commission.[8] John Monkton provided a list of his service and a record of his attempts to secure employment as a post captain, in the hope that he would be promoted to the active list. Since, however, he had not commanded in the current war he was told that he 'cannot by law' be promoted to the active list. His requests for employment, and the fact that he had commanded at sea from 1799 to 1801, meant, however, that his appeal to be made a superannuated rear admiral succeeded.[9] Captain Alexander Wilson wrote from Wexford applying for this position 'however painful it may be to my feelings to give up my claim to promotion which it has ever been my study to deserve'. Wilson, a post captain on the Egyptian expedition of 1800–1801, had not applied for a ship after 1805 because he was employed in the Sea Fencibles in Ireland. The Board's decision was recorded with a magnanimous flourish: '*Let him have the Yellow Flag*.'[10] By mid-August 1814 nine recently passed-over officers had secured commissions as superannuated rear admirals.[11]

Although eligible senior captains had nothing to do but wait their turn to become rear admirals, some particularly ambitious officers canvassed for promotion when they approached the top of the post captains' list. In early April 1794, for example, the future Lord Keith asked to be made a flag officer following his distinguished service in Lord Hood's ultimately unsuccessful Toulon expedition. The king was consulted and Keith was duly promoted on the twelfth of that month at the bottom of the list of rear admirals of the Blue. In November 1795 when Admiral Hotham was commanding the Mediterranean Fleet, Nelson wrote directly to Lord Spencer seeking appointment as a commodore in recognition of his command of a small squadron in Valdo Bay. The first lord regretted that he was not able to 'gratify' Nelson's wishes because his service was likely to be short-lived and there were already a large number of flag officers on the Mediterranean station.[12] Nelson kept Spencer informed of his achievements and when Sir John Jervis took over the Mediterranean command, recruited him to his cause. Jervis told Spencer that Nelson was 'very ambitious' to be promoted to flag rank even though he would forego his pay as a colonel of Marines. Spencer would not consider another promotion in 1796 but he endorsed Jervis's requests to appoint Nelson as commodore with a captain under him.[13] He was appointed rear admiral in the regular promotion of late February 1797. Sir James Saumarez made his ambitions for promotion to flag rank known to his commander-in-chief and was promoted rear admiral at the foot of the list in early 1801. In this promotion, William Waldegrave became admiral of the Blue, a promotion that he had sought at the end of November. Although he had not made a mark in the military aspects of his service as governor and naval commander at Newfoundland, Waldegrave's father was an earl and his wife a niece of the king. This combination of attributes was enough to secure promotion as the last of the new admirals of the blue.[14] However, while some officers and their patrons canvassed the Board, many officers played the essentially passive role taken by Rear Admiral George Murray in late 1806. Murray told his friend Rear Admiral John Markham that 'as some old admirals have lately dropped off, I hope we will come in for vice in the next promotion'.[15]

The last place in a promotion often signalled the Board's particular interest in that officer's elevation. Because the promotion of eligible post captains was on the basis of seniority, at least some of those higher up the list and hence in range for promotion came into the flag ranks on a rising tide of Admiralty favour generated by a more illustrious colleague below them. A particularly marked example of this process occurred in October 1808. Lord Mulgrave, the first lord, told Admiral Lord Gambier that there was to be a limited promotion to rear admiral of the Blue to recognize Captains Sir Richard Keats's and Sir Samuel Hood's roles at the second Battle of Copenhagen. In order to achieve this objective, however, Mulgrave had to promote seven other officers. Keats, the last promoted, was two places below Hood, whose distinction was buried in an otherwise undistinguished list.[16]

Interest (understood broadly to include support based on professional friendship and esteem) influenced the timing of promotion to flag rank and the speed of advancement through the ranks. It is significant that almost all of those who were the last person promoted to each of the flag ranks in the years 1793–1815 were important names, well-connected, well respected, holding major commands or the most prestigious roles as subordinate flag officers. Gardner, Keith, Waldegrave, Cotton, Warren, Saumarez, Keats and Pellew all appeared at the foot of the lists of those promoted rear admiral of the Blue, with Gardner, Waldegrave, Seymour, Nelson, Calder, Markham and Keats occupying this position in promotions to vice admiral of the Blue. Lord Hood, Duncan, Gardner, Keith, Waldegrave, Cotton and Warren were last named in cohorts promoted to admiral of the Blue.

The requirements for recent service at sea brought patronage to bear indirectly on flag promotions. Many officers with only limited interest struggled to secure post commands and since this prevented them meeting the eligibility criteria for promotion to the active list it played an indirect role in condemning them to the Yellow Squadron.[17] The number of superannuated rear admirals was relatively small in most wartime promotions, as were the portions of those passed over entirely. There were, however, exceptions. In the three promotions of 1794 approximately 35 per cent in the promotion range were passed over and in 1804, 30 per cent suffered this fate. A further 15 per cent were consigned to the Yellow Squadron. By contrast only 10 per cent of post captains with the appropriate seniority failed to be promoted to the active list in 1797, 1809 and 1812. In 1799, 20 per cent of those within the range ended their careers as superannuated rear admirals and in 1805 the figure dropped to a wartime low of less than 5 per cent.

While interest seemed to have a direct positive role in the timing of flag promotions, and an indirect punitive one in relation to service-related eligibility rules, the absence of interest was not enough on its own to frustrate post captains' flag ambitions. Similarly, as long as captains avoided unfavourable court martial verdicts, professional competence played no direct role in promotions to, or progression through, flag ranks. Captain Wilkins, who was otherwise eligible for flag rank, was passed over entirely in the 1814 promotion following a court martial for showing contempt to Vice Admiral Wells at Sheerness in March 1809. He appealed to the Board with Wells's support and was given a commission in the Yellow Squadron.[18] By contrast, a notoriously incompetent officer such as Collingwood's bête noire Captain Philip Stephens was promoted commander and post captain in the first half-year of the war and his interest secured him commands at sea. These appointments exposed his alarming inadequacies as a seaman and disciplinarian but they meant he satisfied the eligibility criteria. Stephens was promoted rear admiral of the Blue in 1813 and died an admiral of the Red.[19]

Occasionally, when a promotion was in the offing, senior captains were asked if they wished to be included in it. In July 1810 Charles Yorke put this question to Captain Sir Robert Barlow, who had a senior position in the civil administration of Chatham

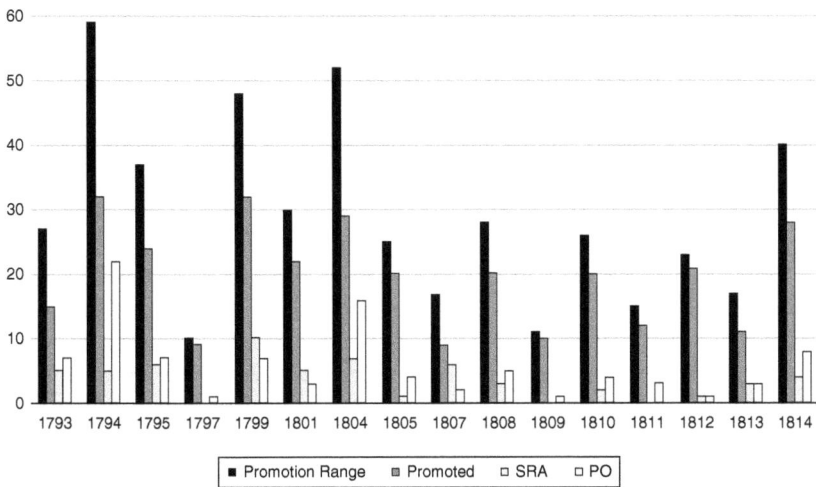

Figure 9.1 Flag promotion outcomes, 1793–1814.

Notes: Promotion range: indicates the seniority of the most junior post captain promoted to flag rank in a given promotion. Promoted: officers gaining flag rank in a given promotion. SRA: officers appointed superannuated rear admirals in a given promotion. PO: passed over; that is, post captains within the promotion range who are not appointed to flag rank or made superannuated rear admirals.

Sources: Compiled from: Cowles, *History*, IV, 192–5, V, 39–43; *Steel's List of the Royal Navy*, 1973–1815; Syrett and DiNardo, *Commissioned Sea Officers*. These figures combine the three promotions of 1794; the range is taken from the post captains' list prior to the first promotion in April.

Dockyard. Barlow deliberated for a few days and then, after a 'severe conflict', declined promotion because of family responsibilities. With a sick wife and five daughters to look after, he was unwilling to accept a promotion that required him to be available to serve at sea.[20] When Captain Nicholas Browne neared the top of the captains' list in 1811, Lord Mulgrave enquired whether he wanted to be made rear admiral at the next promotion, since he would have to give up his appointment overseeing the erection of new semaphore stations up through Essex to Harwich. Browne, perhaps mindful of the risk of delaying promotion, opted to become rear admiral of the Blue.[21]

If flag promotion and advancement up the list was largely a matter of routine for most senior officers, admirals still had notable ambitions open to them. Their primary objective was to secure employment since that provided opportunities for private enrichment through prize money and for establishing claims to royal honours and pensions through distinguished service. The big prizes were commands-in-chief (particularly those on strategically significant and potentially lucrative stations), followed by commands of detached squadrons (still under the commander-in-chief but with a degree of autonomy and the possibility of glory and independent notice) and then subordinate flag roles in large fleets. In their heyday the Channel and Mediterranean Fleets regularly provided employment for up to half a dozen flag officers of varying degrees of seniority and professional reputation. A similar number were employed on the North American station in 1812–15.

Competition for employment

On the eve of war in early 1793 there were 49 admirals of whom 22 were employed on active service. Flag appointments reached a peak of 37 in 1813 but by this time there were more than 200 admirals on the active list. Following the large valedictory promotion of 1814 and the end of the wars in 1815, 223 admirals nominally contended for a mere 24 appointments. As a result of these imbalances, many flag officers faced a lifetime on half pay, while others hoisted their flags only occasionally and sometimes for very brief periods. Just less than half of those who held admirals' commissions during the war years held active service appointments. Although illness, exhaustion, pique, weakening credibility, death, disablement and shifts in favour and expectations gave rise to a significant turnover in flag commands, it never kept pace with the expectations of those on half pay. For most of the period only 20–30 per cent of those on the flag list at any given time held appointments in one of the fleets or ports.[22]

The competitive environment probably strengthened Lord Spencer's resolve not to offer employment to those who had declined appointments on grounds other than ill-health. This approach discouraged flag officers from presuming to bargain with the first lord and underlined the differing obligations of superannuated flag officers and those still on the active list. Spencer invoked the principle as a pretext for not

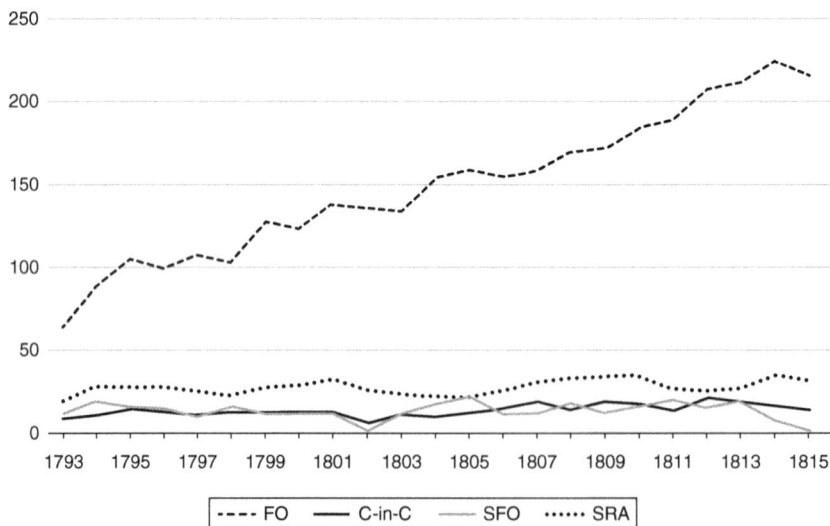

Figure 9.2 Flag officers (FOs), commanders-in-chief (C-in-C), subordinate flag officers (SFOs) and superannuated rear admirals (SRA)s (year end following each promotion), 1793–1815.

Notes: These figures combine the three promotions of 1794; the range is taken from the post captains' list prior to the first promotion in April.

Sources: Compiled from: NA ADM 12/15; Cowles, *History*, IV, 192–5, V, 39–43; *Steel's List of the Royal Navy*, 1973–1815; Syrett and DiNardo, *Commissioned Sea Officers*.

immediately re-employing Lord Keith when his very poor working relationship with Lord Bridport prompted his removal from the Channel Fleet in late 1797.[23] He made his view very clear to Rear Admiral Christian when he made difficulties about being under Cornwallis's command on the West Indian expedition of 1795–96, and when Vice Admiral Sir John Orde refused to accept a subordinate position in the Channel Fleet after his unceremonious and improper dismissal from the Mediterranean Fleet by St Vincent.[24] Sir Hyde Parker and Rear Admiral George Berkeley were unhappy in St Vincent's Channel Fleet in 1800 and were inclined to give up their posts. Parker's brother warned him against this step on the grounds that he would not be employed again, while Berkeley guarded against that risk by presenting his resignation as a consequence of ill health and concern for his wife's. He suffered from gout but his main reason for going ashore was the 'not very pleasant' situation where other flag officers were favoured with detachments that enhanced their opportunities for prizes and glory.[25] The Board agreed to relieve Berkeley but St Vincent, his commander-in-chief, scoffed at the reasons he advanced. He told Spencer that the real cause of the rear admiral's discomfort was fear of keeping station on the Black Rocks off Brest.[26]

William Waldegrave's career was probably affected by his refusal of Lord Spencer's offer of employment in 1800. Following an unhappy period of service under St Vincent in the Mediterranean Fleet, he was appointed naval commander and governor of Newfoundland in 1797. Waldegrave did not distinguish himself in the military aspects of that role and got into jurisdictional disputes with the army commander who was one of the king's sons.[27] On his return to England in 1800, however, he had sufficient residual interest to be offered command at the Cape of Good Hope. His refusal on the grounds of expense and the slim prospects of 'honour or profit' probably explains why he was not offered another command. A few days after declining the Cape Station, Waldegrave thought he had narrowly missed out on another opportunity and still had hopes that Spencer would provide for him: 'When or where I shall be employ'd, I believe Ld. S himself scarce could say, but I have no doubt of my flag flying soon somewhere or other, & for this I must wait patiently.'[28] Waldegrave hoped in vain on this occasion and following subsequent approaches to St Vincent. At one time his prospects seemed rosy – 'if dependence can be plac'd on the word of man, you will ere long hear of my flag once more hoisted' – but an expected offer to replace Rainier on the lucrative East Indian station did not materialize. Waldegrave never secured employment compatible with 'his rank in life & the service' and remained on half pay for the rest of his life.[29]

Vice Admiral Lord Northesk, the husband of St Vincent's niece, suffered a similar fate after declining the Leith command because the costs exceeded the pay and allowances, and it was a miserable place to live. Northesk was supported in these calculations by his uncle-in-law but the decision may well have counted against him in later years. His lacklustre performance at Trafalgar would not have helped.[30] When he canvassed Charles Yorke for employment in late 1810, St Vincent sent a supporting appeal that drew attention to Northesk's status as the only surviving Trafalgar flag officer. These approaches met a cool response. Northesk's aspiration was 'noted for consideration' but there was no 'immediate probability' of a vacancy. He was not employed again until 1827.[31]

Unreasonable prevarication might be as risky as outright refusal. When first lords offered flag officers commands, they did not expect to be trifled with. After rear admiral the Earl of Galloway was offered a junior flag officer's role in the North Sea in September 1810 and declined it because he had urgent personal business on his estates in Scotland, Charles Yorke was prepared initially to cut him some slack. He offered Galloway the same position in March of the following year but when he asked to delay taking up the command so as to conclude his Scottish business, Yorke cast him adrift: 'As circumstances stand at present, my arrangements will not make it necessary for me to call upon your services at Sea for some time, and you will accordingly have sufficient leisure to go into Scotland & regulate your Private Affairs without interruption.'[32] This period of leisure extended until the end of the war.

While eligibility for promotion to the flag was relatively straightforward, the grounds for making flag appointments were far more fluid and complex. Thus Lord Melville declined to give any promise when Vice Admiral Sir Alexander Cochrane enquired about being appointed to the Mediterranean command: it 'must depend on the judgment of the Admiralty at the time, & due consideration also of what may be required for other services, & of the claims & pretensions of other Officers.'[33] When applied in practice across the service, this multifactor consideration produced a pattern in which major commands were held by relatively few officers. A much wider group held minor commands and subordinate roles, sometimes of very limited duration. The consolidated record of flag appointments up to 1808 shows that nineteen flag officers held commands of less than six months and twenty-five held single commands. Some longer periods of continuous employment resulted from series of short-term commissions in the same command. For example, Vice Admiral John Holloway held a succession of twelve commissions as commander-in-chief in the Downs from May 1804 to April 1807 before being appointed to the command and governorship of Newfoundland.[34]

It is not possible to determine the true demand for flag employment since some of those who offered their services to the Board presumably did so as a matter of form rather than because they really wished to go to sea again. Even allowing for this possibility, however, and for those who relied on patrons to make the case for them, unemployed admirals' correspondence suggests that the demand was significant. When war recommenced in 1803 the Board acknowledged fifty-five offers of employment in a single week and in the course of a month more than eighty admirals petitioned St Vincent's Board for less than thirty commands and subordinate positions.[35] The most fulsome of these appeals was from Admiral Roddam, an early supporter of Collingwood. Now in his seventies, he told the Board that 'no man in His Majesty's Dominions can more earnestly hope to see Victory, or take part in supporting the Honour of the British Flag than myself'. For good measure, Roddam threw in praise of St Vincent, the 'noble head of the Board'.[36] Enthusiasm and a well-directed compliment were not enough to offset age and counterproductive seniority; Roddam remained on half pay at his estate in Northumberland. Saumarez and Collingwood were exceptions to the rule that those who rushed to offer their services offered them in vain. They were first out of the blocks in March 1803 and secured employment almost immediately. Their success, however, owed far more to their professional standing, and to a perceived dearth of able flag officers, than to quickness in staking a claim.[37]

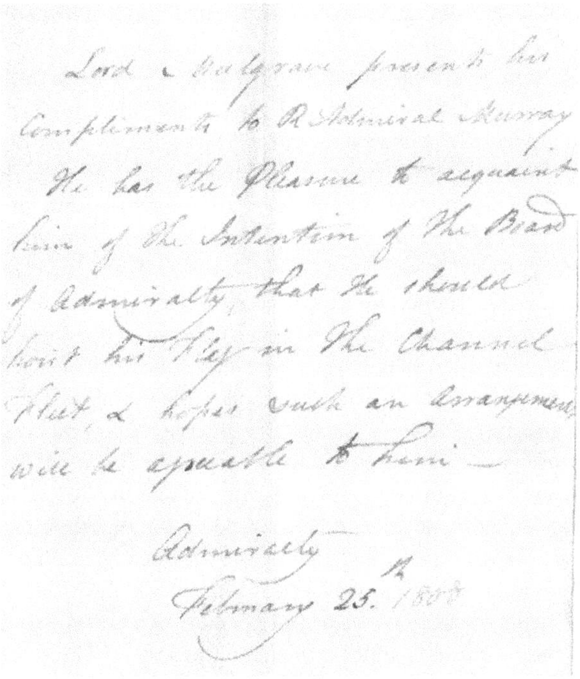

Lord Mulgrave presents his Compliments to R. Admiral Murray. He has the Pleasure to acquaint him of the Intention of the Board of Admiralty, that He should hoist his Flag in the Channel Fleet, & hopes such an Arrangement will be agreeable to him —

Admiralty
February 25th 1808

Plate 5: Many unemployed admirals dreamed of receiving an invitation to take up a post at sea. This offer from Lord Mulgrave to Vice Admiral George Murray in February 1808 was respectfully declined on the grounds of ill health.

The extensive promotion that followed Trafalgar swelled the pool of unemployed admirals by twenty. Rear Admiral William Kelly, one of the beneficiaries, combined acknowledgement of his elevation with an offer to serve 'in any part of the world'. Kelly's appeal to the Board was followed over the course of the next few months by twenty other applications, including two from Rear Admiral Edward Edwards who had also applied for employment on the outbreak of war.[38] So too had Vice Admiral Moriarty. He wrote three further letters declaring his willingness to serve, advising the Board that he was preparing to leave Kerry to come to London 'to wait upon their Lordships' and later notifying it of a change of residence.[39] The big promotion of 1810 gave rise to many letters of thanks and many offers to serve. The enthusiasm shown on this occasion, however, palled into insignificance against that prompted by the valedictory promotion of thirty-two post captains in June 1814. These men were prominent in a veritable avalanche of sixty applications at the beginning of the Hundred Days in March 1815.[40]

Some admirals made direct approaches to ministers, the first lord or a friendly naval commissioner, rather than merely signalling their willingness to serve by a formal letter to the Board. The Channel Fleet was particularly hotly contested in the Revolutionary Wars. Bridport lobbied hard to replace Howe, and St Vincent declared his hand to Keith as he was leaving the Mediterranean command in 1799. Before Bridport's command ended, his second, Vice Admiral Sir Alan Gardner, told him that he had written to the Earl of Chatham and the prime minister 'expecting their good offices' with the king.[41] As we have seen, these representations were unsuccessful.[42] Vice Admiral Berkeley was more fortunate. He used his connection with Sir Charles Pole, a professional member of the Board, and with the prime minister, Lord Grenville, to assist his manoeuvres for a position of 'due seniority'. Having secured the Halifax command, he lobbied for Grenville's support in resisting the Board's demands to leave England immediately and campaigned to enhance the status of his squadron by increasing the number of significant ships allocated to it.[43] In the late 1790s Sir Charles Pole secured his friend Vice Admiral William Young's support for a bid to succeed Waldegrave as naval commander and governor general of Newfoundland. Young, a member of the Board, told Pole that while his expression of interest had been well received by Lord Spencer, the vacancy would not occur for a few months so nothing was being promised. Spencer gave Pole an assurance of appointment after a 'satisfactory' interview a few months later. He was subsequently chosen by St Vincent to replace Nelson in the Baltic and Saumarez in the Mediterranean, and served briefly again in Newfoundland in 1802. In late 1805 Lord Barham made encouraging noises and Pole served on the Board for eight months in the following year. Towards the end of 1806, however, when he declined appointment as second-in-command in the Channel Fleet, St Vincent told the first lord that this was not a matter for regret: '[H]e lacks the firmness, and steady perseverance of an officer fit to encounter the various difficulties incident on this service.'[44] From this stage Pole's stock dropped. Numerous written and personal approaches to Lord Mulgrave over the course of 1807 and 1808 met with the standard response that 'flag arrangements' precluded favourable consideration of his requests for employment.[45] Pole was admiral of the fleet for a few months before his death in 1830 but he never served at sea after his return from Newfoundland in 1802.

Even when flag officers were exceptionally well-placed, appointments did not always run smoothly. In early September 1810 Rear Admiral Sir Samuel Hood, fourth in command in the Mediterranean Fleet under Sir Charles Cotton, told Charles Yorke that although he had never sought an appointment he now wished to be considered for a command, preferably in the East Indies. Two weeks later Hood received an offer of the Leeward Islands command (which he had held as a commodore from 1802 to 1805) and wrote to say he would accept it provided that the East Indies station was not in prospect. Hood's return from the Mediterranean was delayed while he waited for his successor to arrive on the station. In the meantime Yorke, who consulted Lady Hood and Lord Bridport, Sir Samuel's elderly cousin, thought he would decline the command. Yorke gave the appointment to Sir Francis Laforey, a close friend of his brother's, who was at this time a naval commissioner on the Board. The news of this change of tack stunned Hood. He wrote that his 'pen cannot describe the mortification and disappointment I experienced' on receiving it. Given the circumstances, Hood's remonstrance seems remarkably restrained. Yorke, however, declined to take responsibility for the debacle, telling Hood and his wife that she and the family were to blame. He undertook, however, to consider Hood for future vacancies.[46] The first lord's role in this unfortunate transaction was hindered to some degree by slow communications. He may also, however, have thought it expedient to retain an officer of Hood's superior abilities in the Mediterranean rather than send him to a less important command. When Hood took up the Jamaica command in April 1811, his stay there was very short because he soon received his first preference. The East Indian appointment proved a mixed blessing: Sir Samuel died of malaria on the station in 1814.

Yorke's courteous notifications of recall were sometimes resisted. The Prince De Bouillon reacted strongly when congratulations on promotion to vice admiral were paired with notice of his recall from the Channel Islands' command. He was 'mortified that this accession of rank should after forty years perseverance ... paralized the best prospect I ever had of attaining distinction in the Service to which those years have been devoted'. De Bouillon, who had been involved in espionage earlier in his career, told the first lord that he expected the Channel Islands to be 'insulted by the Enemy this year' and there was a grave risk in removing an officer of his experience. As he had made little prize money and his property was tied up on the continent and employment was particularly important, he asked to be considered for a new appointment appropriate to his rank. It is unclear whether the argument from strategy or need carried most weight, but shortly after receiving De Bouillon's appeal Yorke wrote to tell him that 'upon further consideration' the Board had 'superseded' its 'intention of relieving you from your Command for the Present'.[47]

Seniority played a variable and sometimes complex role in making flag appointments because first lords had to try to work round the constraints produced by the clumsy system of flag promotions.[48] Seniority might be seen as a proxy for experience but it provided no guarantee of either competence or *relevant* experience. Because the service was so hierarchical and competitive, however, flag officers perceived their seniority as a signifier of dignity and professional standing. In practice, however, seniority was a card to play rather than a token of fixed value. Spencer appointed Rear Admiral Christian to the West Indian expedition of 1795–96 because his recent experience on the Transport Board would prove useful when working with the army in addressing its logistical challenges. Significantly, the first lord resisted suggestions that Christian should command the naval forces in the West Indies because he had only very recently been promoted to flag rank and would be seen as too junior for the role.[49] When Nelson was appointed to command a detached squadron in the Mediterranean in 1798, however, Spencer ignored the strident claims of more senior officers.[50]

Despite their frequent offers to serve, the prospects of the long-term unemployed grew dimmer as time wore on. They lacked opportunities to demonstrate their capacities for flag command and were considered too senior for minor roles. Once Moriarty became a vice admiral in 1805 his appeals were almost bound to fall on deaf ears. The same was true of another frequent supplicant, Peter Aplin. He had never been employed as a flag officer so his offer to serve in late 1812 when he was an Admiral of the Blue was fruitless.[51] Even officers who had secured significant employment faced more limited options when they became more senior. Thus the poor fit between Lord Radstock's ambitions and his prospects of employment was aggravated by his rise through the flag ranks. He may just have been employable as a rear or vice admiral, but not when he became an admiral of the Blue. Sir Charles Cotton was clearly aware of the adverse implications of promotion. When he became a vice admiral of the Red, Cotton told his wife that the next promotion step (to admiral of the Blue) would mean giving up his subordinate role in the Channel Fleet because he would be too senior to continue in it. Sir Alexander Cochrane suffered this fate when the squadron he commanded in the West Indies was significantly reduced in size in 1812.[52] From 1805 he enjoyed a long period commanding the Leeward Islands and then at Jamaica, during which he had played an important role as Duckworth's second at the Battle of San Domingo and worked effectively with the army to take a number of enemy colonies, including the French possessions of Martinique and Guadeloupe. But while Cochrane's situation seemed settled, it was not without its risks. His son claimed that his interest in London was dwindling with his prolonged, health-sapping absence, and his rising seniority meant his options would soon be limited to hotly contested plum jobs such as the Channel command: 'You are now completely banished from the World, your relations, and from those who might be inclined to serve you and in a short time will be almost unheard and forgot.'[53] The warning was prescient. Within a year Cochrane faced the unwelcome prospect of prolonged unemployment because a vice admiral was too senior to command what had now become a secondary station.[54]

The anointed: Howe, Hood, Bridport, St Vincent, Duncan, Cornwallis, Keith, Nelson, Collingwood, Cotton and Pellew

Although there was a numerical oversupply of flag officers during the war years, successive first lords believed their options were worryingly limited. This perception, due in part to the fact that those appointed to the active list remained on it regardless of age, fitness and motivation, was also a consequence of the operation of the system of flag promotion. In early 1799, William Young mourned the death of a flag officer who he compared most favourably with those who avoided their duty or exercised it 'most carelessly'.[55] During the next war St Vincent, having once treated flag ranks as a dumping ground for inadequate post captains, now urged Thomas Grenville to renew the 'barren list of admirals' by making a flag promotion that would embrace admirable captains, 'great seamen abounding in resources who disdain putting a farthing in their pockets which does not justly belong to them'.[56] Grenville fretfully asked his brother how he could 'weed the list of Admirals. It is a list of incurables'.[57] Successive promotions did not meet the need. Four years later Lord Mulgrave complained that there were no officers of Collingwood's 'long experience and peculiar qualification' to succeed him in the Mediterranean. By the time the second Lord Melville became first lord in the closing years of the war, it was difficult to find strong candidates to fill the professional places on the Board.[58]

As a result of the first lords' perceived lack of options, the major commands of the war years were filled by a very limited number of men belonging to three generations of flag officers. The first cohort (represented here by Howe, Hood and Bridport) was made up of men who were senior figures when the war began and had held major commands in earlier wars. They were followed by St Vincent, Duncan, Cornwallis and Keith who were already flag officers in 1793 or attained that rank within a year or so of the outbreak of the war. These men passed the baton to a third generation whose flag appointments predated Trafalgar. This group included Nelson, Collingwood, Cotton, Warren, Cochrane and Pellew. All these men owed their careers to judgements about their professional skills but questions of experience, interest and physical robustness also played a role in gaining them prestigious and rewarding appointments that marked the pinnacle of achievement in the service.

While questions of overall competence, experience and psychological fortitude were critical for flag officers holding major commands, first lords' choices were often influenced by interest and the political needs of the moment. At the very beginning of the first war the two major commands went to Lords Howe and Hood. These men, very well-connected veterans, had distinguished themselves in earlier wars and had extensive experience in naval administration. The king and the Ministry thought it so essential to secure Lord Howe's services as commander of the Channel Fleet that it was agreed he could exercise this role from onshore in the winter months if his health made it necessary. Even when age and infirmity proved intractable, Howe experienced some difficulty in being released from this command.[59] Although there was some criticism of Hood's handling of the evacuation of Toulon, his command in the Mediterranean continued until 1795, when it was terminated for political and disciplinary reasons, not because of poor performance at sea, or his advanced age. Howe led the fleet to a significant victory on 1 June 1794 but spent increasing periods ashore as his health deteriorated. From 1795 his second-in-command Lord Bridport often deputized for him and finally took over the chief role in the spring of 1797. Bridport, another veteran of earlier wars, was also in indifferent health. In 1799 he gave way in the Channel command to the younger and more vigorous Earl St Vincent, the most senior of the second generation of leading wartime commanders.

Despite St Vincent's penchant for rough handling subordinates and a disinclination to act quietly under the authority of the Admiralty Board, he was considered virtually indispensable for more than a decade. At the very beginning of the war an appreciation of his professional worth helped overcome party feeling, a close association with the unpopular marquis of Lansdowne, and a reputation for partiality in the disposal of patronage.[60] As Sir John Jervis, he collaborated with General Sir Charles Grey in joint-service attacks on France's West Indian possessions but then ran into squalls of political criticism for his role in the rapacious (some would say, almost piratical) seizure of the property of French non-combatants.[61] Nevertheless, in early 1795 Sir John had only to give the smallest hint to Henry Dundas, the secretary of state for war, who immediately passed it on to Lord Spencer: 'Two words dropped from Sir John Jervis this day at dinner … satisfies me that, if you wish it, the service of the Cape would be his wish.' At the urging of Lord Hugh Seymour, however, Spencer appointed St Vincent to the far more important Mediterranean command. In pressing this case, Seymour, a professional member of the Board, stressed the need to recognize highly superior talent, and encouraged Spencer to discount the political hostility of many members of the Ministry.[62] St Vincent withdrew from the Mediterranean command in 1799, exhausted and in poor health. Even then, however, he was looking ahead with an eye for the biggest prize of all and shared his ambitions with Lord Keith: 'His object is the Channel Fleet. He told me I was so like him I was the only man in England fit for that command.'[63] After a period of recuperation in England St Vincent was, on his own (perhaps not entirely reliable) account, dragged from his sickbed to replace Lord Bridport.[64] Following his term as first lord, St Vincent rejected an offer from Pitt's administration to return to the Channel but took up the role when Lord Grenville's Whigs came into office and served from 1806 to early 1807.[65] Like Howe and Bridport before, St Vincent was allowed to live ashore during the worst of the winter weather.

At the time St Vincent commanded in the Mediterranean, an officer of similar vintage held the important North Sea command. Adam Duncan's appointment came into prospect almost by chance, although professional reputation and family connections played a critical role in it. In May 1794 Duncan wrote to the Earl of Chatham's Board saying that he was 'ready to serve when their Lordships will honour me with their Commands'.[66] This offer, one of dozens the Board received during the course of the year, fell on deaf ears. Duncan's fortunes changed dramatically, however, when the Portland Whigs joined the Ministry in December 1794 and Earl Spencer became first lord. Reviewing the flag list with Henry Dundas in February 1795, Spencer asked why 'Keppel's Duncan' had never been 'brought forward'. Dundas, who was Duncan's wife's uncle, told Spencer that his nephew-in-law was keen to serve. That night he was appointed to command the North Sea Fleet.[67] Duncan held this position until 1800 when he thought he was getting too old for further service at sea. By that stage, he had executed a brilliant finale to his career by defeating the Dutch Fleet at Camperdown.

William Cornwallis was commanding as a commodore in the East Indies when the war began and joined the Channel Fleet in 1794 on promotion to rear admiral. Although appointed to the Leeward Islands command in early 1796 Cornwallis did not see service on that station. He resigned his command later that year after a court martial and did not seek employment during the rest of Spencer's first lordship. When St Vincent became first lord in early 1801, however, he immediately appointed Cornwallis to succeed him in the Channel Fleet. This severe judge of flag officers had long been an admirer of Cornwallis's leadership: '[T]he choice ... while it ensures the confidence of the public from the opinion universally entertained of his zeal and talents, will afford the fullest satisfaction ... of the officers now serving in the Channel Fleet.'[68] Cornwallis held the post until the peace and was reappointed just before war recommenced in 1803. His command was clouded by mounting criticism from within the Board and signs of mental instability but he retained it until 1806.[69]

While Cornwallis contended with operational, strategic and political challenges of the Channel Fleet, Keith applied his highly developed organizational and logistical skills to managing an enlarged North Sea command incorporating three previously independent stations that extended from Scotland down the North Sea to the eastern reaches of the English Channel. Keith was employed for fifteen years as a flag officer and thus had a more extensive record of active service than any of his contemporaries. He strenuously avoided party commitments during the course of the war and built strong working relationships with Henry Dundas, Lord Spencer and William Pitt; although he was a close associate of the Prince of Wales he avoided alienating the king.[70] St Vincent had been Keith's commanding officer when he was rated midshipman, and continued to treat him with complacent chauvinistic superiority: 'You will never find an officer native of that country figure in supreme command, they are only fit for drudgery, Lord Keith is by far the best I ever met with by land or by sea.'[71] Nevertheless, St Vincent served as Keith's service patron, was sometimes unstinting in his praise, and provided Admiralty-based support from 1801 to 1804.

In the mid-1790s Keith had served with distinction at the Cape and in the East Indies and played an important role responding to the fleet mutinies of 1797. Having relieved St Vincent in the Mediterranean in 1799, Keith commanded there until 1801 and led the naval side of the successful expedition to evict the French army from Egypt. As the prospect of a lasting peace faded in early 1803, he put in a bid to return to his former command, believing that his performance and experience gave him a strong claim to it. St Vincent, however, having already promised this post to Nelson, undertook to 'place' Keith in command of the North Sea Fleet when war recommenced. Perhaps thinking of the £112,000 in prize and freight money he had accumulated during his Mediterranean service, Keith was not placated by the offer of a far less lucrative posting. He was 'hurt' that St Vincent had favoured a junior officer when he was willing to serve, and had proved his worth in the post; 'however little I have merited that success ... nothing committed to my charge has ever failed in my hands, and it was from that good fortune, perhaps that I hope for a continuation of the favours I had heretofore experienced.' This claim was largely true but St Vincent may well have raised an eyebrow when Keith wrote that he hoped his services had been important to the state but that 'to my private emolument', they were 'much less than has been supposed'.[72] Although the North Sea station lacked the glamour of the Mediterranean command and offered little prospect of a fleet action or spectacular prize money, the threat of an invasion across the Channel, which was a much-feared possibility, made it of vital importance.[73] Keith went ashore in 1807 but by October 1811 he seems to have been getting restless and wrote to Charles Yorke seeking the Portsmouth command. If Keith hoped to benefit from Prince of Wales's regency, he was initially disappointed. The first lord's evasive response noted that the incumbent's term did not finish until the following January. Within a few months Keith had done much better.[74] In late February 1812 when Sir Charles Cotton died in post, he replaced him in the Channel command. This appointment provoked Vice Admiral Thomas Byam Martin to expressions of disappointed ire: 'professional employment loses all its gratification if only to be obtained by interest, or a sneaking, dirty importunity'.[75] Keith, who held the Channel command until 1814 and during the Hundred Days, was the last survivor of his cohort. By the time he finally struck his flag in 1815 Duncan was long dead and St Vincent and Cornwallis (who were both older) had been in retirement for close to a decade.

The third wartime generation were post captains in 1793 and had sufficient seniority to achieve flag rank by the close of the eighteenth century. Nelson was the most prominent member of this group and its shortest lived. He was employed for almost all of his seven-year career as a flag officer, held two of the major commands and was prominent in four of the most important fleet actions of the French Wars. St Vincent welcomed Nelson's retention on the Mediterranean station when promoted rear admiral, and revelled in his audacious bravery at the Battle of Cape St Vincent. He endorsed Spencer's decisions to place a detached squadron under Nelson's command in 1798 and to appoint him as Sir Hyde Parker's second-in-command of the North Sea Fleet in late 1800. Following the victory at Copenhagen in early 1801 and Hyde

Parker's recall, the challenge was to keep Nelson at sea. St Vincent, with a blithe disregard of accumulative injuries, told the king that Nelson was 'in the habit of complaining of ill-health'. He noted sardonically, however, that following Parker's recall, Nelson had 'received considerable benefit from the additional responsibility that has recently been thrown on him, and will … no doubt, be able to continue in the command'.[76] Nelson's North Sea command was followed by increasingly reluctant peacetime service on a specially formed Downs' Command, where St Vincent anticipated that his skill and energy would make a major contribution to advancing preparations to thwart invasion attempts from across the Channel. Even at that stage, however, the first lord had Nelson lined up for the Mediterranean Station. Although the appointment was not made formally until mid-May 1803, St Vincent advised Nelson of it in February 1803.[77]

Collingwood worried about being unemployed when he was promoted rear admiral in 1799 but was almost immediately appointed to a subordinate flag role in Keith's Mediterranean Fleet. He then joined Cornwallis in the Channel until the peace. On the renewal of war in 1803, Collingwood's sense of duty overcame his love of domesticity and he was among the first to offer his services to the Board. He was immediately appointed to serve under Cornwallis in the Channel Fleet and then joined his close friend Nelson in the Mediterranean. He served with distinction at Trafalgar, and was confirmed as Nelson's successor shortly thereafter. During the course of this command, Collingwood learned how hard it was for conscientious and highly competent officers to be relieved of their positions, even when their health required it. He died at sea on the way home in 1810 after a long struggle with his professional conscience. It was rumoured that Lord Mulgrave had delayed Collingwood's recall in order to stave off an unwelcome bid for the command from the Duke of Clarence, and some of his enemies speculated that he might face public censure for having done so.[78]

Sir Charles Cotton shared his friend Collingwood's strong sense of domestic attachment and his commitment to serve while the war lasted. He was reported to have never actively sought employment or advancement.[79] After he became a flag officer in 1799 Cotton held subordinate commands in the Mediterranean and Channel Fleets. St Vincent and Cornwallis thought highly of his capability, but he was not well regarded by Thomas Grenville, first lord from 1806 to 1807.[80] On St Vincent's recommendation, however, Grenville was prepared to offer Cotton the command at Jamaica, which he declined out of 'dread of climate'. An offer of Newfoundland was accepted but for reasons which are clear not taken up.[81] These transactions were designed to get Cotton out of the way so Saumarez could be brought in as St Vincent's second and his alleged pretensions to the Channel command squelched.[82] Cotton's career certainly flourished after Grenville left the Board. Lord Mulgrave appointed him commander-in-chief at Lisbon in 1808 and then as Collingwood's successor in the Mediterranean. A year later, when Charles Yorke (a neighbourhood friend whose family seat was a few miles from Cotton's house at Madingley) gave her husband the Channel command, he wrote a warm letter of congratulation to Lady Cotton on her husband's appointment to this 'honourable and important station'.[83] Sadly, he did not live to enjoy this honour for very long, succumbing to a stroke in late February 1812.

The flag officers discussed thus far so dominated the major commands during the French Wars that little scope was left for their contemporaries and younger colleagues to realize ambitions for sustained employment in the most prestigious posts. Lord Gardner briefly attained the Channel command but only at a time when age and the wear-and-tear of hard service had quite undermined his health. Sir John Warren was twice appointed to the North American command. Although this station assumed increased size and importance because of the conflict with the United States, the chance came in very difficult circumstances when Warren was too old and ill to benefit from it. He was succeeded by Sir Alexander Cochrane who had enjoyed a long period of command on the Leeward Islands.

Keith's return to active service at the head of the Channel Fleet in 1812 blighted the prospects of Martin and other contenders. Indeed, only one officer promoted to the flag in the Napoleonic Wars had the opportunity of a prolonged spell in a prime command. Having commanded for five years in the East Indies and far more briefly in the North Sea, Sir Edward Pellew, benefiting no doubt from the support of his patron the Duke of Northumberland, succeeded Cotton in the Mediterranean Command in 1810 and served through until the end of the war.

Thwarted ambitions: Sir John Duckworth, Sir James Saumarez and the pursuit of 'honourable' employment

Given the Board's reluctance to employ those who declined offers of employment, flag officers usually took what they were offered. Some of them, however, gave private and public voice to what they saw as unjust treatment at the hands of the Board and the 'degradation' occasioned by it. Duckworth's and Saumarez's careers are cases in point.

From the time that Commodore Duckworth commanded the naval attack on Minorca in 1798, he was rarely unemployed but neither his standing nor his interest was sufficient to secure the appointments to which he aspired. Duckworth's command at Jamaica (1801–1805) coincided with the end of the Revolutionary War and when he asked to be relieved from this expensive burden St Vincent brusquely ordered him to remain until the Board decided otherwise.[84] He was aggrieved that the timing of its decision prevented him from benefiting from Spain's entry into the war. Thinking no doubt of the vast riches Sir Hyde Parker had accumulated in the closing years of the Revolutionary War, Duckworth complained bitterly to St Vincent and Vice Admiral Sir John Colpoys on being displaced at such a time by a more junior admiral and wrote also to the secretary of the Board. Using a stock phrase in his epistolary grieving, he told William Marsden of the 'poignancy' of his feelings at the Board's 'harsh measures'.[85]

In early 1806 Duckworth's squadron pursued a French Fleet from the Mediterranean to the West Indies and subsequently defeated a formidable force of French ships-of-the-line off San Domingo. If this action had failed, or even if his squadron had not made contact with the French, Duckworth may well have had to answer to the Board for having acted without orders from Collingwood, his commander-in-chief. Duckworth was aggrieved that this action did not put him in line for a more prestigious command. A year later he wrote to the Duke of Northumberland and the Earl of Westmoreland conveying his mortification when Rear Admiral John Purvis was preferred to command a squadron off Cadiz. He also told the first lord how 'grieved, disappointed, disheartened' he was at this further injustice. A few days later, the news of Sir James Gambier's appointment to command in the Baltic compounded his acute sense of ill usage. Duckworth found temporary relief in making an intemperate protest to Lord Mulgrave but the first lord was disgusted by the communication and it did nothing to enhance his prospects.[86] In 1809 he again complained to Northumberland when Sir Richard Stratchan was appointed to command the ill-fated Scheldt expedition.[87] Since Northumberland saw these rebuffs as expressions of the animus of *his* political and personal enemies, he did not tire of what might otherwise have been a wearisome correspondence.

Duckworth was appointed to the Newfoundland Command and governorship in 1810 but continued to hanker after more active commands. In early 1811 he made a bid to succeed Cotton in the Mediterranean, telling Charles Yorke that he was prepared in the meantime to serve as second there or in the Channel. The first lord told Duckworth that his 'arrangements' for flag appointments did not allow him to take up these offers but his attempt to soften this blow by favourable reflections on Sir John's career was taken as a signal inviting further remonstrance. In a tart reply Yorke pointed out that it 'cannot be expected that these Arrangements should ever meet with general concurrence', suggesting that if he *had* appointed Duckworth to one of these positions, flag officers senior to him 'would have conceived' themselves 'aggrieved by such a determination'.[88]

For much of his career, Duckworth's frustrations were shared with Sir James Saumarez. He was appointed to the Baltic command in 1808 but up to this point had

Plate 6: Admirals Sir John Duckworth (left) and Sir James Saumarez rose to the highest rank in the service, amassed significant prize money and were awarded substantial state pensions. While their careers seemed successful, however, they struggled to attain the appointments and recognition to which they thought they were entitled.

often been painfully aggrieved when his professional expectations were not fulfilled. In common with other evangelically inclined officers, Saumarez saw recognition and advancement as extending his crusading mission within the Navy, and providing assurance of divine endorsement of his efforts.[89] As Hannah More told Gambier, 'I cannot but think that, in these days of lamentable irreligion, it augurs well for our country when rulers select good men for great public situations ... [S]o far from disqualifying persons from high and perilous offices, properly, it inspires them with great vigour and superior energy.'[90] More's advice would have struck a reassuring chord with Saumarez but as his track of worldly recognition did not run as smooth as Gambier's, his Christian fortitude was tested severely. Saumarez's ambition was displayed quite openly to his superiors and confidingly supported by his wife. She encouraged her husband's aspirations and consoled him when they were frustrated, reminding him where worldly goods and recognition stood in the hierarchy of Christian values: '[A] much richer recompense than Wealth can bestow ... awaits a conscientious discharge of the Station allotted thee by Providence.'[91]

Saumarez was prominent among Nelson's 'band of brothers' in Aboukir Bay, and served as second-in-command. In his dispatches, however, Nelson, who had earlier been told that Saumarez was very anxious to go home, treated his captains as equals and made no reference to Sir James's valiant example in fighting his own ship, or his role in leading the fleet when Nelson was wounded.[92] Saumarez resented this lack of notice deeply. Three years later, when reviewing Nelson's role at the Battle of Copenhagen, he turned the 'band of brothers' rationale against his former commander to offer a backhanded compliment on his most recent triumph. This victory placed Nelson 'in superior point of view than any of his former Actions – that of Aboukir in particular in which he had really no claim to extraordinary Merit, no more than in common with the Captains of his Squadron, altho' all the honours fell on him exclusively.'[93]

By the turn of the century Saumarez believed that his superior performance and seniority merited flag promotion and sought his commander-in-chief's support in pursuing it. St Vincent lobbied Lord Spencer and Evan Nepean on his behalf and responded to anxious queries about the timing of the next promotion.[94] Saumarez's promotion on New Year's Day 1801 was not the bitter-sweet prelude to unemployment. He was ordered to hoist his flag on *Caesar*, his late command, and enjoyed early success in his new rank. In mid-1801 he led a squadron that, after a failed attack on Spanish ships-of-the-line off Algeciras, inflicted significant damage on them as they sought to join the rest of the fleet in Cadiz. Saumarez was fêted at Gibraltar and in London, appointed a knight of the Bath and received fulsome congratulations from St Vincent, the new first lord. His wife revelled in this sign of Divine favour: 'I cannot but gratefully acknowledge the hand of Providence in a continuation of that protection he has so significantly experienced during his Life.'[95]

On this occasion, as on a number of others, however, Providence did not deliver on Saumarez's worldly expectations. The changed strategic situation prompted St Vincent to greatly increase the squadron by additions from Ireland and North America and to replace Saumarez by Vice Admiral Pole: '[W]e lament most exceedingly your place on the list of Admirals would not justify our fixing you in the chief command: knowing as I do your zeal and honourable feelings, I persuade myself you will see the propriety of this measure in the way it strikes us.'[96] Evan Nepean claimed that the increased size of the command required two flag officers and since Saumarez was at the foot of the list, that person must be senior to him.[97] Saumarez, not consoled by these explanations, fired off a sharp public letter of protest. 'Their Lordships will I trust forgive me for observing that after the signal success that attended the attack of 12th July … I cannot help feeling mortified to find myself deprived of the Command of the Squadron their Lordships had been pleased to place under my Direction.' St Vincent, not appeased by Saumarez's closing assurance that his 'utmost endeavours will be exerted for the Good of His Majesty's Service,'[98] responded in very decided terms:

> I cannot sufficiently express my surprise at the contents of your public and private letters upon the subject of Vice-Admiral Pole being sent out with the reinforcement, the more so as you were before in a much more subordinate situation than you are now placed in, being removed from fourth in command to second, and I persuade myself that you will, long before this can reach you, have seen the great impropriety of your public letter.[99]

St Vincent emphasized his displeasure by not approving Saumarez's acting appointments and referring them to the tender mercies of Lord Keith, his commander-in-chief at the time of the action. Saumarez was particularly stung when a number of his recommendations for warrant officers were set aside.[100] There was more discomfort to come. Saumarez believed that he was acting on Admiralty orders at the time of the battle and was thus entitled to all of the flag officers' prize money. Keith resisted this claim and when the matter went to court in 1804, it found in favour of him and the other flag officers of the Mediterranean Fleet. This decision cost Saumarez £5,033, exclusive of legal expenses.[101]

Six months before her husband received the first lord's painful rebuke, Martha Saumarez told him of a rumour circulating among their service friends ashore that he was to be appointed to the Mediterranean command on Lord Keith's anticipated retirement from it.[102] When Saumarez was offered a peacetime appointment to the station, however, he declined to accept it.[103] St Vincent was, in effect, inviting Saumarez to forego the comfort of living with his family, and to bear all the expense of a peacetime command with the certain prospect of being superseded on the outbreak of war. Saumarez had to wait until the peace collapsed in 1803 before he was given the momentarily important, domestically convenient but not prestigious command of the Channel Islands squadron. He stepped aside briefly from this command in 1806–1807 to serve as St Vincent's second in the Channel Fleet, returning to it when Lord Gardner took the chief command there and Saumarez faced being displaced by Duckworth. If this episode looked like a repetition of the blow Saumarez had suffered in 1801, the setback was only temporary. Having declined the East Indies command on health grounds, Saumarez accepted command of the Baltic Fleet in 1808. The strategic importance of the Baltic at this stage of the war meant that this was a major and particularly demanding command.[104] In light of Saumarez's earlier disappointment in the Mediterranean command, it is ironic that his Baltic appointment was openly resented by Duckworth on the grounds of his seniority.

Conclusion

When the Board made flag appointments, it had to consider how far the skills and temperaments of particular officers matched the distinctive requirements of the station for which they were being considered. As we have seen, the number of officers entrusted with the key commands of the Channel, Mediterranean and North Sea Fleets was relatively small, but a wider group were thought to possess the skills and fortitude required on less critical stations and to serve as subordinate flag officers across the full range of the Navy's global responsibilities.

The intensification of competition and the tendency for rewards to be accumulative – employed admirals possessed opportunities to distinguish themselves and increase their chances of other, more prestigious, appointments – produced a bifurcation of the list of flag officers. Admirals who were regularly employed, and particularly those who distinguished themselves at sea, stood apart from those who were unemployed for most, and in many cases all, of their flag careers. Although these officers' lives did not necessarily fall into the void conjured up by the bleak characterization of biographical dictionaries – 'promoted but never hoisted his flag', 'never employed again' and so on – they were undoubtedly and finally removed from the concerns, influences and hectic press of business that marked the lives of their more successful contemporaries. Moreover, since they ceased to have the power to make appointments, they were deprived of an important means of participating directly in the patronage network and in the operation of service interest.

While the challenge of wartime command in wartime set competence at a premium, interest continued to play a role in advancing flag officers' careers. St Vincent proved a lukewarm friend to Duckworth and while the Duke of Northumberland encouraged his complaints, he was more active in advancing Pellew's career. Saumarez was arguably a more distinguished captain and fleet commander than Lord Gambier but lacked access to the political connections among the Pitts that no doubt assisted Gambier to the Channel command. It is significant that Duckworth and Saumarez were always prime movers in their own cause, a sign of weakness in the patronage network. Their position contrasts with that of Sir John Orde. When St Vincent left office he rallied his forces. The admiral and his rich and well-connected half-brother Lord Bolton made 'various propositions' to the new first lord that secured his appointment to the lucrative command of a squadron operating off Cadiz in 1805.[105]

Admirals' Ambitions: Wealth and Honour

I am beyond measure grieved that such elevated minds as your Lordship and Lord Grenville's should for one moment conceive, had I only my salary to exist upon, that money could be any remuneration.
　　　　　—Vice Admiral Sir John Duckworth on hearing that he was to be offered a pension and not a peerage after his victory off San Domingo, 6 February 1806[1]

Although flag officers on active service had to contend with taxing physical and mental demands, employment opened up the prospect of significant material and honorific rewards: prize and freight money, peerages, knighthoods, pensions and sinecures. Honorific rewards were entirely discretionary but an appreciation of their exemplary value meant that in practice they were only available to flag officers who had seen extensive distinguished active service. As with flag employment, their distribution was subject to the fluid combination of superior performance, good timing, political imperatives and interest that applied to appointments. Prize and freight monies were the least affected by the full range of these considerations since they depended ultimately on having the good fortune to hold commands when freights were commissioned, treasure ships intercepted or captures made.

Prizes

Admirals were entitled to disproportionately large shares of prize and freight money. Until 1808 commanders-in-chief received an eighth of the value of prizes taken by ships under their command. In that year the share was reduced to a twelfth.[2] When one subordinate flag officer was involved, he received a third of the commander-in-chief's allocation; where there was more than one subordinate, they shared a half of his eighth or twelfth.[3] Flag officers on joint service expeditions shared booty from captured enemy territories with their army counterparts but these gains might be made at the cost of future prize revenue on their command. Sir Alexander Cochrane noted that British seizures of West Indian islands drove enemy shipping from those waters and Sir Samuel Hood made the same point following the capture of Java.[4]

Flag officers' prize income is hard to estimate. Payments could be delayed by legal disputes and were often made in instalments as vessels, cargoes, their stores and fittings were sold and disputes about entitlements settled. Records show multiple streams of settlement payments derived from captures made on various stations over many years. Wealth from prizes, freight and booty fell into three common patterns. First, there were spectacular prizes that resulted from single actions, the capture of treasure ships or from freights. Thus Lord Hood's share from the short-lived occupation of Toulon, and the capture and destruction of the French ships trapped there, was approximately £14,000. His brother Lord Bridport received £20,000 from Spanish treasure ships captured during his Channel command. Sir John Warren and seven other subordinate flag officers each received £2,500 for bullion and later payments of about the same amount for other cargo, hulls, stores and head money for prisoners.[5] St Vincent gained about £8,000 as commander-in-chief when the French Fleet was defeated in Aboukir Bay in 1798. Although Nelson received only £2,000 as a subordinate flag officer, the highly relieved directors of the East India Company made him a gratuitous payment of £10,000, which he did not have to share with his colleagues.[6] On this occasion the prize money was derived from an Admiralty estimate that took account of the complete destruction of many enemy ships. Duncan's share of Camperdown prize money was more than £18,000.[7] The Navy Board's estimate of over £320,000 as the value of captured enemy shipping after Trafalgar included payments for prizes destroyed in the storm that followed the battle. Collingwood's share of this largesse was about £40,000. He also received £3,500 for a treasure ship captured on his station. Windfalls of this kind were more a matter of luck and favourable positioning than valour, and sometimes benefitted relatively undistinguished officers. Rear Admiral John Gell, for example, who served only briefly at sea, received £18,000 for a Spanish treasure ship early in the Revolutionary War. Sir John Orde's prize revenue when he commanded off Cadiz in 1804–1805 included £10,000 from a treasure prize.[8] Orde's command had been carved out of Nelson's and the latter was understandably aggrieved that he did not share in these captures. Later, however, one of Nelson's captains captured a treasure ship that netted him a similar return as commander-in-chief.[9] There were also some spectacular one-off gains for freight payments, one of which yielded Sir Alexander Cochrane between £18,000 and £20,000 for a single shipment when he commanded on the Leeward Islands.[10]

The second major mode of prize accumulation occurred during service on notoriously 'rich' stations where many valuable prizes were available for capture. Lord Keith made £60,000 during a relatively short period of service at Cape Town and the East Indies, and Vice Admiral Peter Rainier accumulated £250,000 during his lengthy command in the latter of these stations. Keith's appetite for prize money was a subject of rueful critical comment by his colleagues, with Nelson quipping that he 'loved a little money, and a great deal much better'.[11] Although Keith is estimated to have made between a quarter and half a million pounds in prize money, he never thought himself over-rewarded and told St Vincent that the personal benefit of his service was exaggerated.[12] Rainier was far more grateful and modest. He left £25,000 to the Chancellor of the Exchequer in his will in acknowledgement of the 'generous bounty of the national establishment of the royal navy, in which I have acquired the principal part of the fortune I now have.' He noted that this fortune 'has exceeded my merits and pretensions'.[13] The East Indies also proved a lucrative hunting ground for Rear Admirals Pellew and Troubridge. Pellew made approximately £100,000 there out of a total prize income that probably exceeded £200,000. He complained that Troubridge's appointment to a command on the more lucrative eastern part of the station had cost him £53,000 by early 1807. The family loss was compounded by £23,000 that had gone to Troubridge's son and would have gone to his own.[14] Flag officers also did well on the West Indian stations. St Vincent and Hyde Parker were enriched greatly on the Leeward Islands and Jamaica commands, and during his time on the latter Sir John Duckworth added to the fortune of £75,000 he had accumulated as a subordinate flag officer in the Mediterranean.[15] Cochrane's prizes from the Leeward Islands and Jamaican commands during the Napoleonic War funded the purchase of extensive properties in Trinidad worked by slave labour.[16]

Finally, while other stations might not have provided returns that matched those of the East and the West Indies, at certain stages the accumulation of large numbers of small prizes made them profitable as well as honourable employments. For example, between August 1797 and March of the year following, and before any payments were made for captures at Camperdown, Admiral Duncan received more than £2,400 as his share of freight and prize money on the North Sea station. The bulk of this income came from a multitude of low-value vessels and cargoes. Similarly, Sir James Saumarez's captains snapped up many small prizes in the Baltic in 1807–1809, with his share amounting to approximately £20,000.[17] Warren's command of the North American station during the war of 1812 was not his most glorious moment in the service but in less than two years a steady accumulation of prizes netted close to £15,000.[18] The value of flag officers' prize money is apparent when expressed in yields in government stock and compared with the half pay they received when commissions ended. Thus Saumarez's relatively modest £20,000 produced an annual return of between £600 and £1,000 to augment half pay of £504.

Given the amounts at stake, the disrupted sequencing of communications which affected flag officers' place in command structures and the labyrinth of eighteenth-century English law, it is not surprising that there were a number of protracted and expensive disputes between flag officers over prize money. Some of these cases were resolved in favour of commanders-in-chief. Thus Sir James Saumarez went to law with Keith in an unsuccessful attempt to vindicate his claim to a commander-in-chief's share of prizes taken by his squadron off Cadiz in 1801. Collingwood withstood a challenge from Duckworth arising from his successful action off San Domingo in early 1806. Although Duckworth had left the Mediterranean without Collingwood's authorization, he was ruled to be still under his command when the action took place. While the rights of commanders-in-chief prevailed in these cases, the claims of subordinate flag officers were upheld in a judgement of Lord Eldon in mid-1800. His decision in favour of Vice Admiral Sir William Parker and other flag officers in the Mediterranean command meant that they were entitled to share a freight which St Vincent thought belonged solely to him.[19] In another case dating back to late 1799, Nelson benefitted from an appeal decision by the King's Bench. The court ruled that since St Vincent was on leave, he could not claim a commander-in-chief's share of prizes captured by

Nelson's squadron. This decision was worth £14,000 to Nelson.[20] Some cases dragged on for years. Duncan's claim to the Camperdown prizes was not challenged but when he died in 1804 a costly dispute with his second-in-command in the attack on the Scheldt in 1799 remained unresolved.[21]

Because Nelson was a subordinate flag officer at the battles of Cape St Vincent, the Nile and Copenhagen, his prize revenue seemed incommensurate with his contributions to these triumphs. His declared indifference to lucre helped him cope with frustrations arising from straightened domestic financial circumstances, but it also reflected a determination (common among his colleagues) to present prize income as a consequence of valuable service, rather than the incentive for energy and commitment.[22] In Nelson's case this stance derived from an ideal of chivalric honour in which personal ambition and the disinterested fulfilment of noble duties tended to be fused.[23] By contrast, St Vincent took a strictly professional view not tinged by romantic inclinations. He professed a wish to depersonalize disputes between flag officers and present them as resolutions of issues of principle that were for the good of the service. In a similar vein, Duncan pressed unsuccessfully for his dispute to be pursued through an action against the prize agents rather than his colleague.[24]

Occasionally, however, flag officers were accused of overstepping the mark that separated a grateful acceptance of the monetary prizes of war from an unscrupulous and dishonourable pursuit of them. Keith had to fend off claims about his handling of prize money and the probity of agents whom he favoured, and St Vincent faced considerable public and parliamentary criticism over his seizure of the property of enemy non-combatants during his West Indian command.[25] Six Alexander Cochrane got into difficulties when he took slaves freed from captured ships to work on his plantation and was accused of brutally re-enslaving them. He defended himself against these charges (made by evangelical anti-slavery campaigners in England) by claiming that he was providing a disinterestedly humane solution to a temporary problem.[26] Cochrane rode out this criticism, but in some circles continued to be suspected of mercenary motives. American interests seem to have been behind later accusations that he had diverted freed slaves who had volunteered for service in the Navy to work on his property.[27] Given his immense standing and influence, the Duke of Wellington's criticism of Cochrane's motives for promoting the attack on New Orleans at the end of the war – 'The expedition to New Orleans originated with [Cochrane] … and plunder was its object' – was potentially more damaging.[28] As we have seen, however, the only flag officer to face formal service charges arising from prize or freight business was Vice Admiral Charles Stirling.[29]

Honours and ambition

If employment at sea enhanced admirals' prospects of sharing in valuable prizes and freights, it also provided opportunities to gain royal honours, pensions and sinecures. These rewards were valued by the service because they fostered a 'spirit of emulation' that encouraged commitment in the face of persistent hardship and intermittent danger. For the ministers responsible for their allocation, they offered a means of reaping political advantage from the achievements of flag officers and the public enthusiasm generated by them. Royal honours were the acme of flag officers' aspirations. Those who won the highest titles frequently received sinecure appointments and pensions as well. Although these rewards recognized leadership in important fleet actions, and distinguished sustained service, their timing was often influenced by political or other considerations not always related directly to an officer's service record.

The ennoblement of distinguished naval officers was relatively recent, and even with extended opportunities arising during a prolonged period of conflict, the number of naval peers remained low relative to the burgeoning cadre of flag officers.[30] British and (from 1801) UK peerages bestowed the right to sit in the House of Lords at Westminster and were more prestigious and highly prized than Irish peerages. St Vincent, Duncan, Nelson, Barham, Collingwood, Gambier and Pellew were elevated directly to the House of Lords. Collingwood's title recognized his role at Trafalgar and there was some discussion between Lord Barham and the prime minister about taking advantage of this glorious occasion to ennoble other senior and well-performing flag officers. Barham thought that peerages for Admiral William Cornwallis and Sir Peter Parker, the admiral of the fleet, would be well received in the service but that other 'retrospects' would not. Nothing came of this discussion.[31] Lords Bridport, Gardner, Hood and Keith used Irish peerages as steppingstones to British ones. Three other flag officers, Hothan, Graves and Waldegrave, had to settle for Irish titles. Over the course of the two wars, eleven admirals were raised to one of the first three orders of the British and UK peerages, becoming barons, viscounts or earls. Alexander and Samuel Hood, Nelson, Keith and Pellew were made barons and then viscounts. St Vincent became a viscount some years after receiving an earldom so that the lesser title could descend to an heir who was not 'of his body'. Since very large fortunes and extensive landed estates were thought necessary to support the dignity of the upper reaches of the British peerage, flag officers were practically precluded from becoming marquises or dukes. The only naval duke was Clarence, son of George III. Even below these ranks, however, flag officers' private means were rarely sufficient to support a peerage, so state pensions and sinecures augmented private fortunes acquired through inheritance, marriage or prize payments.

Baronetcies (hereditary knighthoods) ranked below peerages in orders of precedent and desirability; thirty-three flag officers received this mark of distinction during the wars, a few of whom (Middleton, Gardner, Pellew and Saumarez) were subsequently raised to the peerage. Thirty-eight flag officers held non-hereditary knighthoods and seventy-seven were made knights of the Bath over the war period. At one stage in their careers, Nelson, Duckworth and Sir Hyde Parker favoured the 'red ribbon' over a baronetcy. Nelson owned no real property at the time and Hyde Parker's older brother was already a baronet. After the Battle of Copenhagen he may have had a peerage in mind and certainly regarded his ignominious recall by St Vincent as putting an end to such a prospect.[32] As we shall see, Duckworth's rationale was more complex and smacked of pique.

The initial naval creations were in 1794, immediately after the first major fleet action of the war, the 'Glorious' First of June. On this occasion, two senior subordinate flag officers (Alexander Hood and Thomas Graves) became Irish barons. Their commander-in-chief, Lord Howe, who was already a British earl, asked to be made a member of the Order of the Garter. When the Duke of Portland put pressure on Pitt to secure the first vacancy for himself, the king reluctantly agreed to the prime minister's suggestion that Howe be offered a marquisate instead. Howe's cool decline of this offer raised him in the king's estimation and he determined that Howe should get the next vacancy in the Garter order.[33] Graves's Irish title incorporated his family name but Alexander Hood, whose elder brother Samuel had already claimed the title 'Lord' Hood, became Baron Bridport. Hood became a British baron in 1796 when he gave up his place as MP for Westminster, and a viscount in 1800. Bridport joined him in this rank when he retired from the Channel command in 1800 to make way for St Vincent. His elevation rewarded sustained service and eased the transition to unemployment. As the Earl of Chatham gave Bridport private notice of this honour six weeks before the Duke of Portland sent a formal letter, it is highly likely that the Hoods' close relationship with the Pitts played a role in securing it.[34] In the course of the next few years, Alan Gardner (who was made a baronet after Howe's victory), William Hotham, who succeeded Lord Hood in the Mediterranean command, and George Elphinstone (Lord Keith), who had prevented the recapture the Cape of Good Hope, were made Irish peers. Gardner's honour recognized long and distinguished service but there may also have been an element of compensation for having been passed over for the Channel command in 1799. There was certainly a compensatory consideration when he was translated to the British peerage in 1806 following his displacement as the ministerial candidate for the City of Westminster.

Keith's Irish award was unremarkable in terms of his achievements, although its timing caused difficulties by placing him above Sir John Jervis, under whom he had served as a midshipman. Hotham's elevation was, however, a source of angry embarrassment to Lord Spencer. The king reacted with uncritical enthusiasm to Hotham's minor and incomplete action against the French off Hyéres Island, ignoring the fact that he had just been replaced by Sir John Jervis because his disciplinary and operational performance was inadequate. Partly for this reason, and also because of intra-service relativities, Pitt and Spencer regarded Hotham's elevation as most undesirable. Spencer, who did not know of the proposal until it was too late to resist it, had a very frank conversation with Pitt that was relayed to the king. This award was seen as 'an affront' to the first lord. He was also acutely aware of how it would be perceived by far-better-performed flag officers such as Sir John Jervis and his backers, who included the politically influential Marquis of Lansdown.

Spencer is reported to have told Pitt that if Hotham's peerage was 'to be understood to be for naval pretensions, [it] would in itself produce no good effect in the Navy'.[35] He responded by urging Pitt to persuade the king to make Jervis a British peer, telling him that the admiral's 'merits have been so eminent in point of activity and of restoring discipline, that he might naturally be hurt at not receiving some mark of favour at this time'.[36] Jervis was offered a barony before news of the action off Cape St Vincent had reached London. In the wake of the victory, the king accepted Spencer's forceful suggestion to go two steps further and make Jervis an earl.[37] Sir John was not inclined to self-deprecation so there is every reason to believe that his immediate reaction to his accelerated ennoblement was sincere. It had, he told a friend, done great violence to my feelings, for I dread of all things the imputation of vanity, and although the partiality of my friends places the events of the 14 Feb[ruary] on a level with the illustrious victories of Keppel, Rodney & Howe, I cannot bring my mind up to the comparison, and I really do feel oppress'd with the praise bestowed on it.[38]

The new earl applied the same logic when evaluating his subordinate flag officers' desserts. St Vincent told Evan Nepean that 'Entre nous – the Admirals are evidently disappointed that the same honours, which followed Lord Rodney's & Lord Howe's successes, and are not conferred on them'.[39] The officers concerned were William Parker, Charles Thompson (the illegitimate son of a baron) and William Waldegrave, a younger son of an earl. William Parker apparently had an ambition to become vice admiral of England. Thompson resented the fact that he was only to be a baronet and initially declined the honour on the grounds that it had never been conferred on a second-in-command in such a large and successful action. This characteristically ungracious move probably meant that he aspired to become a peer. Both he and Waldegrave looked back at the honours bestowed on the younger Hood and Graves after Howe's action and thought they were being short-changed. Spencer did not agree. He did not mention Thompson's reservations to the king – on the grounds that it would be 'disagreeable' if he was the only flag officer who did not receive a reward – and he reluctantly became Sir Charles Thompson, Bart.[40]

Waldegrave's pretensions were more tenacious. He told Spencer that it was 'not in my power to acquaint your Lordship that I feel myself either honour'd or flattered' at the prospect of becoming a baronet. In a letter written the following day, Waldegrave audaciously urged Spencer not to react hastily to his earlier communication trusting 'that on calm deliberation, my conduct, on this occasion will appear equally becoming the Officer and the Man'. He assumed, following a suggestion from his mischievous and duplicitous commander-in-chief, that the offer 'originated in a hurry, but that it will be properly settled … before my arrival in England'.[41] At one stage, Waldegrave momentarily overcame his reservations and agreed to accept a baronetcy, but then changed his mind. In a written explanation furnished at Spencer's request, Waldegrave attributed his volte-face to his family's views. The prospect of one of their number being a baronet was 'wholly repugnant to their feeling'. It was an honour those 'most dear' to him 'could never view but in the light of a degradation' of the superior precedential status he enjoyed as an earl's son. Waldegrave asked Spencer to explain his position to the king and tried to put a courteous face on his refusal by insisting that he would 'ever consider his most gracious approbation of my conduct … as an ample reward for my service on that memorable day'.[42]

Any expectation that Spencer and the king would immediately correct their 'mistake' proved groundless, even though Waldegrave's wife was the king's niece, and the couple were regular visitors at Windsor.[43] The vice admiral kept up his campaign for a peerage but was not created Baron Radstock in the Irish peerage until returning from the governorship of Newfoundland. At this time Waldegrave campaigned vigorously but vainly for a major active command and some of his colleagues believed that the peerage was compensation for not being offered one. Waldegrave, keen to scotch this rumour, told his son that it was given in recognition of his role at the Battle of Cape St Vincent '*not* by way of compensation for not hoisting my flag'.[44] This explanation was consistent with his view that there had been a mistake, and probably also with the perception that the offer of a baronetcy unfairly placed his contribution to St Vincent's victory below those Bridport and Graves had made to Howe's.

While Waldegrave viewed the prospect of being a baronet as a 'degradation', Admiral Duncan, a far more able officer who had shown fine judgement and resolution of character in dealing with mutinies in his fleet, would have been very pleased to have been offered one. He wrote to Henry Dundas on this question in May 1797. Dundas later told Duncan that he had taken the matter up with Lord Spencer and William Pitt, who agreed to recommend a baronetcy, and a knighthood of the Bath to signal the military basis of the distinction. Before Duncan was informed of these decisions, however, the

Plate 7: Admiral Adam Duncan was commended as the most handsome and least vain officer in the Royal Navy. When he led the North Sea fleet to a decisive victory over the Dutch Fleet off Camperdown in late 1797, a grateful government made Duncan a viscount and awarded him a pension of £3,000pa.

king suggested he be offered an Irish peerage in recognition of his effective containment of the Dutch Fleet and his handling of mutinous crews off Yarmouth.[45] Duncan, given a choice of these options, plumped for the peerage.[46] Discussions began about the title he would bear, but before this matter could be settled, his fleet triumphed over a powerful Dutch force at the Battle of Camperdown. When news of this spectacular and very welcome victory reached London, a more prestigious British title replaced the Irish one. As Henry Dundas put it, '[A]n Irish title won't do now.'[47] Dundas was doubly pleased with this outcome since he had prefigured it. He told Duncan that he hoped the Dutch admiral would 'give you a fair opportunity … Lord Texel would be a very good counter-part to Lord St Vincent'.[48] In the event, the title in the British peerage, Viscount Duncan of Camperdown, gave the prime minister an opportunity to express his regard for Duncan through a good-natured classical joke. Pitt suggested Lucan's 'Clarum et *Venerabile* Nomen' as Duncan's motto. It allowed for a play on the name of his flagship (*Venerable*) and emphasized the compliment to him: 'Illustrious and *revered* name'.[49] In a charmingly enthusiastic letter to his niece, now Lady Duncan, Dundas took unalloyed pleasure in the triumph, and, ever the politician, made a playful bid for some credit in having made it possible:

> [W]hen you first conceived your attachment to the Admiral when Captain Duncan, … [you] applied to me to speak to your Father, that before doing so I made it a special condition that you would never directly or indirectly use any influence to induce him to give over his profession. Do you now repent that I made that condition, and that you made that promise?[50]

By contrast, Thomas Grenville, another political ally, presented the victory as a triumph for the Grenville-Spencer interest: 'Joy to you, my dear Lord Spencer. I have just heard the news of your victory … [s]urely this is great news. Our family interest have [*sic*] made Duncan a Viscount and have pursued their victory by an attack upon the Texel.'[51] One of his relatives, however, complained that the ministry had not done enough. Lady Mary Duncan challenged Dundas with the claim that '[r]eport says my nephew is only made a Viscount', reminded him of the political significance of the victory, compared Duncan's achievement with that of St Vincent and emphasized how timely it was: 'Please to recollect what a chicken-hearted way all the nation was in, low spirited by the war, murmuring at the taxes … grumbling and dissatisfied in every county.'[52]

Keith pursued honours as vigorously as he pursued appointments and prize money. Shortly after becoming an Irish baron, and having been highly effective in bringing mutinous crews to order at the Nore and Plymouth, he decided to strike while the iron was still hot, pressing his case for an English peerage. He referred to his role in dealing with these mutinies – 'neither … pleasant or brilliant but perhaps not less important' – and suggested that his honorific rewards did not compare with those conferred on his colleagues:

> [W]hen I look around and find other officers who have been successful in chief command and even some in subaltern situations have been rewarded by peerage,

an honour extremely desirable if creditably attained; may I therefore request your Lordships recommendation to the Minister provided you think me deserving and if through your Lordship I am fortunate enough to obtain his consent perhaps now or at the close of the war is a time when little inconvenience would be felt whilst I should be excessively gratified.

Keith told Spencer that he had already sounded out the Duke of Portland and Henry Dundas and won their support.[53] Since only Duncan, Hood and St Vincent had received English peerages thus far during the war, Keith was pitching pretty high. Not surprisingly, his bid met with a very circumspect response from Lord Spencer, who noted that in light of Keith's recent elevation to the peerage of Ireland, the current application 'appears perhaps a little premature'. After praising Keith for his role in suppressing the mutinies, he made it clear that he had not yet done enough to merit the distinction he craved: '[I]f any opportunity should offer itself of a more brilliant nature I have no doubt of you making good use of it.'[54] Keith did not let the matter rest there, telling his sister shortly afterwards that he would 'put Dundas and Portland in mind of their [promise] by and bye'.[55] In the event, the timing of Keith's creation as a British peer more or less coincided with the peace in late 1801, by which time he had added a successful expedition against the French Army in Egypt to his laurels. Towards the end of the war, in 1814, he became a viscount, assisted no doubt by his long friendship with the Prince Regent. Keith's ongoing usefulness to his royal patron had recently been affirmed when he and his daughter acted to secure compromising correspondence and gifts from a disreputable junior army officer with whom the prince's daughter had been romantically involved.[56]

While neither Waldegrave nor Thompson thought that a baronetcy was a fitting reward for their contributions to the victory off Cape St Vincent, Nelson declined that honour because he seemed most unlikely to have a son and did not have a fortune sufficient to support the title. He asked for, and was granted, a knighthood of the Bath. This preference had a bearing on the king's reaction to news of the spectacular victory over a French Fleet off the coast of Egypt in September 1798. Although feeling an inexpressible 'degree of joy' at this triumph, the king told Lord Spencer that a peerage was 'quite out of the question' and that Nelson should receive a 'handsome pension'.[57] Spencer obviously regarded the king's suggestion as politically and financially obtuse, telling him that 'an honorary as well as a pecuniary reward will naturally be earnestly looked for by the public on an achievement of a magnitude like the present'. He refrained from making the equally obvious point that concerns about Nelson's capacity to support a title would be alleviated by a pension. In the circumstances, however, Spencer might have thought it unwise to press the king too far and recommended a barony of Great Britain. Even so, the king was said to have resented having his hand forced and greeted Nelson coolly at court on his return.[58]

The strained terms in which Spencer conveyed this news to Nelson – 'the highest honour that has ever been conferred on an officer of your standing in the Service and who was not a commander in Chief' – hinted embarrassment at a compromise that was depreciated by the hero's wife and some friends. Lord Hood, his old 'sea daddy' (who had no reason to love Lord Spencer), stirred the pot by blaming him unfairly for the outcome and raising the family's expectations. He told Nelson that he was 'much mortified your well-earned honours were not carried higher, particularly as Mr. Pitt told me ... that you would certainly be made a Viscount, which I made known to Lady Nelson'.[59] Nelson finally gained this step in the peerage in 1801, following his crucial role in the destruction of the Danish Fleet at the Battle of Copenhagen.

Keith and Nelson both eventually obtained what could reasonably be expected given questions of relativity, personal wealth and the king's views. Sir James Saumarez's pursuit of a peerage was far more protracted. Having been knighted in 1793 after one of the earliest successful frigate actions of the war, Saumarez doggedly pursued advances in heraldic status. His ambition was no doubt sharpened by the marks of royal favour bestowed on his fellow officers and by his pride in his family's ancient connections to the high aristocracy of France. Looking back on Nelson's reward, and seeing junior officers such as St Vincent's favourite, Captain Thomas Troubridge, being made a baronet in late 1799, Saumarez clearly believed that his rightful claims had been neglected.[60] In late July 1800, almost two years after the battle, he raised the matter with St Vincent, under whom he was then serving in the Channel Fleet.

On 29 July St Vincent wrote to Saumarez enclosing a copy of a letter he had sent to Lord Spencer. This correspondence throws interesting light on Saumarez's ambitions and on the role of service interest in the reward system. St Vincent made a case for Saumarez in terms of his merits and justified sense of entitlement, but also referred to his own professional and reputational stake in seeing him rewarded. 'My dear Lord', he wrote,

> I need not describe to your Lordship the Merit of Sir James Saumarez, which cannot be surpassed. In a Conversation I accidentally had with him last Evening, I learnt that his ambition had been much disappointed in not being created a Baronet, and he thought I was wanting, in not pointing to this Object, in the Letter I had the honor to write Your Lordship by him, after the Battle of the Nile, where he was second in Command; and he also conceives, that Your Lordship led him to hope, this Mark of approbation of his Services, would have been conferr'd upon him. May I therefore trespass upon Your indulgence, to request you will bring it about, if possible, as nothing can gratify me more, than that Officers, who have signalized themselves under my Auspices, should be amply rewarded.[61]

This appeal was successful, although Saumarez had to wait until the final days of Spencer's First Lordship to receive confirmation of it.[62] Having secured this objective, he immediately gained the king's permission to use his ancestors' 'supporters', that is, the figures that support the heraldic shield in a coat of arms. A pedigree from 1331 was provided in evidence of his claim.[63]

The decision on the baronetcy followed on the heels of Saumarez's promotion to flag rank on New Year's Day. After commanding at the successful action off Gibraltar, he received a further sign of royal recognition when he was selected to fill a vacancy in the Order of the Bath. Unfortunately, the lustre of this honour was tarnished by the news of his displacement by Vice Admiral Pole. In any case, it fell short of his ambitions.[64] Before receiving news of this award, Saumarez had written to St Vincent seeking a peerage and a pension to support it. By early September 1801, though concerned at the first lord's lack of response, he still seemed relatively sanguine about the outcome, telling his wife that if his expectations were met the pension would offset a potential loss of £5,000 in his prize dispute with Lord Keith. He cheered her with the prospect that they would then be able to afford a new carriage and enhance their domestic establishment.[65] When St Vincent's announcement of Saumarez's appointment to the Order of the Bath blasted these hopes, Lady Saumarez encouraged her husband to see the 'cordon rouge' as an instalment against a more fitting honour, and reminded him that 'everything … is in the hands of a superior Power who will order everything for the best'.[66] Sir James's reaction to the news was less resigned than his wife's. He told her that the outcome 'makes me more than ever thankful that our dear Boy is not to be in a Service, which is subject to so many Instances of Injustice as I have experienced'.[67]

Although Saumarez served with distinction as commander-in-chief on the critical and challenging Baltic station between 1808 and 1812, major honours continued to elude him. In mid-1810 he sent the king a long account of his service but nothing came of this heavy hint.[68] By mid-1814, he was admiral of the Blue, and had received the degree of doctor of civil law (*honorus causus*) from the University of Oxford, but remained a baronet. Spurred by the contrast between the warmth of his reception by the crowned heads of Europe gathered in England and his lowly position in orders of precedence, Sir James laid his case before Lord Liverpool, the prime minister.[69] He reminded Liverpool that he had won the 'marked approbation' of the British government for his conduct in the Baltic and had been praised by the emperor of Russia, the monarchs of Prussia and Sweden, and Prince Metternich, the *eminence grisé* of Austrian diplomacy. Saumarez combined an exculpating reference to the tragedy unfolding at his home in Guernsey, where a daughter lay close to death, with a hope that his merits would be recognized: 'Your Lordship will I am persuaded make due allowances for the anxiety of my Mind on the present occasion, and that in the high Rewards conferred upon Officers for their Services during the long and glorious War, I shall also be found deserving the Mark of His Royal Highnesses Favour'.[70]

In 1815 Saumarez was made a Grand Cross of the Bath and he was later appointed to the lucrative and wholly honorific posts of rear- and vice admiral of England. However, the long quest for a peerage did not conclude until 1831. This late echo of fame almost certainly owed something to contemporary political considerations. In writing to congratulate him, the First Lord, Sir James Graham, stressed the role the Whig Prime Minister Lord Grey had played in promoting the measure.[71] Following the highly charged reform bill election of March 1831, which saw a turbulent contest for one of the Plymouth seats between officers whose careers went back to the Napoleonic War, Lord Grey may have wished to distinguish a flag officer from the same era who had strong Whig credentials and could be expected to vote with the government on the Reform Bill.[72] Saumarez's elevation thus happily addressed the honour of the service, his undoubted merits and the exigencies of parliamentary politics. The newly minted Lord de Saumarez received many letters of congratulation from fellow admirals of his generation. The redoubtable Sir Isaac Coffin provided a pithy summary of a theme that ran through almost all the congratulatory messages: Saumarez at last enjoyed a distinction 'so long, so unjustly and so ungenerously withheld'.[73]

Sir James's decision to lobby Lord Liverpool in 1814 was almost certainly triggered by the recent announcement that Sir Edward Pellew, who was his junior, was to be raised to the peerage as Lord Exmouth. Ironically, there is no evidence that Pellew was actively pursuing a peerage at this time. His immediate objective appears to have been the Order of the Bath, an honour Saumarez had received more than a decade before. Early in 1812 Pellew was sufficiently aggrieved to talk of resigning the Mediterranean command because the first lord had not responded to the Duke of Northumberland's suggestion that he receive this honour. The Duke continued to press Pellew's case through his connection with the Duke of York but nothing immediately came of it.[74] In early May 1814, however, when the matter finally appeared to be settled, the decision was unexpectedly trumped by the offer of a peerage. The award of a pension of £2,000pa no doubt turned the knife in Saumarez's wound.[75]

These developments would have been equally galling to Sir John Duckworth. When he led the naval side of the Minorca expedition in early 1798, he believed his contribution gave him a good claim to a baronetcy. Although St Vincent clearly doubted the strength of Duckworth's case because he had acted under orders rather than holding an independent command, he half-heartedly brought the matter to Lord Spencer's attention, fearing that Duckworth would abuse him as lukewarm 'for the service' if he did not. He hedged his bets, however, telling Spencer that 'I ... leave his pretensions with your Lordship, whose superior judgement, and experience in these matters, will determine what is right to be done, upon the occasion'.[76] Spencer's judgement coincided with St Vincent's, so Duckworth went unrewarded. His disappointment would no doubt have been sharpened by the knowledge that later in the same year St Vincent supported Vice Admiral Coffin's bid for a baronetcy on the grounds that it would 'accelerate his union with Miss Bootle'.[77]

In mid-1801 when St Vincent was first lord and Duckworth was commanding at Jamaica, he dealt directly with his aspirations for royal honours. Duckworth's claims arose from a series of successful collaborations with the army during which a string of French, Danish and Swedish possessions were seized. St Vincent initially intended to recommend Duckworth for a baronetcy, believing this to have been an earlier object. Having heard from one of Duckworth's friends that he would prefer to be nominated to the Order of the Bath, he sought the king's approval for this honour. When subsequent information suggested that Duckworth's preference was for the more highly ranked hereditary honour, St Vincent reported with regret that it was too late to pursue that.[78] St Vincent's information, or perhaps its sequencing, turned out to be an unreliable guide to Duckworth's preferences. He really wished to become a knight of the Bath rather than a baronet, so in that sense he got what he wanted. In the course of making this point, however, Duckworth rejected the offer of a baronetcy in terms that doubtless displeased both the first lord and the king. He displayed his usual lack of tact by airing his resentment at the earlier failure to secure this honour and indicating that he was now entitled to a higher mark of hereditary distinction. Duckworth complained that while the army commanders were to be offered the 'red ribbon', he was only to be given a belated baronetcy, noting bitterly that 'the Admiral is at last to be a Baronet'. '[S]uch a lukewarm attention my Lord implies rather Censure than Compliment.' He could not 'face such a wound when I consider my Exertions equal to my compeers'.[79]

Duckworth was not present at Trafalgar but had hopes of securing an Irish peerage following his fleet action off San Domingo early in 1806. He had already raised this prospect in May 1805, when he presented a peerage as a mark of royal favour which would dispel the cloud cast by the indignity of being court martialled over his grossly excessive Jamaican baggage, and facing the suspicious scrutiny of HM Customs when it was landed.[80] The victory off San Domingo became the starting point of a sustained campaign to receive recognition for his achievements, to vindicate himself, and what he saw as the honour of the service. Duckworth's initial plea was rejected, allegedly because of the scale of the action and because he was under Collingwood's orders. Lord Barham, the first lord, also hinted that it was believed that the initiative to pursue the French came from Sir Alexander Cochrane rather than his temporary commander-in-chief.[81] When Duckworth was offered a consolation pension of £1,000pa, and St Vincent made a (probably insincere) attempt to placate him by describing it as 'a more substantial reward' than a peerage, his junior colleague was incensed.[82] He retailed St Vincent's mercenary comfort to his friend the Duke of Northumberland, who responded with consoling patrician outrage at the low mercantile instincts of those who would offer it: 'Honours and distinctions are the objects of military men ... not ... dirty pounds, shillings and pence.'[83]

A year later, Duckworth sent a six and a half page letter to Lord Howick, advancing precedents to counter claims that he was not entitled to a peerage because he acted under Collingwood's orders, denying that he was really under Collingwood's orders at all, and comparing the relative force of the fleets and the number of prizes taken. Having earlier sought appointment as St Vincent's second-in-command in the Channel, he now declared himself unfit to take it up: 'my feeling wounded, and degraded, I am not equal to the important charge.'[84] In a subsequent interview with Howick, Duckworth thought he had extracted a promise that he and Lord Grenville would recommend him for the next vacancy in the Irish peerage. He subsequently wrote to Grenville reminding him of this undertaking.[85]

Over the years that followed, Duckworth sought unsuccessfully to persuade Lord Mulgrave, the Duke of Portland, and Spencer Percival to redeem Howick's promise and tried to enlist the support of St Vincent and Lord Henry Petty, as well as the Duke of Northumberland.[86] In mid-1814, having recently accepted the baronetcy declined scornfully twelve years before, Duckworth made a final bid for a peerage. He appealed to Lord Liverpool by letter and in an interview, reminding him of Howick's promise, his long years of honourable service and his victory off San Domingo. In reply, Liverpool told Duckworth that he had communicated his request to the Prince Regent and been commanded to tell him that 'His Royal Highness does full justice to your Service on the Occasions to which you refer. But he feels it nevertheless quite impossible under all the Circumstances to comply with your Request'. It would have been cold comfort to Duckworth to be told that other officers (probably a reference to Saumarez and Warren) had received the same response to their recent applications.[87] Although Duckworth was made a Grand Cross of the Bath in 1815 and continued in employment after the war, he died a baronet.

At the beginning of 1815 a separate military order of the Bath was created. It contained three divisions, the first of which, Military Knights Grand Crosses (GCBs), was restricted to flag officers and their army equivalents. The second division was that of Military Knights Commanders (KCB) and the third Military Companions (CB). The new order was not constrained by the numerical limitations of the original order and a large creation was announced at the beginning of the year. This move no doubt did something to smooth the hurt feelings of those whose claims for other honours had fallen on deaf ears. Sixteen flag officers were made GCBs, with the army taking the other forty-three places in the order. Fifty-eight naval officers became KCBs. The Navy were represented in the higher division by a number of figures who appear in this book: St Vincent, Keith, Warren, Colpoys, Duckworth, Saumarez, Samuel Hood, Northesk, Strachan, Alexander Cochrane, Keats, Young, Lord Hood, Onslow, Cornwallis, Radstock and Berkeley. Gambier, Pole, Calder, Bickerton, Exmouth, Eliab Harvey and Hallowell took the highest positions among the flag officers in the second division.[88]

The Duke of Northumberland cruelly teased Duckworth about whether the GCB was really a mark of distinction, and St Vincent showed his dislike of being placed in such mixed company by describing the KB as 'an honourable distinction', pointing to names on the list of GCBs that 'degraded' it, and declining for many years to wear the new insignia.[89] Cornwallis's reaction was quite different and equally in keeping with his character. Induction into the Order of the Bath closed an episode that had opened twenty years before when he was offered a Knighthood of the Bath following a brilliant fighting retreat in the Channel. On this occasion, Cornwallis declined the honour. He stuck to his guns when Spencer told him that the king was keen for him to accept it so as to signal to 'the World ... that Merit such as you have displayed ... is the best and strongest claim to a Distinction of this kind'.[90] For Cornwallis, it seems, questions of recognition were calibrated by an independent sense of personal and professional honour which determined that he would accept rewards only when he thought they were truly deserved. He despised unmerited honours, remarking scornfully that half the peerage were 'living on the reflected glory of their forebears'. Honours were 'very well in their way, but ... [w]orth makes the man, and want of it the fellow'.[91] Cornwallis may have been prepared to accept a Grand Cross in 1815 because he thought his achievements were well placed in relation to those of his naval peers in the Order. Be that as it may, his letter of thanks to the Board was marked by the understated pride that had led him to decline the earlier offer. Cornwallis said that he was too old and infirm to attend the investiture, but expressed his appreciation of the Prince Regent's 'consideration in noting any little service it may have been in my power at any time to have performed *and* which has long since passed away'.[92]

The creation of the new divisions gave scope for recognition on a scale that piqued the competitive instincts of some of Cornwallis's colleagues. Lord Gambier and his friends may have been surprised to see Duckworth, Onslow, Radstock and Berkeley favoured over him for a Grand Cross but as he attained this status in June 1815, his comparative dignity was soon restored. Momentarily for Gambier, and lastingly for some other flag officers, the numbers of flag officers in the higher divisions of the new order was likely to have made exclusion particularly galling. In the wake of the supplement to the *London Gazette* that announced the new-modelling of the Order, the Board received a number of letters of complaint.[93] The most aggrieved of these was from Vice Admiral William Otway. Three days after the *Gazette* appeared, he wrote to express his disappointment and draw the Board's attention to a long record of service. He subsequently forwarded letters of support from the assembly of the Island of St Vincent, from the Earl of the same name, and from Cornwallis, but all to no avail.[94] Otway and other disappointed flag officers were no doubt particularly mortified at not even being made knights commanders since this division included a number of post captains.

Pensions

When admirals were raised to the peerage it was common for additional financial provision to be made for them in the form of a pension for life, and sometimes for two lives, so as to provide for peers' widows and children, and allow their dynasty to become established. These arrangements were necessary because the private for-tunes of the recipients were usually insufficient to support their elevated status. That was particularly the case for Collingwood, Duncan, Gardner, Nelson, and St Vincent. Collingwood was highly relieved to receive a pension when he was made a baron because the storms that struck after Trafalgar wrecked many of the captured ships and seemed set to have a detrimental impact on prize money. As things turned out, the government agreed to pay prize money on the basis of an evaluation. The value of the pension was increased by a provision that allowed Lady Collingwood £1,000pa and each of his daughters £500pa after his death.[95] James Gambier was an exception to the general pattern, having declined a pension after the Second Battle of Copenhagen. He was reputed to have moral scruples over a campaign that gave rise to 2,000 civilian casualties, and could only be justifiable by reference to the uncomfortable doctrine of raison d'etat.[96] Gambier had no children and was content to uphold the dignity of his peerage from a modest house. As he had spent so long at the Board his prize money was probably not very significant.[97]

Pensions paid to naval peers were substantial. For example, the £3,000pa that Duncan, Nelson and St Vincent were each receiving in 1805 represented the income on a capital sum of £60,000 invested in 5 per cent annuities, and closer to £100,000 in 3 per cent consolidated funds. The daily income of £8 8sh handsomely exceeded the full pay of the most senior flag officers. Admirals receiving pensions continued to draw full pay and allowances when in employment, and half pay when they were not. Subject to the king's approval, which seemed to have been granted as a matter of form, they also received the financial benefits of any sinecures or posts that they held. A few flag officers were awarded pensions on account of severe wounds received in the king's ser-vice. Even with these additions, however, the number of admirals receiving pensions remained low. In June 1795 only three of the ninety-nine flag officers on the active list were in receipt of pensions. By early 1799 eleven were receiving pensions out of a list that had swelled to more than one hundred and thirty. Recipients included St Vincent and Duncan who had £2,000pa (and were shortly to receive a further £1,000 from the Irish Exchequer), and Nelson, who *Steel's* listed as receiving £1,000. Sir Thomas Palsey who lost a leg at the First of June wrote to the Board asking for their Lordships'

'Patronage and Protection' and was duly awarded a pension of £1,000pa.[98] Only fourteen of the one hundred and eighty flag officers on the active list in 1810 were receiving pensions and most of these were awards of a few hundred pounds for wounds received earlier in their careers. By 1814 only five flag officers were receiving naval pensions of £1,000 or more. A further three officers had state pensions from other sources.

Lord Howe (who was already an earl and very rich) declined a pension after the First of June and was also reported to have given his prize share of £16,000 for the benefit of the wounded.[99] Graves received a pension of £1,000pa after that battle but for a severe wound rather than to support his Irish peerage. He had a substantial estate in Cornwall and sufficient capital to leave his wife an annuity of £900pa on his death. Bridport did not receive a pension and neither he nor his brother were given one when they became British peers in 1796. In light of subsequent practice, the treatment of the Hoods appears anomalous. Bridport received £500pa as treasurer of Greenwich Hospital and it seems that this, along with his pay and other private and public income, was thought sufficient to support a British peerage. He was obliged to give up the treasurership in 1799 when appointed lieutenant general of Marines but by this time he was receiving £1,000pa as vice admiral of England.[100]

Lord Hood had not made a vast fortune from prize money and only had a modest estate in Hampshire but was in receipt of a life income of £1,000pa as governor of Greenwich Hospital. In late 1798, however, he wrote to William Pitt asking for a pension, drawing attention to his achievements relative to other officers of 'my standing'. He pointed out that Lady Hood, who held a peerage in her own right, would be reduced to living on £800pa if he predeceased her.[101] The government's response was to grant Lady Hood a pension for life of £1,000. In January 1800, however, her husband was granted a pension of £2,000pa 'for services', with provision for £1,500 for his widow which would pass on her death to Hood's heir. This award, which was not reported in *Steel's List*, appeared spasmodically in parliamentary reports of pensions charged against the 'Four and A Half Per Cent Leeward Islands Duties' and was paid by Treasury warrants.[102] In 1807 Bridport and Hood made approaches through the Duke of Portland to secure additional financial recognition from the Crown. Lord Hood reported the duke as having said that 'as we were raised to the dignity of British Peers, and as a reward for public service, that our pretensions to His Majesty's favour, were fair and good'. He succeeded in having his pension extended for three lives so that his immediate descendants would have the benefit of it but there is no parliamentary record of provision for his younger brother.[103]

St Vincent and Duncan do not appear to have initiated formal appeals for pensions when they were raised to the peerage. Rather, grateful (and relieved) first lords took up the running, making enquiries about their private fortunes and reporting the results to the king. When deciding the amount of awards, some consideration was given to ensuring that they were equitable and did not become a source of jealous disgruntlement. Thus claims on behalf of St Vincent and Duncan were considered together, with Pitt telling the king that as St Vincent's income was as little able to support his rank as that of Lord Duncan, '[h]e therefore presumes that your Majesty will think him entitled to a similar provision'.[104] These pensions, like those later awarded to Nelson, Collingwood, Duckworth, Strachan and Saumarez, were authorized by acts of parliament as civil list pensions paid from the Consolidated Fund. They were listed in *Steel's*. The £1,000 portion of St Vincent's and Duncan's pensions that were authorized by the Irish Parliament were paid in Dublin and put recipients to the trouble of having an Irish banker.[105]

When Nelson became a baron after the Battle of the Nile, the king and the Ministry knew that he would need a pension to support his new rank. He was duly granted £2,000pa that was to extend to heirs to his barony. Some friends and members of Nelson's family were disappointed that he had not been given a more elevated rank in the English peerage but there does not appear to have been any immediate disquiet on the pension.[106] In March 1803, however, when appointed to command the Mediterranean Fleet, Nelson (now a viscount) was extremely worried about his financial affairs and raised the matter with the prime minister, Henry Addington, providing him with a statement of annual income, expenditure, major assets and debts.[107] After paying the interest on his mortgage and on another substantial debt incurred when fitting out for his last two commands, providing an allowance of £1,800pa to the estranged Lady Nelson and meeting other family obligations, Nelson was left with £768pa to live on. Having initially made a case for extending the pension so that it might be enjoyed by his brother and nephews, if they should be his heirs, Nelson then raised the separate question of an additional pension of £1,000pa from the Irish Exchequer:

> I presume to make only one remark: Was it, or not, the intension of his Majesty's Government to place my rewards for services lower than Lord St Vincent or Lord Duncan? I had the happiness to be a sharer of the glory of the 14 th February; and I had the honour to command the Fleet which gained the Victory of the Nile, which, till that of Copenhagen, was, I believe, the most complete one ever obtained.[108]

Nelson was mistaken in linking the extension of the pension to his viscountcy since that title, unlike the barony, could pass only to heirs of his own body.[109] The (unsuccessful) appeal to Addington involved two further difficulties, the first of which concerned relativity with the awards made to Duncan and St Vincent. Since Nelson's viscountcy could only be transmitted to an heir of his body and there seemed no prospect of that, his heirs would be barons, not viscounts so the comparisons with the provision for St Vincent's and Duncan's heirs was not valid. It seems significant that Keith, Collingwood and Pellew were all awarded pensions of £2,000 on becoming barons, which suggests that sum was seen as appropriate pension for those on the lowest rung of the English peerage. In any case, the figures provided to Addington make clear that Nelson enjoyed an income from pensions that was almost identical to those of Duncan and St Vincent. In his statement, Nelson listed a sum of £2,000 from an 'exchequer pension for the Nile' and a further £923 'Navy pension for loss of one arm and one eye'. Taken together, these pensions amount pretty much to the sums provided for Duncan and St Vincent, with the difference reflecting standard deductions for income tax and Greenwich Hospital funds.

In addition to questions of relativities, Nelson's letter to Addington raised the question of his overall financial situation and, obliquely at least, whether it was fitting for someone in his situation to have a disposable private income of only £768pa. This amount was significantly above the £465pa half pay of a vice admiral, and while less than the full pay of an officer of that rank, would not be burdened with the expenses of employment. It was also exclusive of interest payments on debts, and commitments to his family. Nelson, however, was not only the most fêted flag officer of his day, he was also a viscount and these considerations clearly made a difference. Nevertheless, the reference to a payment of £1,800pa to Lady Nelson must surely have told against his bid for an enhanced pension. Insofar as Nelson's appeal to Addington rested on financial need relative to his station in life, he was, in effect, asking the government to increase the income he derived from state pensions, already on a par with two of his illustrious contemporaries, so that he might live apart from his wife and provide a separate establishment for himself and his mistress. One may admire Nelson's candour in disclosing the source of his financial difficulties, and his boldness in expecting that his irregular domestic arrangements would be taken into account. It is not surprising, however, that this cause did not gain the prime minister's official support and seems never to have been raised with the king. Nelson's contemporaneous attempts to secure a pension for Lady Hamilton also ran into the sand.

Keith was granted a pension after the successful conclusion of the expedition to Egypt when he became an English baron. Given his princely prize money, this award presumably reflected considerations of equity rather than need. It also owed something to a general awareness of Keith's determination to press for his due. When St Vincent found out that Keith's army counterpart was to receive an English peerage and a pension, he wrote to the prime minister warning him that it would be perilous to ignore Keith: '[Y]ou and I shall be attacked most virulently.' If Addington took the point, Keith will have joined Nelson and St Vincent on the short list of well-pensioned flag officers, with a pension of £2,000pa for life.[110] Questions of relativity may also explain why Pellew was awarded a pension of that amount. Where flag officers were concerned, differential treatment raised the prospect of complaints of 'degradation' and a loss of reputation in the eyes of the service. Duckworth was offended at being offered a pension without a peerage but those who received a peerage without a pension might well feel slighted in comparison to their colleagues, even if they were rich enough to support the honour. There was certainly no question about financial need in Pellew's case as he had made a fortune in prize money when commanding in the East Indies.

Saumarez's pursuit of a pension, like his bids for a peerage, relied largely on his own direct efforts. When trying to secure St Vincent's support for his elevation to the peerage late in 1801, he also sought a pension of the value of those awarded initially to Duncan, Nelson and St Vincent. When the prospect of a peerage receded, Saumarez did not give up hope of a pension in recognition of his recent victory. His earlier disappointments clearly made him wary, however. Noting the vote of thanks he had recently received from Parliament, he speculated pessimistically that 'this may make them consider £1,000 a Year adequate, or probably they will not vote anything whatever'. Mentally preparing himself for the worst, he went on to tell his wife that 'I should consider either as very inadequate and unless £2,000 a Year is voted I shall think myself very ill requited for a whole Life devoted to my Country and the signal services it has pleased the Almighty to make me instrumental in rendering it'. In keeping with this acknowledgement of divine instrumentality, Saumarez earmarked any addition to his income from this source for extending their '[p]ower to do the good we wish', rather than for the fine carriage and enlarged establishment that had been before his eyes when a peerage still seemed a possibility. As a baronet, Saumarez would not have felt the need to maintain the same style of living as a peer.[111] For that reason, of course, and considering recent precedents, Saumarez was bidding pretty high. Nevertheless, when it failed, he did not let the matter rest. Almost a year later he bailed up the first lord in London who reported on the meeting to Addington: 'Sir James Saumarez in a conversation I had with him yesterday, amongst other grievances, stated his disappointment at not having a pension given to him to support the titles conferred upon him.'[112] The 'amongst other grievances', a telling indication of St Vincent's strained patience with Saumarez's expressions of frustrated entitlement, probably refers to the peerage and the slighting offer of a peacetime command. The amount mentioned at this stage was £1,000pa but in the event Saumarez was granted a pension of £1,200pa. Though this sum fell well short of his aspirations, it nevertheless represented the income on a capital sum of between £24,000 and £40,000 and was in line with pensions paid to flag officers who were knights rather than peers. It was more than double a vice admiral's half pay. Four years later Duckworth reluctantly accepted a pension of £1,000pa, and Sir Richard Strachan was awarded a similar sum following his capture of French ships that had escaped from Trafalgar.

Although Saumarez was persistent in pursuing a substantial pension, it would be a mistake to treat his expectations as venal, or otherwise inconsistent with his piety. Before taking up the Baltic command he declined an offer of the East Indies station, even though it had proved a gold mine to other flag officers posted there. Moreover, there is no indication that Saumarez's decision-making in the Baltic was influenced by prize opportunities.[113] As in Duckworth's case, the pursuit of honours and pensions was motivated primarily by professional pride and a determination (reflected in their references to awards bestowed on other colleagues) to be treated fairly. In addition, however, Saumarez's correspondence with Martha indicates they shared Hannah More's view that public recognition of godly officers' achievements showed that bravery and professional excellence aligned with evangelical ideals of Christian leadership.

Sinecures

In common with other participants in the Georgian patronage network, flag officers hoped to augment their income by holding sinecure offices. Two sets of sinecures were the preserve of senior sea officers: the senior positions in the administration of Greenwich Hospital, and three generalships in the Marines. The governorship of Greenwich Hospital carried a handsome salary of £1,000pa, which compared very favourably with an admiral's half pay of about 60 per cent of that figure. With the king's permission, half pay could be claimed by those holding sinecure appointments. The governor was entitled to accommodation in the governor's apartments at Greenwich and allowances for table, coals and candles. The substantive duties of managing the hospital were in the hands of a lieutenant governor drawn from among half-pay post captains. The governor presided over the institution, performed ceremonial duties, and if active, might have a role in determining its overall direction. Flag officers also held the treasurership of Greenwich Hospital. This office attracted a salary of £500pa, with accommodation at Greenwich and the usual allowances. Since the substantive duties could be performed by a deputy remunerated from a portion of the salary, officers could hold the post while they served at sea.

There were only two governors of Greenwich Hospital during the war years. Admiral Sir Hugh Palliser died in office in 1796, having held the post since 1780. In March 1796 Admiral Lord Hood applied to Spencer for the position and was granted it. Hood told Henry Addington that he had stayed in the country after his dismissal from the Mediterranean command to avoid questions that might embarrass government, and perhaps this forbearance encouraged Spencer to look more favourably on his application than he might have done.[114] He certainly reminded Hood of the black mark of the previous year when telling him he recommended appointment to the king because he had given a promise to the previous first lord, the Earl of Chatham, and wished to show 'attention' to him as brother of the prime minister, and to give appropriate recognition for Hood's prior service'.[115]

In 1799 Vice Admiral John Payne leveraged his friendship with the Prince of Wales to secure the treasurership of Greenwich Hospital grudgingly relinquished by Bridport on becoming vice admiral of England. Vice Admiral Young observed that 'while this will not be considered as the reward of distinguished merit ... it effectively prevents the contest, among those who have distinguished themselves, to determine whose merit is greatest'.[116] When Payne's health began to fail in late 1803 and a number of his fellow flag officers showed an interest in succeeding him, merit did not play a role in the selection process. As we have seen, St Vincent dashed the hopes of flag officers by reverting to what he claimed was the standard practice of appointing treasurers from the captains' list. After the death of his nominee, the treasurership fell to Admiral Sir John Colpoys who held it throughout the rest of the war. Colpoys, who was on the Admiralty Board when the vacancy occurred, clearly did not share his friend St Vincent's scruples about flag officers being appointed to the post.

Commissions as colonels of marines with handsome salaries of £800pa were given to favoured post captains but had to be relinquished on promotion to flag rank. Senior flag officers could aspire to hold a lieutenant generals' commission in the Marines which was worth £1,200pa. During the war years Barrington, Bridport, Palliser, Sir Peter Parker and St Vincent held one of these commissions. Gardner became the first major general in 1794, for which he received £1,000pa. Collingwood succeeded him in late 1808 when the Board was keen for him to continue in the Mediterranean command. He welcomed this mark of distinction from the king, but was chagrined that the ministry thought 'such an excitement necessary to retain me'.[117] This comment suggests that Collingwood had not sought the appointment. As he received news of it from the Duke of Northumberland, whose son was under his protection, the Duke probably played a role in proposing him for it.[118] At £3pd the position was significantly more lucrative than the half pay of a vice admiral (£1/10) or admiral (£2pa). The venerable Admiral John Forbes, who was general of Marines when war began, was succeeded in the office by Lord Howe, and then Admiral the Honourable Samuel Barrington who had been promoted to flag rank in the 1770s. On Barrington's death in 1800 Bridport was appointed to this position and retained it until his death in 1814. Since St Vincent had coveted this post earlier in his career, he was unlikely to have been happy to wait so long to enjoy the distinction and the pay of £5pd that went with it.

Early in 1807 St Vincent told an applicant for his interest that '[i]t is a very different thing to have the power of bestowing, & to request favours from others'.[119] This homily reflected an important feature of St Vincent's career. While many flag officers competed openly for appointments, honours and pensions, there is only occasional evidence that St Vincent did so. From an early stage of his career he enjoyed the support of the Earl of Shelburne (later the Marquis of Lansdown), an awkward and not always trusted colleague of the Portland Whigs, but a powerful patron of his protégé. For example, in late 1789 with a change of ministry in the offing, and Admiral Forbes reported to be on his deathbed, St Vincent hinted to Shelburne that this would be a good time to encourage the outgoing first lord to give him generality.[120] Although he jumped the gun on this occasion – Forbes lived until 1796 – St Vincent's friendship with Shelburne meant that he did not have to plead his own cause and his cool, Olympian sense of self-worth remained intact. Rewards that were the anxious objects of other admirals' ambitions seemed to fall into his lap. But while the role of direct supplicant was no doubt uncongenial to St Vincent, it was not entirely unknown. There was at least one occasion on which he put himself in the position of a Duckworth, Keith or Saumarez, by pursuing an unsuccessful application on his own behalf.

In a letter dated 12 May 1797, addressed from his flagship *Ville de Paris*, 'off Cadiz', St Vincent asked Lord Spencer how he might secure appointment as 'Ranger and Keeper' of the Royal Park at Greenwich. The rehearsal of his case moved smoothly from fitting diffidence and deferential gratitude to hardheaded business considerations bearing on the value of the grant to the recipient. It concluded with warm sentiments of service solidarity and the nostalgic glow of early associations that predated St Vincent's naval career but were connected inextricably with it.

> I believe the rangership of Greenwich Park has been long, and is still vacant; but I am ignorant of the propriety of soliciting the King to confer it on me. Should his Majesty be graciously pleased to make the grant, and the Board of Works be directed to put the premises in repair, ... the passing the remainder of my days in the vicinity of the old boys, with many of whom I have served, and amid the scenes of my early youth ... would be a great gratification.[121]

At this stage St Vincent had not been awarded a pension and the Rangership was certainly a plum. The income from the office was £500pa and the 'premises' in which the Ranger lived was Inigo Jones' 'Queen's House'.[122] Spencer's response to St Vincent's enquiry was emphatic and discouraging: 'I understand from very good authority this as with all other appointments of this description are [*sic*] reserved by the King for the Royal Family, and on this account have thought it best not to mention the subject.'[123]

St Vincent let the matter rest for a year and then wrote directly to the king. This appeal repeated almost word for word the sentimental explanation of the earlier approach and added two news lines of argument. The letter was prefaced with a reminder that his claim rested on a lifetime of service: 'My labors and the last drop of my blood are devoted to the defence of your Majesty's sacred person and Government.' More surprisingly, St Vincent presented his residence in the Queen's House as a means of protecting the royal family from threats to its dignity and sense of moral decency. Perhaps drawing on his own experience as a schoolboy at Greenwich, St Vincent warned the king that if members of his family lived in the Park, they would be exposed to the distasteful spectacle of the populace exercising rights held 'since time immemorial' to exhibit 'a scene of frolicksome gambol and indecorous pastime' that 'renders [the Park] a very unfit residence for any branch of the Royal Family'. St Vincent proposed that the king's family should be spared these indignities by his appointment to the Rangership.[124] George III was deaf to this plea, and, consistent with Spencer's information, appointed members of his immediate family to the post.

Although St Vincent never lived in the Queen's House, he perhaps took comfort when George III gifted the property to Greenwich Hospital in 1806 and it became part of the school for pensioners' children. This act of generosity did not, however, spare the blushes of members of the royal family. The Ranger was rehoused in another property within the Park and thus remained exposed to popular indecencies. Still, since the king's bounty fell first to the Princess of Wales (who became notorious for sexual

Plate 8: Rowlandson's 'One Tree Hill' depicts the vulgar frolics from which St Vincent selflessly offered to shield members of the royal family by displacing them as Keeper and Ranger of Greenwich Park.

licentiousness) and then to the Duke of Clarence (the foul-mouthed sailor prince) not much moral sensibility was at risk.

Conclusion

Most of the flag officers who received royal honours, pensions and sinecures had performed with distinction and those who clamoured unsuccessfully for them drew attention to their significant achievements in the service. These appeals invoked ideas of fair allocation that were entirely consistent with the general assumption that royal recognition fostered a spirit of 'emulation' among senior naval officers. At the same time, however, the allocation of royal honours to particular flag officers was subject to the influence of interest and the impact of political considerations. Their role in determining the value and timing of awards is apparent in the contrasting fortunes of Saumarez and Pellew. Pellew's family was under the protection of the Boscawens and the Earl of Chatham was among his early friends. Later in his career he alienated St Vincent but acquired a particularly powerful and enthusiastic backer in the Duke of Northumberland.[125] Pellew nurtured this connection by advancing the career of one of the duke's sons and by keeping his patron up to date with military and diplomatic news when on active service. For his part, Northumberland pressed Pellew's claim for a place in the Order of the Bath and almost certainly encouraged Melville and Liverpool to supplant the *cordon rouge* with a baron's coronet. Northumberland made no bones about the parliamentary interest which he could bring to Pellew's support. Having arranged for the admiral's eldest son to be the member for Launceston, the duke expressed surprise at Melville's 'conduct and silence' over the Order of the Bath and remarked, 'When your son is in Parliament, a little hint perhaps coming from me may even be of some use, under such circumstances, as it will in some measure authorize me to interfere in your affairs at the Admiralty, because we have a vote or two on certain occasions to serve as an allure.'[126] As the duke had a determining role in the election of no less than seven MPs his interest played powerfully and directly on the patronage network.[127]

By contrast, Saumarez's interest was very limited.[128] He had come into the Navy on the basis of Channel Island connections and being at least a nephew, if not a son, of the service. Although Saumarez was highly regarded by the king, their relationship did not extend to the personal friendship which eased the way for Lords Howe, Gardner and Radstock. The latter appears to have been particularly fortunate in his family connections since his service record does not bear comparison with Samaurez's. His performance in the Baltic command was highly commendable but lacked the *éclat* necessary to prompt the ministers to feel the need to reward him at that stage of the war. Finally, while Saumarez's moral rectitude and spotless personal life would have pleased the king, they would have counted for little with the Prince Regent.

The rate of creation among flag officers dwindled during the Napoleonic Wars. There had been seven British and five Irish creations in the French War, with three of the latter subsequently being elevated to a seat in the House of Lords at Westminster. No admiral was chosen to fill a vacancy in the Irish peerage after 1804 and only four men (Barham, 1805; Collingwood, 1805; Gambier, 1807; Pellew, 1814) were made peers of the United Kingdom. These figures contrast sharply with senior army officers' rewards in this period. In the Napoleonic Wars nineteen senior army officers were raised to the British peerage, eight of whom received this distinction in 1814–15. This shift reflected the Army's increasingly prominent role towards the end of the wars, the dearth of fleet actions and the relative size of Britain's military forces. Towards the end of the war the Army had twice the manpower of the Navy and more than twice the number of commissioned officers.[129] The *Naval Chronicle*'s claim that Pellew's peerage and Keith's elevation to viscount showed that the Navy had not been forgotten amid the honours showered on the army would not have been endorsed by disappointed flag officers such as Duckworth, Saumarez, Warren and even Berkeley.[130]

As in other aspects of late Georgian government, the allocation of honours, pensions and sinecures involved both the king and his ministers. The king took a close interest in naval matters and formed his own views on officers' professional capabilities and personal merits. He was the prime mover in Elphinstone's and Hotham's elevation to the Irish peerage, resisted moves to make Nelson a baron after Cape St Vincent and is said to have resented bowing to ministerial pressure after the Battle of the Nile. It is significant that Lord Spencer did not press the case for a viscountcy at this time.

In contemplating recommendations for royal honours and pensions, first lords' susceptibility to interest was balanced by their estimation of the impact of particular rewards on the morale of recipient's colleagues. They also had to take account of political imperatives. Georgian governments relied on the support of loose coalitions associated with sections of the landed classes and powerful trading interests. They also, however, took account of a broader, less clearly defined constituency, summed up in phrases such as 'the feeling of the public'. The wars against France were so prolonged, so costly and so fraught that there was scarcely a year when government did not feel the political need for a major victory at sea. When these occurred, it sought to benefit from the reflected glory of ennobling the triumphant senior flag officer. These considerations meant that timing was critically important and that the longer the achievements of men like Duckworth and Saumarez went unrewarded the less likely rewards became. Spencer's and Dundas's congratulations to St Vincent and Duncan were perfectly good natured and sincere but they were fully aware of the political significance of both victories. Similarly, when Spencer sidestepped the king's declaration that Nelson lacked the financial means to be a peer, he clearly believed that the Ministry would lose face with the service and with the public if Nelson's achievement in Aboukir Bay was not recognized by a peerage.

The wider political significance of royal recognition was illustrated most graphically in the aftermath of Trafalgar. Collingwood, Nelson's gallant second-in-command, was made a baron and given the standard pension of £2,000pa. The main prize – an earldom, a pension of £5,000pa, a £90,000 grant to purchase an appropriate estate and other grants of £2,000 – went to a man of no distinction whose only service at sea was a brief unhappy spell as chaplain on his brother's ship twenty years before. Nelson's grasping, ungrateful and ungracious brother, the Reverend Dr William Nelson, who inherited Horatio's barony under the terms of the original patent, was created the first Earl Nelson in recognition of his brother's services, and endowed with an establishment that far eclipsed his aspirations.[131]

Admirals Afloat

The Treaty has not yet afforded me much comfort – doubts and fears still prevail and I believe will *prevail till my eyes rest on my dear Husband.*
—Lady Martha Samaurez to her husband, Rear Admiral Sir James Saumarez
when his return home was delayed, early April 1802[1]

When admirals commanded at sea, they were immersed in a distinctive way of life that was shaped by conditions on board ship and by their status in the service. Their lives afloat fused friendship, or at least sociability, with the cold reality of authority and hierarchy. Ongoing interactions with members of their staff, including captains of fleets and flag captains, provided opportunities for admirals to act as authoritative hosts to subordinates and, if personalities and inclinations allowed, to mitigate the isolation of their position by creating a distinctive form of domesticity. At the same time, however, flag officers naturally looked – through memory, shared feelings and written communications with their families – to the domestic realms they had left behind.

Earls Howe and St Vincent were allowed to spend the winter months ashore when they commanded in the Channel in old age, and some other 'home' commands involved periods of residence ashore, regardless of the age or health of the officers involved. When Lord Keith held an enlarged North Sea command in the early years of the Napoleonic War, for example, his flagship was moored off Ramsgate and he lived ashore. Vice Admiral Otway took his family with him to Leith as did Sir Richard Kingsmill and Lord Gardner when they commanded the Irish station based at Cork. Life in Ireland had distinct social advantages. Both men were popular figures among the Irish gentry and aristocracy and made social calls among them when their duties allowed.[2] Rear Admiral George Berkeley's wife went with him to Halifax when he took up the North American command in mid-1806.[3] Two of the flag officers who commanded in the Channel Islands during the war – Sir James Saumarez and Admiral Charles Duc de Bouillon – lived ashore when operational requirements permitted. Port admirals on the mainland also lived ashore in comfortable, well-appointed official houses. For the overwhelming majority of flag officers, however, an appointment on active service necessarily meant separation from their families and immersion in a distinctive way of life on board their flagships.

Domestic economy at sea

Admirals may have eaten some of the victuals supplied by the Naval Board, but from what little we know of their catering arrangements, it is clear that they preferred to live on their own supplies. In late August 1795 Lord Bridport advanced the unwelcome prospect of having to eat the seamen's ration of salt meat as an indication that the Board had prolonged his cruise beyond what he could reasonably be expected to endure. At this stage the fleet had been at sea for two and a half months.[4] Flag officers supplemented their supplies by sharing with their colleagues on station. If within reach of families and friends at home, they might also receive foodstuffs organized by them. Thus when Bridport and Sir Alan Gardner served in the Channel Fleet in the mid-1790s, they assisted one another to maintain supplies of fresh food. On one occasion Gardner regretted that he could not supply Bridport with hay because his meagre stock was needed to keep his surviving cow alive. Gardner told Bridport he had just killed his last sheep. His commander-in-chief responded by sending him some of his own dwindling flock. In acknowledging this gift, Gardner reported gratefully that it would keep his officers in 'good humour' for a week or so. He hoped that friends in England would soon replenish his flock so that he could return the favour. When Saumarez served off Ushant and in the Baltic, his friends and family supplied him with pork, venison, hearts, salmon, porter, butter and biscuits, and his wife sent a cow to ensure a supply of fresh milk. Flag officers on inshore stations also benefitted from fresh produce grown on isolated islands.[5]

Upon receiving appointments at sea admirals moved from half pay to full pay and also received an allowance (known as 'compensation') for servants who had in the past been carried on the books of their flagship. In the early stages of the wars, commanders-in-chief were paid 'table money' of £1 a day, later increased to £1/10. Over the period, the net value of pay and compensation varied depending on rates of income tax, and the offsetting impact of a 10 per cent increase in flag pay effective from 1 May 1806 (Table 11.1). The pay and compensation of admirals was double that of rear admirals. Before income tax was introduced, admirals, vice admiral and rear admirals on full pay received (inclusive of compensation) £1,529, £1,068 and £752pa, respectively, with their actual remuneration being calculated on the basis of a daily rate set for twelve, twenty-eight-day lunar months. After 1806 the annual after tax rates were £1,482, £1,037 and £713. Commander-in-chiefs' table money increased their annual service income by £504. There were some local variations to these standard rates. Flag officers commanding at Jamaica were paid as if they were full admirals, to take account of the cost of living on that station and the need to maintain a house and entertain on shore.[6] The East India Company made a hefty payment of £3,000pa to commanders-in-chief on that station in recognition of the costs of the post and the added responsibilities of working with the Company and its officers. It might also have been intended to focus their minds on protecting the Indian trade rather than on pursuing prizes.[7]

The apparent financial benefits of employment were offset to some degree by expenses incurred when serving afloat. Flag officers were expected to entertain senior members of their retinue and official guests and invite officers of their flagships to breakfast or dine with them. In some cases these expenses were thought to be unreasonably

Table 11.1 Flag pay and compensation

	Flag pay	Comp.	Deduction	Nett	Less 10%*	Less 5%*
1793–1805						
ADM	1176	396	43	1529	1376	1453
VA	840	258	30	1068	961	1015
RA	588	186	22	752	677	714
1806 onwards						
ADM	1294	396	43	1647	1482	N/A
VA	924	258	30	1152	1037	N/A
RA	649	186	22	813	732	N/A

Source: Compiled from tables in NMM RAI/6, NA ADM 1/582.

Note: Values rounded to nearest pound in all cases.

* Income tax was charged at 10% from 1799 to 1802 and from 1806, and at 5% from 1802 to 1803.

onerous. The key variables were the price of provisions on particular stations and the taste and disposition of the flag officer concerned. When Sir John Duckworth's command at Jamaica was prolonged into the peace and pay could no longer be augmented by prize money, he complained to St Vincent of the ruinous expenses of the post and asked (unsuccessfully) to be relieved from it. The Board added insult to injury by declining to meet a claim for nine months' house rent. Duckworth was particularly incensed that he was expected to bear the costs of entertaining senior army officers with whom he was working, claiming it had cost him £450 to support three generals and their staff on a joint operation in southern Martinique in mid-1801.[8] A decade later, Vice Admiral Sir George Berkeley found the Lisbon station a very expensive appointment: '[A]s Every Article of Life is much dearer than in England ... I do not conceive it possible to keep a decent Table *even on Board* for less than £2,000 a year.'[9] In this case a 'decent Table' was one fit to receive senior army officers and officials of Britain's Portuguese ally. Despite his complaints about the cost of serving at Jamaica, Duckworth took advantage of the posting to accumulate a mountain of exotic consumer goods, which he shipped home on the frigate *Acasta*. Details of this cargo were listed in court martial papers when Duckworth was obliged to defend himself before a court martial on charges of using a king's ship for private trade. It included large quantities of alcohol, mahogany tree trunks, slabs of other exotic timber, barrels of limes, forty pounds of arrowroot, between eight and ninety pounds of snuff, thirteen casks of guinea oil and a hogshead of cocoa nuts.[10]

While admirals were expected to entertain officers serving on their flagships, views differed on whether it was necessary or desirable for them to extend their hospitality to other members of the fleet. Captain Edward Codrington praised Nelson's warm yet strategic entertainment in the months before Trafalgar, 'these social arrangements which binds his captains to their admiral'.[11] Nelson's unusual ability to uphold authority while encouraging informality among his subordinates, his generous table and fine wines, all helped the cause and enhanced the social value of these occasions for flag officers and captains alike.[12] Codrington had complained bitterly when Collingwood had discontinued Nelson's practice and made unfavourable comparisons with Sir Robert Calder's revival of it.[13] He recalled with warm appreciation a convivial meeting after a court martial on Sir Robert's flagship. 'It was really a most animating sight; an admiral surrounded by twenty of his captains in social intercourse, showing a strong desire to support each other cordially and manfully in the event of a battle taking place.'[14]

Since Collingwood appreciated that 'ship-visiting' provided relaxation when officers were forbidden to go ashore during re-victualling and refitting off the British coast, it is not clear why he thought this practice inappropriate in operational situations. He certainly lacked Nelson's spontaneous social skills and as his long Mediterranean command wore on, a desperate concern to bring the French to action might have made him intolerant of practices that compromised his fleet's capacity to respond instantly to unfolding developments. An unsympathetic marine officer who served under Collingwood at this time was critical of the 'old fractious Admiral's' practice of putting to sea at half a moment's notice: 'as if the D[evil] was at him' the admiral 'set all sail possible, and without *signal* or other *notice*, away he went'.[15]

Collingwood's view on ship visiting at sea followed St Vincent's forceful example. When he was feuding with his flag officers and captains in the Mediterranean in the late 1790s, St Vincent suspected that troublesome subordinate flag officers took advantage of these occasions to cabal and incite disaffection among the captains under their command. Sir John Orde was a frequent target and it is possible, as Collingwood suggested, that St Vincent's resentment at Orde's magnificent 'style of living' may have been a contributory factor.[16] To be both upstaged and undermined was too much for a man of St Vincent's temperament. During his final command in the Channel in 1806, he only entertained officers from other ships at the beginning and end of cruises, when the fleet was in port.[17] St Vincent was thought to have a congenital dislike of ostentation and probably approved of Admiral Phillip Patton's demand that captains should set an example of simplicity in their furnishing and culinary arrangements so as to turn the attention of their junior officers 'from mean and little concerns to the perfection of the whole machine'.[18] This stricture might also have applied in an attenuated way to subordinate flag officers, with commanders-in-chief having pre-eminence in formal entertainment as in all other facets of their command.

St Vincent's views on entertaining and ship visiting were not due to parsimony. He was reputed to be a generous host and certainly spent lavishly during the course of his last command.[19] Before putting to sea in early March 1806 his agents paid more than £700 (sixteen months' table money) to merchants in Portsmouth for provisions, glassware, crockery and kitchen equipment for his flagship *Hibernia*. The bills presented by Portsmouth tradesmen point to elaborate and varied dining. In addition to livestock, cured meat and vegetables, they itemize large quantities of confectionary (milk chocolate, sugar, candy, currants, grapes, almonds) for dessert courses, as well as a range of spices, including black pepper, Jamaica ginger, allspice, nutmegs, cloves, cayenne, tarragon and twelve canisters of 'currie' powder, presumably used to enliven dishes made from hashed and salt meat. The extensive range of cooking utensils include various pie, pudding and patty pans and a box of pastry cutters.[20] Admirals' chefs had to contend with very variable weather but in other respects they were set up with stoves and cooking utensils on a par with those available to their colleagues onshore.[21] Judging from a record of Admiral Digby's menus from 1781, these supplies and utensils would have enabled St Vincent's chef to prepare elaborate and extensive meals for the sustenance and entertainment of his guests.[22] Digby entertained commissioned officers and 'young gentlemen' from *Prince George* on a daily basis. The admiral and his guests regularly ate roast ducks, roast mutton, potatoes, and gooseberry and cherry tarts and apple pie. Fresh vegetables (cabbages, cauliflower, carrots and turnips) were still being served in the third week of an eight-week passage.[23]

St Vincent's and Duncan's wine orders indicate that their guests were served a range of fortified and non-fortified wines, including St Vincent's 'best claret' from Bordeaux, and Duncan's 'Lisbon', a superior red wine from Portugal. When commanding in the Channel in mid-1800, St Vincent sent imperious instructions to a wine merchant at Bordeaux for between forty and fifty dozen bottles of 'best claret'. He showed a lordly disregard for expense, 'I regard not the price', and for the state of hostility between Britain and France: 'I do not think the first consul would object to it.'[24] Allowing for variations of availability, conditions, taste, wealth and inclination, the fragmentary surviving evidence suggests that flag officers' tables demonstrated at least some of the attention to culinary comforts demanded by such a determined bon vivant as Parson Woodforde.

As a general rule, and to the extent that the requirements of the service allowed, it was expected that flag officers would be assigned a ship appropriate to their status, conducive to their comfort and consistent with operational requirements. Disagreements on how far these considerations were reflected in particular allocations were sometimes a cause of tension between first lords and flag officers. As we have seen, the inferior accommodation of frigates was a significant factor in events leading to Admiral Cornwallis's court martial in 1795.[25] Before joining St Vincent in the Mediterranean in 1798 Vice Admiral Orde wrangled with Lord Spencer when his expectation that he would hoist his flag in *Leviathan* were unfulfilled.[26] Although Nelson was pleased to see the back of Calder in the late summer of 1805, he was careful to ensure that unfortunate officer went home to face a court martial in a dignity-preserving ship-of-the-line, rather than in the frigate that had been insensitively suggested by the Board.[27] It was characteristic of Lord Duncan's constrained sense of entitlement that Lord Spencer had to press him to shift his flag into a more comfortable vessel when he was commanding off the Texel in mid-1797. Duncan made light of rain that was driven into his cabin by the sharp north-easterly winds that whipped off the North Sea.[28] By contrast, Duckworth complained bitterly about the condition of the *Royal George* and of a professional member of the Board's brusque manner in responding to his concerns. Such treatment was 'truly humiliating to the feelings of a Flag Officer'.[29] At about the same time, the Board was also receiving sharply worded complaints from George Berkeley about being hurried off to his command at Halifax in a frigate with a convoy in tow. He tried unsuccessfully to recruit the prime minister, Lord Grenville, in his campaign to resist this 'indignity' to his rank.[30]

In order to live in appropriate style and comfort, many flag officers paid close attention to furnishing their quarters and recruiting specialized staff. When St Vincent appointed Cornwallis to command the Channel Fleet in 1803 he obligingly sent a naval vessel to convey furniture and other stores to his flagship at Plymouth. Cornwallis returned the favour by offering his furniture and stores to St Vincent when he took over the Channel command in early 1806. These transfers usually involved a sale and purchase, but Cornwallis seems to have been willing to gift them to his successor.[31] In the event, St Vincent demurred graciously: 'Many thanks for all your goodness to me. I have got everything I want, and am as comfortable as these wooden walls will permit.'[32] We don't know how St Vincent's quarters on *Hibernia* were furnished but judging from the display of Nelson's furniture in the Museum of the Royal Navy, they would have been equipped with a large dining table, writing desk, easy chairs and sofas, a sideboard, chests of drawers and closets for clothes, a sleeping cot and wash stand.

Flag officers' shipboard living arrangements included the recruitment of specialized non-military personnel. In addition to secretaries and their clerks who helped admirals deal with their service correspondence and prize business, they retained expert domestic personnel, including chefs and stewards to prepare and serve their food and to manage their domestic arrangements. Some flag officers also kept musical ensembles to enhance their status as hosts and gratify their personal aesthetic tastes. Duckworth was said to have delayed his departure to join Nelson's fleet – which meant he was not present at Trafalgar – while he awaited the arrival of an ensemble of personal musicians.[33] When Sir Charles Cotton came ashore in early 1807, he asked the Board for permission to turn his band of sixteen players over to Saumarez's *San Josef* at his successor's request, and at the end of the war when Sir Sidney Smith struck his flag he asked for two Sicilian musicians to be discharged from the service.[34]

Companionship at sea

Naval regulations gave captains complete authority over all members of their ships' companies and elevated them above all those with whom they served. While these requirements were thought necessary to maintain discipline in the service, they meant that captains were surrounded by men who held them in awe, and lacked companions who were not subject directly to their control. Depending on their personalities, this position could induce a sense of isolation and loneliness. It is easy to see why Codrington resented Collingwood's discouragement of ship visiting, and why he and his fellow captains welcomed the opportunity that courts martial provided to dine among their peers when judicial duty was done. Paradoxically, while the status and authority of flag officers entirely overshadowed that of post captains, these Neptunes of squadrons and fleets were often less isolated socially than those who reported to them. Although they had no equals, they were surrounded by staff members – first captains, flag captains and secretaries – who worked in close physical proximity to them and formed the shipboard equivalent of a flag officer's household. As with intimate subordinates ashore – domestic chaplains, the steward of an estate or a trusted agent – these men dined at the admiral's table as a matter of course. They were joined from time-to-time by captains who had business to transact on the flagship, by wardroom officers and 'young gentlemen' (midshipmen and masters mates) with sharp appetites and very limited means of satisfying them.

Judgements on whether these engagements crossed the boundary between well-fed but dull and uneasy duty and deferential conviviality varied. It was said that Vice Admiral Waldegrave's officers did not look forward to the prospect of dining with him. He was on friendly terms with Nelson, Saumarez and Collingwood but the tendency to stand on his dignity as the son of an earl, which motivated his refusal of a baronetcy in 1797, may well have made him an uncomfortable host to his inferiors in the service and in society. By contrast, while St Vincent was not above exercising a rough tyranny over his subordinate flag officers and captains, he kept a well-stocked store-room and when the mood took him could be an agreeable, courtly and generous host. His authoritarian jocularity provided amusement for some of his subordinates, albeit at the expense of others.[35] In addition to teasing those under his authority, St Vincent amused himself by challenging his officers to wagers. On 12 August 1795 when the installation of the Directory in France prompted rumours of a peace, he bet Captain Saumarez £100 that an agreement would be signed on that day and that hostilities would cease a month later and settled early when proved entirely wrong.[36] It says much for a commander-in-chief's capacity to determine the terms of social engagement that an evangelical officer was drawn into such a wager and hazarded several months' pay.

Nelson struck up warm personal and professional relationships with a number of his flag captains but Captain Thomas Masterman Hardy seems to have come closest to fulfilling his ideal. It has been noted that Hardy's calm temperament balanced Nelson's more mercurial and excitable disposition. He was also supremely competent, workmanlike and robust, which meant that he was able to relieve his admiral of unnecessary tasks that would have added to the physical and psychological strain of his role and distracted him from concentrating on strategic considerations.[37] Nelson invited Hardy to Merton as 'one of our true friends', and left him his telescopes, 'sea glasses' and a bequest of £100.[38]

Saumarez's relationships with his intimate subordinates were congenial. In his first appointment as an admiral, he got on very well with his flag captain, Jaheel Brenton. As Saumarez told his wife, Brenton 'is both an excellent officer, and agreeable as a Companion which makes the Evenings lose their former Ennui'. He and Brenton were both pious officers and shared a taste for divine services on Sundays. They did not sup together but took wine and water in the evenings and chatted amiably. When serving in the Channel Fleet in early 1807, Saumarez's sea routine involved breakfast at 8:30, dinner at 3:00 and companionable wine and water from 8:00 to 9:00. He always invited his flag captain, three wardroom officers and one or two 'young gentlemen' to share dinner with him.[39]

One way to increase the prospect of acceptable company at sea was to secure the appointment of a relative or close friend as flag or first captain. When Lord Gardner took command of the Channel Fleet in 1807, the first lord agreed that his son should be his captain of the fleet. In seeking this appointment, Gardner told Charles Yorke how important it was that he had 'a friend in whom I can confide and who will on all occasions second my wishes, and give me honest and unbiased opinion'.[40] Sir Charles Cotton no doubt had these benefits in mind when he asked Yorke to appoint his brother-in-law Captain Rowley first captain in mid-1810. On this occasion, however, the request was not granted. He was told that Rowley was too low on the captains' list to warrant such an appointment.[41] Cotton had earlier enjoyed the company of Sir Samuel Hood when they served together in the Mediterranean and regretted his departure to take up a command in the West Indies. 'He is always good humoured and in spirits.'[42]

But while flag officers' close interactions with their staff might enhance the quality of life in the twilight zone where personal and professional considerations intersected, they also carried risk. Admirals and their flag captains sometimes experienced barely unmanageable tensions arising from the demands and expectations of flag officers and captains' habit of reigning supreme within their own ships. George Murray had originally shied away from being Nelson's first captain in 1803 because he did not wish to compromise their mutual respect by taking on a 'service' that 'very frequently terminated in disagreement between the admiral and the captain'.[43] In response, Nelson waived any right to immunity from Murray's future protestations. Whether for that reason, or because of the personalities involved, or because the occasion never arose, their friendship withstood the test. Other arrangements did not prove so robust. Duckworth had questioned Spencer's decision to appoint Captain Richard King (the son of an admiral who was also MP for Rochester) to be his flag captain because he seemed unlikely to tolerate Duckworth's ways of doing things. Within a week these fears were confirmed and he asked for King to be replaced.[44] Even when there was a strong preexisting relationship between a flag officer and his captain, the pressures of working together might give rise to tensions that threatened a close, long-term friendship. Captain John Whitby's experience as Cornwallis's flag captain in the Channel Fleet is a case in point.

Cornwallis had taken a strong interest in Whitby's career since meeting him in the East Indies in 1790. He was delighted when his protégé returned to home waters in late 1803, telling the captain's wife that 'of all the people in the world he is the person I wish to have with me.... [I]n Torbay two winters ago, I was always unhappy if it was not in his power to come aboard'.[45] When Cornwallis's command ran into political and strategic difficulties from late 1804, however, Whitby's relationship with his service patron was placed under great pressure. Whitby and Vice Admiral Sir Charles Nugent, Cornwallis's first captain, competed for their commander-in-chief's attention and feuded with one another. At the same time, Cornwallis's behaviour became increasingly erratic. In late 1805 Whitby complained to his wife that Cornwallis and Nugent were effectively running his ship, leaving him to deal with punishments and suffer the opprobrium of the officers and crew for doing so. Cornwallis seemed oblivious to the damage he was doing, and while compromising Whitby's professional prospects, continued to treat him as a warm personal friend. As expectations that Cornwallis was to be superseded mounted, and he failed to take any steps to find his flag captain another command, Whitby felt increasingly isolated and insecure.[46] Theresa Whitby's interventions on her husband's behalf added to the immediate difficulty of the situation although they seem to have proved effective ultimately.[47]

Collingwood did not respect the flag captain who served under him at Trafalgar, finding him a source of aggravation rather than companionable support.[48] For the most part, however, he seems to have been well served by his flag captains and he got on very well with two of his subordinate flag officers, Vice Admiral Cotton and Rear Admiral Purvis. Collingwood also took great pleasure in the theatrical and operatic recreations of his ship's company. He told his wife that 'assemblies, concerts and plays' were their only common experiences: 'We have an exceedingly good company of comedians, some dancers that might exhibit at an opera, and probably have done so at Sadlers Well, and a band consisting of very fine performers.'[49] His most constant and faithful companion was, however, a large dog called Bounce. He told his daughters that he sung Bounce to sleep when he seemed despondent with a parody from *Much Ado About Nothing*: 'Sigh no more, Bounce, sigh no more / Dogs were deceivers never; Through ne'er you put one foot on shore, / Trust to your master ever.'[50] When the dog died towards the end of Collingwood's Mediterranean command, he felt the loss sharply:

> You will be sorry to hear that my poor dog Bounce is dead. I am afraid he fell overboard in the night. He is a great loss to me. I have few comforts, but he was one, for he loved me. Everybody sorrows for him. He was wiser than [a good many] who hold their heads higher and was grateful [to those] who were kind to him.

Collingwood had earlier reported that his dog was afflicted severely with rheumatism; that would have made it difficult for him to respond to the roll of the ship, or breaking seas.[51] It is also possible that one of Bounce's compassionate admirers among the 'people' helped the dog over the side to put the poor creature out of its misery.

Home thoughts when abroad

Most flag officers' surviving correspondence consists of their private and public interactions with the Board and with other contacts in the patronage network. They also corresponded with business agents and with family members and close friends. Agents who represented them in official transactions over pay and prize money, assisted in the supply of clothes and provisions and helped in personal arrangements concerning their families and dependents. For example, Ramsey and Williamson of Leith, who were Duncan's general agents, and dealt with prizes brought in for condemnation at that port, also advanced money to Lady Duncan for household expenses, kept an eye on building work on the admiral's new house in George Square, Edinburgh, and secured accommodation for his oldest son Robert when he went to Edinburgh with his tutor to study.[52] Personal regard and financial necessity meant that Nelson was very reliant on his agent Alexander Davison in the final years of his life.[53] Although the details of flag officers' business with their agents reflected their distinctive professional interests and were complicated by absence from home, they involved dependencies that were commonplace among men of their class and station.

Some of admirals' family correspondence related directly to domestic arrangements afloat. In addition to providing foodstuffs, family members arranged for clothing and linen to be supplied in bulk. Nelson's seagoing outfit in April 1798 included two dozen silk and cambric handkerchiefs, a dozen cravats, half a dozen Genoa velvet stocks and thirty numbered towels. Some of his correspondence exudes irritation at hurried embarkations and miscarried arrangements, aggravated on one occasion by Nelson's comment that 'I can do very well without these things, but it is a satisfaction to mention them'.[54] Two years later Lord Keith asked his sister to arrange for him to be

sent a dozen table cloths and sixteen napkins.[55] Family members could help in making these arrangements but they were essential to addressing the far more challenging
matter of coping with the emotional demands of long periods at sea or on foreign
stations.[56] Those serving in the Channel Fleet were occasionally able to obtain a few
days' leave ashore with wives and children who lived on the south coast, or travelled
there in the expectation of an opportunity arising. For the most part, however, flag
officers' contacts with their families were dependent on the mail services organized
by the government, and the goodwill of colleagues in the service who arranged for
letters to be carried out to them.[57] Letters took months to reach some foreign stations
and were subject to the hazards of the weather and the chance of enemy capture. They
often arrived out of sequence or in batches that had been written over several months.

Collingwood, Cotton, Murray and Saumarez might be taken to represent a much
larger group of flag officers who were highly successful in performing their wartime
duties and spent long periods at sea, but whose strong domestic inclinations made
them long for peace and an honourable release from service. As Collingwood put it
when forwarding letters to Mrs Murray, her husband was in 'good spirits but like all
[of] us, who have good wives at home leave them with regret and indulge the hope that
the day will come when we may enjoy our own fire sides in Peace – it is to make that
Peace sweet and secure that we suffer these privations'.[58] Collingwood's domestic attentions focused on his wife Sarah and their two daughters. When he was a senior post
captain, he had praised Sarah for supporting him in his desire to serve his country and
not subjecting him to 'teazing' complaints about his absence from home. Her forbearance had already been put to the test by a five-year separation. Collingwood's admiration for her 'exemplary and honourable' 'patience and equanimity' was matched by a
fervent expectation of the time when these sacrifices would no longer be necessary.[59]
When he spent a short time ashore following his promotion to rear admiral in early
1799, Collingwood revelled in the quiet joys of domesticity but also declared himself
impatient 'to be in the exercise of my profession .... There is a nothingness in a sailor
ashore at such a time that will, if it last long, weary me'.[60]

These ideas were not inconsistent but rather pointed to the need for an honourable,
and hence sustainable, peace. As things turned out, Collingwood hardly had time to
grow weary of home. He was soon appointed to a subordinate role in the Channel Fleet
and remained at sea up to, and indeed beyond, the signing of the peace preliminaries
on 1 October 1801. During these two and a half years he scarcely put foot on shore,
noting wistfully in August 1801 that this was 'the third summer that I have hardly seen
the leaf of the trees, except through a glass at a distance of some leagues'. This depriva-
tion was to some degree self-inflicted as Collingwood chose to remain on board to
set an encouraging example to his captains when they were ordered to stay on ships
moored inshore.[61] He saw his wife and older daughter briefly at Plymouth in March
1801 but for the most part relied on letters from Sarah (which have not survived), and
the pleasure of discussing his children in correspondence with other members of his
family and close friends.

During the Peace Collingwood spent eighteen contented months at home in
his comfortable town house in the Northumbrian market town of Morpeth, tending his extensive garden and taking a close enlightened interest in nurturing his

daughters' education. In late 1804, however, he was appointed to the Channel Fleet under Cornwallis and subsequently joined Nelson's Mediterranean Fleet. From thenceforth, he was separated from his family forever. Having served as Nelson's second at Trafalgar, and secured St Vincent's warm praise for his conduct in the aftermath, he remained in command of the Mediterranean station until a couple of days before his death. Collingwood's correspondence from the last years of his life is marked by poignant, characteristically stoic, commentary on his unrelieved service at sea. He told Murray how much he missed his daughters and regretted that they had been deprived of a father's 'caresses and love'. Collingwood tried, however, to make light of his loss by joking that he would only know his girls now if parents' recognition of their offspring was instinctive. He doubted whether such a faculty existed, or would be beneficial if it did. It 'would not be for the general convenience of the world. Providence has been equally good to us in the faculties it has given us and in those it has withheld'.[62]

Collingwood was relieved that the girls had inherited his wife's 'gentleness of disposition' rather than the barely suppressed 'acidities' that sometimes marred his own. He did not want them speaking with 'an uncouth provincial dialect and corrupt pronunciation' but thought their personal and intellectual development, 'their hearts, their minds', far more important.[63] Although markedly conservative in his politics, Collingwood's views on female education were not far removed from those of Mary Wollstonecroft. He railed against 'fine ladyism', empty-headedness and idleness. When he was at home between the wars he taught his daughters languages, writing and composition, geometry and arithmetic. He stressed the importance of acquiring a disposition marked by humanity, good sense and rationality and developing an independent sense of right and wrong. The girls' education should 'improve the benevolence of their hearts and direct it [sic] to have a knowledge of the world and how to be independent in it, in every condition of life, for independence consists more in the temper of the mind than in outward possessions'.[64] He disliked the moral and intellectual atmosphere of female boarding schools, and, fearing that his daughters would pick up bad card-playing habits and a competitive taste for finery, vowed to bring them home when he returned from his Mediterranean command.

These worries about his daughters' education suggested a lack of confidence in Lady Collingwood's firmness in these matters. As Collingwood's last command dragged on, he also became concerned about his wife's financial management and toleration of her father's unhelpful interference in their affairs. He was particularly incensed that his father-in-law had made him a shareholder in a dubious Newcastle fire insurance company. Collingwood saw this connection as a stain on his honour and a threat to his reputation in the service, and demanded that his name be removed from the company's books: 'It is an undertaking for speculators and adventurers who have nothing to lose. I would rather lose the money than not show my resentment'.[65] Collingwood was becoming rich from prize money and bequests, enjoying in his last years an income of almost £7,000pa from pay, table money, pension and dividends.[66] He left a handsome fortune of more than £160,000.[67] He nevertheless worried about money and his financial affairs were complicated by an inheritance he shared with other members of his family, and by wrangles with the Duke of Northumberland's agent over a right of way. These matters all played a role in Collingwood's correspondence with his family at home.

Sir Charles Cotton served under Collingwood in the Mediterranean Fleet and succeeded him in that command. Collingwood told Cotton that he kept his daughters' letters on his table and 'when I am sad – and I am often sad – I think I find comfort and consolation in reading them – they seem to convey a promise of future happiness'. The two flag officers looked forward to family visits in the comfort of peace: 'Whenever I go on shore – it will be forever – and I hope My dear Sir at Madingley and at Thriston we may look back to the days we have seen – with delight that they are past.'[68] A few letters from Cotton's daughters are in his papers in the county records office at Cambridge. When Cotton was a junior flag officer serving in the Channel Fleet in late 1799 he received a charming letter from his youngest daughter Philadelphia (Philly), written over two days in a lovely clear hand. She congratulated her father 'most sincerely on your safe arrival to Torbay …. Mamma and Maria join me in love to you and in our best wishes for your return to Madingley'. Later, when Cotton was serving in the Mediterranean, Maria, the older daughter, passed on news of their social life, with detailed accounts of concerts in the Senate House at Cambridge and a ball at the Red Lion which kept her up until four in the morning.[69] If Cotton saw the *Morning Post's* account of his friend Collingwood's funeral, he would also have read with pride a notice of his daughters' presentation at the Queen's Drawing Room that appeared in the same issue of that newspaper. It was reported that their 'dresses of white satin and crepe tastefully ornamented with wreaths of green and white flowers … attracted universal admiration for their elegant and juvenile simplicity'.[70]

Probably thinking of his predecessor's extended period of service in the Mediterranean, Cotton feared prolonged absence from home and regretted lost opportunities to ride and walk over his estate with his children. He dwelt longingly on a missed harvest thanksgiving service in Madingley Church:

> All day yesterday & the day before my beloved family were uppermost in my Thoughts … [T]he Pew at Church where all were assembled … the Pride of the Lady of the Manor, the grateful thanks to Providence for all Blessings received … with a thought now & then, with a Prayer for the only one of the family absent.

These poignant thoughts did not displace more practical considerations, however. Cotton advised his wife on routines for the younger children, stressing that they should be warned to stay away from ponds on the estate and not to go fishing unless an adult was with them. Lady Cotton seems to have taken an active role in the management of the estate while her husband was at sea. He sent her detailed instructions on repairs and improvement to his property, enquired eagerly after the condition of his livestock, and assured her that 'everything is interesting that I receive from you'.[71]

Sir James Saumarez and his family shared Collingwood and Cotton's longing for peace.[72] His wife Martha, a lively and loving correspondent, sent him family news and reassured him of the mutual consolation of their devotion to one another and their willing resignation in the face of God's providence. Her letters included touching vignettes of their children. Martha wrote to tell him that their youngest daughter

Cartaret, at this time a child of four, had woken her mother to tell her with delighted laughter that she had just seen her father and *Caesar* in a dream. 'I wish my *eyes* had been as good!'[73] The admiral's son and a friend held mock courts martial over which the younger James Saumarez presided, in the way he imagined his father did.[74] In a very different vein and during a prolonged period of particularly foul weather in the spring of 1801, Martha told her husband that 'I send up many an earnest prayer to Heaven … & with gratitude acknowledge that it is owing to the Divine Goodness thou dost not fall into misfortunes "like other men" tho' encountering *seeming* greater Perils than they'.[75] Saumarez longed desperately for letters from his wife and became anxious when their flow was disrupted by adverse conditions, or by the capture of vessels carrying mail to the fleet. When commanding the inshore squadron off Brest, he complained bitterly of Cornwallis's apparent inattention to mail arrangements, condemning it as 'unpardonable'.[76] Martha seemed calmer, presumably because if anything happened to him there were a range of public and private sources through which the awful news would travel, while her husband wholly relied on his wife for private news of the well-being of their family.

When Saumarez was promoted rear admiral in early 1800, he spent two months with his family in rented accommodation in Sidmouth but appointment to a subordinate role in the Mediterranean Fleet marked the start of a period of uninterrupted service that did not end until mid-1802. The news that the peace negotiations had begun in earnest at the beginning of October 1801 launched Martha Saumarez on an excited wave of capital letters, exclamation marks and appeals to divine providence.

> THE PRELIMINARIES OF PEACE are Signed!!!!!!! – Oh may God in his infinite mercy grant that Happiness & Content may now be the Fruits of those Labours & Toils thou hast been enduring for nine long years.

Over the coming months, however, the couple's patience was tested sorely. When Saumarez's service was prolonged after the Treaty of Amiens was signed on 25 March 1802, his wife wrote to tell him that 'doubts and fears still prevail and I believe *will* prevail till my eyes rest on my dear Husband'. Martha's letters were sent through Captain Sir Thomas Troubridge of the Admiralty Board.[77] He was personally sympathetic but official information from the Admiralty was vague and ambiguous. The rumour that Saumarez was to be appointed to command in the Mediterranean complicated the situation and prompted Martha to make plans to travel to Gibraltar with her oldest child to see him. Their letters from this period show more signs of open agitation, low spirits and stress than during the war years.[78]

Although Martha Saumarez's letters are dominated by family news, religious reflections and warm expressions of spousal affection and support, she also found time to share service gossip with her husband and to pass judgement on his colleagues and their wives. This news usually derived from her stays in Bath where she kept company with other sea widows and half-pay admirals. Over 1801–1802 Lady Saumarez's naval acquaintance included Mrs Bertie, Ladies Bickerton, Cotton, Mitchell, Nelson and St Vincent, Admiral and Mrs Thornbrough, Lord Hood, Sir John Colpoys and Sir Sydney Smith. She told her husband that the latter was 'greeted with all the distinction even his vanity could wish'.[79] Thornbrough, however, was condemned for being too fond of good company shortly after his wife's death. Martha noted sardonically that the admiral 'seems to have no difficulty practicing the duty of resignation'.[80] Nelson's personal conduct in the Mediterranean and the implications of this for Lady Nelson were subjects of keen interest. Martha alluded to rumours of Nelson's life in Naples, but was angry at what she saw as Lady Spencer's thoughtlessly cruel hints to Lady Nelson. She thought it 'very wrong to mention things to [Lady Nelson] that tend to no good but to irritate and mortify her'.[81] Rumours attached to Admiral Mitchell's sexual and financial affairs made him the object of Martha Saumarez's censure, and his wife an object of pity. Lady Mitchell was 'a pleasing woman, & looks deserving of a better Partner than, it seems, has fallen her lot'. She reported that Mitchell had been described as '*comme un vaut thien*, qui aime la Compaigne des Dames *a la Nelson*, & of a disposition extremely extravagant. *We* have not been much deceived, for the more I saw of him the less I lik'd him'.[82] Fallen women were also held up for mutual disapproval. Lady Saumarez noted that the divorced wife of St Vincent's heir was shunned by her mother's acquaintance when she appeared among them with no fitting show of repentance for her adulterous conduct.[83]

A few years earlier Lady Nelson had been more accommodating towards this woman, and so too had Lady St Vincent. Fanny told her husband that Lady St Vincent 'spoke very humanly and tenderly of the unfortunate Lady Elizabeth Ricketts' and asked him to 'lean on the poor woman's side' if St Vincent ever raised the subject with him. These were early days in the unfolding of news of Lady Rickett's affair with Captain Hargreaves, however, and Martha Saumarez's reaction may have been more typical after a court case in February 1799. Captain Rickett was awarded £1,000 damages for Hargreaves's adulterous relationship with his wife. He had sought £20,000 and when the jury determined on a small fraction of that sum after only ten minutes of deliberation, it is safe to assume that it accepted Hargreaves's plea that the very young captain of militia had, at least in part, been encouraged by the slightly older daughter of an Irish peer.[84]

When Lady Nelson was in Bath in early 1797, her husband was serving under St Vincent in the Mediterranean. She relied on naval connections – Vice Admiral Young at the Board and Martha Saumarez – to arrange for the passage of letters to him. Lady Nelson reported meetings with naval acquaintance, including Admirals Dickson, Barrington, Stanhope and Sawyer, who passed on second- or third-hand, and hence usually dated and unreliable, news of Nelson's whereabouts. They also exchanged service speculation on pending honours. Fanny told Nelson that the word in Bath was that it was 'certain' that Elphinstone (Keith), Hotham and Jervis would be raised to the peerage. The day after the Battle of Cape St Vincent she passed on (inaccurate) information that Jervis was to become an Irish peer.[85]

Fanny Nelson provided her husband with excited accounts of the enthusiastic public reception of his singular role in the battle, and told him of the congratulations that had come to her from Lords Hood and Howe and other members of the naval community at Bath. Duncan was reported to have jocularly praised Nelson by saying he had abandoned any ambition for a meeting with the French because his exploits would never match Nelson's. But while Fanny was highly gratified by the public adulation of

Nelson, the accounts of his most daring exploits worried her. She told her husband that he had 'done desperate actions enough. Now may, I, indeed I do beg, that you never board again. *Leave* it for *captains*'.[86]

In Lady Nelson's letters to her husband she encouraged his ambitions and sense of entitlement. Thus when Lord Keith told Fanny that Nelson was to be given the 'red ribbon' of the Order of the Bath, she was far from satisfied: 'I expect they will give you a handsome pension, if they do not you must ask for it. They cannot refuse.'[87] Fanny underestimated the considered, even stubborn, way in which the king dealt with these matters, and it was not until late in the following year that Nelson's triumph in Aboukir Bay gave Lord Spencer the leverage necessary to persuade the king to raise Nelson to the lowest step in the British peerage and approve the standard pension of £2,000pa.[88] By that time, however, Fanny's ambitions for her husband had expanded. Encouraged by Lord Hood, she again complained that his rewards were inadequate. In the months before the battle, however, unfounded rumours of actions had unsettled Fanny. She told her husband that she longed for a peace that would preserve him from fresh dangers and remove the stress she felt at his ongoing exposure to them.[89] Reports of the great victory at the Nile that circulated in England in advance of the official dispatches and reliable information of casualties, heightened Fanny's anxiety: 'The newspapers have tormented me in regard to the desperate action you have fought with the French fleet.'[90] Late the next year, when Keith was leaving to supersede St Vincent in the Mediterranean command, Fanny expected her husband to return home. She wrote to tell him that his new carriage was waiting for him: '[I]t is really elegantly neat ... I will not use the chariot that I may have the pleasure of seeing you get in it.'[91] These hopes were dashed by Nelson's growing attachment to Emma Hamilton.

Lady Hamilton's letters to Nelson have not survived but his side of the correspondence gives a sense of the pain of separation. In five letters written between September 1804 and January 1805 but not received until March 1805, Emma seems to have pressed Nelson to take a leave of absence that had been approved by the Board. She proposed travelling to Gibraltar to see him. Nelson gently reminded her that she 'supposes things that are impossible' and tried to explain why he was unable to fall in line with her fervently stated wishes. In the last years of his life with Lady Nelson, Fanny's letters had been full of news of renovations to 'Round Wood', the house they had purchased outside of Ipswich. Home improvement also played a role in Emma's correspondence. Nelson and Emma undertook extensive alterations to Merton Place during the Peace of Amiens but this project was not complete when he went back to sea. Judging from Nelson's correspondence, Emma sent progress reports, discussed future developments and warned when it would be necessary to apply to Alexander Davison, his deep-pocketed and long-armed agent, to advance money to cover costs.[92] Nelson, who was hard-pressed for ready money at this stage of his career, expected to repay his agent when pending prize payments were settled.

The importance attached to naval officers' correspondence with their families was reflected in the willingness of friends and colleagues to carry letters on their behalf, or forward them to those who would. It also prompted sharp criticism of commanding officers who were thought to pay insufficient attention to the delivery and despatch of private letters. Martha Saumarez shared her husband's disgust at Cornwallis's apparent disregard for this aspect of what she clearly saw as his duty. The criticism itself may have been fair, but the attribution of it to the myopic insensitivity of a confirmed bachelor was not. Cornwallis never married but during his last command he corresponded with the shore-bound member of what had, in effect, become his family. Captain Whitby married Theresa Symonds in 1801 and they had a daughter shortly thereafter. When he went back to sea in 1803 Mrs Whitby and her daughter moved into Cornwallis's house, where the highly capable sea widow quickly became an indispensable source of practical and emotional support to him. Theresa superintended the farm and oversaw renovations to the enlarged farm house where the admiral had settled. She guarded Cornwallis's property rights jealously, keeping a sharp eye on those who trespassed on his shooting while he was away at sea. Towards the end of 1805 she was in dispute with a neighbouring property owner on Cornwallis's behalf, forcefully advising him to sign a letter of warning: you 'must take the matter up in a regular way ... you must either suffer it always or prevent it at once'. Mrs Whitby told Cornwallis that the offender 'has behaved in so ungentlemanlike a manner ... that I feel quite justified in considering nothing but what may be advantageous to you'. In the spirit of this declaration, she urged Cornwallis to pursue a contemplated land purchase that they knew would 'discomfort' this adversary. Theresa wrote detailed accounts of farming and property business and reported on the behaviour of servants. She also told Cornwallis how much she and her daughter missed him and her husband. Like Martha Saumarez and Lady Cotton, she longed for the end of the war. 'I wish this tiresome sort of Warfare was over with all my heart – happy indeed shall I be to welcome you once more to Newlands.'[93]

Conclusion

Families, friends and agents went to considerable trouble and expense to ensure that flag officers at sea had access to supplies of food and drink that were fitting for men of their status and, no doubt, satisfied their personal expectations. Their capacity to do so was constrained by available resources and always subject to the competing demands of wartime active service. For many admirals the material comforts available at sea had a significant bearing on personal well-being and morale. They also, however, played a role in flag officers' fulfilment of their social obligations to those under their command. These obligations required them to balance the demands of official conviviality with those of general disciplinary authority. As in other aspects of his leadership, Nelson was particularly adept at maintaining this balance. Officers such as Collingwood who had trouble in doing so risked exacerbating the sense of loneliness arising from long separation from wives and children at home. As a result, they were even more heavily reliant than other flag officers on written communications with their immediate family, and on the opportunities that correspondence with other relations and close friends gave for sustaining memories of their loved ones and prompting comforting images of returning to live among them.

Admirals Ashore

[A]s I am in the Country and still on Crutches, I cannot help not only wishing, but regretting that I had not the honour of sporting my other leg on such honourable service under your Lordship's command.
    —Admiral Sir Thomas Pasley (who lost a leg at the Battle of First June 1794) to Lord Bridport after his action against the French off Ile de Groix, 23 June 1795[1]

When flag officers struck their flags and went ashore they re-entered the social strata from which they sprang, or to which they had ascended through marriage or professional accomplishments. In some cases their fortunes depended on the financial fruits of their professional lives but in many other respects the land-bound lives of late Georgian flag officers did not differ from those of other men of their wealth and social standing. They kept houses in London and the countryside, superintended their property, and, as health, taste and opportunity dictated, visited, dined, attended assemblies and balls and killed game birds, fish and foxes. Fourteen admirals, including St Vincent, Keith and Charles Stirling, were Fellows of the Royal Society but of these only the Duc De Bouillon, William Bentinck and William Bligh seemed actively engaged in scientific pursuits.[2] Many flag officers were substantial landowners or significant figures in provincial towns and watering places, and played leadership roles as members of the local elite. In some cases, they were also members of the House of Commons. Their engagement generally mirrored the uneven levels of attendance and participation which characterized Georgian parliaments, but some flag officers, not surprisingly, showed an interest in naval affairs that came before the House. Sir Charles Pole, who never served at sea after 1802, had leisure to take his parliamentary duties as the member for Newark (1802–1806) and Plymouth (1806–18) seriously. He spoke regularly on naval matters and was a staunch defender of St Vincent's draconian reforms of naval administration. Captain John Markham also defended the former first lord. When he attended the House as a rear admiral, his contributions were focused almost entirely on the Navy. The same was true of Sir John Orde. As MP for Yarmouth (IOW) he was a staunch ministerialist who spoke against moves to condemn the expeditions against Copenhagen and the Scheldt. Ironically, given his turbulent transactions with St Vincent, Sir John disapproved of Lord Cochrane's attempt to continue his feud with Admiral Lord Gambier through hostile parliamentary motions.[3]

But while admirals ashore lived much like other men they continued to be affected by their careers in the service. Half-pay flag officers of the Blue, White and Red Squadrons remained subject to the direction of the Board, and even members of the Yellow Squadron were not wholly free of its influence. They were liable to be called on to perform services on the Board's behalf and to attend important ceremonial occasions with other admirals and state dignitaries. These obligations, and the lasting effects of early entry to the service, prolonged isolation from other sections of the community, and friendships forged by shared hardship and the working of patronage and service interest produced a lasting sense of collective identity which survived flag officers' return to life ashore.

Homes of the admirals

Flag officers came originally from across Great Britain and Ireland and a few hailed from North America and the Caribbean. When they went ashore, some returned to their old homes but a significant number settled, understandably enough, in the southern and south-western counties of England. Some flag officers' homes were grand and ancestral, others were grand and *noveau* and many were substantial and comfortable. Where and how flag officers lived ashore depended not just on their inclinations but on the accidents of birth and inheritance, the romantic or mercenary vagaries of marriage and the extent of service-related income from prizes, sinecures and pensions.

Several flag officers lived in style on properties that had come to them though their families. Admiral Roddam, Collingwood's early service patron, resided at Roddam Hall, an estate he had inherited in Northumberland. Sir Charles Cotton, the fifth baronet, owned an extensive property in Cambridgeshire that had been in his family for generations. In 1804 Sir Charles's income was almost £4,000, of which only about £1,100 came from his active service pay and allowances. The balance was made up of dividends from investments in the public funds, profit on land farmed by him and £2,000 in rents. Most of the rental income derived from land in Cambridgeshire, but Cotton also owned commercial property in East Smithfield, London.[4] He and his family lived in Madingley Hall, a fine sixteenth-century house set in seven acres of garden and grounds designed by Capability Brown.

Sir Eliab Harvey, who also came from a wealthy landed family, inherited its property at Rolls Park in Essex when he was still a midshipman with wild oats to sow. Showing the taste for risk that later made him a hero of the Trafalgar action, the youthful Harvey lost £100,000 in a single gambling session at the Cocoa Club. When he boldly declared that he would sell his estate to settle this debt of honour, his opponent (whether through good nature, sportsmanship or calculation is not clear) agreed to settle for £10,000 and hazard the rest on the toss of a coin. Horace Walpole said that the offer came from the gamester Mr O'Birne, but the *London Chronicle* reported that Harvey begged for one last chance to either save the situation or ruin himself entirely. In any case, young Harvey's luck momentarily returned and while he lost £10,000, he retained his family estate. When he was older, but scarcely any wiser, he retired to Rolls Park when another act of extreme rashness put an end to his active service career.[5]

Plate 9: Vice Admiral Sir Charles Cotton's prize money and flag pay supplemented a handsome income from inherited property. His substantial estate in Cambridgeshire included Madingley Hall, a fine Elizabethan house set in seven acres of gardens designed by 'Capability' Brown.

Sir Thomas Pakenham was also the beneficiary of family property. His elder brother gave him an estate in the vicinity of the ancestral home at Castlepollard, County Westmeath, and he came into other substantial property in Ireland and Hampshire through marriage.[6] Pakenham never served at sea as a flag officer, but having held the sinecure offices of surveyor-general and lieutenant general of the Irish Ordnance while a post captain, he had the good fortune to be appointed master general in 1800. This post carried a handsome salary of £1,500pa. When it was abolished as a result of the union of Great Britain and Ireland in 1801 Pakenham received compensation of £1,200pa for life.[7] He had seen volunteer service against Irish rebels in 1798 but that was the end of any active military engagement. Pakenham spent the rest of his life as a country gentleman, managing his estate and overseeing the cultivation of a large garden.[8]

Lord Howe, a bold fighting officer and accomplished service politician, died 'very rich'.[9] He married an heiress and his fortune was boosted by a four-year tenure of the highly lucrative post of treasurer of the Navy, other service sinecures and rich prize winnings. He had a country property near St Albans with an imposing house, Porter's Lodge, designed by Sir Richard Taylor. This architect was also responsible for the interior of Howe's London house in Grafton Street.[10] St Vincent had been poor for much of his life, but he married well and acquired through his wife Martha a substantial country house called Rochetts near Brentford, in south Essex. Prudential financial management, prize money and sinecures boosted St Vincent's fortune and allowed him to purchase the lease of a substantial London town house in Mortimer Street, off Great

Portland Street. Some of its furniture and decoration, including models of the *Royal William* and *Lion*, were of naval provenance, having been purchased for just under £300 from Admiral Sir Samuel Barrington's estate.[11]

A combination of prize money and a prosperous marriage also set Vice Admiral Sir Robert Kingsmill up for a very comfortable retirement after his command of the Irish station from 1795 to 1800. Prize earnings on this station were steady rather than spectacular but Kingsmill was still receiving substantial sums after giving up the command. He accumulated more than £30,000 in government stock and in addition to his half pay enjoyed an income of about £2,300pa from a substantial landed property in Hampshire he had inherited through his wife.[12] Kingsmill, who had no children to support, enjoyed an income even more comfortable than that of Sir Charles Cotton. Lord Duncan's family property in and around Dundee was modest compared with Cotton's and Kingsmill's estates but when he went ashore his income was boosted significantly by the fruits of his successful career in the service. He had half pay of just over £600pa, a £3,000 pension, residual prize payments, which amounted to £600 in his first year ashore, and dividends from invested prize funds of about £1,200.[13]

Sir Hyde Parker's and Lord Keith's huge prize earnings allowed them to live ashore in considerable style. Parker, a younger son, came ashore to a substantial estate in Suffolk and a town house in London purchased from a fortune acquired as commander-in-chief at Jamaica in the 1790s and at the Battle of Copenhagen. Keith's prize earning may have neared half a million pounds, he probably had a pension of £2,000pa and his second marriage was to an heiress. He is said to have settled a ducal income of £30,000 on his only daughter and certainly invested heavily in property.[14] His English properties included a town house in Harley Street and Purbrook House, built to a grand design of Sir Richard Taylor, on the northern slopes of the Southdown Hill, half a dozen miles north of Portsmouth. Keith also invested heavily in Scottish property, including an estate called Tulliallan where he lived after the war.

Lord Hood's relatively modest prize earnings were sufficient to fund the purchase of Catherington House, a small country residence a few miles north of Keith's splendid property. Hood retreated to Catherington when dismissed from his command in 1795, and his brother Lord Bridport stayed there when he had leave from the Channel command in the late 1790s. By that time, however, Hood's main residence was in the well-appointed governor's apartments in Greenwich Hospital. These quarters were close enough to London for Hood to keep in touch with the founts of information and interest but they also exposed him to the depredations of 'London housebreakers'. They broke into his apartments in September 1807 and left with four of the admiral's silver tea and coffee pots and three dozen spoons.[15] Hood's brother Lord Bridport had an income from half pay, sinecures and prize earnings sufficient to purchase Cricketts, a substantial house in Dorset. Running true to form, however, he continued to hanker after what he could not have. Shortly after his retirement, Lord Glastonbury's splendid Burton Pynsent estate in Somerset took Bridport's fancy and Hood handsomely offered to advance him £14,000 that had just come to hand from his Toulon prize money. Even with this assistance, however, Bridport could not meet Lord Glastonbury's asking price of £50,000. As he regretfully told his brother, the property was 'far beyond my reach or the reach of any part of my family to purchase'.[16]

Plate 10: A small portion of Lord Keith's quarter million pound prize money was sufficient to cover the purchase of 'Purbrook House', near Portsmouth. This spectacular Italianate building was designed by Sir Roger Taylor.

Duckworth had been desperately poor as a half-pay post captain in the 1780s but regular employment during the French and Napoleonic Wars brought significant prize income. That and a prosperous second marriage allowed him to advance his sons' careers by purchasing commissions in the army and investing in an estate in Wear, near Exeter. Duckworth reported spending almost £1,500 on the property in 1805 and later claimed that the cost of repairs to what he described as a 'great house' left him 'drained at every pore'.[17] Unlike Duckworth, Vice Admiral Peter Rainier, who came from a family of small provincial merchants, showed no inclination to set himself up as a country gentleman even though he returned from the East Indies loaded with a fortune of quarter of a million pounds. He had houses in London and in Bath, thus establishing quarters in two of the most powerful urban magnets of half-pay flag officers. After many years' service in the East Rainier suffered from the cold, damp climate of Bath. The 'native climate … has been fully equal to my expectations, having experienced enough cold & rheumatism to remind me of the change throughout the autumn and winter'.[18] Lord Radstock also seems to have preferred to live close to town rather than invest in a distant country estate. He lived in considerable style at Twickenham surrounded by notable works of art.[19] In 1801 he boasted that his collection of Flemish painting was superior to that of the Duke of Buckingham. The Duke of Northumberland's agent had discussions with him in 1808 about purchasing one of his prize Italian pieces. One hundred and fifteen pictures from Radstock's collection, including many fine works by Dutch, Italian and Flemish masters, fetched more than £23,300 when they went to auction in London in 1826.[20]

In common with many members of the middle and upper classes, flag officers who were not resident in the capital gravitated there for the winter season, renting houses or taking lodgings. From time to time, they were listed by newspapers at significant events of the 'fashionable world'. In addition to attending private parties and balls, half-pay admirals, along with their subordinates, waited on the first lord to press their case for appointments or honours, and to seek his interest on behalf of friends.[21] Loyal devotion, a taste for high society and a wish to keep oneself in the minds of the direct and indirect dispensers of good things prompted admirals to attend the Royal levees and the Drawing Rooms.

When Sir James Saumarez was serving at sea, his wife sometimes joined other sea widows (including Lady Nelson and Lady Calder) at Bath. There they kept company with half-pay admirals and their wives who had come to see and be seen, and to take the waters for gout and other afflictions. Rainier's obesity probably made residence at Bath a medical as well as a social necessity but he was no reclusive invalid. He was well enough integrated into local society to serve on the committee of the Harmonic Society, a gentlemen's dining and glee club. Members and guests entertained themselves with the help of 'professional' singers. Performances at a meeting in late 1814 'set the tables on a roar' and there is no reason to suppose that earlier meetings were any tamer.[22] There was plenty of naval company in the city. The *Bath Chronicle* noted the arrival of a stream of flag officers, including 'Admirals' Buckner, Alpin, Pakenham, Gambier, Chamberlayne, Duckworth, Young, Stirling, Man and Pickmore.[23] When Vice Admiral Sir George Berkeley arrived in Bath in the summer of 1808 he was honoured at a dinner attended by 100 gentlemen of Gloucester. He sat as a member for that county so the dinner was likely to have been as much a tribute to the family's electoral interest as to his standing in the service.[24] Vice Admiral Arthur Philip, the distinguished and humane first governor of New South Wales, resided at Bath in his retirement. His half pay was boosted by a pension of £500pa for his Australian service and he was able to lay out £2,200 to purchase the lease of an elegant house in a fashionable part of the town.[25] Other flag officers visited rival watering places. Vice Admiral Jackie Payne, a great friend of the Prince of Wales, was depicted in a contemporary print taking in the bracing sea air of Brighton. St Vincent, Saumarez and Rear Admiral Sir Richard Keats were among those who visited the increasingly fashionable spa at Cheltenham. St Vincent found the place dull beyond belief but endured it on account of his wife's increasingly precarious health. He wrote encouragingly to Keats about the national importance of medical benefits of the waters. 'Considering you as I do and that you are public Property; the preservation of your health is most important and I trust that it will be perfectly restored by the Effects of Cheltenham Water.'[26]

Flag officers' half pay (around £300 to £600pa depending on rank before 1806 and then £370–670) was several hundred pounds short of the annual income necessary to demonstrate middle-class affluence by keeping a carriage (Table 12.1). Indeed, as the cases of Sir Charles Knowles and Vice Admiral Moriarty indicate, flag officers who were largely reliant on their half pay could be hard-pressed to keep up their station in the world. Knowles was not initially employed after his promotion to rear admiral in 1799 and his exclusion from active service seemed likely to continue while St Vincent, who had hounded him out of his ship in 1797, headed the Board. By the time St Vincent left office in 1804, however, another fifty-eight admirals were below Knowles on the list, so he could not demonstrate his capabilities as a flag officer by serving in subordinate positions. Knowles lived for another quarter of a century without the

Table 12.1 Flag officers' half pay

	Half pay	Less 10%*	Less 5%*
1793–1802			
ADM	588	529	559
VA	420	378	399
RA	294	265	279
1802–15			
ADM	672	605	638
VA	504	454	479
RA	378	340	359
1815			
ADM	705	635	N/A
VA	546	491	N/A
RA	420	378	N/A

Source: Compiled from Admiralty half-pay records, 1793–1815, NA ADM 25/125–169

Note: Values rounded to nearest pound in all cases.

* Income tax was charged at 10% from 1799 to 1802, and from 1806, and at 5% from 1802 to 1803.

benefit of significant inheritances, capital from prize money, a pension or a sinecure. Life on half pay was not materially prosperous or easy. He shuttled his wife and many children between rented properties and lodgings in Bath, London and various small provincial towns, and spent as much time as possible as the guest of a well-married sister at Vaynor House in Montgomeryshire. When Sir Charles secured belated recognition as a supplementary Grand Cross of the Order of the Bath in 1820, he was hard-pressed to pay the fees and installation costs.[27]

Sylverius Moriarty's life as a flag officer was similarly constrained. He inherited leases on several small properties in County Kerry, the income from which did not amount to more than a couple of hundred pounds a year.[28] There were two sons in the service to assist, and his two daughters required ongoing support. Initially, the vice admiral lived on his own property but in 1808 he removed to England, living first at Sittingbourne and then at the Hermitage, near Rochester in Kent. The house was substantial rather than grand, but the cost of living there seems to have been beyond the vice admiral's slender means.[29] On his death in 1809 friends of his daughters secured an annual grant of £100 from government to provide for them.

Although Vice Admiral Sir George Murray was far from being a naval grandee, the material quality of his life in Chichester demonstrated the benefits of supplementing half pay with modest private means. Murray inherited property from his father who was a wine merchant and his wife Anne (Nancy), the daughter of a prominent figure in Chichester, may have brought some property into their marriage. As a frigate captain under Sir John Warren in the Channel from 1794, and a veteran of Cape St Vincent and Copenhagen, Murray came into a reasonable share of prize money. He left almost £25,000 (representing an annual income of between £850 and £1,000) to his widow and only son.[30] Although one of Murray's friends among the prosperous burghers of Chichester teased him about the house that he had built there, referring to it as 'the Admiralty', it did not compare to the splendid metropolitan and rural properties at the disposal of many of his colleagues.[31] Nevertheless, Murray and Nancy lived comfortably, keeping a carriage and entertaining their personal friends in the service. Sir George was mayor of Chichester in 1815 and a long-standing alderman of the city. His promotion of the Tory cause in borough elections put him on friendly terms with the aristocratic Lennox family who lived at nearby Goodwood Park.[32] He and his wife were active in support of local musical occasions and were leading members of a book club whose holdings formed the basis of the Chichester Library Society. Although not numbered among the 'blue lights' of the service, Murray had evangelical inclinations and was a foundation subscriber to a chapel in the town.[33]

In late 1802 when he was still a captain, Murray had gone out of his way to visit Nelson and Lady Hamilton at their house at Merton and received a warm letter of thanks from his late commander. Nelson's response was coloured by resentment at what he saw as the neglect of 'those who I thought were my firm friends some of near 30 years standing who have never taken that trouble', and his awareness that this was a consequence of his highly irregular relationship with Sir William Hamilton's wife.[34] Nelson and Emma lived at Merton Place during the Peace of Amiens, having bought the house in the summer of 1802. The vice admiral's approach to the purchase was 'sailor-like' in its speed, directness and open-handedness. Nelson told his solicitor that

Plate 11: Vice Admiral Sir George Murray built this substantial house in the centre of his native city of Chichester. One of his friends dubbed it 'the Admiralty'.

'I never knew much got by a hard bargain. I approve of the Gentleman's plan that went to see an estate, bought it as it stood, Dinner on the Table, the former owner eat as his guest'.[35] Opinions varied on the fundamental soundness of the house – the surveyor condemned it as 'an old paltry small dwelling of low stories and very slightly built' – but both Sir William Hamilton and Nelson thought it charming. Nelson and Emma made changes to the internal layout that gave the house a memorably light and spacious air. By buying adjacent fields they trebled the size of the estate to just over 160 acres.[36]

Lord Barham did not serve at sea as an admiral but had faced many prolonged challenges in the treacherous waters of naval administration. When he quit the first lordship he retired to Barham Court in Kent with evident relief, and a marked determination to shake off transitional obligations as soon as possible.[37] This was a handsome house and Barham had kept the adjacent farm in his own hands. William Wilberforce was amazed by the intellectual and physical vigour of his 85-year-old friend. He waxed

Plate 12: A sketch view of Nelson and Emma Hamilton's house, Merton Place. Like other flag officers, Nelson used his prize money to purchase a property appropriate to his newly acquired social status. These earnings were not sufficient, however, to avoid debt and financial strain.

eloquent on the beauty and utility of a property that had been as carefully husbanded as the resources that Barham controlled at the Navy and Admiralty Boards. Barham Court was 'the most perfect specimen … in England of the *ferme orneé*' and 'also one of the most profitable of farms'.[38]

Admiral Cornwallis was also an agricultural improver. He purchased his 'farm' at Milford-on-Sea in 1801 and lived quietly there on his retirement in 1806. He was a wealthy man, enjoying an annual income of about £2,000 from money invested in government stock and receiving, in addition to his half pay, close to £350 from the sinecure post of rear admiral of England.[39] Captain Whitby's wife directed significant improvements made to 'Newlands' when Cornwallis was at sea with the Channel Fleet and when she was away from home after his retirement, he kept her abreast of farm business. He reported on the state of harvests, the progress of the wool clip and the repair of hedges, shared his anxieties about the choice of winter crops and the lack of rain, his irritation with the impertinence of a neighbouring landholder's tenant and his more tolerant reaction to wild horses from the New Forest that strayed on to his property.[40]

Unfinished business

When admirals went ashore, they had a range of ongoing business relationships with the Board and other government agencies. As we have seen, many of them wrote seeking employment, and requested the commissioners' interest to advance their friends' careers. Even when not seeking favours, they had to establish eligibility when their half pay was due. The Board posted newspaper notices of flag officers' six-monthly half pay dates but did not take any active steps to pay them. Rather, it waited for admirals' or their agents to claim their half pay. In order to do so they had to furnish sworn affidavits affirming that they were not in receipt of a salary for holding a public office and subscribed to the thirty-nine articles of the Church of England. They were then authorized to draw bills for the sums owing, making the appropriate deduction for income tax.

In the early stages of unemployment, flag officers dealt with residual official business. On leaving their commands, they submitted their journals to the Board and claimed arrears of full pay and compensation, table money, and reimbursements for stationery, postage, shore accommodation and other cash payments made in the line of duty. These claims were subject to close scrutiny.[41] In early 1813, for example, Admiral Sawyer was engaged in a correspondence over £400 house rent at Halifax, Nova Scotia. This claim was initially disputed by the Board because a reorganization of the North American commands in 1812 meant that Sawyer ceased to be a commander-in-chief and lost his entitlement to accommodation ashore. After Sawyer pointed out that he had leased the house in good faith, the Board reluctantly agreed to accept the charge but stressed that it should not be considered a precedent.[42]

Flag officers spent months and sometimes years wrangling over payments that stood as an imprest against outstanding pay, half pay and allowances. These encumbrances were a consequence of the complexity of active service business and communication delays and their resolution was impeded by the creaking accounting and settlement systems of the various boards whose sign-off was required.[43] Admiral Lord Hotham was quickly relieved of anxiety over a huge imprest of £52,645 arising from his Mediterranean command but other officers waited years for imprests to be removed.[44] Keith struggled heroically with the Navy Board over expenses incurred on the Egyptian expedition of 1800–1801 and did not obtain a settlement until 1808. Principle, pride and in some cases avarice or financial necessity prompted extensive correspondence. The mighty were not immune to the threat of imprests. When St Vincent relinquished the Channel Command in early 1807 and came ashore for good, the Board wrote to him about a charge for £31 1sh originating from early in 1806.[45] After Lord Barham left the Board in February 1806, he instructed his agent to secure papers relating to secret service monies advanced to Sir Sidney Smith in 1805. Barham, who had a great deal of experience of these matters from the Board's perspective, noted that he 'may be called into account for ordering it'.[46]

Even when money was not outstanding and accounts were settled, the Board expected unemployed flag officers to supply information and furnish documentation on transactions that had occurred years before. These enquiries taxed aging memories and record-keeping arrangements. In late 1802, for example, Keith, had to respond to questions on the grounding of the *Argonaut* at the Cape of Good Hope in October 1796. Three years after Admiral Bertie's successful expedition against the Isle de France in 1808, he was fending off claims that he had purchased unsuitable vessels during the course of the operation. Vice Admiral Berkeley was questioned on the appointment of two supernumerary assistant surgeons after he left the command at Lisbon in 1811. Sir Edward Pellew's elevation to the peerage as Lord Exmouth did not spare him from the Board's inquisitorial correspondence. He was questioned on the purchase and sale of a French schooner, and asked to account for expenses that had arisen when transporting an Austrian archduke and his wife.[47]

Unemployed flag officers needed the Board's permission to take government appointments or travel abroad. Despairing of being offered employment, Rear Admirals Charles Calmady and Francis Parry wrote to the Board in 1798 seeking leave to take command of units of cavalry volunteers formed to protect their neighbourhoods in the event of an invasion.[48] In the next war, Sir Isaac Coffin made a number of requests to attend to his North American property. While there, he shared his views on the navigation of the St Lawrence and the inadequacy of its defences with the Board.[49] There was a flood of applications to visit Europe when peace came in May 1814. Officers applied to travel to Geneva, France, Belgium and the Netherlands on personal business. When Berkeley asked to live abroad to restore his health, the Board insisted on knowing where he was going. It received a tetchy letter saying he was returning to Lisbon where he had been stationed during the war. At the end of the year, the recently promoted Rear Admiral David Milne asked permission to travel to Bordeaux to bring his children home. His wife, who had been living there for the sake of her health, had died, leaving their young children stranded.[50]

Given the complexity of flag officers' official business transactions and the tenacity of the Board, it is not surprising that these matters sometimes pursued them to the grave and beyond. In July 1806, for example, the Board was still pressing the late Rear Admiral Thomas Frederick's representatives to produce papers relating to a ship he had commanded nine years before.[51] Even when the Board had no claim on an admiral's estate, the practice of claiming pay in arrears meant flag officers were always owed money at the time of their death. As a result, the Board received numerous requests from executors and widows to waive the affidavit requirement. These requests were sometimes starkly and conclusively annotated 'DEAD'. As the first two decades of the nineteenth century wore on, a number of the admirals featured in this study made their last appearance in the unemployed Admirals records as posthumous claimants of half pay without an affidavit, 'which', as one of their agents pointed out, 'by reason of … death cannot now be obtained'.[52] These letters signalled that Hyde Parker, Rainier, Troubridge, Roddam, Pasley, Chamberlyne, Drury, Peter Parker, Cotton, Man and Hotham had slipped below a horizon that was beyond the piercing eyes of their lords commissioners of the Admiralty.[53]

Occasional employment

Before leaving their final terrestrial soundings, half-pay admirals on the active list were subject to ongoing Admiralty demands for occasional administrative, advisory, judicial and ceremonial service. Some of these duties were substantial. George Berkeley and Arthur Philip, for example, conducted searching inspections of the Sea Fencibles on the English coast in 1804–1805 and submitted a series of detailed reports to the Board.[54] Berkeley's and Philip's roles lasted for several months and the level and detail of reporting paralleled that expected of flag officers serving at sea. It was more common for the Board to rope in unemployed admirals for much shorter periods of temporary duty. Following his return from the East Indies in late 1808, for example, Pellew was asked to advise the Board on the Indian naval establishment and supplying ships on that station. In April 1809 he submitted an extensive memorandum that ran to more than fifty pages. Two years later the Board drew on Sir John Warren's recent experience when it was considering the management of the American stations.[55] In mid-1812 Sir Roger Curtis and Sir Charles Pole were asked to join Gambier and

Duckworth on a committee to consider the division of prize money on joint service expeditions. Curtis wrote from Gatcombe in the Isle of Wight asking to be excused, saying he had little knowledge of expeditions or the distribution of prize money in general. Pole accepted 'most cheerfully' but he was writing from London which would have made his attendance relatively easy.[56] Over the latter part of the Napoleonic War, the Board also called on flag officers to observe and report on trials of a range of potentially interesting innovations. They duly attended demonstrations of the relative merits of copper powder barrels, alternative cartridges, various ordnance pieces, models of new ships and new codes of signals.

When unemployed admirals were 'desired' to take up these temporary assignments the requests had the force of an instruction. The Board could be insistent. Rear Admiral Sir Richard Keats was a brilliant and well-connected flag officer but the fact that he came ashore in late 1812 to recover his shattered health did spare him from the Board's forcefully expressed attention. When Keats declined attendance at an ordnance experiment on the Sussex coast in December 1812 because of the state of his health, the Board responded sharply. John Croker, the secretary, told Keats that as the service would take so little time and involve so little trouble and no fatigue, his explanation was 'not quite satisfactory to their Lordships'. Keats, stung by this insensitive and high-handed communication, responded at some length and with barely concealed indignation:

> Although it may not be generally deemed strictly decorous to remonstrate with a superior authority against its decision, I nevertheless feel so much in receiving the present severe reproof, and so perfectly convinced that it is unmerited, that I trust I shall be held excusable for now particularly stating what I confess on reckoning their Lordships confidence, did not appear to me to be necessary in my former letter.

Keats detailed the fragility of his health and referred to the opinion of his knighted physician. For good measure he mentioned that a couple of days before he had been so 'indisposed' that he had retired early from a dinner at Croker's house. The Board accepted Keats's explanation but noted grumpily that he should have made the position clear in his earlier letter. On the same day it continued to disturb the rear admiral's recuperation with a momentous question about the arrangement of stewards' storerooms on board ship.[57]

In order to minimize delays in holding courts martial, the Board turned to half-pay admirals to take a role in these proceedings. They were members of the courts that tried Cornwallis, Parker, Duckworth, Calder, Harvey, Gambier and Stirling. As with other services for which they were summoned, attendance at courts martial was not voluntary. In November 1801 Collingwood was pleased to be at sea in Bantry Bay and thus not available for the court martial of his brother-in-law, Sir William Parker. Rear Admiral Sir Samuel Hood had to appeal on the grounds of ill health against being required to serve on the court which tried Lord Gambier in 1809.[58] When half-pay admirals attended courts martial, they were entitled to claim for expenses they incurred. As with other official financial transactions, however, that might become a source of embarrassment. When Vice Admiral John Wells sat on a court martial at Deal in 1810, his claim of £12 expenses incensed the Navy Board. In retaliation, it refused to authorize full pay due from Wells's subsequent appointment to the Nore command at Sheerness until the matter was dealt with to its satisfaction.[59]

Ceremonials

The limited and occasional duties performed by half-pay admirals did something to mitigate the risk of professional detachment resulting from prolonged and, in some cases, perpetual unemployment. In addition to participating in regular court ceremonials such as the levees and 'drawing rooms', flag officers had three opportunities during the wars to take their place among their colleagues in important official processions through London. The first, in late 1797, celebrated victories at sea during the early years of the French Wars; the last two, in early 1806 and 1810, mourned Nelson and Collingwood.

When the news of Camperdown arrived in London in late October 1797, Thomas Grenville suggested to Lord Spencer that a victory parade would help to maximize the benefit to their political friends.[60] The king had a similar idea but he saw it in terms of national thanksgiving rather than partisan celebration. The post-Camperdown event provided an opportunity for the traumas of fleet mutinies to be soothed symbolically in a celebration in which ordinary seamen and marines, as well as admirals and other dignitaries, played a part.[61] The organizers were careful to ensure that images of unity were not compromised by rivalry between flag officers. Because no such event had been commissioned to mark the Battle of Cape St Vincent in 1797, or Lord Howe's victory in 1794, Grenville's initiative was broadened into a celebration of 'general fleet' actions in which at least one enemy ship-of-the-line had been taken. Flag officers who had commanded at these actions, or been present at them, were offered seats in St Paul's Cathedral and invited to participate in a procession from the Admiralty. The details were settled in something of a hurry. Forceful invitations went out to flag officers on 13 December for an event on 19 December. The Board received many letters of acceptance but several officers, including Admiral Thomas Graves, sent apologies. He wrote to the Board from Cornwall, explaining that he could not travel the 224 miles to London in the time available.[62]

Graves missed an unprecedented 'spectacle' that the *Times* thought was enlivened by 'the recollection of the ever-memorable events which gave rise to it'.[63] He also missed a very early start on a midwinter's day, the prelude to six and a half hours of processing, singing, sermonizing and praying. Participants gathered in Palace Yard at seven in the morning and the procession of admirals, other officers, marines and seamen began to make its way to St Paul's at eight. The rigours of the full programme were presumably too much for Lord Howe's advanced age and poor health, so he was represented in the procession by Sir Robert Calder, his flag captain on the Glorious First of June. Howe took part in the ceremonies in St Paul's, however, joining his slightly younger colleague Duncan in presenting colours to the Dean. St Vincent (who was at sea) was, ironically, given his view of this officer's performance in the battle and thereafter, represented by

Sir Charles Thompson.[64] Bridport and Keith, who were also at sea, were represented by Lord Hotham and Captain Douglas. *The Times* made much of the royal family's role in the celebration but admirals held pride of place behind them.

The return of Nelson's body for burial early in 1806 was the major naval ceremonial of the war. The obsequies included a lying in state at Greenwich Palace, with Nelson's old friend Lord Hood, the governor of the Hospital, playing a leading role in overseeing the arrangements. The invitations went out in late December 1805 and were followed by an avalanche of acceptances. Some officers, however, were forced to decline on health grounds. Gout was often mentioned but that was not what prevented St Vincent attending. He wrote in early January, referring to the return of a common affliction, 'violent inflammation' of the eyes.[65] Six of the most senior admirals led by Sir Peter Parker were selected as pall bearers. Since Parker was admiral of the fleet and Nelson's early patron, there do not appear to be any grounds for seeing St Vincent's absence as an offended response to Parker's role. If a naval first lord was to have the place of honour among the living, then Lord Barham, the incumbent who had supported Nelson most effectively in his last command, would appear to have had the strongest claim. How far St Vincent's illness really precluded his attendance remains a moot point. He is said to have hated 'show' and was certainly on bad terms with a number of his colleagues[66] but that was nothing new. The former first lord's plea of illness was not merely a convenient fiction. St Vincent had been suffering from an eye infection for at least two weeks and had to rely on his wife to write his letters. By the end of the month he was so sorely afflicted with swollen legs that he attended the King's Drawing Room in Lady St Vincent's invalid chair.[67]

Plate 13: Nelson's coffin is carried down the Thames from Greenwich on its way to the Admiralty and St Paul's Cathedral. The funeral provided an opportunity for unemployed flag officers to join their more fortunate colleagues on an important ceremonial occasion.

After lying in state for three days in the Painted Hall in Greenwich amid huge crushes and barely controlled crowds, Nelson's body was taken in a waterborne procession up the river on 8 January. It spent the night at the Admiralty and was transferred the next day into a funeral car shaped like a boat that headed a vast procession to St Paul's. Sir John Orde, Lord Radstock, Vice Admiral Sir Isaac Coffin and Sir Charles Pole were prominent as official mourners. The crowds on the streets were immense, and the cathedral was packed solid with the official party, privileged ticket holders and those who had been fortunate enough to gain admittance after a long wait outside.

Given Orde and Nelson's recent mutual antagonism, it seems ironic that Sir John was one of the pallbearers, decked out in a special black cloak provided by the Lord Chamberlain's Office.[68] Orde ran true to form by engaging the Admiralty and Lord Chamberlain's Office in an irritated (and probably highly irritating) correspondence on his official dress.[69] More frustration followed on the day of the funeral. Orde arrived at the pall bearers' assembly point to find that his name had been omitted from the list. Fortunately, one of the other admirals did not turn up, so Sir John took his place. This blunder gave rise to further carping correspondence with William Marsden at the Board that was copied to Lord Barham.[70]

One of Nelson's recent biographers has described the service in St Paul's as 'long and sombre'. Lady Bessborough's very fine (and often quoted) observation probably best captured the mood of the vast numbers of ordinary people who lined the streets of the

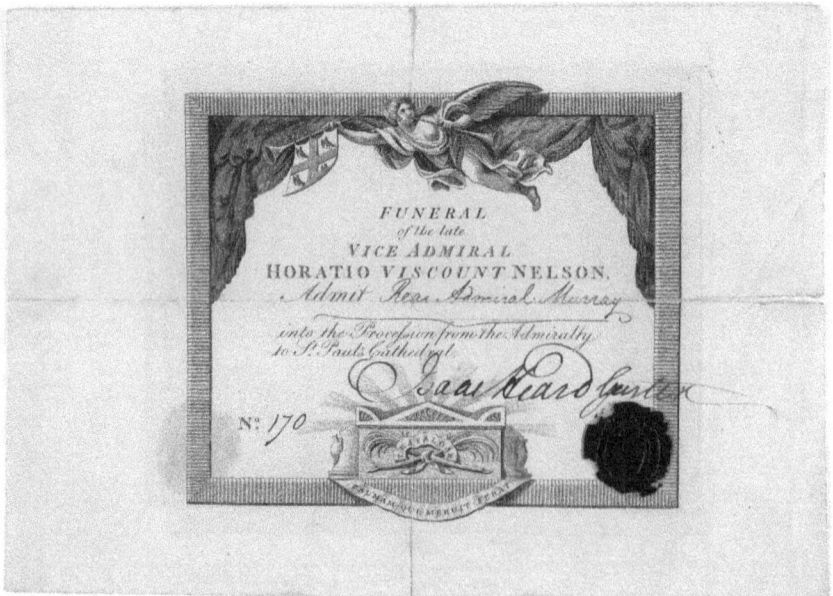

Plate 14: Rear Admiral George Murray was one of scores of admirals living in Britain and Ireland who were invited to participate in Nelson's funeral in January 1806. The admission card ensured that he had a privileged position in the proceedings.

city. In the recent past the 'mob' had 'huzzard' Nelson's carriage as he moved around the capital. It now stood in mute respect.

> Amongst many touching things the silence of that immense Mob was not the least striking; they had been very noisy. I was in a house in Charing Cross, which look'd over a mass of heads. The moment the Car appear'd which bore the body, you might have heard a pin fall, and without any order to do so, they all took off their hats. I cannot tell you the effect this action produc'd; it seem'd one general impulse of respect beyond anything that could have been said or contriv'd.[71]

Collingwood's funeral was also a significant public event although as befitted his place in Nelson's shadow it was not on the same scale. The procession began at Greenwich where 500 pensioners lined the route to the main gate. The coffin, made by Cardinal Wolsey for his own burial but never used and recovered from a lumber room at Windsor on the king's orders, was placed in a hearse drawn by six horses.[72] This funereal vehicle, decorated with Collingwood's arms, and what the press reported as 'trophies emblematic of his victories', was followed by eight mourning coaches and a number of 'gentlemen's carriages'. Three civilian first lords (Grey, Mulgrave and Grenville) were in the procession and St Vincent overcame his dislike of 'show' to honour an officer whom he admired unreservedly. Sir Peter Parker and Admiral Harvey were named in the press as being among the thirty odd 'other Admirals and Captains' who had served with Collingwood.[73] The procession made its way to St Paul's where the *Morning Post* reported 'the greatest confusion prevailed ... in consequence of the pressure of the crowd'. Collingwood's old school fellow, now Lord Chancellor Eldon, remarked on the number of sailors in the crowd and their affectionate respect for their former commander. Eldon helped one of these men gain access to St Paul's and was greatly affected by his grief: '[W]hen it came to throwing some earth on the coffin ... he burst past me and threw himself into the vault.'[74]

These large-scale commemorations served a range of public and personal purposes and it was fitting that flag officers and other naval personnel played a prominent role in them. They had taken part in the victories celebrated in late 1797 and had been colleagues, and in some cases friends, of those whose lives were commemorated in 1806 and 1810. Thompson's role as St Vincent's representative in the post-Camperdown procession and Orde's appointment as one of Nelson's pallbearers signified that these celebratory and solemn occasions rose above the personalities of those directly or indirectly involved. The Admiralty's invitations might thus be seen as being addressed to admirals as a class rather than to individuals. These ceremonies also, however, provided unemployed flag officers with opportunities to express a sense of collective professional identity by taking their place among their peers on important public occasions.

Networking

If unemployed admirals still hoped for appointments, offices, pensions or honours, their networks remained essential to them. Even if they were resigned to living on half pay and private means, however, there were still strong incentives for maintaining contact with their service colleagues and related connections. Habits of clientage and patronage were ingrained and constantly reinforced by the appeals of family members, friends and followers. Flag officers with sons in the service were likely to be particularly active in seeking to advance their careers, utilizing their personal and professional friendships and the powerful consideration accorded to 'sons of the service'. Information was one of the currencies of the patronage network and it continued to be valued by admirals ashore. Unemployed admirals often maintained a personal and political interest in strategic, operational and political developments, and were keen to secure well-informed unofficial reports of unfolding events. Finally, dependencies fostered through patronage and service interest, and warm friendships resulting from mutual admiration and shared service, forged strong personal bonds which continued to be important when admirals went ashore.

In retirement Lord Hood had the disposal of patronage arising from the governorship and retained sufficient residual interest to encourage senior officers to invite applications from him. Thus when Lord Gambier was about to take over command of the Channel Fleet he told Hood that 'I need not say how glad I shall be to execute any friendly offices within my power towards such persons under my command in whose welfare you take an interest, or in any way to accommodate your wishes'.[75] Residence at Greenwich Hospital made it easy for Hood to travel up the river to London to keep in touch with those who might assist his friends in the service. In common with other well-connected individuals, he also received reports on political and military developments from dutiful clients. Hood's informants included Admiral Domett who had been Lord Bridport's flag captain in the 1790s and served on the Admiralty Board for five and a half years from mid-1808. Hood assiduously relayed gossip on appointments and other service matters to his brother in Dorset. In the autumn of 1798 he received a stream of unofficial information on Nelson's pursuit of the French Fleet and was later kept informed on speculations about major commands. Hood told Bridport that Lord Gardner was no longer fit for service at sea being 'quite broken down' and that Collingwood was being scouted to replace him in the Channel Fleet. He subsequently reported Collingwood's death – you will 'I am sure grieve at hearing that Lord Collingwood arrived a corpse at Spithead' – and speculated with some relish that this might spell trouble for Lord Mulgrave, whose failure to relieve him earlier 'will be reflected on'.[76] Having been closely involved in making the arrangements for Nelson's lying in state at Greenwich, Hood took an informed interest in the funeral arrangements for Nelson's warmest friend in the service. Regular visits to Bath for the sake of his gout and rheumatism provided Hood with opportunities to keep company with service friends and their wives and, on one occasion in 1809, to make a carefully paced five-day detour to see his old friend Cornwallis near Lymington.[77]

On leaving office St Vincent seems to have taken a self-denying ordinance on the patronage of his successors. The reasons for this were various. He explained his disinclination to advance requests to Grenville on the grounds that he was not closely acquainted with him and claimed that Lord Barham was so partial that his friends would be ignored while he reigned at the Board.[78] He later warned his sister that 'as I have no intercourse with the Admiralty [under Lord Mulgrave] parry all questions put to you upon the subject of the Navy'.[79] In Howick's case St Vincent was reluctant to crimp his old friend's patronage. In spite of these protestations, however, he made a few exceptions, reserving the general right to make 'fair representations of the merits of officers, who distinguish themselves under my auspices'. He also continued to favour those with particularly powerful friends such as George Seymour, son of his old friend Lord Hugh, grandson of the Marquis of Hertford and a protégé of the Duchess of Northumberland.[80]

Cornwallis went into deep retirement in 1806 when he gave up the Channel command and his seat in parliament, but was not without residual interest in the service. He was diffident about its impact but used what influence he still possessed to advance Mrs Whitby's brother's career. In the late summer of 1807 he waited anxiously for a letter from Lord Melville and scanned *Steel's List* for news of the young man's promotion to lieutenant. This step was obtained in August 1807 but advancement thereafter was slow. Six years later, Cornwallis felt uncomfortable at the prospect of writing to the first lord, telling Mrs Whitby that any further approach would be a 'teaze and more likely to do harm than good'. He did write, however, and Lieutenant John Symonds was advanced to commander, the beneficiary of a timely intervention which ensured that he made that important step in the last promotion of the war.[81] Two years after his retirement, Cornwallis received an open offer of accommodation from a flag officer who had benefited from his assistance earlier in his career. Sir Richard King, one of Gambier's subordinates in the Channel Fleet, offered to take any of Cornwallis's 'young friends who wish to join' and told him that 'I can never forget your great kindness to me'.[82]

While Hood, St Vincent and Cornwallis stood at the head of the hierarchy of unemployed flag officers, Sir George Murray had a lower place in it. He had no prospect of being raised to the peerage, and as the son of a wine merchant was not even numbered among the gentry. He was, nevertheless, an admired and popular senior officer with an extensive network of service friends. In retirement he corresponded with a range of flag officers, including Berkeley, Coffin, Drury, Markham, Otway, Stopford and St Vincent, with captains, and naval wives, including Lady Hardy, the wife of Nelson's flag captain at Trafalgar and daughter of his neighbour Berkeley, and Lady Northesk, wife of Admiral Earl Northesk and niece of St Vincent. Murray emerges from this correspondence as a highly valued figure in the naval reaches of the patronage network, a conscientious backer of sons of the service and promoter of the careers of his followers. His role in these transactions was underwritten by personal integrity and sociability, as well as professional reputation. Murray's friends' trust in his judgement seemed boundless. When Captain Bedford heard that Vice Admiral Otway was considering buying Murray's carriage, he wrote to say that he would consider taking it off Murray's hands if Otway did not. Bedford did not 'profess to be any judge of Wheels, Springs etc, etc, therefore if you are inclined to part with it tell me if you think it in a fit state *without any thing being done to it* to proceed on a journey of six or seven hundred miles in a bad Country'.[83]

Murray's naval correspondents provided him with information about the theatres of war in which they were serving and maintained the service tradition of commenting freely and sharply on the performance of their superiors and colleagues. Both

Berkeley and Hardy reported on the situation at Lisbon in 1810, with the former venting his frustration at the behaviour of the British and Portuguese political elites, and the rapacious ingratitude of Sir Roger Curtis. Berkeley had been a friend to Curtis in the past but the ingrate was now whinging about his workload, interfering with ships under Berkeley's command and, to add insult to injury, using that as grounds for claiming £1,000 prize money.[84] Sir Isaac Coffin kept Murray up with the play in Anglo-American relations. He accurately predicted the outcome of what he saw as the insolent and unwise behaviour of the Royal Navy on the American coast: 'Our officers forget it is a *foreign* Country & play all kinds of tricks & when complaint is made shuffle it off as well as they can.'[85]

Berkeley and Coffin corresponded with Murray as equals in the service and as old friends. He also received correspondence from more junior officers with whom his personal relationship was equally cordial. When he was a midshipman Peter Heywood survived initial condemnation as one of the *Bounty* mutineers and succeeded in rebuilding his career after receiving a pardon.[86] He attained post rank in 1804 and served as Murray's flag captain during his only command at sea. Heywood felt sufficiently comfortable in their relationship to write Murray a witty letter exposing the procrastinations of the port admiral at Portsmouth. It was headed 'Portsmouth Harbour – at last'. Delay in seeing his friend and patron was a particular cause of frustration. Heywood assured Murray that when he received leave 'the first course I steer will be to Chichester'.[87]

Coffin also looked forward to enjoying Murray's hospitality. He told Murray that he and his wife planned to set off from London at the end of April 1811, stopping at Petworth and then coming on to Chichester to 'eat your Mutton' and, no doubt, to sample Murray's impressive cellar. Coffin told Murray 'you may *retain* us as long as you think us agreeable'. After the visit he was warm in his thanks and gallant in his recollection of Murray's wife's hospitality: Nancy 'made my spouse as much in love with her as I am & have been for *thirty five years*'.[88] Murray and his family in turn benefitted from the hospitality of his naval friends. Thus Vice Admiral Markham pressed him to come to Lewes: 'you will find a warm house and sincere friends come when you will'. When his nephew visited London in mid-1811, Sir Edward Pellew assured Murray that he shall 'gladly shake his hand'.[89]

Murray had a particularly close relationship with the late Rear Admiral Sir Thomas Troubridge's son, Captain (Edward) Sir Thomas Troubridge. Murray had waited anxiously for news of the elder Troubridge, at the Cape in 1807 when he was overdue from the East Indies in *Blenheim*. So too did St. Vincent. Having initially thought the fears of disaster were exaggerated, by early 1808 he was gravely apprehensive over the fate of both his protégé and his niece's son, whom Troubridge had taken on board.[90] *Blenheim* foundered in a hurricane and neither the admiral nor any of his shipmates were ever seen again. Murray took on a quasi-paternal role when Troubridge's heir came ashore in 1808. Markham and St Vincent also had an ongoing interest in the young man's affairs and welfare. The rear admiral had put his son in the way of significant prize money in the East Indies and on his death the younger Troubridge inherited a substantial flag officer's share of rich prizes. Pellew put the joint share they made at his expense at £76,000.[91] Wealth and indifferent health meant the young Sir Thomas was not eager to return immediately to active service, so Murray's support was not needed to secure a command at sea. He helped in other ways, however. In late November 1809 Murray assisted in settling the late rear admiral's estate and was trustee for his daughter, Charlotte. She expressed warm appreciation of his guidance: 'Indeed my dear Adm we are all *very much* obliged for all your kindness.'[92]

In the following year when Troubridge was to marry Anna Maria Cochrane, a daughter of the vice admiral, he sought Murray and Nancy's approval: 'I have now all I wish for and hope I shall not be disappointed in my prospects of Happiness. It is impossible for any Girl to have a better disposition & I think my Mama Murray will forgive me when she knows her.' He also told them of his anticipation of St Vincent's response to the news of the unusually generous settlement he had made his future wife: 'I have written to Lord St Vincent & expect his answer will begin by calling me a damn fool.'[93] Shortly after their marriage, Anna Maria persuaded Troubridge to accompany her to the West Indies where her father had an extensive estate. Troubridge told Murray that although he regarded the step as the 'extreme of folly' it was a matter of marital necessity: 'I am truly sorry I am obliged to go but as I must the sooner it's over the better.'[94] Unbeknown to Troubridge, Markham took an even less enthusiastic view of the scheme. In a comment which sheds interesting light on intra-service scales of regard and esteem, Markham confided to Murray:

I fear for Thomas T with respect of his marriage as his going to the West Indies with the Cochrane family is throwing himself away completely, and becoming their appendage[. M]ore could not be asked or expected if one who had married was altogether dependent for support on them, and he will never hereafter be allowed to act for himself after he is trammelled among all these Scotch speculators – his sun is set if he goes.

St Vincent was even more damning about the whole Cochrane clan. He told Lord Howick its members 'are not to be trusted out of sight, they are all mad romantic, money-getting and not truth-telling'.[95] Markham's censure did not prejudice Murray against the newly-weds. He helped Troubridge arrange a passage to the West Indies in a government store ship, and forwarded information on an English estate in which the young man was interested. Years later Murray was still keeping St Vincent up to date with Troubridge's doings.[96] The former first lord seemed less impressed by the son than he had been by the father. His oracular response to claims about the therapeutic benefits of the Scottish winter air for rheumatics was that 'the philosophy of Sir Thomas Troubridge passes my understanding'.[97]

In retirement St Vincent continued to cast a sharp judgemental eye on fellow flag officers. He praised 'my friend Philip' for his role as governor of New South Wales and continued to find fault with his old adversary Vice Admiral Young, when he was commander-in-chief at Plymouth. Young had allegedly given thirty of St Vincent's nephew's prime seaman to a friend and provided 'thirty Potatoe [*sic*] digging Paddy's in Lieu'.[98] Admiral Charles Wolseley's failings were personal and moral rather than professional. When he swindled Miss Crutchley out of £2,000 by promising to marry her, St Vincent took a role in protecting her fortune and the honour of the service. He told his sister that Wolseley had been 'forced' to pay the interest on this sum and insure his life to secure the principal, insisting that the insurance should not be allowed to 'drop'.[99] This gallant solicitude did not extend to Sir Robert Calder and his wife. St Vincent allowed his scepticism over Calder's professional capabilities to provoke a cruel jest on his former flag captain's personal misfortunes when his wife was committed: Lady Calder 'had no dread of anything but seeing Sir Robert'. He subsequently accused Sir Robert of manoeuvring to secure a large bequest from Admiral Roddam, abusing him to his sister as 'a vain foolish man, who sets himself up as an Idol of Flattery, and there are sycophants in abundance, who will worship him for his good cheer'.[100]

St Vincent passed on rumours of the collapse of Lord Gardner's health and speculated (correctly) that he would never go to sea again.[101] Gardner was shortly to join a growing list of flag officers whose representatives would need to seek a dispensation from the Board if they were to collect their final entitlement of half pay. In retirement St Vincent observed dispassionately the falling away of his less robust colleagues. In April 1808 he told his sister 'the last winter has been very fatal to the List of the Navy'. He named seven flag officers who had died recently, with Roddam and Rainier among them. As Wolseley was also on the list, the risk of unpaid insurance premiums was short run and Miss Crutchley presumably recovered her money.[102] While keeping a watchful eye on the duplicitous Admiral Wolseley, St Vincent also observed the last blundering steps of Sir Nigel Gresley. Gresley, a superannuated rear admiral, died in 1808, leaving inadequate support for a 'brood' of illegitimate children and three legitimate daughters. St Vincent suspected his estate was greatly encumbered and noted with wry contempt: 'Sir Nigel got through a great deal of money in a muddling way'.[103]

Scenes from domestic life

Once flag officers were living ashore their correspondence dwindled, and insights into their domestic lives are fragmentary and fleeting. Regrettably, we have no way of knowing how Keith occupied himself while living among the architectural splendours of Purbrook House – although we know he entertained the Duke of Clarence there towards the end of the wars[104] – or how Knowles and Moriarty, at the other end of the scale, survived on their very modest incomes. However, Nelson's persistent celebrity has helped ensure the survival of material on his life ashore, and occasional glimpses also emerge of the domestic lives of a few of his contemporaries.

The purchase of Merton Place, improvements to the property, and the cost of living and entertaining there, placed Nelson's fragile finances under considerable pressure. He had to borrow to meet repayments on the purchase cost, and his share of the living expenses – up to £1,800pa – consumed the lion's share of his pension and half pay.[105] The impact of Nelson's relative lack of capital was exacerbated by cash flow problems resulting from the substantial provision of £1,800pa for Lady Nelson and drain on his income arising from his ducal property at Bronte in the Kingdom of Naples.[106] Emma's decision to fill Merton with Nelsonian memorabilia was repugnant to some of their acquaintance – Lord Minto, for example, found the idea that Nelson should allow his house to be made into a 'mere looking-glass to view himself all day' distasteful – and others sneered at the *ton* of their entertainment.[107] These critical views were not universal, however.[108] Nelson's family became somewhat reconciled to his new domestic arrangements, and, as a result, he and Emma enjoyed a visit from his very elderly father, and frequent ones from his brother and sisters and their children. Some people whom Nelson had numbered among his service friends kept away, but others including Samuel Hood, George Murray, Alexander Ball and Thomas Hardy visited.[109] Moreover, while the purchase of land around Merton and the construction of appropriate outbuildings strained Nelson's finances, it provided opportunities for the hero of Cape St Vincent, the Nile and Copenhagen to engage in a spot of hobby farming. Under the superintendence of Emma and her very capable mother, the Merton estate ran a few cattle, grew hay to feed them in winter, kept pigs and chickens and raised fruit and vegetables for the table.

Cornwallis was a more serious farmer. When Mrs Whitby was away from home Cornwallis wrote to her on farm business and, probably with little Theresa in mind, passed on news of animal life around his property. Thus in the spring of 1818 he told her that although the birds had 'forsaken the place', 'the squirrels are about as usual and a Hare was before the window this morning'.[110] If Cornwallis's bluff manners corresponded to one maritime stereotype, his affection for a pet parrot called 'Poll' conformed to another. The bird's antics provided amusement to the ageing seaman. In August 1813 Cornwallis asked Mrs Whitby to tell her daughter that 'Poll is well and full of play'. Earlier, however, he had used the parrot as a means of drawing Mrs Whitby's attention to his own feelings of loneliness when she was away from home: 'I take as much notice of it as I can without letting it pinch me too hard with kindness.'[111] The old admiral's loneliness was mitigated to some extent by personal superintendence at a school he supported, and by the prospect of a visiting theatre company from Drury Lane. 'The players are come!' he excitedly exclaimed in a letter from 1817. He ventured on entertaining in Mrs Whitby's absence, but that could be a source of anxiety when it seemed that many of those he had invited to a party were unable to come.[112]

As Cornwallis had never married, Mrs Whitby and her daughter provided a surrogate family for him. He was as concerned as any natural uncle or parent when Theresa contracted whooping cough and he marvelled at the clarity of her handwriting: 'if everyone wrote so well' he would not need reading glasses.[113] By contrast, his surviving brother's complaints were received with amused incredulity. The brother in question was James, the splendidly vain-glorious Lord Bishop of Lichfield and Coventry, referred to simply and sardonically as 'the Bishop'. The admiral joked about his brother's failing memory and told Mrs Whitby that his letters were a tonic: 'I have got a letter from the Bishop which makes me laugh in the midst of my problems for he has written and talked so much about the fatigues of a Bishop's Life that he now really seems to believe it himself.'[114] While his brother was still facing the hazards of active service in the East Indies and the Channel, Bishop Cornwallis retreated from Lichfield to a house in Richmond. His account of the hardships of ecclesiastical life may have arisen from the many hundreds of confirmations he had to perform on his triannual visitations of his diocese.[115]

As governor of Guadeloupe in 1809–10 Sir Alexander Cochrane also had one foot onshore in Trinidad where he owned plantation estates worked by slaves. He claimed to have spent £75,000 on the purchase and development of these properties,[116] and £20,000 came from a freight payment which Cochrane had assigned nominally to his son and intended to repay out of the profits of the business. In order to achieve this objective, he managed the estate keenly and seemed at times to have sailed very close to the wind. The African Institution, the successor of the Anti-slavery Association, accused him of taking slaves liberated from enemy ships to work on his estate and raised questions about this in one of its annual reports to parliament. Cochrane wrote to the first lord to defend himself against these charges and heap abuse on the anti-slave lobby, those 'demagogues ... of the many *self-created societies* that now exist in England'.[117] He claimed that the people concerned were left on his hands and that, in the absence of instructions from government, he had them shipped to his estate for their own good. He denied emphatically that he had treated them as slaves and declared his willingness to give effect to any official plan for their future well-being, provided he was compensated for the money he had lavished on them. Nothing came of these charges, or of later, highly implausible, claims that Cochrane and Sir John Warren colluded to sell slaves out of captured ships.[118] Cochrane professed to be in favour of the abolition of the slave trade but subscribed to the pro-slavery mantra that those on his estates were treated far better than labourers in England. He had purchased slaves at Guadeloupe in early 1812.[119]

St Vincent kept in touch with political and service allies in retirement but his letters to his sister provide the best insights into this chapter of his personal life. From its early stages his retirement was clouded by his wife Martha's increasingly unsettled mental state. In the summer of 1807, St Vincent told his sister that his wife was nervous and suspicious, and that when they had visited Cheltenham she stayed in the house of the famous Dr Jenner.[120] This pioneer of small pox vaccination had a large house in the town from which he ran a successful and fashionable practice. Over the course of the next year Lady Vincent's suspicions developed into paranoia focused on the clergy. In March 1808 St Vincent recounted an incident in church when his wife imagined that the officiating clergyman's warnings of the wages of sin were directed specifically at her. Her condition seemed to improve over the next couple of weeks, with St Vincent describing her as being 'much more calm and compos'd'. He trusted that 'her terrors of Capital Punishment at the hands of the Clergy now subside'. In the following month, however, he had difficulty persuading his wife to leave Rochetts because she was afraid she would never be able to return: '[T]he poor thing is so full of chimeras, it is extremely difficult to shape one's conduct towards her'.[121] Martha became increasingly demanding, requiring her husband's constant presence and refusing to eat if he was not in attendance. At times it seemed as if the scourge of flag officers and captains was intimidated by his wife's demands and suspicions.[122] Later, Lady Vincent became convinced that her husband was having an affair with her companion. In these circumstances, visits to London were something of a relief. His guests in Mortimer Street included a two-man delegation from Dublin that presented him with the Freedom of the Guild of Merchants. It was a merry occasion: 'I ... gave my two Irish friends, the best Batchelor's dinner, I could, and their skins full of the best wines I ever had, and happily, I am not the worse for the share I took in it'.[123]

As St Vincent's health deteriorated, he spent an increasing proportion of his time at Rochetts and exercised his skills as a host there. Early biographers, who were personally familiar with this stage of his life, thought that his temper mellowed as he got older. Josiah Tucker, his future biographer, observed that he seemed prepared to tolerate lapses by his servants that would have incurred sharp rebukes if committed by service personnel.[124] St Vincent's days at Rochetts were enlivened by admiring members of younger generations, including Captain Edward Brenton, a follower and his first biographer, and Miss Ellis Cornelia Knight, the daughter of an admiral and later a lady-in-waiting. She provided a picture that would have astounded the earlier victims of his duplicitous authoritarianism. In a memorial verse signed 'Rochetts, 17 December 1823', Miss Knight mourned

That sportive wit, that energy of mind,
That solid judgement, and that taste refined,
That warm benevolence, that converse sweet,
And all that vivified this calm retreat![125]

Once admirals came ashore they were spared the pains of long separation from their families but had to confront the personal trials of family life. As we have seen, both Calder and St Vincent had to deal with their wives' mental illness. In the early years of his retirement from active service, Saumarez lost two daughters to illness. In 1808, when he was about to take command of the Baltic squadron, his daughter Mary was so dangerously ill that her condition precipitated a breakdown of her father's mental health. Lord Hood told his brother Bridport that Sir James had recently been locked in a bout of melancholy that 'so deranged ... his mind' that he had to be 'put under restraint'.[126] This crisis passed but four and a half years later Mary's sudden death prompted Saumarez to ask Lord Melville to be relieved of his command so he could return to Guernsey to comfort his family. Within two years tragedy struck again.

In March 1814 Saumarez travelled to England with his wife and two surviving daughters. The admiral was to receive the honorary doctor of laws at Oxford and to pay his respects to the king of France and other about-to-be restored crowned heads who were gathered in London. After a brief stay in the capital, Sir James travelled on to Oxford and his wife returned to Guernsey with her daughters. Shortly thereafter, Cartaret, the younger daughter, became seriously ill. Over the following weeks as her condition deteriorated, Lady Saumarez wrote a heart-wrenching 'Retrospect', an account of her attempt to meet this tragedy in the spirit of being 'directed by what might occur'.[127] Cartaret died on 19 June 1814 in her twentieth year.[128] Sir James had received his DCL at Oxford on 16 June and set off for Guernsey immediately after the ceremony. He landed on the island two days after his daughter's death, came ashore unrecognized and made his way to their house, where, as Lady Saumarez recorded in her diary, '[t]he clos'd shutters revealed the agonising truth to the hopes of the tenderest of Fathers'.[129] Martha Saumarez reflected on the scenes of 'flattering distinction' that her husband had just left and consoled herself that 'had our hearts been set on the

pomps & vainglory of this world how would it have increas'd the bitterness of an affliction which so powerfully proclaimed *their* ... delusions'.[130]

Epilogue: war's end

When the French Wars came to an apparent end in the spring of 1814 flag officers got
a taste of things to come.[131] Employment opportunities were constrained greatly and
life ashore on half pay became the norm. In 1813 thirty-seven admirals held active
commands. By November 1814 that number had dropped to twenty-four, seven of
whom were employed on the North American station.[132] Two of these officers were
commodores and all but one of the rest were rear admirals whose flag rank dated from
1812–14. The only senior officer was Vice Admiral Sir Alexander Cochrane, the commander-in-chief. He had been an admiral since 1804.

By 1816, when the American and French Wars were finally over, only sixteen admirals were employed on active service. The fact that all but two of them were commanders-in-chief was a consequence of a sharp contraction of the Navy's size, range
of activities and geographical reach. By 1816 naval personnel numbered a quarter of
the wartime peak in 1813 and the fleet had shrunk at an even greater rate.[133] Not only
were there far few admirals on active service but those who were employed tended
to be drawn from the junior flag ranks. The limitations of postwar commands, the
absence of prize money and opportunities for glorious service and perhaps the blunted
appetites of those who had carried the weight of flag command during the wars tended
to give recently promoted admirals an advantage in the employment market. This is
apparent in the postwar careers of the junior flag officers on the North American station in late 1814. Sir George Cockburn, who served with particular distinction there
was commander-in-chief at Cape Town in 1816, before returning to England to take a
seat on the Board. He became a formidable service politician. Sir Charles Rowley commanded at the Nore from 1815 to 1818 and then in Jamaica from 1820 to 1823. After
serving with Lord Exmouth on the Algerian expedition of 1816, Rear Admiral David
Milne returned to North America as commander-in-chief from 1816–19. Sir Edward
Codrington's experience more nearly matched that of the flag ranks as a whole. He was
unemployed for ten years after his North American service.

A few veterans held commands in the immediate postwar period but usually in
shore-based roles they would not have sought while the wars continued. Sir John
Duckworth's last command was as port admiral at Plymouth, not too far from his
estate on the outskirts of Exeter. He remained attentive to the duties until his death
at the end of August 1817. Lord Exmouth, Sir Alexander Cochrane and Sir James
Saumarez were his successors in this command. Sir Richard Keats continued in his
role as governor general and commander-in-chief of Newfoundland until 1816. After
a period in retirement he was appointed governor of Greenwich Hospital in succession
to Sir John Colpoys who died in the post in 1821.

Lord Exmouth's command at Plymouth was preceded by a rare spell of belligerent
service. Exmouth led apparently successful negotiations with the Barbary states over

the treatment of their Christian populations before it transpired that the Dey of Algiers had authorized the murder of two hundred Christian fishermen. Exmouth, by this time an admiral of the blue, led a retaliatory expedition of British and Dutch warships that arrived off Algiers in the late summer of 1816. After a devastating seven-hour bombardment that completely destroyed the Dey's naval forces and inflicted severe damage on Algiers, the city was surrendered to Exmouth. Twelve hundred Christian slaves were liberated and the Dey brought to due order. Exmouth returned to a hero's welcome and was given a step up in the peerage to join Lord Keith as a naval viscount.

Keith gave up the Channel command in 1814 but resumed it during the Hundred Days. Having gone ashore for good after seeing General Bonaparte off to St Helena, he gave up his interesting grand house at Purbrook and concentrated his attention and his money on his estate in Scotland. For other veterans such as Hood, Bridport and St Vincent, the days of active service were long past. Hood died early in 1816, having lived to triumph in the successful conclusion of the wars in which he and his brother had played significant early roles. He sent Lord Bridport 'hearty' congratulations 'on a day you have so well deserved to see'.[134] On Bridport's death in early May 1814, a month after receiving his brother's affectionate praise, St Vincent finally secured the post of general of Marines that he had long coveted. He lived to enjoy it until 1823.

If the end of the war signalled the termination of the employment prospects of most flag officers, it also put a sharp brake on progression through the flag ranks. Promotion to admiral was the pinnacle of realistic ambition for flag officers and carried significant monetary benefits for those whose inheritances, marriages, pensions or sinecures had not put them beyond the reach of financial concerns. As we have seen, the frequency and scale of wartime promotions greatly increased the speed of advancement through the flag ranks and particularly favoured those promoted early in the war.[135] The career trajectories of these officers are in marked contrast to those made rear admiral in the valedictory promotion of 1814. These men, a fourth generation of wartime flag officers, included Edward Codrington, Home Popham and Charles Rowley. They waited twenty-two and a half years to advance from rear admiral to admiral, by which time thirteen of their thirty-one cohort colleagues had already died. Delays in promotion to the next rank cost rear admirals £126pa and vice admirals £149pa from 1815.[136]

Sir William Hargood's brief career on active service illustrates the impact of the end of the war on those who might have been regularly employed had hostilities continued. He had fought at Trafalgar and enjoyed the strong support of the Duke of Clarence, through whose interest he gained appointment as second-in-command at Portsmouth a month after his promotion in 1810. In late March 1813 Hargood was appointed to command in the Channel Islands. By this stage of the war he found, in the words of his memorialist, 'comparatively little food for his active mind'. After briefly testing his resolve against local smugglers with a side-line in supplying information to the French, he was ordered to strike his flag in May 1814. Hargood became a vice admiral in the big promotion of June 1814 and was created KCB early in the New Year. He waited sixteen years for promotion to admiral of the blue and saw no further active service. Having married quite late in life he was said to have had few regrets about the end of his active service career and settled down happily to enjoy life ashore.[137]

Conclusion

From 1793 to 1815 the lives of British admirals were affected profoundly by the prolonged and often desperate challenges posed to their country's security, prestige and trade by the armed forces of revolutionary and Napoleonic France. The number of flag officers increased markedly over the course of the wars and in a real sense it became easier for senior officers to achieve that rank. This development, which also made it easier for senior officers to move up through flag ranks, was partly a response to the need to refresh the list of admirals to meet the operational demands of global warfare. Many of those on the admirals' list in 1793 were already beyond active service and those who were at their peak when the wars began had careers that extended back to the mid-century. As a result of the exceptional physical and psychological demands of high command, and the duration of the French Wars, the most senior ranks of naval leadership passed through four generational cycles before lasting peace came in 1815. Lord Keith was the only man who saw active service as a flag officer across the span of the wars. This feat rested on an unusual confluence of natural, institutional and behavioural factors: age, seniority when the war began, interest, ability, ambitious drive and resilience. Keith was still commanding at sea when the final generation of wartime flag officers (promoted in 1814) embarked on attenuated careers of active service in the remaining months of war. This veteran of the 1794 promotion finally struck his flag in August 1815.

Senior officers serving at sea in the late Georgian Navy faced significant physical hardship and were subject to high levels of psychological stress. Operational requirements, prolonged periods of service at sea and the weight of professional, political and public expectation made flag command an onerous burden that sapped the physical and mental resources of even the most robust officers. These pressures were in part a consequence of an increasingly widely held view that the disciplinary requirements of wartime service would only be met if flag officers were committed to an ethos of vigorous professionalism. Earl St Vincent articulated this ethos with characteristic forcefulness in the Mediterranean and Channel Fleets in 1796–1801 and he found an effective, if more considered, ally in Lord Spencer at the head of the Admiralty Board. Spencer had been brought in when it became clear that the Earl of Chatham's diffident approach to the role was inconsistent with the sharpening expectations of the government and the public. St Vincent's campaign was epitomized by his strictures on getting ships to sea as soon as possible, and his blunt and zealous attention to all that that implied for logistical planning and fleet discipline. This imperative was not entirely new but it assumed a heightened significance in the face of the unfolding strategic situation. It received widespread endorsement among politicians involved with the Service and the highly effective senior captains who became the leading lights of the second and third generation of wartime admirals. Their reaction to the less urgent practices of the first generation (Lords Howe, Hood, Hotham and Bridport) in the early years of the Revolutionary Wars signalled a significant shift in ethos of the Service.

This shift saw increasingly overt attention paid to flag officers' exercise of authority and the emergence of heightened expectations of their disciplinary role. St Vincent was an early and highly influential contributor to discussions about admirals' responsibilities, capabilities and dispositions. He propagated measures that emphasized their disciplinary responsibilities and the need to ensure that a habit of obedience was ingrained throughout the service, up to and including officers of flag rank. The practical application of this doctrine in the Mediterranean and Channel Fleets in the late 1790s led to clashes between flag officers that disrupted their working relationships. At the same time, St Vincent, Bridport and Cornwallis were sometimes inclined to question the Board's instructions and show reluctance to comply with them. Questions about the need for flag officers to exhibit a tightly focused commitment to the disciplinary ethos of the service assumed a heightened significance after the two 1797 fleet mutinies in home waters and related flare-ups on other stations. Admirals showed varying degrees of skill and determination in responding to these challenges and the events themselves lent credence to claims that it was essential for flag officers to model discipline in their commands and ensure that all members of the service were consistently subject to it. Incidents of mutinous conduct on the lower deck continued throughout the wars but never on the scale of the late 1790s. Open conflicts between flag officers, their commanding officers and the Board also virtually ceased in the Napoleonic Wars as later generations of flag officers seemed far more reluctant to challenge their superiors openly.

Increases in the scale of the Navy's operations and personnel enhanced its role in the Georgian patronage network. Flag officers were active participants in this network, utilizing their interest for the direct benefit of their friends and connections and also seeking access to the interest of those who were better placed to advance the careers of their clients. But while opportunities for promotions and appointments extended significantly, there were burgeoning fields of aspirants motivated by the prospects of honourable and profitable employment in a popular war and more flag officers to press their cases. Admirals looked to first lords to assist their friends but these officeholders were subject to a range of mutually exclusive imperatives. Many of these demands arose from the patronage network but some were a consequence of the widely recognized need to pay some attention to questions of basic competence and merit when appointing men to positions of responsibility in the Royal Navy. As a result, appointments and promotions were often a source of tension between flag officers and their political masters.

Patronage relationships were as important for the ambitions of admirals as they were to those below them in the service hierarchy. Their aspirations focused on securing profitable employment and public recognition of superior contributions through royal honours, pensions and valuable sinecure offices. As with more junior appointments, however, interest worked in fluid combination with other considerations. The fulfilment of admirals' ambitions depended upon first lords' assessment of professional ability and standing, and government's perceived need to encourage emulation among flag officers and reap political advantage from their triumphs. Admirals had made their way up through the ranks of an intensely competitive service and many had been highly successful post captains. Competitive instinct and sense of self-worth were important motivating forces in the professional lives of many flag officers, prompting them to seek opportunities for major command at sea and for enrichment and public recognition.

In practice, however, first lords' perception of the limited pool of talent available to them meant that the most prestigious posts were tightly held. Moreover, while employment and prize money were available throughout the period, the changing shape of the war had an important impact on flag officers' access to the highest and most sought-after royal honours. These rewards depended on relative judgements on the brilliance of an officer's performance, and on the political and strategic circumstances in which it occurred. In the first decade or so of war, admirals commanded in a number of strategically and politically significant fleet actions and they and some of their subordinate flag officers were well rewarded for their achievements. While the Navy operated on the same scale during the second half of the wars and continued to play a critical role, the Army moved into the strategic and political limelight. It was far bigger than the Navy and there were no large-scale fleet actions to set alongside the army's triumphs in the Peninsular, France and finally Belgium.

Admirals had experienced the hardships of shipboard life and prolonged separation from friends and family as they made their way up through the ranks. By 1793, however, this experience was relatively distant for most of them as they had seen little or no service since the end of the American War in 1783. Admirals' financial means allowed them to enjoy a quality of material comfort on board ships, which was, subject to the needs of the service, roughly comparable with that enjoyed by men of their class who lived ashore. Moreover, while flag officers' status set them apart from their subordinates, commonality of background and professional interests made it possible for them to recreate a sphere of deferential sociability to enliven their leisure hours and alleviate their isolation. Even with these advantages, however, admirals' lives were punctuated by long periods in which the satisfaction of doing their duty and the prospect of reaping the rewards of active service at sea were in constant tension with the emotional ties of home and family life.

When officers went ashore on half pay their situation changed significantly. As we have seen, the category 'half-pay flag officer' embraced three distinct groups, the largest of which was made up of a growing number who had never seen active service at flag rank and probably never would. A second group was made up of admirals who had seen service but had come ashore because their health was broken irreparably, or they were too old to contend with the mental and physical demands of flag command, or had shown that they lacked the managerial skills, judgement, leadership and 'nerves under responsibility' necessary for high command in times of war. These men were silently, informally but irrevocably consigned to the ranks of perpetually unemployed admirals. The position of officers in these first two groups bore some similarities to that of officers who were formally superannuated as rear admirals although they continued to be eligible for promotion and were still formally on the active list. The third group of flag officers was made up of those who, having been recently promoted to, or employed at that rank, still had some prospect of seeing active service in future. Time would tell how these officers' careers would develop and whether their aspirations were realistic. From their perspective, however, life ashore was viewed as an interlude in an ongoing career of active service. These officers' cultivation of first lords, members of the Admiralty Board and extra-service patrons and their periodical written declarations of their willingness to serve were, in their eyes at least, more than a matter of form.

While those who still had reasonable prospects of employment had the strongest and most direct incentives for high levels of ongoing professional engagement, other land-based flag officers continued to be affected by their membership of the service. In many cases it determined their place in the social hierarchy of conventional society and had an impact on their material prosperity ashore. In addition, however, half-pay flag officers retained a range of formal and informal institutional connections with the Navy. Accountability for past decisions and past expenditure did not cease when admirals struck their flags, and the continuation of half pay depended on active compliance with the Board's requirements. Unemployed flag officers were still subject to the Board's summons to assume short-term duties ashore, serve on courts martial and join their colleagues in service ceremonials. To these formal commitments were added informal connections arising from naval friendships and ongoing participation in the patronage network on behalf of their friends.

Once the wars ended, opportunities for active service diminished markedly and the incentives to seek it weakened. In these circumstances, the lives of admirals changed irrevocably. Employment was intermittent and even less evenly spread than in war time, and life ashore became the normal condition for the large cadre of flag officers generated during more than two decades of war.

Appendix: Biographical Notes of British Admirals, 1793–1815[*]

[Key: Lt: lieutenant; Cmd: commander; PC: post captain; Com: commodore; RA: rear admiral; VA: vice admiral; ADM: admiral; AF: admiral of the fleet; FO: flag officer; SFO: subordinate flag officer; c-in-c: commander-in-chief; CM: court martial; MP: member of parliament; Bart: baronet; Kt: knight; KB: knight of the Bath; KCB: Knight Commander of the Bath; GCB: Grand Cross of the Bath; YS: younger son of a peer.]

Aplin, Peter (1753–1817) Lt 1776, Cmd 1778, PC 1780, RA 1799, VA 1805, ADM 1810. Service as a PC in American War. Never employed as a FO.

Berkeley, George (1753–1818) YS Earl of Berkeley. Lt 1772, Cmd 1778, PC 1780, RA 1799, VA 1805, ADM 1810, surveyor general of the Ordnance 1789–95. Service as PC in American War. Subordinate commands in Channel Fleet 1800–1801; c-in-c North America 1806–1808, where he caused a diplomatic incident by firing on the *Chesapeake*, Lisbon 1808–12. MP Gloucestershire 1783–1810. KB 1813, GCB 1815.

Bertie, Albemarle (1755–1824) Lt 1777, Cmd 1780, PC 1782, RA 1804, VA 1808, ADM 1814. C-in-c Cape of Good Hope 1808. Bart 1812, KCB 1815.

Bowyer, George (1740–99) Lt 1758, Cmd 1761, PC 1762, RA 1793, VA 1794, ADM 1799. SFO Channel Fleet 1793–94; lost leg at Battle of First June 1794. Bart 1794.

Buckner, Charles (1735–1811) Lt 1756, Cmd 1761, PC 1766, RA 1793, VA 1794, ADM 1799. C-in-c Nore during 1797 mutinies.

Calder, Robert (1744/5–1818) Lt 1762, Cmd 1779, PC 1780, RA 1799, VA 1804, ADM 1810. Captain of the fleet at Battle of St Vincent 1797. Commanded off Cape Finnesterre 1805, CM 1805, c-in-c Plymouth 1810–12. Kt 1797, Bart 1798, KCB 1815.

Carnegie, William (1756–1831) Seventh Earl Northesk. Lt 1777, Cmd 1780, PC 1782, RA 1804, VA 1808, ADM 1814. SFO Channel Fleet 1801. Undistinguished third-in-command at Trafalgar 1805. KB 1806, GCB 1815, RA of Great Britain 1821.

Christian, Hugh Cloberry (1747?–98) Lt 1771, Cmd 1778, PC 1778, RA 1795. Commanded main West Indian Expedition convoy 1796, second-in-command Cape of Good Hope 1797, c-in-c 1798. KB 1796.

Cochrane, Alexander Inglis (1758–1832) YS Earl of Dundonald. Lt 1778, Cmd 1780, PC 1782, RA 1804, VA 1809, ADM 1819. Superintended landing of troops on Egyptian coast 1801 as Com, SFO Channel and Mediterranean 1803–1804, c-in-c Leeward Islands 1805–10, second-in-command Battle of San Domingo 1806, captured

[*] Compiled from Marshall, *Royal Naval Biography*, ODNB, Ralfe, *Naval Biography*, Syrett and DiNardo, *Commissioned Sea Officers*.

Martinique 1809 and Guadeloupe 1810, Gov Guadeloupe 1810. C-in-c North America 1814–15, oversaw withdrawal of British forces from North America 1815. MP Stirling Burghs 1800–1802, 1803–1806. KB 1806, GCB 1815.

Coffin, Isaac (1759–1839) Lt 1776, Cmd 1781, PC 1782, CM 1788, restored to list 1789, RA 1804, VA 1808, ADM 1814. 1795 Commissioner of Navy at Corsica, and at Lisbon 1796; Commissioner at Halifax yard 1799 and Sheerness 1801–1805. Bart 1804.

Collingwood, Cuthbert (1748–1810) Lt 1775, Cmd 1779, PC 1780, RA 1799, VA 1804. Early employment as PC in American War and in West Indies under Nelson. Took part in Battles of First June 1794, Cape St Vincent 1797. Com with command of Cadiz blockade 1797, Brest blockade as SFO 1799–1802, and off Atlantic coasts of France and Spain 1803–1805; second-in-command Trafalgar 1805, c-in-c Mediterranean 1805–10. Died during return voyage; buried St Paul's Cathedral near dear friend Nelson. Received three gold medals in course of twenty-two years of war. Major general of Marines 1809, UK baron 1805.

Colpoys, John (1742–1821) Lt 1762, Cmd 1770, PC 1773, RA 1794, VA 1795, ADM 1801. SFO Channel, active against Spithead mutineers 1797, c-in-c Plymouth 1803, 1804–1805, Admiralty Board, 1805–16, Treasurer Greenwich Hospital, 1816– Governor Greenwich Hospital. Kt. 1798, GCB 1815.

Cornwallis, William (1744–1819) YS First Earl Cornwallis. Lt 1761, Cmd 1762, PC 1765, RA 1793, VA 1794, ADM 1799. Distinguished early service as PC. C-in-c East Indies 1788–94, SFO Channel 1794–95, c-in-c Leeward Islands 1796, Channel Fleet, 1801–1802, 1803–1806, ably managing the blockade. CM 1796. MP for Eye 1790–1807. RA Great Britain 1796, VA United Kingdom 1814, GCB 1815.

Curtis, Roger (1746–1816) Lt 1771, Cmd 1776, PC 1777, RA 1794, VA 1799, ADM 1804. Distinguished service in American War. Howe's Captain of the Fleet at the Battle of First June 1794, c-in-c Cape of Good Hope 1800. Commission for revising the civil affairs of HMN 1805–1807, c-in-c Portsmouth 1809–12. Bart 1794, GCB 1815.

Domett, William (1752–1828) Lt 1778, Cmd 1782, PC 1782, RA 1804, VA 1809, ADM 1819. Served at Battle of First June 1794, Bridport's flag captain in Channel Fleet. Admiralty Board 1808–13, c-in-c Plymouth 1813. KCB 1815, GCB 1820.

Duckworth, John Thomas (1748–1817) Lt 1771, Cmd 1779, PC 1780, RA 1799, VA 1804, ADM 1810. Com Leeward Islands 1796, and 1798 (under St Vincent) commanding the naval element at recapture of Minorca. C-in-c Leeward Islands 1801–1805. As SFO under Collingwood successfully engaged French force off San Domingo 1806, second-in-command Channel Fleet 1807, Governor and c-in-c Newfoundland 1810–12, Port Admiral Plymouth 1813–17. MP New Romney 1812–17. KB 1801, Bart 1813, GCB 1815.

Duncan, Adam (1731–1804) Lt 1755, Cmd 1759, PC 1761, RA 1787, VA 1793, ADM 1795. Important share in capture of Belle Ile 1761 and Havana 1762. Joined Channel Fleet under Keppel 1778 and played prominent role in disputes with VA Palliser. C-in-c North Sea 1795–1800, blockaded Texel 1795–97, defeated Dutch Fleet at Battle of Camperdown 1797. As senior admiral successfully undertook naval part of Helder expedition 1800, with surrender of Dutch at Texel. Struck his flag April 1800, greatly admired for his courage and integrity. Viscount 1797.

Elphinstone, George Keith (1746–1823) Lt 1770, Cmd 1772, PC 1775, RA 1794, VA 1795, ADM 1797. Fought in Seven Years and American Wars and with Lord Hood at Toulon 1793–94. SFO in Channel Fleet 1794, and led squadrons that captured the Cape Colony in 1796 and prevented its recapture a year later; after playing an important role in supressing 1797 mutinies, appointed to succeed St Vincent in the Mediterranean in late 1799, after serving as his second-in-command. Led naval forces in successfully landing in Egypt 1801, c-in-c North Sea 1803–1807, Channel 1812–14 and 1815. Keith's prize earnings were legendry. MP Stirlingshire 1796–1803. Closely connected with the Prince of Wales. Irish baron (Keith) 1797, UK baron 1803, viscount 1814, KB 1794, GCB, 1815.

Forbes, John (1714–96) YS Third Earl of Granard. Lt 1731, Cmd 1737, PC 1737, RA 1747, VA 1755, ADM 1758, AF 1781. General of Marines 1763–.

Gardner, Alan (1742–1808/9) Lt 1760, Cmd 1762, PC 1766, RA 1793, VA 1794, ADM 1799. Served in West Indies, playing important role in Battle of Granada 1779 and in Battle of the Saints 1782. Commanded squadron in West Indies 1793. Took part in Battle of First June 1794; second-in-command Channel Fleet during 1797 mutinies. C-in-c Ireland 1800–1805, Channel Fleet 1807–1808. Admiralty Board 1790–95. Major general Marines 1794. MP for Plymouth 1790–96, Westminster 1796–1806. Bart 1794, Irish baron 1800, UK baron 1806.

Gell, John (c.1740–1806) Lt 1760, Cmd 1762, PC 1766, RA 1793, VA 1794, ADM 1799. Present as junior flag officer under command of Lord Hood at occupation of Toulon 1793.

Graves, Thomas (1725–1802) Lt 1743, Cmd 1754, PC 1755, RA 1779, VA 1787, ADM 1794. Second-in-command to Howe, Battle of First June 1794. Irish baron 1794.

Hargood, William (1762–1839) Lt 1780, Cmd 1789, PC 1790, RA 1810, VA 1814, ADM 1830. Fought at Trafalgar. Second-in-command Portsmouth 1810, c-in-c Channel Islands in 1814. KCB 1815, GCB 1831.

Harvey, Eliab (1758–1830) Lt 1779, Cmd 1782, PC 1783, RA 1805, VA 1810, ADM 1819. Commanded *Téméraire* at battle of Trafalgar. SFO in Channel and off Finisterre 1806 under St Vincent and in Channel Fleet under Gambier 1808. Renowned for his intemperate character. CM 1809 and dismissed from service; reinstated in rank and seniority 1810. MP Essex 1802–12. Inherited Bart 1779, KCB 1815, GCB 1825.

Holloway, John (1744–1826) Lt 1771, Cmd, PC 1780, RA 1799, VA 1804, ADM 1809. Distinguished service in the American war. C-in-c Downs 1804–1807, commander and governor at Newfoundland 1807–10.

Hood, Alexander (1726–1814) Lt 1746, Cmd and PC 1756, RA 1780, VA 1787, ADM 1794. SFO Battle of First June 1794; Howe's second-in-command Channel Fleet 1794–95, 1796–97; c-in-c during Spithead Mutiny 1797 and in charge of blockade of Brest 1797–1800. Treasurer, Greenwich Hospital 1776–99. MP Buckingham 1790–96. Lieutenant general of Marines 1799, general of Marines 1800–. Kt 1788, Irish baron (Bridport) 1794, British baron 1796, viscount 1800.

Hood, Samuel (1724–1816) Lt 1746, Cmd 1754, PC 1756, RA 1780, VA 1787, ADM 1794. Appointed c-in-c Mediterranean and Toulon 1793, achieved notable victories, including French surrender of Corsica 1794. Dismissed from command 1795. Admiralty Board 1788–95. Governor Greenwich Hospital 1796–. MP Westminster 1784–96. Bart 1779, Irish baron 1782, British viscount 1796, GCB 1815.

Hood, Samuel (1762–1814) Lt 1780, Cmd 1782, PC 1788, RA 1807, VA 1811. Extensive distinguished service as a PC 1793–1807. SFO Mediterranean 1807, Baltic Fleet 1808, second-in-command at Corunna during re-embarkation of army 1809, briefly c-in-c West Indies 1811, and then East Indies where he died in post. Joint commissioner for government of Trinidad 1802. MP Bridport 1807–12. KB 1808, Bart 1809.

Hotham, William (1736–1813) Lt 1755, Cmd 1756, PC 1757, RA 1787, VA 1790, ADM 1795. Second-in-command to Lord Hood in Mediterranean 1793, during Hood's absence commanded in two inconclusive battles 1795; relieved in that year by Sir J. Jervis. Irish baron 1797.

Jervis, John (1735–1823) Lt 1755, Cmd 1759, PC 1760, RA 1787, VA 1793, ADM 1795, AF 1821. Extensive service in earlier French and American Wars. Commanded fleet sent to secure West Indian Islands 1794, replaced Hotham as c-in-c Med 1795, commanded at Battle of Cape St Vincent 1797. Responded with severity to mutinies of 1797. Commanded in Mediterranean with Keith 1797, struck his flag 1799. Commanded Channel Fleet 1800–1801 during Brest blockade, and 1806–1807. First Lord of Admiralty 1801–1804. MP Chipping Wycombe 1790–94. Lieutenant general of Marines 1800 and general of Royal Marines 1814–. British earl (St Vincent) 1797, KB 1782, GCB 1815.

Keats, Richard Goodwin (1757–1834) Lt 1777, Cmd 1782, PC 1789, RA 1807, VA 1811, ADM 1825. Protégé of Duke of Clarence. Served with distinction as a PC 1793–1807. Missed Trafalgar but accompanied Duckworth in the victory off San Domingo 1805. SFO in Baltic 1807–1809, on Scheldt expedition in 1809 and off Cadiz 1810–11, second-in-command to Cotton in Mediterranean 1811; invalided home 1812. Governor and c-in-c Newfoundland 1813–16. Major general Marines 1818–, Governor of Greenwich Hospital 1821–. Kt 1807, GCB 1815.

King, Sir Richard (1730–1806) Lt 1745, Cmd 1756, PC 1759, RA 1787, VA 1793, ADM 1795. Governor and c-in-c Newfoundland 1792–94 and c-in-c at Plymouth during the 1797 mutinies. MP Rochester 1794–1802. Kt 1784, Bart 1792.

Kingsmill, Richard Brice (1730–1805) Lt 1756, Cmd 1761, PC 1762, RA 1793, VA 1795, ADM 1799. C-in-c Irish station 1793–1800. Bart 1800.

Knowles, Charles Henry (1754–1831) Lt 1776, Cmd 1777, PC 1780, RA 1799, VA 1804, ADM 1810. Served as PC during French Wars in North American and Mediterranean commands. Took part in Battle of St. Vincent 1797. Never employed as FO. Inherited Bart 1777, supplementary GCB 1820.

Laforey, Francis (1767–1835) Lt 1789, Cmd 1790, PC 1793, RA 1810, VA 1819, ADM 1830. Served in Battle of Trafalgar; c-in-c Leewards Island 1811–14. Inherited Bart 1796, KCB 1815.

Laforey, John (1729?–96) Lt 1748, Cmd 1755, PC 1758, RA 1789, VA 1793, ADM 1795. Service as a PC in earlier French and American Wars. Naval commissioner

Leeward Islands station 1779 and at Plymouth Dockyard from 1783. C-in-c Leeward Islands station 1789–93. Captured Tobago 1793. Re-appointed Leeward Islands command 1795. Superseded 1796, died at sea on voyage home. Bart 1789.

Man(n), Robert (c.1748–1813) Lt 1768, Cmd 1776, PC 1777, RA 1794, VA 1799, ADM 1804. Served in American War of Independence. Brought squadron in Mediterranean back to England in 1796 without Jervis's authorization. No further active service but Admiralty Board 1798–1801.

Markham, John (1761–1827) Lt 1780, Cmd 1782, PC 1783, RA 1804, VA 1809, ADM 1819. Served in West Indies with Jervis (later St. Vincent) 1793, and then in Channel Islands and on French coast. No active service as FO. Admiralty Board 1801–1804 when identified closely with St Vincent, and again 1806–1807. MP for Portsmouth 1801–18.

Martin, Thomas Byam (1773–1854) Lt 1790, Cmd and PC 1793, RA 1811, VA 1819, ADM 1830, AF 1849. Served as PC on coast of Ireland, in West Indies, off Brest, and coast of France, 1798–1808 and Baltic from 1808 to 1812. Second-in-command at Plymouth 1812–14; deputy comptroller of Navy 1815; comptroller 1816–31, VA United Kingdom 1847, ADM Fleet 1849. Kt 1814, KCB 1815, GCB 1830.

Murray, George (1759–1819) Lt 1778, Cmd 1782, PC 1782, RA 1804, VA 1809. Present at Bridport's action against French off L'Orient 1795. Participated in battle of St Vincent 1797, led the fleet into action at Copenhagen 1801. Nelson's first captain in *Victory* off Toulon 1803 to 1805 and in chase to West Indies 1805. C-in-c naval operations against Buenos Aires 1807, returned home 1808. Mayor of Chichester 1815; KCB 1815.

Nelson, Horatio (1758–1805) Lt 1777, Cmd 1778, PC 1779, Com 1796, RA 1797, VA 1801. Served with distinction as PC in East Indies and West Indies and with Hood in the Mediterranean 1793–95. Lost eye in army siege of Calvi 1794 and arm in attack on Minorca 1797. Played a notable role in Battle of St Vincent 1797, and at the Battle of the Nile 1798. Hoisted flag in Channel fleet under St Vincent 1800 and then showed decisive leadership during Battle of Copenhagen 1801. C-in-c North Sea 1801, Downs 1801 (July–October), Mediterranean 1803–, died in Battle of Trafalgar, October 1805. KB 1797, UK baron 1798, viscount 1801.

Onslow, Richard (1741–1818) Lt 1758, Cmd 1761, PC 1762, RA 1793, VA 1794, ADM 1799. Port Admiral Portsmouth 1796 and second-in-command to Duncan in North Sea Fleet from late 1796. Leading role in battle of Camperdown 1797. Bart 1797, GCB 1815.

Orde, John (1751–1824) Lt 1774, Cmd 1777, PC 1778, RA 1795, VA 1799, ADM 1805. Active in American War of Independence; governor Dominica 1783. Returned to naval duties 1793, presided over courts martial of Nore mutineers 1797, then joined St Vincent's Mediterranean fleet, as third-in-command and then fourth-in-command; sent home following bitter dispute with his c-in-c. Commanded squadron off Cadiz 1804–1806. MP for Yarmouth Isle of Wight 1807–12. Bart 1790.

Packenham, Thomas (1757–1836) YS Baron Longford. Lt 1776, Cmd 1779, PC 1780, RA 1799, VA 1804, ADM 1810. Never hoisted flag on active service as admiral but took part in suppression of rebel forces in Ireland 1798. Held sinecure offices in Irish ordnance. GCB1820.

Parker, Hyde (1739–1807) YS of an admiral who was lost at sea. Lt 1758, Cmd 1762, PC 1763, RA 1793, VA 1794, ADM 1799. Extensive and notable service in earlier French and American wars. SFO under Hotham and then Jervis in the Mediterranean 1794–96; c-in-c Jamaica 1796–1800; St Vincent's second-in-command in Channel 1800. C-in-c North Sea fleet which won Battle of Copenhagen 1801, but credit went to Nelson and Parker was recalled soon afterwards. Refused court of enquiry and never served again. Kt 1779.

Parker, William (bap. 1742–1803) Lt 1766, Cmd 1773, PC 1777, RA 1794, VA 1799. Com and c-in-c Leeward Islands station 1787–90. Distinguished service as PC in early stages of French war. C-in-c Jamaica 1795; took effective part in Battle of St Vincent as third-in-charge 1797, but later fell into dispute with c-in-c St Vincent. Appointed c-in-c Halifax station 1800 but recalled a year later for sending two ships to West Indies contrary to Admiralty orders. Defended CM late 1802. Bart 1797.

Pasley, Thomas (1734–1808) Lt 1757, Cmd 1762, PC 1771, RA 1794, VA 1795, ADM 1801. Played distinguished part as FO in Battle of First June where he lost a leg. C-in-c at the Nore 1998, Plymouth 1799. Bart 1794.

Patton, Philip (1739–1815) Lt 1763, Cmd 1778, PC 1779, RA 1795, VA 1801, ADM 1805. Commissioner Transport Board 1794. Second-in-command to Keith in the Downs 1803–1804; Admiralty Board 1804–1806. Author of books of advice to PCs.

Payne, John Willett (1752–1803) Lt 1777, Cmd 1779, PC 1780, RA 1799. Played distinguished part in Battle of First June 1794. Intimate friend of Prince of Wales. Treasurer Greenwich Hospital 1799–. MP Huntingdon 1787–1796.

Pellew, Edward (1757–1837) Lt 1778, Cmd 1780, PC 1783, RA 1804, VA 1808, ADM 1814. Captured French frigate *Cleopatre*, the first such victory of French wars 1793; commanded detached section of western frigate squadron 1797–. Appointed East Indian command 1804–1808, c-in-c Mediterranean when he worked effectively with Lord Wellington 1811–14. MP Barnstaple 1801–14. Kt 1793, Bart 1796, UK baron (Exmouth) 1814, UK viscount 1816, KCB 1814, GCB 1815, VA UK 1832.

Pole, Charles Morice (1757–1830) Lt 1777, Cmd 1778, PC 1779, RA 1795, VA 1801, ADM 1805. Service as PC early in French Wars under Hood and Howe. SFO on Christian's convoy to West Indies 1796, and under Bridport in the Channel in 1797 where he was ineffectual in bringing Spithead mutineers to obedience. C-in-c Newfoundland 1800, 1802, Baltic 1801. Commissioner on Naval Inquiry into abuses in Civil Administration 1802–1803, when St Vincent was first lord; Admiralty Board 1806. MP Newark 1802–1806 and Plymouth 1806–18, spoke regularly and independently on naval affairs. Bart 1801, KCB 1815, GCB 1818.

Popham, Home Riggs (1762–1820) Lt 1783, Cmd 1794, PC 1795, RA 1814. Launched unauthorized attack on Buenos Aires 1806. MP Yarmouth, Isle of Wight 1804–1806, Shaftesbury 1806–1807, Ipswich, 1807–12. KCB 1815.

Purvis, John Child (1747–1825) Lt 1778, Cmd 1781, PC 1782, RA 1804, VA 1809, ADM 1819. Collingwood's second-in-command in Mediterranean, 1806–1807, commanded squadron off Cadiz 1807–10, acting c-in-c (March–May 1810) after Collingwood's death.

Rodham, Robert (1719–1808) Lt 1741, Cmd 1746, PC 1747, RA 1778, VA 1779, ADM 1793. No active service during French Wars. A patron of Collingwood.

Rowley, Charles (1770–1845) Lt 1789, Cmd 1794, PC 1795, RA 1814, VA 1825, ADM 1841. Served in North Sea, Mediterranean, Walcheron expedition, off Cadiz, in Adriatic, and at capture of Fiume and Trieste 1813. Admiralty Board 1834–35. Bart 1836, KCB 1815, GCB 1840.

Rowley, Samuel (d. 1811) Cmd 1781, PC 1799, RA 1801, VA 1805, ADM 1810.

Saumarez, James (1757–1836) Lt 1778, Cmd 1781, PC 1782, RA 1801, VA 1806, ADM 1814. Served with distinction as Cmd and PC during American War, in Bridport's action off Ile de Groix, the Brest blockade, and reinforcing Jervis before his action off Cape St Vincent 1797. Senior captain in Nelson's squadron, ex-officio his second-in-command during Nile campaign 1798, entrusted with Brest blockade 1799. In 1801 led successful capture of Spanish ships off Algeciras. Hoisted flag at Nore 1803, then assumed command at Channel Islands. Second-in-command Channel Fleet under St. Vincent 1807; appointed to lead Baltic command and continental blockade 1808–12, which he did with skill and diplomacy. RA UK 1819 and VA 1821, General of Marines 1832. Kt 1793, Bart, KCB 1801, GCB 1815, UK baron, 1831.

Smith, (William) Sydney (1764–1840) Lt 1780, Cmd 1782, PC 1783, RA 1805, VA 1810, ADM 1821. C-in-c South American 1808, reprimanded and returned home 1809 after attempting to raise an authorized Portuguese attack on Spanish forces. This episode typical of record of wilful behaviour which irritated colleagues and superiors. Second-in-command to Pellow in Med 1812–14. MP for Rochester 1802–1806, KCB 1815, GCB 1838.

Stirling, Charles (1760–1833) Lt 1778, Cmd 1780, PC 1783, RA 1805, VA 1810. Extensive experience as PC including role in Saumarez's action off Algeciras and off Cape Finisterre with Calder 1805. Naval commissioner at Jamaica, 1803–1804. Participated in siege of Montevideo as FO, c-in-c Cape of Good Hope 1806–10 and Jamaica 1811–13. Recalled 1813, partial defence of CM charges for providing a convoy for private profit 1814; remained on half pay without further promotion.

Thompson, Charles (1740–99) Illegitimate son of a baron. Lt 1761, Cmd 1771, PC 1772, RA 1794, VA 1795. Extensive service in earlier French and American Wars. SFO in Leeward Island 1794–95 under Sir John Laforey with whom he quarrelled sharply. After brief service in the Channel 1796, joined Jervis's Mediterranean fleet in 1796 where (after a dubious contribution to the Battle of Cape St Vincent) another dispute with his superior resulted in being recalled in 1797. Further service as SFO in Channel Fleet 1798–99, resigned because of ill health. MP Monmouth 1796–99. Bart 1797.

Troubridge, Thomas (c.1758–1807) Lt 1781, Cmd 1782, PC 1783, RA 1804. Early friendship with Nelson, later taken up by Jervis as service protégé. Troubridge accompanied Nelson on ill-fated Santa Cruz mission and was in the squadron which destroyed French fleet in Aboukir Bay; Troubridge missed the action, however, as his ship struck shoal ground in early manoeuvres. Leading role in force that retook Naples 1799. St Vincent's flag captain in Channel Fleet 1800 and joined him on the Admiralty Board 1801. Shared command of East Indies with Pellew 1805–1806 was very lucrative but resulted in great acrimony. Appointed c-in-c Cape of Good Hope 1806, lost at sea en route 1807. Admiralty Board 1801–1804, MP Yarmouth 1802–1806. Bart 1799.

Waldegrave, William (1753–1825) YS Third Earl of Waldegrave. Lt 1772, Cmd 1775, PC 1776, RA 1794, VA 1795, ADM 1802. Distinguished service in West Indies and North America. Served in Mediterranean 1793 with Hood at Toulon. Third-in-command at battle of St Vincent 1797. Governor and c-in-c Newfoundland 1797–1800. Irish baron (Radstock) 1800. GCB 1815.

Warren, John Borlase (1753–1822) Lt 1778, Cmd 1779, PC 1781, RA 1799, VA 1805, ADM 1810. Distinguished service as frigate captain in the early stages of the Revolutionary Wars. SFO under St Vincent off Brest and under Keith off Cadiz 1800–1801. Ambassador to Russia 1802–1804. C-in c North American squadron at Halifax 1807–11. C-in-c amalgamated North America, Jamaica and Leeward Islands station in War of 1812–13. MP Nottingham 1797–1806, Buckingham 1807. Inherited Bart 1775. KB 1794, DCL University of Oxford 1814, GCB 1815.

Notes

Introduction

1 Roger Knight, *Britain against Napoleon: The Organization of Victory* (London: Penguin, 2014).
2 Admirals were only assigned to a Red Squadron from 1806.
3 NA ADM 1/579, 21/2/1799.
4 There is a collection of Saumarez's stamped commissions in SRO SA3/2/1/9–20.
5 See Table 11.1 below.
6 See Chapter 9 and Table 12.1.
7 Brian Lavery, *Nelson's Navy: The Ship's, Men and Organisation 1793–1815*, revised edn (London: Conway, 2012), 99, says there were 168 flag officers on the active list in 1814. The date upon which this figure is based is not given and that is important given deaths and the timing of a promotion. Even allowing for the thirty-two promotions in early June 1814, however, this figure seems to exclude surviving flag officers who were promoted before the wars and between 1793 and 1802. The figure given here (and referred to elsewhere) includes those who were still alive at the time of the 1814 promotion, as listed in Cowles, *History*, IV, 191–5; V, 39–43.
8 See Figure 9.1 below.
9 These figures are derived from Cowles, *History*, IV, 191–5; V, 39–43.
10 Rodger, *Command of the Sea*, xxii, lists sixteen but one of them was commanded by a commodore in the East India Service.
11 Cowles, *History*, V, 10.
12 James Davey, *In Nelson's Wake* (London: Yale University Press, 2015), 313–18.
13 See pp. 37–8 below.
14 Cowles, *History*, IV, 191–5; V, 39–43.
15 A few officers near the top of the list who were serving in civil appointments as naval commissioners or governors were not considered for promotion until they returned to the active list. As discussed below, a number of officers were 'passed over' entirely.
16 Evan Wilson, *A Social History of British Naval Officers 1775–1815* (Woodbridge: Boydell Press, 2017), 83–6; Michael Lewis, *A Social History of the Navy 1793–1815*, 2nd edn (London: Chatham, 2004), 31–45.
17 See pp. 152–5 below.

Chapter 1

1 NMM YOR/3, #31, 6/10/1810.
2 *Regulations and Instructions Relating to His Majesty's Service at Sea* [1806] (London, 1808), I, ch. 2, III, ch. 4; I ch. 1.
3 HRO 19M61/4204, 12/3/1795.

4 Gordon C. Bond, *The Grand Expedition* (Athens: University of Georgia Press, 1979), Appendix B.

5 Evelyn Berckman, *Nelson's Dear Lord* (London: Macmillan & Co, 1962), 43.

6 SRO 93/6/2/3 (877/53), 14/8/1803, ff16–17 and October 1803, ff30–1.

7 SRO HA93/6/2/4 (877/103), f24 5/10/1807.

8 NLS Ms 2340, 23/3/1813.

9 BL Add Ms 35195, f4, 5/7/1794; Dorothy Hood, *The Admirals Hood* (London: Hutchinson, 1943), 164–5.

10 BL Add Ms 31167, f33, 16/6/1799.

11 Lord Camperdown, *Admiral Duncan* (London: Longman's Green & Co, 1898), 254, 332.

12 Nicolas, *Nelson's Dispatches*, VI, 258, 4/11/1804, and see pp. 75–7, 244 below.

13 Andrew Lambert, *The Challenge. Britain against America in the Naval War of 1812* (London: Faber, 2012), 260.

14 *Spencer Papers*, IV, 19, 29/10/1800.

15 For an account of St Vincent's professional relationships between 1797 and 1801, see Chapter 4 below. Roger Morriss raises the interesting possibility that dietary deficiencies may have played a role in prompting flag officers' extreme behavior; Roger Morriss, ed., *The Channel Fleet and the Blockade of Brest, 1793–1801* (London: NRS, 2001), 521–2.

16 NMM WYN/103, 13/7/1799, 31/7/1799.

17 Keele UL, 16/9/1805. See Margarette Lincoln, *Representing the Royal Navy: British Sea Power, 1750–1815* (Aldershot: Ashgate, 2002), 69–73, for the turning political tide against Cornwallis.

18 BL Add Ms 35196 ff179–80v, 24/8/1795.

19 Nicolas, *Nelson's Dispatches*, VI, 475, 20/7/1805; Oliver Warner, *The Life and Letters of Vice-Admiral Lord Collingwood* (London: Oxford University Press, 1968), 290–1.

20 SHC DD/CPL/30, Autobiographical Material, 58–63.

21 For example, between May 1798 and April 1799 Lord Duncan purchased eighty-two dozen bottles of wine, port and sherry and two casks of Lisbon wine; NWMS, Duncan Papers DUN/17, M19995.2.114, f39, 23/3/1798, f43 15/5/1798.

22 Roger Knight, *The Pursuit of Victory* (London: Allen Lane, 2006), 216; G. Cornwallis-West, *The Life and Letters of Admiral Cornwallis* (London: Robert Holden, 1927), 250.

23 See p. 38 below.

24 BH Lans 6(1), f94, 6/2/1795.

25 C. E. Vulliamy, *The Onslow Family, 1528–1874* (London: Chapman & Hall, 1953), 243.

26 R. G. Thorne, *House of Commons, 1790–1820* (London: Secker and Warburg, 1986), V, 5.

27 *Markham's Letters*, 205–206, 5/11/1806.

28 See James Davey, *In Nelson's Wake* (London: Yale University Press, 2015), 39.

29 SRO, SA/3/21; H. W. Hodges and E. A. Hughes, *Select Naval Documents* (Cambridge: Cambridge University Press, 1927), 213, 4/2/1805.

30 Leyland, *Blockade of Brest*, II, 207; BL Add Ms 31167, f178, 25/1/1801.

31 *Markham's Letters*, 53, 22/5/1806.

32 BL Add Ms 31167, ff108–108v, 20/6/1800, f114, 3/7/1800, f219v, 2/6/1806.

33 See Rodger, *Command*, 487–8.

34 Hodges and Hughes, *Select Naval Documents*, 213, 4/2/1805.

35 Iain Gordon, *Admiral of the Blue: The Life and Times of Admiral John Child Purvis, 1747–1825* (Barnsley: Pen & Sword, 2005), 91–2.

36 Leyland, *Blockade of Brest*, I, 256–7 and n1, 25/1/1804.

37 NLS Ms 2345, f2v-3, 25/3/1814; Ms 2348, ff4–5, 1/4/1814.

38 NMM DUC/5, 28/8/1799, 31/8/1799, 16/9/1799.

39 NMM DUC/8, 20/2/1802, 29/3/1802; BL Add Ms 31165, ff138–138v, 6–7/12/1806, f140v, 8/12/1806, 153–153v, 7–8/1/1807.

40 Janet Macdonald, *Feeding Nelson's Navy* (London: Chatham, 2004).

41 *Spencer Papers*, II, 37, 18/7/1796.

42 James Davy, '"Within Hostile Shores": Victualling the Royal Navy in European Waters during the French Revolutionary and Napoleonic Wars', *International Journal of Maritime History*, 21:2 (2009), 246–8.

43 Nicolas, *Nelson's Dispatches*, VI, 17, 14/5/1804, 141–2, 7/8/1804. See also Janet Macdonald, 'Two Years Off Provence: The Victualling and Health of Nelson's Fleet in the Mediterranean, 1803–1805', *MM*, 92:4 (2006), 443–54.

44 Colin White, 'A Man of Business: Nelson as Commander in Chief Mediterranean, May 1803–January 1805', *MM*, 91:2 (2005), 180–1.

45 *Collingwood's Correspondence*, 232–8, 12/1/1808, 1/2/1808, 9/2/1808, 19/2/1808.

46 Davy, '"Within Hostile Shores"', 248–9.

47 NMM WAR/118, ff4–6, 4/7/1808; the tender documents are not foliated. The records for 1812–14 cover 280 folio sheets, most of which were dealt with by Warren.

48 Davy, '"Within Hostile Shores"', 250.

49 *Geo III c35.*

50 NA ADM 25/125, 126, 128, 130, 132, 134, 136, 138, 140, 144, 158, 160, 162, 164, 166, 169.

51 NA ADM 2/1091, ff50–2, 23/2/1802, f200, 23/4/1804, f242, 8/8/1804.

52 NMM DUC/11, 26/6/1805.

53 Nicolas, *Nelson's Dispatches*, VI, 17, 14/5/1804, 369–72, 18/3/1805.

54 NLS MS 2297, f136, 19/2/1813.

55 NA ADM 1/582, 19/8/1808.

56 NMM RAI/8, 22/2/1803.

57 Ibid., 10/3/1807, RAI/6, f211, 12/10/1799.

58 NA ADM 1/582, 16/7/1807, 27/5/1808, 2/3/1809, 18/3/1809, 30/3/1809; emphases in the original.

59 See p. 143 below.

60 ADM 1/582, 18/7/1807, 21/7/1807.

61 Ibid., 18/71807, 21/7/1807(St Vincent); ADM 1/583, 2/12/1811, 6/8/1812 (Berkeley).

62 ADM 1/581, f160, 26/5/1805; ADM 2/1092, f51, 7/6/1805, ADM 1/58, f177, 16/6/1805; f237, 24/8/1805.

63 See John Creswell, *Generals and Admirals: The Story of Amphibious Command* (London: Longmans, Green & Co, 1952), 88–117.

64 NLS MS 2569, 4/10/1800, 19/2/1801.

65 See Robert K. Sutcliffe, *British Expeditionary Warfare and the Defeat of Napoleon, 1793–1815* (Woodbridge: Boydell Press, 2016), 124–5.

66 Quoted Dorothy Hood, *The Admirals Hood* (London: Hutchinson & Co, 1943), 155.

67 See pp. 215–16 below.

68 BL Add Ms 31167, f4, 6/12/1798.

69 Creswell, *Generals and Admirals*, 95–7; NMM, DUC/25, 13/7/1801; and see pp. 215–16 below.

70 *Spencer Papers*, IV, 134, 29/10/1800.

71 *Keith Papers*, II, 142–52.

72 BL Add Ms 41852, f70, 25/10/1800.

73 *Spencer Papers*, IV, 139, 25/12/1800.

74 See Piers Mackesy, *British Victory in Egypt, 1801: The End of Napoleon's Conquest* (London: Routledge, 1995), 151–2, 166, 208–209, 230.

75 CRO 588./c. 74, 22/7/1808; quoted Davy, *In Nelson's Wake*, 187.

76 Carl A. Christie, 'The Royal Navy and the Walcheren Expedition of 1809', in Craig L. Symonds, ed., *New Aspects of Naval History* (Annapolis: United States Naval Institute, 1981), 190–200.

77 Creswell, *Generals and Admirals*, 117.

78 Herbert Maxwell, ed., *The Creevey Papers: A Selection from the Correspondence & Diaries of the Late Thomas Creevey, M.P.* (London: John Murray, 1906), 133.

79 NLS MS 2297, f59v, 9/3/1809, ff77–8, 9/2/1810.

80 CRO 588./c. 74, 22/7/1808; NMM, YOR/2, # 19, 4/8/1810, 23/9/1810; Christopher D. Hall, *Wellington's Navy: Sea Power and the Peninsular War, 1807–1814* (London: Chatham Publishing, 2004), 77–110.

81 NA ADM 1/341, 1/6/1809; Hall, *Wellington's Navy*, 108.

82 NLS MS 3420, 3/9/1813; Hall, *Wellington's Navy*, 215–17.

83 *Martin's Letters*, III, 1–58.

84 BL Add Ms 31166, ff119–23, 31/1/1796; Nicolas, *Nelson's Dispatches*, V, 349–51, 9/1/ 1804.

85 *Markham's Letters*, 100–101, 4/4/1807; Warner, *Admiral Lord Collingwood*, 185–6.

86 NMRN, MSS 259/1, 10/5/1797.

87 NMM, DUC/5, 30/4/1799.

88 *Spencer Papers*, II, 47–8, nd August 1796.

89 See Piers Mackesy, *The War in the Mediterranean, 1803–1810* (London: Longmans, Green & Co, 1957), 394–6, for a highly favourable assessment of Collingwood's diplomatic role.

90 BL Add Ms 40098, ff125–53.

91 *Collingwood's Correspondence*, 233, 12/1/1808.

92 DCA Letter Book 1795, 9/8/1795, 3/9/179514/9/1795.

93 Sir John Ross, *Memoirs and Correspondence of Admiral Lord de Saumarez* (London: Richard Bentley, 1838), I, 191.

94 See Anthony Ryan, 'An Ambassador Afloat: Vice Admiral Sir James Saumarez and the Swedish Court, 1808–1812', in Jeremy Black and Philip Woodfire, eds, *The British Navy and the Use of Sea Power in the Eighteenth Century* (Leicester: Leicester University Press, 1988), 237–58.

95 SRO SA 3/2/6 Misc. Papers, 1845–1975.

96 SHC DD/CPL/30, Autobiographical Material, 49.

97 Knight, *The Pursuit*, 323–7.

98 *Keith Papers*, II, 37, 19/4/1799; 128, 15/9/1800.

99 Quoted ibid., 62.

100 Nicolas, *Nelson's Dispatches*, V, 112–13, 1/7/1803.

101 Walter Vernon Anson, *The Life of Admiral Sir John Borlase Warren* (London: Simpkin, Marshall, Hamilton, Kent & Co, 1914), 152–3.

102 Castalia Countess Granville, *Lord Granville Leveson Gower* (London, 1916) I, 490, 12/11/1804, II, 37, 1/1/1805.

103 NLS MS 2571, f87, 3/6/1806, f105, 1/7/1806.

104 Ibid., f133, 135 19/7/1806.
105 Knight, *Britain against Napoleon*, 241.
106 See p. 56 below.
107 'Biographical Memoir of the Late Sir Charles Cotton, Bart., Admiral of the White Squadron', *Naval Chronicle*, XXVII (1812), 371–5.
108 CRO 568/c. 94, 24/8/1808.
109 DCA Letter Book 1795, 24/3/1795.
110 See p. 83 below for Keith's difficulties over prizes and provisioning.
111 BL Add Ms 31167 f70, 10/6/1799.
112 Newman Collingwood, *Correspondence* II, 287–8; *Collingwood's Correspondence*, 180.
113 NMM YOR/3, #31, 6/10/1810; *St Vincent's Letters*, II, 391, 8/12/1803.
114 DCA Letter Book No. 2 1798–1800, f13, 5/6/1798, f25, 21/6/1798.
115 *Keith Papers*, III, 23, 22/6/1803.
116 *Barham Papers*, III, 301, 27/3/1805.
117 NLS MS 2340 (Official correspondence to Warren handed on to Cochrane on assuming the command), f76, 17/5/1813.
118 NWMS DUN/20, f97, 27/3/1800.
119 Nicolas, *Nelson's Dispatches*, VI, VII.
120 N. A. M. Rodger, *The Admiralty* (Lavenham: T. Dalton, 1979), 24, 87–8; Knights, *Britain against Napoleon*, 303.
121 See Morriss, 'Introduction', *Channel Fleet*, 11–15.
122 *Spencer Papers*, IV, 168, 30/5/1798.
123 See Peter A. Ward, *British Naval Power in the East 1794–1805: The Command of Admiral Peter Rainier* (Woodbridge: Boydell Press, 2013), 61–84, for Rainier's relationship with the EEC.
124 NMM RAI/6, RAI/7.
125 BH Lans (6), II, f346, 29/11/1801.
126 Nicolas, *Nelson's Dispatches*, VI, 103, 9/7/1804; V, 214, 27/9/1803; 429–30, 26/2/1804; VI, 239, 13/10/1804.
127 Nicholas Tracy, 'Sir Richard Calder 1745–1818', in Peter Le Fevre and Richard Harding, eds, *British Admirals of the Napoleonic Wars* (London: Chatham, 2005), 204–205.
128 *Collingwood's Correspondence*, 236, 19/2/1808.
129 John D. Grainger ed., *The Royal Navy in the River Plate, 1806–1807* (Cambridge: Scholars Press/NRS, 1996), ix–x.
130 Ward, *British Naval Power in the East 1794–1805*, 43, 45–6.
131 C. Northcote Parkinson, *Edward Pellew: Viscount Exmouth, Admiral of the Red* (London: Methuen: 1934), 354; Alnwich, DNP Ms 63ff1–2, nd 1806.
132 See pp. 145–6 below.
133 NLS Ms 2327 f118, 5/2/1815.
134 See p. 102 below.
135 *Barham Papers*, III, 303–304, 27/3/1805, 305, 307, 20/5/1805, 21/5/1805.
136 BL Add Ms 40096 ff25–25v.
137 See Mackesy, *War in the Mediterranean*, 168n2.
138 See Lincoln, *Representing the Royal Navy*, 60–73, for the political context of the Navy's operations.
139 *Spencer Papers*, II, 44, 31/7/1796; 46, 1/8/1796.
140 BL Add Ms 31167, f177, 21/1/1801.
141 NMM MSS/94/034, ff 26, 20/7/1780; BL Add Ms 36708, ff1–14, 1797–1801.

142 NLS MS 2264 f40, 30/9/1799.

143 *Keith Papers*, III, 23, 22/6/1806.

144 *St Vincent's Letters*, II, 383, 14/10/1803, 387–8, 24/11/1803, 389–90, 3/12/1803, 391, 8/12/1803.

145 Nicolas, *Nelson's Dispatches*, V, 47–9, 8/3/1803, 23/4/1803, 59–60, 10/8/1803, 173, 24/8/1803, 215–16, 27/9/1803, 224, 6/10/1803.

146 NLS MS 2297, f136, 19/2/1813; Leyland, *Blockade of Brest*, II, 211, 16/3/1805; *Markham's Letters*, 79–101.

147 Wiltshire and Swindon History Centre, Lord Hood's Letters, 9/35/168, f499a, 7/10/1808.

148 DNM, Ms G/4/64, 15/9/1805, G/4/78, 16/3/1808, G/4/97, 18/10/1809, G/4/141, 21/7/1813, G/4/142, 4/8/1813; DNP, Ms 63, ff75–8, 30/4/1806, ff177–9, 30/9/1806; Alnwick Syon Miscellanea, Ms G/5/1–13, 12/9/1807–16/4/1809.

149 *St Vincent's Letters*, II, 369, 4/7/1803.

150 SRO HA 93/6/2/3 (877/53), 22/8/1803.

151 Leyland, *Blockade of Brest*, I, 52–3, 110–19, 9/8/1803, 30/7/1803.

152 See Davy, *In Nelson's Wake*, 230–53; Andrew Lambert, *The Challenge* (London: Faber, 2012), 198–228.

153 Leyland, *Blockade of Brest*, xxiii, xl, 200, 10/11/1803, 122, 13/8/1803.

154 NMM DUC/25, 25/7/1800, 22/2/1801, DUC/11. See Lincoln, *Representing the Royal Navy*, 96–104, for the trading interests' role in recognizing its achievements.

155 DCA 6/4/1795, May–June 1795; Letter Book No 2, 1798–1800, f17, 11/6/1798; Davy, *In Nelson's Wake*, 138.

156 Lady Bourchier, ed., *Memoir of the Life of Admiral Sir Edward Codrington, With Selections from His Public and Private Correspondence*, 2 vols (London: [sn], 1873), I, 51, 30/9/1805.

157 See pp. 162–5 below.

158 NLS MS 2340, f14v-16, 18/11/1812, f39, 9/1/1813.

159 See note 2 above for examples of the language of urgency in the 1806 *Regulations*. The section on flag officers' duties in the 1787 edition is brief, procedural and conveyed in passive language.

160 H. W. Dickinson, *Educating the Royal Navy: Eighteenth- and Nineteenth-Century Education for Officers* (London: Routledge, 2007), 33–46.

161 Ibid., 29–32.

162 On Murray, see Barry Aldridge, *My Dear Murray: A Friend of Nelson*, 2nd edn (Chichester: published by the author, 2014), 9; St Vincent: 9. NMRN, MSS 259/1, f 7, 9/3/1773. Duncan: NWMS M1995.2.76.

Chapter 2

1 BL Add Ms 31164, f129, 29/11/1806.

2 J. Ross Dancy, *The Myth of the Press Gang* (Woodbridge: Boydell Press, 2015), 187–8; Dancy offers a statistically based corrective to the conventional picture, arguing that only about a third of ships' companies were pressed into the service.

3 Lans 6(1), f90, 22/1/1795.

4 NA ADM 3/126, 18/2/1801.

5 See p. 60 below.

6 See p. 30 above.

7 BL Add Ms 31167, f108, 20/6/1800, f157, 4/11/1800.

8 BL Add Ms 31167, f33, 16/6/1799.

9 NMM MSS/94/034, Jervis to Shelbourne, ff 26–26v, 20/7/1780.

10 *Spencer Papers*, II, 42, 27/7/1796.

11 CRO, Cotton Papers, 588/c.71, 11/11/1805.

12 NMM WYN/104, 19/3/1799; BL Add Ms 41852, 25/10/1800.

13 Hardin Craig, 'Letters of Lord St Vincent to Thomas Grenville 1806–7', in Christopher Lloyd ed., *Naval Miscellany*, IV (London: NRS, 1952), 482, 16/11/1806.

14 Ibid., 476, 21/10/1806.

15 Ruddock F. Mackay and Michael Duffy, *Hawke, Nelson, and British Naval Leadership* (Woodbridge: Boydell Press, 2009), 93–8.

16 A. M. W. Stirling, *Pages & Portraits from the Past, Being the Private Papers of Sir William Hotham, GCB*, 2 vols (London, 1919), I, 39–40.

17 See pp. 79–81 below.

18 See p. 79.

19 BL Add Ms 37608, ff10–10v, 24/10/1800.

20 See p. 11 above.

21 *Barham Papers*, III, 254, 25/6/1805.

22 James Greig, ed., *The Farington Diary by John Farington, R. A.*, V, 116, 19/2/1809.

23 *Spencer Papers*, II, 442–3, 1/5/1798.

24 BL Add Ms 31167, f26v, 16/4/1799; *Markham's Letters*, 30–1, 3/11/1803.

25 BL Add Ms 31167, f32v, 10/5/1799.

26 See p. 81 below.

27 Roger Morriss, *The Channel Fleet and the Blockade of Brest, 1793–1801* (London: NRS, 2001), 514, 517, 21 and 27/6/1800.

28 NMRM, MSS 259/4 f36, 24/6/1800.

29 NMM MSS 94/034 f. 4v, nd; f. 26, 20/7/1780; f. 48v.

30 *Spencer Papers*, II, 37, 18/7/1796.

31 BL Add Ms f178–178v, 26/1/1801.

32 *St Vincent's Letters*, I, 339, 29/3/1801. This declaration was prompted by the prevalence of the practice of appointing acting lieutenants who had not served their time and passed the examination.

33 Rodger, *Command*, 476–8, 487–8.

34 Hardin Craig Jnr, 'Letters of Lord St Vincent', 472, 6/2/1806.

35 BL Add Ms 31167, F180, 2/2/1801.

36 Morriss, *Channel Fleet*, 563–4, 26/9/1800.

37 *Spencer Papers*, II, 210–12.

38 BL Add Ms 31167, f158, 11/11/1800.

39 Margarette Lincoln, *Naval Wives and Mistresses* (Stroud: History Press, 2011 [2007]), 75–7.

40 *Markham's Letters*, 420, ?1801.

41 *Collingwood's Correspondence*, 69, 2/7/1795, 111, 12/1/1800.

42 Ibid., 81, 22/2/1797.

43 See pp. 74–80 below.

44 *Collingwood's Correspondence*, 89–90, 3/12/1798 and 91, 16/12/1798.

45 Quoted Roger Knight, *Britain against Napoleon: The Organization of Victory 1793–1815* (London: Penguin, 2013), 103n.

46 *Collingwood's Correspondence*, 100, 17/8/1799; *Keith Papers*, II, 41, 30/7/1799.

47 Morriss, *Channel Fleet*, 454–5.

48 Ibid., 596, 8/12/1800.
49 Ibid., 514, 21/6/1800 and 517, 27/6/1800.
50 Ibid., 516–17, 27/6/1800.
51 SRO, SA/3/1/2/1, 22/3/1801.
52 Ibid.; on the importance of St Vincent's familiarity with the details of the Channel fleet, see *St Vincent's Letters*, I, 240, 9/3/1801.
53 BL Add Ms 31164 f16v, 4/12/1800, 31167 f183v, 9/2/1801.
54 For Pellew's performance in the House of Commons, see Knight, *Britain against Napoleon*, 223.
55 Pat Crimmin, 'Sir Thomas Troubridge c1749–1807', Peter Le Fevre and Richard Harding, eds, *British Admirals of the Napoleonic Wars* (London: Chatham, 2005), 305–6, 311–12.
56 Cf. ibid., 320.
57 C. Northcote Parkinson, *Edward Pellew, Viscount Exmouth, Admiral of the Red* (London: Methuen, 1934), 367, 10/7/1807; 372–3.
58 Colin White, 'A Man of Business: Nelson as Commander in Chief Mediterranean, May 1803–January 1805', *MM*, 91:2 (2005), 175–94.
59 Nicolas, *Nelson's Dispatches*, V, 199, 8/9/1803.
60 Ibid., VI, 354, 11/3/1805.
61 Gerald Jordan and Nicholas Rogers, 'Admirals as Heroes', *Journal of British Studies*, 28 (1989): 216–18.
62 Nicolas, *Nelson's Dispatches*, VI, 108–109, 12/7/1804.
63 Ibid., 90, 30/6/1804.
64 Ibid., 276, 20/11/1804.
65 Ibid., 446–7, 5/6/1805; 141–2, 7/8/1804.
66 Ibid., 211, 4/10/1804.
67 Mackay and Duffy, *British Naval Leadership*, 210–11.
68 Colin White, *Nelson: The New Letters* (Woodbridge: Boydell Press, 2005), 53, 59, 18/6/1801.
69 N. A. M. Rodger, 'Nelson and the British Navy: Seamanship, Leadership and Originality', in David Cannadine, ed., *Admiral Lord Nelson: Context and Legacy* (Houndsmills: Palgrave, 2005), 26.
70 Nicolas, *Nelson's Dispatches*, VI, 386, 30/3/1805.
71 Ibid., 126, 1/8/1804.
72 Ibid., 353, 10/3/1805.
73 *Collingwood Correspondence*, 36, 22/7/1793.
74 Ibid., 53, 3/8/1794.
75 Ibid., 43, 2/3/1794.
76 Ibid., 108, 5/12/1799.
77 Ibid., 36, 22/7/1793.
78 Ibid., 112, 8/4/1800.
79 See Tony Barrow, *Collingwood's Northumbrians: Old and Valuable Officers* (Rainton Bridge: Business Education Publishers, 2010), 47–75, for an account of Rotheram's career and his service under Collingwood.
80 *Collingwood's Correspondence*, 82 n1, nd.
81 See Geoffrey Murray, *The Life of Admiral Collingwood* (London: Hutchinson, 1936), 114.
82 Lady Bourchier, ed, *Memoir of the Life of Admiral Sir Edward Codrington* (London: [sn], 1873), I, 47, 5/9/1805.
83 Hugh Owen, 'Cuthbert, Lord Collingwood', in Le Fevre and Harding, *British Admirals*, 154–5.

84 M. D. Hay, ed., *Landsman Hay: The Memoirs of Robert Hay, 1789–1847* (London: Rupert Hart-Davies, 1953), 66.

85 *Collingwood's Correspondence*, 191, 12/9/1806.

86 Ibid., 227, 1/12/1807.

87 Quoted Murray, *Collingwood*, 109; emphasis in the original.

88 *Collingwood's Correspondence*, 273–4, 18/4/1809.

89 Bourchier, *Codrington*, I, 47, 5/9/1805.

90 Ibid., 46–7, 4/9/1805.

91 Ibid., 96, 10/3/1806.

92 Anne Parry, *The Admirals Freemantle* (London: Chatto and Windus, 1973), 76, 28/11/1805.

93 NMM, COL/14, 15.

94 Robert Blake, *Evangelicals in the Royal Navy 1775–1815: Blue Lights and Psalm Singers* (Woodbridge: Boydell Press, 2008), 84–5.

95 For recent treatments of aspects of these officers' careers, see Gareth Atkins, 'Christian Heroes, Providence and Patriotism in Wartime Britain, 1793–1815', *Historical Journal*, 58 (2015), 393–414, and 'Religion, Politics and Patronage in the Late Hanoverian Navy, c1780–c1820', *Historical Research*, 88 (2015), 272–90.

96 Blake, *Evangelicals*, 198.

97 Michael A. Lewis, ed., *A Narrative of My Professional Adventures (1790–1839) by Sir William Henry Dillon, KCH., Vice-Admiral of the Red*, 2 vols (London: NRS, 1953), I, 97–104.

98 Blake, *Evangelicals*, 72–3, 194–5.

99 SRO HA 93/6/2/4 (877'103), 28/9/1808; emphasis in the original.

100 Blake, *Evangelicals*, 190–5.

101 See Lewis, *Dillon's Narrative*, I, 93n3, 98–9, 105–106, 107–108, 168.

102 Ibid., I, 96.

103 See pp. 85–7 below.

104 *Martin's Letters*, I, 326–7, 17/7/1807, 330n2, 336.

105 Ibid., I, 30–1, II, 48, 27/8/1808.

106 See pp. 183–4 below.

107 Lewis, *Dillon's Narrative*, I, 99, 104.

108 Sir John Ross, *Memoirs and Correspondence of Admiral Lord de Saumarez* (London: Richard Bentley, 1838), I, 184, 183.

109 Ibid., 184–5; emphasis in the original.

Chapter 3

1 *Spencer Papers*, II, 26, 23/6/1796.

2 Roger Morriss, *The Channel Fleet and the Blockade of Brest 1793–1801* (London: NRS, 2001), 27, 56, 1/2/1795, 57–8, 11/2/1795; Michael Lewis, ed., *A Narrative of My Professional Adventures by Sir William Dillon* (London: NRS, 1953), I, 146.

3 *Spencer Papers*, II, 494, 23/12/1798. St Vincent had earlier praised Murray to the first lord; see 92, 22/7/1797, 486, 12/11/1798.

4 *Markham's Letters*, 36, 17/2/1806, 56, 26/6/1806.

5 See pp. 74–80 below for St Vincent's disputes with his flag officers, c1797–1800.

6 *Markham's Letters*, 227, 12/12/1806.

7 Ibid.

8   Ibid., 210, 11/11/1806.

9   Ibid., 211, 16/11/1806.

10 Ibid., 227, 12/12/1806

11 Ibid., 233, 23/12/1806.

12 Ibid., 251–2, 27/11/1807

13 John D. Grainger, ed., *The Royal Navy in the River Plate, 1806–1807*
    (Aldershot: Scholars Press/NRS, 1996), 254, suggests that Murray and other naval
    commanders involved exaggerated their success in maintaining the health of the
    troops in their convoys.

14 *Markham's Letters*, 244, 14/2/1807; 247, 15/3/1807.

15 Ibid., 252, 255, 27/3/1807.

16 Ibid., 269–70, 10/4/1807.

17 Ibid., 291, 18, 7/1808.

18 Grainger, *River Plate*, 254.

19 *Markham's Letters*, 299, 8/7/1807. The attribution is conjectural because the signature
    initials are indistinct.

20 WSRO, AM 760/1/31, 25/2/1808; AM 760/1/122, 19/8/1810; AM 760/1/123, 27/9/
    1810.

21 *Spencer Papers*, II, 15, 23, 31–2, 39–40.

22 *Spencer Papers*, II, 23, 21/41796, 31, 12/7/1796.

23 Ibid., 25–6, 23/6/1796.

24 Ibid., 42, 27/6/1796.

25 Ibid., 27, 23/3/1796; 28, 2/7/1796.

26 Ibid., 49–50, 24/8/1796.

27 Ibid., 58–60, 9/10/1796.

28 Ibid., 86–9, 30/12/1796

29 Ibid., 72, 11/11/1796.

30 *Spencer Papers*, II, 88–90, 2, 4/1/1797.

31 Peter Le Fevre offers a detailed rebuttable of the view that Parker was a lacklustre
    officer, pointing out that he served very effectively in a number of commands,
    including providing relief for St Vincent in the Channel Fleet; '"Little Merit will be
    given to me": Admiral Sir Hyde Parker (1739–1807) and the Diplomatic Build-up to
    the Battle', in Stephen Howard, ed., *Battle of Copenhagen 1801: 200 Years* (Shelton: The
    1805 Club, 2003), 1–29. He did not, however, enter into his North Sea command with
    any great enthusiasm.

32 *St Vincent's Letters*, I, 318–19.

33 Melford Hall, Hyde Parker Papers, F75/18, 6/10/1800; F75/21, 25/11/1800; F75/22, 29/
    11/1800.

34 Ibid., F76/2, 27/3/1801.

35 *St Vincent's Letters*, I, 83, 5/3/1801.

36 Ann Parry, ed., *The Admirals Freemantle* (London: Chatto & Windus, 1971), 53, 11/3/
    [1801].

37 *St Vincent's Letters*, I, 86, 11/3/1801.

38 Ibid., 89, 5/4/1801.

39 Ibid., 89–90, 17/4/1801.

40 Le Fevre, '"Little Merit"', 25.

41 Roger Knight, *The Pursuit of Victory* (London: Allen Lane, 2005), 389.

42 Hyde Parker Papers, F42/2.

43 Ibid., F75/27, 28, 22/5/1801.

44 Ibid., F86/2, *Hyde Parker's Defence* (1801), 9, 1.
45 William Hunter, *A Few Reflections on Recent Events, Concluding with A Defence of Sir Hyde Parker's Convention with Denmark* (London: John Stockdale, 1801), 31. Hunter appears to have been unknown to Hyde Parker. This pamphlet is in the Hyde Parker Papers, F86/3.
46 NA ADM 2/1091, f 90, 4/2/1803.
47 *St Vincent's Letters*, I, 78–9.
48 Le Fevre, '"Little Merit"', 20–1.
49 Ibid., 21–2.
50 Ibid., 22–3.
51 NNM WDG/11/1/13, 21/12/1800.
52 See Nicholas Tracy, 'Sir Robert Calder, 1745–1818', in Peter Le Fevre and Richard Harding, eds, *British Admirals in the Napoleonic Wars* (London: Chatham, 2005), 197–217.
53 Ibid., 204–205.
54 *Barham Papers*, III, 267, 17/8/1805.
55 Ibid., 262.
56 *Morning Post*, 22/8/1805.
57 NA, ADM 1/5371, 30/9/1805.
58 NA ADM 1/5371, record of Calder's count martial, not paginated.
59 Ibid.; emphases in the original.
60 Ibid.
61 Nicholas Tracy, 'Sir Robert Calder's Action', *MM*, 77:3 (1991), 267; *Martin's Letters*, I, 73–6.
62 Quoted Knight, *The Pursuit*, 499.
63 Tracy, 'Calder', 214.
64 See pp. 242–3 below.
65 See Lady Bourchier, ed., *Memoir of the Life of Admiral Sir Edward Codrington* (London: [sn], 1873), I, 48, 10/9/1805 for Codrington's comment and Duke of Buckingham and Chandos, *Memoirs of the Court and Cabinets of George the Third* (London: Hurst and Blackett, 1854), III, 446, 30/9/1805 for Freemantle's.
66 *Martin's Letters*, I, 73–4; cf. Knights, *The Pursuit*, 495.
67 Buckingham and Chandos, *Memoirs*, IV, 100, 25/11/1806.
68 Tracy, *Naval Chronicle*, IV, 334; NMM YOR/3, #2, 14/4/1811, 17/4/1811, 22/4/1811.
69 See p. 201 below.
70 NA ADM 1/5442, Vice Admiral Stirling's Court Martial, 7/5/1814–9/5/1814, not paginated. Unless indicated otherwise all references to the trial are from this document.
71 NMM WAR/54, f12, 3/8/1812, 16/9/1812.
72 *Markham's Letters*, 300, 17/7/1806.
73 James Ralfe, *The Naval Biography of Great Britain* (London: Whitmore and Fenn, 1828), IV, 275.
74 James Ralfe, *Historical Memoirs of Admiral Charles Stirling with Notes and Observations by Vice-Admiral Stirling* (London: L. Harrison, 1826), 24–7, 28n, 60–2.
75 See Thomas Malcomson, *Order and Disorder in the British Navy, 1793–1815* (Woodbridge: Boydel, 2016), 150–2. Malcomson's account includes useful detail on the trial and context but it does not discuss Stirling's claims about his relationship with Wolley, the equivocal verdict and sentence, the absence of witnesses and O'Grady's motivation.

76 Charles Stirling, *The Case of Vice Admiral Stirling. With an Appendix Containing the Minutes of the Court Martial and Mr Const's Observations* (Chertsy: William Slater Castell, 1821), 27–8.

77 Ibid., 32–3; Ralfe, *Charles Stirling*, 53.

78 NMM WAR/35, ff209–10, 3/4/1813.

79 NA ADM, ff105–6, 23/2/1814.

80 NMM WAR/54, 27/2/1813.

81 NA ADM 2/932, ff254–5, 10/4/1813; ADM 1/264, ff76–8, 18/6/1813.

82 NA ADM 1/264, f86, 19/6/1813, which identifies the date of recall as 12 April; Ralfe, *Charles Stirling*, 69–70. Warren first raised the matter with Stirling in a letter dated 3 April but did not forward Wolley's letter and ask for a full explanation until 1 June, at which time he told Stirling that he had also forwarded it to the Admiralty; NMM WAR/35, ff209–10, WAR/54, 1/6/1813, not foliated.

83 Gerald Jordan and Nicholas Rogers, 'Admirals as Heroes', *Journal of British Studies*, 28 (1989), 201–24.

84 NMM, Sir Charles Pole's Papers, WYN/104, 21/8/1798.

85 Bourchier, *Memoir*, I, 48, 10/9/1805.

86 See pp. 29–30 above.

Chapter 4

1 NLS MS 2569, 13/5/1801.

2 *Markham's Letters*, 410, 8/2/1806.

3 *Spencer Papers*, I, 205, 5/11/1795.

4 Michael Duffy, '… All Was Hushed Up: The Hidden Trafalgar', *MM*, 91:2 (2005), 216–18.

5 BL Add Ms 31167, f140, 10/8/1800.

6 *Barham Papers*, II, 82–149, for correspondence relating to this episode.

7 Ibid., 415, 24/7/1795.

8 NMM THO/2e MS57/101, 14/6/1795. This collection is made up of copies of papers that Thompson gathered to use in an anticipated court martial on his return to England in 1796.

9 Ibid., 7/7/1795.

10 Ibid., 9/7/1795.

11 James Ralfe, *The Naval Biography of Great Britain* (Boston: Irvington, 1972 [1828]), I, 237–18.

12 NMM THO/2e MS57/101, 9/7/1795.

13 Ibid., 9/7/1795.

14 Ibid., 10/7/1795, 11/7/1795.

15 *Barham Papers*, II, 415–16, 24/7/1795.

16 NA ADM 1/579, 24/3/1796.

17 *London Gazette*, 24 June 1796.

18 NA ADM 1/579, 21/6/1796, 3/7/1796.

19 NA ADM 2/1090, f93, 4/7/1796, f94, 7/6/1796.

20 NA ADM 1/579, 9/7/1796.

21 NA ADM 2/1090, f95, 12/7/1796, f96, 15/7/1796.

22 See pp. 72–3 above.

23 See Colin White, 'The Battle of Cape St Vincent, 14 February 1797', in Stephen Howarth, ed., *Battle of Cape St Vincent 200 Years* (Shelton: The 1805 Club, 1998), 51.

24 See p. 193 below.
25 *Spencer Papers*, II, 411 9/7/1797.
26 Ibid., 409, 1/7/1797.
27 Denis Orde's *Nelson's Mediterranean Command* (Barnsley: Pen & Sword Maritime, 2014 [1997]) provides a detailed account of his ancestor's career.
28 Sir John Orde, *Copy of Correspondence, &c Between The Right Hon. The Lords Commissioners of The Admiralty, The Right Hon. The Earl of St Vincent, K.B, The Right Hon. Earl Spencer, K.B. and Vice-Admiral Sir J. Orde, BART* (London, 1802), 101, 11/12/1797.
29 Orde, *Nelson's Mediterranean Command*, 89–90.
30 Edward Pelham Brenton, *Life and Correspondence of John, Earl of St Vincent, G.C.B, Admiral of the Fleet*, 2 vols (London, 1838), I, 373–5, 396.
31 Evelyn Berckman, *Nelson's Dear Lord: A Portrait of St Vincent* (London: Macmillan, 1962), 161–70, provides a good summary of the dispute with Orde.
32 Cf. Kathrine Orth, 'Sir John Orde, 1751–1824', in Peter Le Fevre and Richard Harding, eds, *British Admirals in the Napoleonic Wars* (London: Chatham, 2005), 80.
33 BL Add Ms 31167, 17/2/1799.
34 See pp. 46–7 above.
35 Brenton, *Life of St Vincent*, I, 399, 16/6/1798, 407, 6/9/1798; emphases in the original.
36 *Spencer Papers*, II, 473, 28/9/1798; BL Add Ms 31167, f5, 20/12/1798. For Orde's governorship, see Orth, 'Sir John Orde', 73–6.
37 Orde, *Copy of Correspondence*, 18; emphasis in the original.
38 Ibid., 5–8; *Spencer Papers*, III, 24–6; 6–7/10/1799; for a recent reference to this episode, see Mark Barton, 'Duelling in the Royal Navy', *MM*, 100:3 (August 2014), 288.
39 *Spencer Papers*, III, 27–8, 28/5/1798.
40 Ibid., 28–9, 13/8/1798.
41 Brenton, *St Vincent*, I, 412, 6/12/1798.
42 *Spencer Papers*, III, 33, 13/2/1799.
43 BL Add Ms 31167, f 3, 6/12/1798.
44 BL Add Ms 31167, f 25v, 27/3/1799.
45 BL Add Ms 31167, f 112v, 2/7/1800.
46 Julian Gwyn refers to Parker's recall but not to St Vincent's likely role in it or to their previous dispute; Julian Gwyn, *Frigates and Foremast: The North American Squadron in Nova Scotia Waters, 1745–1815* (Vancouver: UBC Press, 2003), 96–7.
47 NA ADM 3/144, 24/2/1801.
48 NA ADM 3/126/f129–30, 25/4/1801.
49 NA ADM 3/126, f129–30, 25/4/1801.
50 NA ADM /5359.
51 Ibid.
52 BL Bridport Papers, Add Ms 35201, f76, 28/3/1800.
53 *Spencer Papers*, III, 310, 2/5/1800, 315–16, 20/5/1800.
54 Ibid., 310, 5/5/1800.
55 Ibid., III, 315, 20/5/1800.
56 See pp. 177–8 below.
57 *Spencer Papers*, III, 313–14, 19/5/1800.
58 Ibid., 316, 8/6/1800.
59 Ibid., 317–18, 7/8/1800.
60 Ibid., 318–19, 9/8/1800; 320–1, 12/8/1800.
61 *Keith Papers*, II, 272, 9/3/1801.
62 Ibid., 286–8, 21/4/1801.
63 Ibid., November? 1800.

64 Ibid., 297, 11/5/1801; NLS MS 3022, f28, 4/5/1801

65 *Keith Papers*, II, 295, 11/5/1801.

66 Ibid., 294, 9/5/1801.

67 Ibid., 296 n1.

68 Ibid., 298–9, 12/5/101.

69 Ibid., 301–302, 15/5/1801; NLS MS 2569, f153, 8/6/1801.

70 NLS MS 2569, f172v, 19/7/1801.

71 *Keith Papers*, II, 331–3, 349.

72 Ibid., 311–12.

73 NLS MS 2568, f149, 5/6/1801; f109, 29/8/1801.

74 *Keith Papers*, II, 292, 10/5/1801.

75 See Kevin D. McCranie, *Admiral Lord Keith and the Naval War against Napoleon* (Gainesville: University of Florida Press, 2006), 116, 119.

76 Ibid., 297.

77 *Keith Papers*, II, 308, 309n1, 27/5/1801, 29/5/1801.

78 John Marshall, *Royal Naval Biography* (London: Rees, Orme, Brown and Green, 1823), I.2, 480.

79 *Keith Papers*, II, 296, 13/5/1801.

80 *St Vincent's Letters*, I, 221–2, 4/4/1801.

81 Ibid., 231, 8/10/1802.

82 NA ADM 2/1091, f76, 18/2/1802.

83 See p. 239 below.

84 *Keith Papers*, III, 390ff.

85 This account of the first day of the court martial is taken from the report in the *Times*, 23 May 1809. Harvey's brief statement of defence was reproduced verbatim in the *Times* of 24 May.

86 *Times*, 24 May, 3.

87 James Greig, ed., *The Farington Diary by John Farington, R.A.*, 5 vols (London, 1922–25), V, 173, 26/5/1809.

88 Tracy, *Naval Chronicle*, IV, 203.

89 Chatterton, *Memorials*, II, 306, 328.

90 See Orth, 'Sir John Orde', 69–72.

91 *Barham's Paper's*, III, 303–308, 27/3/1805, 20/5/1805, 21/5/1805, 22/5/1805.

92 NMM Pole Papers, WYN/104, 18/3/1799, 19/3/1799.

93 Sir Lewis Namier and John Broke, *The House of Commons, 1754–1790*, 3 vols (London: HMSO, 1964), I, 281, II, 86, for Berkeley's relationship with the Beauforts and their electoral interest; Thorne, *House of Commons*, I, 47, and V, 366, for Thomson's relationship with the Beauforts.

94 Tracy, *Naval Chronicle*, IV, 247. Aspinall, *Correspondence of George III*, V, #4111, 540–1, 10/3/1810.

Chapter 5

1 NMM WYN/103, 31/7/1799; emphases in the original.

2 C. I. Hamilton, *The Making of the Modern Admiralty. British Naval Policy-Making, 1805-1927* (Cambridge: Cambridge University Press, 2011), 6–14, 27–34.

3 Dorothy Hood, *The Admirals Hood* (London: Hutchinson & Co, 1934), 152–5.

4 BL Bridport Papers, Add Ms 35195, f152v, 8/5/1795.

5 Castalia Countess Granville, *Lord Granville Leveson Gower (First Earl Granville) Private Correspondence 1781–1821* (London: 1916), I, 69, 31/10/1793.

6 Michael Duffy, *Soldiers, Sugar and Seapower: The British Expeditions to the West Indies and the War against Revolutionary France* (Oxford: Clarendon Press, 1987), 24–5.

7 *Spencer Papers*, I, 210, 8/2/1796.

8 *Spencer Papers*, I, 169, 12/10/1795; John E. Talbott, *The Pen & Ink Sailor: Charles Middleton and the King's Navy, 1778–1813* (London: Frank Cass, 1998), 139–40.

9 *Spencer Papers*, I, 169, 12/10/1795.

10 Ibid., 167–8, 12/10/1795.

11 Ibid., 170, 12/10/1795.

12 Ibid., 171, 16/10/1795.

13 Ibid., 178, 20/10/1795.

14 Ibid., 180–1, 22/10/1795.

15 Ibid., 180, 22/10/1795.

16 Ibid., 6, 14/12/1794. Given Dundas's promotion of amphibious expeditions and Middleton's dislike of them, the latter's confidences to the former seem particularly maladroit.

17 Ibid., 51, 1/7/1795.

18 *Barham Papers*, II, 20, 26/4/1781.

19 Ibid., 182–3.

20 *Barham Papers*, II, 421, 23/10/1795; *Spencer Papers*, I, 183, 25/10/1795.

21 See N. A. M. Rodger, *The Admiralty* (Lavenham: T. Dalton, 1979), 82–3.

22 *Barham Papers*, II, 421, 25/10/1795; Hamilton, *Making of the Modern Admiralty*, 31–2, for the evolution of this position.

23 *Barham Papers*, II, 424–8, 9/11/1795.

24 Ibid.

25 Ibid., 428–9.

26 Ibid., 427.

27 Ibid., 429, 430.

28 Ibid., 430.

29 Ibid., 429–30.

30 Hamilton, *Making of the Modern Admiralty*, 8–11.

31 *Spencer Papers*, I, 193–4, 31/10/1795.

32 Ibid., 202, 5/11/1795; 209–10, 2/2/1796; 216, 25/2/1796; 217, 25/2/1796.

33 NMM, Waldegrave Papers, WDG/6/1/1, 3/11/1795, 6/2/1, 7/11/1795, 6/3/1/, 10/11/1795.

34 *Spencer Papers*, I, 212, 15/2/1796.

35 Ibid., 221–2, 17/3/1796.

36 Ibid., 227, 2/4/1796.

37 G. Cornwallis-West, *The Life and Letters of Admiral Cornwallis* (London: Methuen, 1927), 340.

38 Ibid., 334–5.

39 Ibid., 328–9.

40 Ibid., 330.

41 Ibid., 339.

42 NA PRO30/11/275, nd, but before the trial since Cornwallis anticipates it.

43 *Spencer Papers*, I, 229; a draft but indicative of Spencer's view of the matter.

44 Ibid., 224, 1/4/1796; NA PRO 30/11/275.

45 Aspinall, *Correspondence of George III*, II, #1187, 290, 7/1/1795.

46 Hood, *The Admirals Hood*, 163–4, 166.

47   Sir John Barrow, *The Life of Richard Earl Howe* (London: John Murray, 1838), 2.
48   See p. 34 above.
49   Roger Morriss, ed, *The Channel Fleet and the Blockade of Brest, 1793–1801* (London: NRS, 2001), 50, 17/12/1794.
50   Ibid., 51, 24/12/1794.
51   Ibid., 51–2, 26/12/1794, 52, 28/12/1794.
52   Ibid., 53, 6/1/1795.
53   Ibid., 58, 28/2/1795.
54   BL Add Ms 31597, f10, 17/4/1796.
55   Morriss, *Channel Fleet*, 89, 5/6/1795, 126, 15/9/1795.
56   BL, Bridport Papers, Add Ms 35196, f137, 1/8/1795.
57   Morriss, *Channel Fleet*, 100, 27/7/1795, 103, 31/7/1795.
58   Ibid., 107–108, 9/8/1795.
59   Ibid., 109, 15/8/1795; BL, Add Ms 35196, f168, 15/8/1795.
60   Morriss, *Channel Fleet*, 110, 16/8/1795.
61   Ibid., 110, 18/8/1795; emphasis in the original.
62   Ibid., 136, 22/10/1795.
63   Ibid., 61, 28/4/1795.
64   Aspinall, *Correspondence of George III*, II, #1244, 341, 4/5/1795.
65   See Hood, *The Admirals Hood*, 154 for Nelson's reaction.
66   Morriss, *Channel Fleet*, 62, 4/5/1795; *Spencer Papers*, I, 31–2, 3/5/1795.
67   Andrew Lambert, *Admirals* (London: Faber and Faber, 2011), 180–1; BL Add Ms 35195, f141–2, 28/4/1795.
68   Morriss, *Channel Fleet*, 262–3, 8/8/1797.
69   Ibid., 217–19, 5/1/1798.
70   BL Add Ms 31167, f141v, 20/8/1800; emphasis in the original.
71   Ibid., f18, 10/2/1799.
72   Ibid., f10, 6/12/1798.
73   Ibid., f11, 23/1/1799.
74   See pp. 141–2 below.
75   See Robert Blake, *Evangelicals in the Royal Navy, 1775–1815* (Woodbridge: Boydell Press, 2008), 190–224, for a detailed account of Gambier's religious aspirations as a sea officer.
76   Ibid., 194.
77   BL Add Ms 36708, f 4–4v, 5/5/1797.
78   BL Add Ms 37608, f 9, 28/8/1800.
79   NMM, WYN/104; WYN/104, 21/8/1798.
80   BL Add Ms 37608, f 10, 24/10/1800, f12, 17/12/1800.
81   C. Northcote Parkinson, *Edward Pellew, Viscount Exmouth, Admiral of the Red* (London: Methuen, 1934), 398, 410; see p. 199 below for a discussion of Pellew's ambitions towards the end of the war.
82   Keele UL, M148/6 (53/6), 4/7/1808.
83   See pp. 29–30.

Chapter 6

1   *Spencer Papers*, II, 206, 17/4/1797.
2   The calorific value of seamen's standard rations (more than 4,000 calories a day) provides a measure of the physical demands of the job; see Janet Macdonald, *Feeding Nelson's Navy* (London: Chatham, 2004), 177–9.

3 See Brian Lavery, *Nelson's Navy: The Ships, Men and Organisation, 1793–1815*, revised edn (London: Conway, 2012), 328.

4 J. Ross Dancy, *The Myth of the Press Gang* (Woodbridge: Boydell Press, 2015).

5 Clowes, *History*, IV, 240–1, 246.

6 DCA Duncan's Letterbook 1798–1800, f 94, August 1798.

7 These cases appear in the lists of ships lost in Clowes, *History*, IV, 548–52, V, 549–55.

8 Stephen Taylor, *Storm and Conquest: The Battle for the Indian Ocean in 1809* (London: Faber, 2007), 228–9, 242.

9 Leyland, *Blockade of Brest*, I, lii.

10 Arthur N. Gilbert, 'The Nature of Mutiny in the British Navy in the Eighteenth Century', in David Masterman, ed., *Naval History: Sixth Symposium of the US Naval Academy* (Annapolis: United State Naval Institute, 1987), 115–16; Rodger, *Command*, 443–5. See Ann Coats's contributions to Ann V. Coats and P. MacDougal, eds, *The Naval Mutinies of 1797: Unity and Perseverance* (Woodbridge: Boydell Press, 2011), 17–37, 39–60, for a recent statement of the industrial action interpretation; and Niklas Frymman, 'The Mutiny on the *Hermione*: Warfare, Revolution, and Treason in the Royal Navy', *Journal of Social History* 44:1 (2010), 159–87.

11 John D. Byrn, Jr., *Crime and Punishment in the Royal Navy: Discipline on the Leeward Islands Station, 1784–1812* (Cambridge: Scholar Press, 1989), 10.

12 G. E. Manwaring and Bonamy Dobreé, *The Floating Republic* (London: Penguin Books, 1937), 269.

13 For a detailed account of the *Hermoine* mutiny and the trials and punishment of men from this ship, see Dudley Pope, *The Black Ship* (London: Secker & Warburg, 1968).

14 Byrn, *Crime and Punishment*, 22–4; examples of the king's exercise of his role appear in his published correspondence: Aspinall, *Correspondence of George, III*, # 1613, 31/8/1797, 618–20, where capital sentences on Nore mutineers were confirmed.

15 See Thomas Malcomson, *Order and Disorder in the British Navy, 1793–1815* (Woodbridge: Boydell Press, 2016), 140–3, 209–10.

16 Gilbert, 'The Nature of Mutiny', 113.

17 Sir John Barrow, *The Life of Richard, Earl Howe, K.G, Admiral of the Fleet and General of Marines* (London: John Murray, 1838), 324.

18 Roger Morriss ed., *The Channel Fleet and the Blockade of Brest, 1793–1801* (London: NRS, 2001), 197, 14/4/1797.

19 *Spencer Papers*, II, 116–17, 21/4/1797.

20 Morriss, *Channel Fleet*, 200, 15/4/1797; if Barrow's account is correct (see above n.17), Bridport's criticism of Howe was disingenuous.

21 Ibid., 207, 18/4/1797.

22 NA ADM 1/107 f262; Conrad Gill, *The Naval Mutinies of 1797* (Manchester: Manchester-Victoria University Press, 1913), 58.

23 Morriss, *Channel Fleet*, 203, 16/4/1797.

24 Ibid., 212, [22/4/1798].

25 NA ADM 1/107, f262, 7/5/1797.

26 Ibid., f274, 9/5/1797.

27 NA ADM 1/107, f293, 11/5/1797, 13/5/1797; emphasis in the original.

28 Gill, *Naval Mutinies*, 58ff.

29 NA ADM 1/107, f269, 9/5/1797.

30 [Anon], *History of the Mutiny at Spithead and the Nore* (London: Thomas Tegg, 1842), 63–5.

31 NA ADM 1/107, f269, 9/5/1797.

32 Gill, *Naval Mutinies,* 66; *Times,* 15/5/1797.
33 Manwaring and Dobreé, *Floating Republic,* 102.
34 Barrow, *Howe,* 333.
35 Mrs Henry Baring, ed., *The Diary of the Right Hon. William Windham, 1784–1810* (London: Longmans, Green, and Co., 1866), 367, 10/5/1797.
36 Morriss, *Channel Fleet,* 228, 10/5/1797; 223, 7/5/1797.
37 Ibid., 228, 10/5/1797.
38 Ibid., 229, 11/5/1797.
39 NA ADM 1/107, f304, 16/5/1797; f342, 28/5/1797.
40 Barrow, *Howe,* 335.
41 Gill, *Naval Mutinies,* 80; see *Times* 17/5/1797.
42 ADM 1/107, f283, 11/5/1797, f305, 16/5/1797; Gill, *Naval Mutinies,* 98, for Howe's role.
43 BL Add Ms 31167, f26v, 16/4/1799; BL Add Ms 75864, f311, 13/8/1800.
44 *Collingwood's Correspondence,* 82–3, 85, 3/6/1797, 7/8/1797.
45 See Barrow, *Howe,* 324.
46 *Collingwood's Correspondence,* 86, 7/8/1797, SHC DD/CPL 30, 16.
47 NA ADM 1/107, f228, 25/4/1797, f230, 26/4/1797.
48 Barrow, *Howe,* 339.
49 Aspinall, *Correspondence of George III,* II, #1545, 572, 15/5/1797. Interestingly, Howe remained concerned about the general state of discipline at this time; Barrow, *Howe,* 345.
50 Gill, *Naval Mutinies,* 115, 138, 143–7.
51 *Keith Papers,* II, 13–14, 6/6/1797.
52 NA ADM 1/728, f414, 22/6/1797, f422, 24/6/1797.
53 BL Add Ms 35198, f56, 28/7/1797.
54 *Keith Papers,* II, 14, 5/7/1797.
55 Ibid.; Lans 6 (1) f134, 5/7/1797.
56 See Earl of Camperdown, *Admiral Duncan* (London: Longmans, Green & Co, 1898), 96–7.
57 *Spencer Papers,* II, 121, 1/5/1797.
58 Quoted Camperdown, *Duncan,* 100.
59 *Spencer Papers,* II, 122, 7/5/1797.
60 Camperdown, *Duncan,* 105–106.
61 *Spencer Papers,* II, 130–1, 14/5/1797.
62 Quoted in Camperdown, *Duncan,* 101.
63 Ibid., 106.
64 *Spencer Papers,* II, 135, 26/5/1797; 138, 27/5/ 1797.
65 Ibid., 148, 5/6/1797; 147–8, 1/6/1797.
66 NWMS DUN/32, 27/5/1797.
67 NWMS DUN/20, f67, 14/6/1797.
68 The account of these events draws extensively on Hubley and Malcolmson, 'The People', Craig Lantle, ed., *The Apathetic and the Defiant: Case Studies of Canadian Mutiny and Disobedience, 1812* (Toronto: Dundurn, 2007), 36–51.
69 NA ADM 1/473, f380–81, 9/6/1797.
70 NA ADM 1/473, f400, 3/8/1797.
71 NA ADM 1/473, f401–402, 6/8/1797.
72 Ibid.
73 NA ADM 1/473, f395–6, 9/8/1797.

74 Hubley and Malcolmson, 'The People', 47.

75 NA ADM 1/473, f27–8, 24/11/1797.

76 See p. 37 above.

77 Richard Harding, 'Sir Charles Knowles, 1754–1831', in Peter Le Fevre and Richard Harding eds., *British Admirals in the Napoleonic Wars* (London: Chatham, 2005), 113–38.

78 Ibid., 127–8, 132–3.

79 *Spencer Papers*, II, 377–8, 29/3/1797, p. 402, 22/5/1797.

80 Sugden, *Nelson: A Dream of Glory* (London: Pimlico, 2012), 732–3.

81 Brenton, *St Vincent*, I, 360.

82 *Spencer Papers*, II, 410, 9/7/1797.

83 *St Vincent's Letters*, II, 263, 11/10/1802.

84 Brenton, *St Vincent*, I, 367.

85 See p. 39 above.

86 BL Add Ms 31167, f115v, 5/7/1800.

87 BL Add Ms 29914, f327, 5/7/1798.

88 BL Add Ms 31167, ff93–4, 10/6/1800, ff96–8, 13–14/6/1800.

89 BL Add Ms 31167, f169v, 112/12/1800; f171, 8/1/1801; f176v, 21/1/1801.

90 BL Add Ms 31167, ff93–4, 10/6/1800, ff96–8, 14/6/1800; Add Ms 37608, f6, 30/6/1800.

91 BL Add Ms 75864, f311 13/8/1800.

92 BL Add Ms 31167, f23, 15/3/1799.

93 ADM 1/248, 28/5/1798; Pope, *The Black Ship*, 260–1.

94 *Collingwood's Correspondence*, 132, 8/11/1801.

95 NA ADM 1/248, 28/5/1798.

96 *Spencer Papers*, III, 286, 11/5/1800.

97 Pope, *The Black Ship*, 260–1.

98 Ibid., 263.

99 Byrn, *Crime and Punishment*, 32, 43–4.

100 David Hannay, *Naval Courts Martial* (Cambridge: Cambridge University Press, 1913), 39.

101 Morriss, *Channel Fleet*, 222, 6/5/1797.

102 Byrn, *Crime and Punishment*, 20.

103 NLS MS 2264, f80v–81, 22/10/1807.

104 NLS MS 2340 (Admiralty Letters Addressed to Sir John Warren, 1812–1814 and delivered to Cochrane on assuming his command), ff153–154v, 4/11/1813, f160, 15/11/1813.

105 Malcolmson, *Order and Disorder*, 172–4.

106 *Spencer Papers*, II, 150, 8/6/1797; DCA Letter Book No 2, 1798–1800, f94, August 1798, f98, 11/9/1798.

107 Quoted Sugden, *Nelson: A Dream of Glory*, 735; emphasis in the original.

108 BL Add Ms 31167, f107v, 25/6/1800, *Collingwood's Correspondence*, 112, 8/4/1800.

109 NMM WYN/104, 27/4/1797.

Chapter 7

1 NLS Ms 2571, f2 6/1/1806.

2 Philip Harling, *The Waning of 'Old Corruption': The Politics of Economical Reform in Britain, 1779–1846* (Oxford: Oxford University Press, 1996), 18–21.

3 N. A. M. Rodger, 'Commissioned Officers' Careers in the Royal Navy, 1690–1815', *Journal of Maritime Research*, 3:1 (2001), 102–105. In 1814 only about half of the commissioned officers on the active list were employed; see Charles Consolvo, 'The Prospects of Promotion of British Naval Officers, 1793–1815', *MM*, 91:2 (2005), 144. The ratio was far less favourable for flag officers.

4 See Michael Lewis, *A Social History of the Navy 1793–1815*, 2nd edn (London: Chatham Publishing, 2004), 218.

5 See C. I. Hamilton, 'John Wilson Croker: Patronage and Clientage at the Admiralty, 1809–1857', *Historical Journal*, 43:1 (2000), 55.

6 BL Add Ms 58987, ff77–8, August 1811, f80, 20/10/1811.

7 Alnwick, DNM Ms G/4/89, 13/7/1809, G/4/92, 20/7/1809.

8 CRO 588/c.85, 8/8/1800.

9 R. G. Thorne, *The House of Commons, 1790–1820* (London: Secker and Warburg, 1986), I, 315.

10 Ibid., IV, 756.

11 Lewis, *Social History*, 210.

12 Alnwick, DNP, Ms 63, f177, 30/9/1806.

13 Alnwick, DNM, Ms G/4/125, 2/4/1811.

14 Thorne, *House of Commons*, II, 187–9. Markham probably helped Carter's son-in-law, Captain John Giffard, to the governorship of the Royal Naval Academy at Portsmouth in 1807.

15 *Markham's Letters*, 374, 15/8/1806.

16 Ibid., 183, 27/7/1806.

17 NA, ADM 1/179, 29/9/1794.

18 *Markham's Letters*, 363, 1/6/1803; Steele was drowned in early 1806 before his interest had advanced him in rank.

19 *Markham's Letters*, 366–7, 26/6/1803, 369, 26/8/1807.

20 NA ADM 1/585, 24/2/1815.

21 *Markham's Letters*, 374–6; *St Vincent's Letters*, II, 94–5, 26/5/1802.

22 *St Vincent's Letters*, I, 373, 2/11/1801.

23 *St Vincent's Letters*, II, 85–93.

24 Thorne, *House of Commons*, II, 199.

25 NLS MS 2265, f171, 31/5/1811.

26 Thorne, *House of Commons*, II, 598; NLS MS, 2265, f244, 14/10/1812.

27 Thorne, *House of Commons*, II, 616–17, III, 457.

28 Peter A. Ward, *British Naval Power in the East, 1794–1805* (Woodbridge: Boydell Press, 2013), 15–19, 80–1.

29 NLS MS 2571, f208v, 1/6/1807.

30 See Tony Barrow, *Collingwood's Northumbrians: Old and Valuable Officers* (Rainton Bridge: Business Education Publishers, 2010), 17–19.

31 *Collingwood's Correspondence*, 27, 14/6/1790.

32 Ibid., 179–80, 17/4/1806.

33 Ibid., 191, 12/9/1806; 238–9, 22/2/1808.

34 Ibid., 289, 13/8/1809. Crespigny's grandfather corresponded with St Vincent; see BL Add Ms 31165 f61.

35 NMM, DUC/5, 5?/3/1799.

36 George P. B. Naish, ed., *Nelson's Letters* (London: NRS, 1958), 459, 18/10/1798.

37 *St Vincent's Letters*, II, 313–14, 5/5/1804.

38 NMM DUC/25, 13/2/1802, 20/11/1802.

39 *St Vincent's Letters*, II, 351, 18/12/1803.

40 Lorna M. Campbell and Heather Noel-Smith, 'You Are a Very Naughty Admiral Indeed', *MM*, 101:2 (2015), 220.

41 *Spencer Papers*, I, 189, 28/10/1795.

42 BL Add MS 31167, f124, 10/7/1800; *St Vincent's Letters*, II, 329, 19/5/1803.

43 *St Vincent's Letters*, II, 212, [16–18]/5/1803.

44 BL Bridport Papers, Add Ms 35200, f 197, 19/8/1799.

45 *St Vincent's Letters*, II, 110, 16/11/1803.

46 Ibid., 111–12, 17/11/1803. Captain Jervis was drowned in the Channel in early 1805 so he did not long enjoy the advantages of his uncle's patronage; *Brest Blockade*, II, 168–9, 26/1/1805.

47 *St Vincent's Letters*, II, 111, 17/11/1803.

48 Ibid.

49 Ibid., 313–14, 5/5/1804; Knight, *Pursuit*, 521.

50 *St Vincent's Letters*, I, 149, 25/4/1802.

51 See C. Northcote Parkinson, *Edward Pellew, Viscount Exmouth, Admiral of the Red* (London: Methuen, 1934), 325.

52 *Markham's Letters*, 370, 23/8/1806, 374, 15/8/1806.

53 Sir John Barrow, *The Life of Richard, Earl Howe, KG, Admiral of the Fleet and General of Marines* (London: John Murray, 1838), 371.

54 *Collingwood's Correspondence*, 108, 5/12/1799.

55 Ibid., 112, 8/4/1800; *Spencer Papers*, II, 78, 16/12/1796.

56 Sugden, *Nelson: The Sword of Albion* (London: Vintage, 2014), 364–9.

57 See p. 159 below for Collingwood's misgivings; Parkinson, *Pellew*, 402, 409. A copy of Vice Admiral Sir Fleetwood Pellew's (unsuccessful) request for a court martial is in the Cochrane Papers, NLS MS 2295, f4, dated 19/4/1855.

58 *St Vincent's Letters*, II, 247–8, 29/4/1802.

59 NLS MS 2264, ff76–7, 9/8/1807, MS 2265, f104v, 26/12/1809; emphasis in the original. The elder Cochrane's comments indicate that Michael Lewis's suggestion that these cases were greeted with 'envy, not censure' requires qualification; see Lewis, *Social History*, 213.

60 Lewis, *Social History*, 205, mentioned this possibility with regard to Howe and Bridport but thought the informal nature of residual interest made it impossible to point to particular instances. For St Vincent, see Aspinall, *Correspondence of George III*, IV, #284, 260, 264.

61 Rodger, *Command*, 508.

62 NWMS DUN/19, f41, 10/11/1799.

63 See Lewis, *Social History*, 203.

64 C. I. Hamilton, *The Making of the Modern Admiralty: British Naval Policy-Making, 1805-1927* (Cambridge: Cambridge University Press, 2011), 6–14, 27–34.

65 Ibid., 8–9.

66 NMM DUC/26, 21/7/1806; the Board member in question was probably Captain Sir Harry Burrard Neale who, Duckworth complained, had written to him 'in a manner truly humiliating to the feelings of a Flag Officer', DUC/26, 20/7/1806.

67 N. A. M. Rodger, 'Patronage and Competence', *Les Marines de Guerres Européenes XVII–XVIIIe Siécles*, 243; cf 'Commissioned Officers', 101–103.

68 *Spencer Papers*, II, 73, 2/12/1796.

69 Ibid., II, 92, 22/2/1797, 95, 7/3/1797.

70 BL Add Ms 75863, f27v, 1/7/1797.

71 Mrs Henry Baring, ed., *The Diary of the Right Hon. William Windham, 1784–1810* (London: Longmans, Green, and Co, 1866), 384, 16/12/1797.

72 NWMS DUN/20, f105, 7/10/1798.

73 NWMS DUN/20, f19, 28/12/1795.

74 NWMS DUN/20, f77, 15/4/1798, f77, 15/7/1798, f 86, 3/13/1799.

75 NWMS DUN/20, f85, 30/11/199; DCA, Duncan Papers, Letter Book 2, 1798–1800, f274, 22/9/1799; DUN/20, f86, 3/12/1799.

76 *Spencer Papers*, II, 452, 12/8/1798; BL Add Ms 31167, f144v, 31/8/1800.

77 Rodger, 'Patronage and Competence', 240–1.

78 Gareth Atkins, 'Religion, Politics and Patronage in the Late Hanoverian Navy, c.1780–1820', *Historical Research*, 88 (2015), 287.

79 R. W. Chapman, ed., *Jane Austen's Letters to Her Sister Cassandra and Others*, 2nd edn (London: Oxford University Press, 1959), 40, 46, 47, 18, 24, 28/12/1798.

80 BL Add Ms 31167, f 20v, 20/2/1799; f26, 13/4/1799.

81 Ibid., f124, 10/7/1800, 17/10/1800.

82 *St Vincent's Letters*, I, 143, 9/9/1801.

83 NMM DUC/8, 7, 10, 12, 18/5/1802; 23/6/1802, 10/7/1802, 28/7/1802, 20/7/1802, 20/9/1802, 18/10/1802.

84 *St Vincent's Letters*, II, 266, 16/11/1802.

85 Ibid., 330, 29/6/1803. Sir William A'Court was a Portland Whig and owned the nomination to a seat in parliament. Lake had until recently been MP for Aylesbury and was a member of the household of the Prince of Wales.

86 Ruddock Mackay and Michael Duffy, *Hawke, Nelson and British Naval Leadership 1747–1805* (Woodbridge: Boydell Press, 2009), 190.

87 Nicolas, *Dispatches*, V: 244, 13/10/1803, 461, 19/3/1804.

88 Ibid., 364, 11/4/1804.

89 BL Add Ms 40098, f43; NMM DUC/26, 7/6/1806; 13/7/1806; emphasis in the original.

90 NMM MID/2/9, 5, 9, 12/7/1805, 30/11/1805.

91 Atkins, 'Religion, Politics and Patronage', 280–90.

92 Newnham Collingwood, *Correspondence*, I, 221–2, 8/11/1805.

93 Anne Freemantle, ed., *The Wynne Diaries 1789–1820* (London: Oxford University Press, 1952), 441, 6/4/1806.

94 NLS MS 2296, f1, 18/9/1805.

95 NLS MS 2571, ff 2, 6, 8, 6/1/1806.

96 Ibid., ff 48–50, 13/3/1806; NLS MS. 2296, f23, 4/8/1806.

97 NLS MS 2296, ff 9–11, 6/5/1806; ff18, 23, 24/6/1806, 4/8/1806.

98 Ibid., ff36–7, 1/12/1806; MS 2297, f1, 11/3/1807.

99 NLS MS 2297, f30, 8/7/1809; f34, 5/7/1809; f36–8, 3/11/1809.

100 Ibid., f38, 3/11/1809.

101 Ibid., f59, 4/3/1809, f80, 27/5/1810.

102 NMM YOR/10, ff1–2, 10/4/1811, 13/7/1811.

103 NLS MS 2345, f1, 10/3/1814, ff2–3, 25/3/1814, f5, 2/4/1814, ff6–7, 24/4/1814, f9, 16/5/1814, f14, 17/7/1814.

104 *Saumarez Papers*, 136, 28/6/1810.

105 Ibid., 139, 25/7/1810.

106 NMM WAR/82, ff3–4, 5, 11, 36–7, 52–3, 4/8/1812, 10/8/1812, 9/1/1813, 26/2/1813.

107 Ibid., f69, 31/5/1813.

108 Consolvo sees interest of all kinds as the major factor in promotions that did not follow service in battle; Consolvo, 'The Prospects', 150–1.

Chapter 8

1 *Markham's Letters*, 183, 27/7/1806.
2 Michael Lewis, *A Social History of the Navy 1793–1815*, 2nd edn (London: Chatham Publishing, 2004), 202.
3 Sir William Dillon, *A Narrative of My Professional Adventures (1790–1839)*, ed. Michael A. Lewis (London: NRS, 1953), I, 137.
4 *Collingwood's Correspondence*, 149, 155; Tony Barrow, *Collingwood's Northumbrians: Old and Valuable Officers* (Rainton Bridge: Business Education Publishers, 2010), 2.
5 'Captain G. M. Mundy, 1797–1809', *Naval Miscellany* V, 288–9.
6 *Collingwood's Correspondence*, 52–3, 9/7/1794.
7 BL Add Ms 35195, f152v, 8/7/1795.
8 Keele UL, Ms 148/6 (53/6), 4/6/1805, 16/9/1805.
9 For example, NMM YOR/3, f72, 26/2/1811 to Campbell in the Downs and f83, 20/3/1812 to Calder at Portsmouth.
10 Ibid., 94–5, 148.
11 [Sir John Orde] *Copy of a Correspondence &c* (London: R. Faulder, 1802), 54.
12 *Spencer Papers*, III, 36, 11/5/1799.
13 SRO SA/3/1/2/3, 16/4/1795.
14 *Naval Chronicle*, VI, 95.
15 Sir John Ross, *Memoirs and Correspondence of Admiral Lord de Saumarez* (London: Richard Bentley, 1838), I, 150.
16 Ibid., II, 28.
17 NMM DUC/26, 22/5/1806, 13/7/1806.
18 Alnwick DNP, Ms 63, f182, 30/9/1806.
19 ADM 1/581, f 462, 15/1/1806.
20 ADM 2/1092, f164, 14/3/1806.
21 WSRO, AM 760/1/56, 57, late February 1809, 760/1/52, 4/11/1810.
22 NA ADM 1/582, 12/1/1807.
23 ADM 1/580, 29/4/1802.
24 Cf. Ellen Gill, '"Children of the Service": Paternalism, Patronage and Friendship in the Georgian Navy', *Journal for Maritime Research*, 15:2 (2013), 149–65. Dr Gill merges these categories to cover cases of officers protecting the sons of family friends and officers promoting their own children's careers.
25 *St Vincent's Letters*, I, 345, 17/5/1801.
26 Ibid., II, 341, 10/6/1803.
27 NWMS DUN/19, f2, 7/10/1803.
28 Ibid., f76, 19/7/1803, f77, 21/8/1803, f78, 26/8/1803, f79, 13/10/1803, f81, 28/10/1803, f98, 4/7/1804.
29 *St Vincent's Letters*, II, 325, 29/11/1803.
30 BL Add Ms 31165, f31, 29/4/1806.
31 WSRO AM 760/1/40, 31/1/1810.
32 Ibid., 760/1/24, 23/6/1810.
33 *Spencer Papers*, II, 393–4, 19/4/1797.
34 NLS MS 2327, f91, 24/10/1814.
35 Ross, *Saumarez*, I, 10.
36 Edward Pelham Brenton, *Life and Correspondence of John, Earl St Vincent* (London: Henry Colburn, 1838), I, 3–4.

37 Nicolas, *Nelson's Despatches*, V, 511, 20/4/1804; emphasis in the original.

38 ADM 1/581, f 44, 4/2/1805. Commander Chamberlayne's appointment took effect on 6 February 1805.

39 Nicolas, *Nelson's Despatches*, V, 59, 17/4/180[3].

40 Hyde Parker wrote to the Board in early 1803 seeking his son's appointment into a vacancy; it was already filled but he was appointed lieutenant in the following year; NA ADM 1/580, 16/1/1803. Orde's son became a commander on 29/4/1802.

41 BL Add Ms 31165, f40, 9/6/1806.

42 *ODNB*, 45, 246.

43 NA ADM 1/582, 8/2/1808, ADM 1/583, 25/12/1812.

44 N. A. M. Rodger, 'Commissioned Officers' Careers in the Royal Navy, 1690–1815', *Journal for Maritime Research*, 3:1 (2001), 104–105.

45 The British losses are summarized in David J. Heppe, *British Warship Losses in the Age of Sail, 1650–1859* (Rotherfield: Jean Boudriot, 1994), 213. French, Dutch, Danish, Russian, Spanish, Turkish and US figures are in Clowes, *History*, IV, 552–61, V, 55–68.

46 *Collingwood's Correspondence*, 256, 261–2, 31/10/1808, 17/12/1808.

47 *St Vincent's Letters*, II, 298–9, 18/6/1803.

48 Oliver Warner, *The Life and Letters of Vice-Admiral Lord Collingwood* (London: Oxford University Press, 1968), 50–5.

49 *Collingwood's Correspondence*, 48–9, 30/6/1794.

50 John Sugden, *Nelson: A Dream of Glory* (London: Pimlico, 2012), 710–13; Roger Knight, *The Pursuit of Victory* (London: Allen Lane, 2005), 347–8.

51 SRO, Saumarez Papers, SA/3/2/1/26, 107.

52 See p. 82 above.

53 Lady Bourchier, ed., *Memoir of the Life of Admiral Sir Edward Codrington* (London: [sn], 1873), 100n1; SHC, Keats' Papers, DD/CPL/31, 19/9/1808.

54 James Ralf, *Historical Memoirs of Admiral Charles Stirling with Notes and Observations by Vice-Admiral Stirling* (London: L. Harrison, 1826), 18n, 22–3n.

55 *Spencer Papers*, II, 472, 23/9/1798.

56 DCA Letter Book 1795, 25/8/1795, 26/8/1795.

57 NWMS DUN/20, f105, 7/10/1798.

58 I am most grateful to Elsie Ritchie of Sydney, NSW, for sharing with me her research into the career of her great, great, great grandfather.

59 *St Vincent's Letters* I, 341, 18/4/1801.

60 *Markham's Letters*, 374, 15/8/1806.

61 ADM 1/581 f 580, 8/11/1806.

62 Quoted Gill, 'Children of the service', 158.

63 *Spencer Papers*, II, 193, 2/10/1797.

64 NMM RAI/7, 29/1/1799.

65 NMM DUC 25, nd February–March 1801.

66 When discussing St Vincent's support for Thomas Troubridge, Michael Lewis presents him as a determined proponent of advancement by merit (*Social History*, 43–4) with 'other considerations a bad second'. His later discussion is more equivocal, however, tending to the view that St Vincent would have adhered to this principle if it had been possible in the circumstances (220, 226–7).

67 *St Vincent's Letters*, I, 335, 1/3/1801; 379, 28/2/1801.

68 Ibid., 335–9; II, 326, 2/1/1804; 321, 30/9/1803.

69 Ibid., II, 275, 15/3/1803.

70 Ibid., I, 340, 6/4/1801.

71 Hardin Craig Jnr, 'Letters of Lord St Vincent to Thomas Grenville 1806–7', in Christopher Lloyd, ed., *Naval Miscellany* IV (London: NRS, 1952), 486, 3/12/1806.

72 Ibid., 474, 17/10/ 1806 and 477, 22/10/1806.

73 NLS MS 2296, f1, 18/9/1805, MS 2321, f12, 24/6/1805.

74 *Martin's Letters*, I, 173.

75 Ibid., I, 173; *Collingwood's Correspondence*, 236, 19/2/1808.

76 *Martin's Letters*, I, 66, 20/3/1795.

77 *Collingwood's Correspondence*, 185, 15/5/1806; Lewis, *Social History*, 224–5.

78 *Collingwood's Correspondence*, 274, 18/4/1809.

79 See p. 146 above.

80 *Saumarez Papers*, 239, 23/7/1812.

81 Quoted in Lorna M. Campbell and Heather Noel-Smith, 'You are a Very Naughty Admiral Indeed', *MM*, 101:2 (2015), 220.

82 *St Vincent's Letter*, I, 338, 28/3/1801; emphasis added.

83 Ibid., II, 266, 5/12/1802.

84 Ibid., I, 303–304, 7/5/1804; 307, 18/3/1801.

85 Craig, 'Letters of St Vincent', 482, 17/11/1806.

86 See above p. 160.

87 NMM, DUC/25, 13/2/1802.

88 *Martin's Letters*, I, 296, 16/10/1801 and see *St Vincent's Letters*, 1, 334, 26/2/1801. Cf Charles Consolvo, 'The Prospects of Promotion of British Flag Officers', *MM*, 91:2 (2005), 141–9.

Chapter 9

1 Melford Hall, Hyde Parker Papers, F75/19, 15/10/1800.

2 BL Add Ms 29914, f342, 9/1/1801.

3 NA ADM 1/580, 23/9/1802, 15/3/1803.

4 NA ADM 3/110, 5/3/1793.

5 NA ADM 1/579, 18/2/1799.

6 NA ADM 1/579, 11/11/1794: Duddington's request was granted immediately. The appeals from 1799 are in ADM 1/579, 16/1/1799, 17/2/1799, 18/2/1799, 19/2/1799 and 20/2/1799. The criteria was enunciated in an annotation to a letter from Captain Halwell, 20/2/1799; *St Vincent's Letters*, I, 342, 23/4/1801; see John Marshall, *Royal Naval Biography* (London: Longman, Rees, Orme, Brown and Green, 1823–35), II, 22, for the regulation requiring service in command of a ship-of-the-line since the Peace.

7 *Martin's Letters*, II, 164. Griffith was promoted rear admiral a year later.

8 NA ADM 1/584, 31/5/1814, 12/6/17814, 18/8/1814.

9 Ibid., 8/6/1814, 12/6/1814, 19/6/1814.

10 Ibid., 10/7/1814, 14/7/1814; emphasis in the original.

11 *Steel's List*, November 1814.

12 George P. B. Naish, ed., *Nelson's Letters to His Wife and Other Documents, 1785–1831* (London: NRS, 1958), 333–4, 15/1/1796.

13 Ibid., 337, 13/7/1796; *Spencer Papers*, II, 21, 28/3/1796; 46–7, 11/8/1796; 57, 29/9/1796.

14 BH Lans 6 (1), f63; the date of the request is not recorded but the letter is from early April and predates the promotion on twelfth of that month. For Saumarez's canvassing of St Vincent, see p. 167 below; for Waldegrave, see NMM WDG/11/1/11, 27/11/1800.

15 *Markham's Letters*, 228, 16/12/1806.

16 Lady Georgiana Chatterton, *Memorials, Personal and Historical of Admiral Gambier GCB* (London 1861), II, 71, 1/10/1807. Mulgrave told Keats of the basis of his promotion; DD/CPL 35 nd.

17 Marshall, *Royal Naval Biography*, II, 22, mentions this 'regulation' in connection with Rear Admiral John Cooke, superannuated in 1814.

18 NA ADM 1/584, 11/6/1814.

19 See p. 137 above for Stephens's interest and references to his deficiencies as a seaman and disciplinarian.

20 NMM YOR/2, # 1, 2, 25/7/1810, 30/7/1810. Barlow became a superannuated rear admiral in 1823 and in 1842 at the age of 82 he finally rejoined the active list as an admiral of the white.

21 ADM 1/583, 27/7/1811, 13/9/1811, 19/9/1811, 29/12/1811. In the event, the Board allowed Browne to retain his appointment until the project was completed.

22 This figure is an approximation (380 flag officers of whom 180 held flag appointments) derived from information in Cowles, IV and V, *ODNB* and *Naval Chronicle*, Marshall, *Royal Naval Biography, Steel's List*, 1793–1815, and the flag appointments up to 1808 which are in NA ADM 12/15. It includes very elderly officers who held flag rank in 1793 and those from the large promotion of 1814 whose opportunities were necessarily very limited. Even when allowance is made for these distorting factors, however, the indicative employment rate is still only just over 50 per cent.

23 Kevin D. McCranie, *Admiral Lord Keith and the War against Napoleon* (Gainsville: University of Florida Press, 2006), 63–4.

24 [Orde], *Copy of a Correspondence*, 89; see p. 97 above for Spencer's forceful 'conversation' with Christian.

25 Melford Hall, Hyde Parker Papers, F75/22, 29/11/1800; BL Add Ms 58987, ff39–40, 31/8/1800.

26 *Spencer Papers*, IV, 6, 17/7/1800, 18, 14/9/1800.

27 NMM WDG/4–14, August–December 1797.

28 NMM WDG 11/1/4, 26/12/1800.

29 NMM WDG/11/2/3, [19]/2/1801; WDG/11/2/5, 3/4/1801. Cf. Ellen Gill, *Naval Families, War and Duty in Britain, 1740–1820* (Woodbridge: Boydell Press, 2016), 109.

30 See Michael Duffy, '"… All Hushed Up": The Hidden Trafalgar', *MM*, 91:2 (2005), 231–2, 236.

31 BL Add Ms 29915, f262, 12/6/1808; NMM YOR/8, ff2–3, 21/10/1810, 22/10/1810.

32 NMM YOR/5, ff1–4, 19/9/1810, 7/3/1811.

33 NLS MS 2265, f201, 1/4/1812.

34 NA ADM 12/15, ff95–6.

35 NA ADM 2/1091, ff92–4, 14–23/3/1803.

36 NA ADM 1/580, 14/4/1803.

37 NA ADM 1/580, 9/3/1803, 11/3/1803.

38 NA ADM 1/580, 9/3/1803, ADM 581 f20, 8/1/1805, f176, 13/6/1805; NA ADM 1/581, ff3337, 356, 359, 378,459, 486–9, 490, 494, 497–8, 515, 521, 528, 530.

39 NA ADM 1/580, 12/6/1803; 1/582, 17/4/1808.

40 Ibid., 1/585, 23/3/1815.

41 BL Add Ms 35200, f76, 28/3/1800.

42 See pp. 79–80 above.

43 NMM WYN/103, 3/3/1806, 7/3/1806; BL Add Ms 58987, f59, 14/2/1806, f68, 2/5/1806.

44 Hardin Craig, Jnr. 'Letters of Lord St. Vincent to Thomas Grenville 1806–7', Christopher Lloyd, ed., *The Naval Miscellany Volume* IV (London: NRS, 1952), 481, 16/11/1806.

45 NMM, WYN/104, 20/6/1799, WYN/105, 20/9/1805, 28/3/1807, 10/7/1807, 29/10/1807, 2/12/1808.

46 Ibid., YOR/7, f9, 4/8/1810, f8 8/9/1809 [actually 1810], f11, 27?/10/1810, f14, 16/12/1810.

47 YOR/2, #54, 2/8/1810, #55, 15/8/1810.

48 Roger Knight, *The Pursuit of Victory* (London: Allen Lane, 2005), 268.

49 Roger Knight, *Britain against Napoleon: The Organization of Victory, 1793–1815* (London: Penguin, 2014), 110.

50 See p. 77 above.

51 NA ADM 1/583, 28/12/1812.

52 NLS Ms 2297, ff97–8, 24/4/1812.

53 NLS Ms 2265, ff165v-66, 17/3/1811.

54 NA ADM 1/584, 16/8/1814. He was also told that an active command was incompatible with the governorship of Guadeloupe.

55 NMM WYN/104, 18/3/1799.

56 Craig, 'Letters of St Vincent', 476, 21/10/1806.

57 Duke of Buckingham and Chandos, *Memoirs of the Court and Cabinets of George the Third* (London: Hurst and Blackett, 1853–5), IV, 100, 25/11/1806.

58 Aspinall, *Correspondence of George III*, V, #4111, 540, 10/3/1810; see Andrew Lambert, *The Challenge: Britain against America in the Naval War of 1812* (London: Faber and Faber, 2012), 112–13, for Melville's difficulties at the Board.

59 Aspinall, *George III*, II, #1187, 290, 7/1/1795; John Henage Jesse, *Memoirs of the Life and Reign of King George the Third*, 2nd edn, three volumes (London: Tierney, 1867), III, 208–209.

60 Castalia Countess Granville, *Lord Granville Leveson Gower* (London: John Murray, 1916), I, 69–70, 31/10/1793.

61 Michael Duffy, *Soldiers, Sugar and Seapower: The British Expeditions to the West Indies and the War against Revolutionary France* (Oxford: Clarendon Press, 1987), 106–14.

62 Tucker, *St Vincent*, I, 142–3; *Spencer Papers*, I, 54, 23/9/1795.

63 *Keith Papers*, II, 36–7, 30/3/1799.

64 *Spencer Papers*, III, 315, 20/5/1800.

65 Tucker, *St Vincent*, I, 252–3.

66 ADM 1/579, unfoliated, 11/5/1794.

67 *Spencer Papers*, II, 177.

68 *St Vincent's Letters*, I, p. 238, 20/2/1801.

69 Andrew Lambert suggests that Gambier may have undermined the Board's confidence in Cornwallis in the latter stages of his command; see 'Sir William Cornwallis, 1744–1819', Peter Le Fevre and Richard Harding, eds, *Precursors of Nelson: British Admirals of the Eighteenth Century* (London: Chatham, 2000), 373.

70 See p. 179 below.

71 Quoted McCranie, *Admiral Lord Keith*, 64.

72 *Keith Papers*, III, 13, 11/3/1803.

73 See Knight, *Britain against Napoleon*, 251ff, for a fine account of this threat and perceptions of it.

74 NMM YOR/9, #32, 7/10/1811, 10/10/1811.

75 NMM YOR/3, #5, 23/2/1812, 26/2/1812; *Martin's Letters*, II, 173, 29/2/1812.

76 Aspinall, *Correspondence of George III*, III, #2424, 24/5/1801.
77 Nicolas, *Nelson's Dispatches*, V, 57, 6/4/1803, 58–9; *St Vincent's Letters*, II, 273–4. See John Sugden, *Nelson: The Sword of Albion* (London: Vintage, 2014), 566, 587, for references to the assumption that Nelson would take the Mediterranean command.
78 Aspinall, *Correspondence of George III*, V, #3755, 150, 8/11/1808; CRO 588/041B, NMM, MKH/505, 194/1810.
79 'Cotton', *Naval Chronicle*, XXVII, 360–1.
80 There is a warm personal letter from St Vincent in the Cotton papers; CRO 588/C. 75, 17/1/1809.
81 Craig, 'Letters of St Vincent', 484, 485 and n3, 28/11/1806, 30/11/1806.
82 Buckingham and Chandos, *Memoirs*, IV, 100, 25/11/1806, 102, 5/12/1806.
83 CRO 588/c.99, 3/4/1811.
84 NMM DUC/25, 14/12/1801.
85 NMM DUC/25, 26/1/1805, 27/1/1805, 6/2/1805.
86 Chatterton, *Memorials of Gambier*, II, 71–2, 1/10/1807.
87 NMM DUC/28, 7/9/107, 12/9/1807, 14/9/1807; DUC/15, 19/7/1809.
88 NMM YOR/4 #8, 9, 2/4/1811, 5/4/1811, 7/4/1811, 15/4/1811.
89 See Gareth Atkins, 'Christian Heroes, Providence, and Patriotism in Wartime Britain, 1793-1815', *Historical Journal* 58 (2015), 393–414; Chatterton, *Memorials of Gambier*, I, 248–9.
90 Chatterton, *Memorials of Gambier*, II, 88, 14/11/1807.
91 SRO SA/3/1/2/1, 1/4/1801.
92 Sugden, *Nelson: The Sword of Albion*, 109–10; Sir John Ross, *Memoirs and Correspondence of Admiral Lord de Saumarez*, II, 409–10; Naish ed, *Nelson's Letters to His Wife*, 406–407, 21/5/1798.
93 SRO SA/3/1/2/1, 26/4/1801.
94 BL Add Ms 37608, 24/10/1800, f10–10v; BL Add Ms 31167, f166v, 2/12/1800.
95 SRO SA 3/1/2, 11/9/1801.
96 *St Vincent's Letters*, I, 209, 13/8/1801.
97 Nepean's letter of 14 August 1801 is printed in Ross, *Saumarez*, II, 28.
98 NA ADM 1/405 # 254, 31/8/1801.
99 *St Vincent's Letters*, I, 211, 2/11/1801.
100 Ross, *Saumarez*, II, 34, 7/10/1801 and see p. 151 above.
101 SRO SA 3/2/5, 4/4/1804, 1/6/1804. Saumarez's agent was very sanguine and relished the contest but his principal did not.
102 SRO SA 3/1/2/1, 26/4/1801.
103 *St Vincent's Letters*, I, 213, 30/4/1802.
104 Tim Voeckler, *Admiral Saumarez versus Napoleon: The Baltic, 1805–12* (Woodbridge: Boydell Press, 2005), 21–4, evaluated the options and judged that Saumarez was the best qualified candidate.
105 G. Cornwallis-West, *The Life and Letters of Admiral Cornwallis* (London: Robert Holden, 1927), 162.

Chapter 10

1 Alnwick, DNP Ms 63, ff75–6.
2 See Richard Hill, *The Prizes of War: The Naval Prize System in the Napoleonic Wars, 1793-1815* (Stroud: Sutton, 1998), 202–04.

3	Graeme Aldous QC, 'Lord Nelson and St Vincent: Prize Fighters', *MM*, 101:2 (2015), 135–55.

4	NMM YOR/7, f19, 1/7/1812.

5	NMM WAR/35, f92, 1802 nd.

6	John Sugden, *Nelson: The Sword of Albion* (London: Vintage, 2014), 112–13.

7	NWMS DUN/17, M.1995.2.114, f37, 23/3/1798, ff56–8, 30/9/1797; f18, 1/1/1798.

8	DRO D3311/1/1; Denis Orde, *Nelson's Mediterranean Command* [1997] (Barnsley: Pen & Sword, 2014), 154.

9	Orde, *Nelson's Mediterranean Command*, 159–60; and Roger Knight, *The Pursuit of Victory* (London: Allen Lane, 2005), 477–8.

10	NLS MS 2265, f104v, 26/12/1809.

11	Peter A. Ward, *British Naval Power in the East 1794–1805* (Woodbridge: Boydell Press, 2013); 231 Nichols, *Nelson's Despatches*, V, 250, 22/10/1804.

12	See p. 179 above.

13	Tracy, *Naval Chronicle*, 1V, 145.

14	See Hill, *Prizes of War*, 223; Ward, *British Naval Power*, 231; Alnwick, DNP Ms 64, ff19–20, 1/2/1807.

15	Hill, *Prizes of War*, 224–5, for Duckworth's prize money.

16	See pp. 251–2 below.

17	SRO SA 3/2/5; Tim Voelcker, *Admiral Saumarez versus Napoleon* (Woodbridge: Boydell Press, 2008), 211.

18	NMM WAR/35, ff191–200, 1/1/1813–10/1/1814.

19	NWMS DUN/17, M. 1995.2.114, f77, 12/6/1800.

20	Hill, *Prizes of War*, 80–2; Aldous, 'Prize Fighters', 149; Sugden, *Nelson: The Sword of Albion*, 356.

21	NWMS Duncan Papers DUN/23, M1995.2.116, f22, 1/1/1801, f28, 30/11/1801, f29, 24/2/1802, f33, 1/6/1803.

22	See Hill, *Prizes of War*, 222–34, for an informative discussion of declared attitudes towards prize money.

23	On Nelson, see Adam Nicholson, *Men of Honour: Trafalgar and the Making of the English Hero* (London: Harper Perennial, 2006), 124–6.

24	BL Add Ms 31167, f100, 19/6/1800; *Keith Papers*, II, 395–6; NWMS Dun/23, M1995.2.116, f32, 24.5.1803.

25	Accusations were made against Keith in 1801 (see p. 83 above) and twelve years later he was still having to defend himself to the second Lord Melville against charges going back to the mid-1790s in the East Indies, protesting his wealth from prize money 'is very different to what is imagined', NLS MS 3420, f44–46, 8, 16/5/1813. For Jervis's West Indian scrape, see Michael Duffy, *Soldiers, Sugar and Seapower: The British Expeditions to the West Indies and the War against Revolutionary France* (Oxford: Clarendon Press, 1987), 106–14.

26	NLS Ms 2297, ff93–4, 15/4/1812, f97, 21/4/1812.

27	Ibid., f103–104, 8/8/1812.

28	Quoted in Eliza Pakenham, *Tom, Ned and Kitty. An Intimate Portrait of an Irish Family* (London: Phoenix, 2008), 134.

29	See pp. 65–8 above.

30	See Rodger, *Command*, 513, for the currency of the practice.

31	*Barham Papers*, III, 333–4, 9/11/1805.

32	Hyde Parker Papers, F75/3, 15/3/1800, F75/27, 22/5/1801. When Parker responded negatively to Lord Spencer's query whether a baronetcy would be an 'object', he assumed this meant that Spencer was promising him a 'red ribbon' and was offended when his claims were overlooked.

33 Aspinall, *Correspondence of George III*, I, #1095, 15/7/1794, 224n2, #1479, 8/12/ 1796, 523.

34 *Spencer Papers*, III: 327, 16/4/1800; BL Add Ms 35201, f95, 25/4/1800, f103, 9/6/1800.

35 Aspinall, *Correspondence of George III*, #1499, 3/2/1797, 539, #1500, 15/2/1797, 540; James Greig, ed., *The Farington Diary by John Farington, R.A.* 5 vols (London: Hutchinson, 1922), I, 198.

36 Aspinall, *Correspondence of George III*, II, #1500, 540, 15/2/1797.

37 Ibid., #1515, 551, 7/3/1797.

38 BM Add Ms 36708.

39 Ibid., 36708, 22/3/1797.

40 T. Sturges Jackson, ed., 'From the Letterbooks of Sir Charles Thompson, Bart, Vice-Admiral', in J. N. Laughton, ed., *Naval Miscellany II* (London: NRS, 1911), 310, 29/3/ 1977, 4/5/1797.

41 NMM WDG/3/6/2, 28/3/1797, WDG/3/7, 29/3/1797.

42 Ibid., WDG/3/9, 17/5/1797.

43 There are references to numerous and prolonged visits in the summer of 1801 in Waldegrave's papers in the NMM (WDG/11/2/15, 9/7/1801, 27/7/1801, 30/7/1801).

44 Ibid., WDG/11/1/13, 26/12/1800; emphasis in the original.

45 NWMS DUN/19, f37, 2/8/1797.

46 NWMS DUN/20, f70, 27/7/1797.

47 *Spencer Papers*, II, 201n1.

48 NWMS DUN/20, f37, 2/8/1797.

49 *Spencer Papers*, II, 195, 12/10/1797.

50 NWMS DUN/19, f38, 16/10/1797.

51 *Spencer Papers*, II, 196–7, 13/10/1797.

52 George W. T. Omond, *The Arniston Memoirs: Three Centuries of a Scottish House, 1571–1838* (Edinburgh: David Douglas, 1887), 251, 18/10/1797.

53 Roger Morriss, *The Channel Fleet and the Blockade of Brest 1793–1801* (London: NRS), 256–7, 20/7/1797.

54 Ibid., 260, 30/7/1797.

55 BH Lans 6 (1), f145, 2/9/1797.

56 A. Aspinall, ed., *The Letters of George IV, 1812–1830*, 3 vols (Cambridge: Cambridge University Press, 1938), I, #339, 387, 395, 396, 418, 434, 435, II, #547A.

57 Aspinall, *Correspondence of George III*, III, 134–5, 3/10/1798.

58 Ibid., 135, 4/10/1798; Knight, *The Pursuit*, 347.

59 Nicolas, *Nelson's Dispatches*, III, 75; George P. B. Naish, *Nelson's Letters to His Wife* (London: NRS, 1958), 458, 18/10/1798; Dorothy Hood, *The Admirals Hood* (London: Hutchinson, 1942), 197.

60 Sir John Ross, *Memoirs and Correspondence of Admiral Lord de Saumarez* (London: Richard Bentley, 1838), I, 222–3.

61 SRO SA3/2/1/25.

62 SRO SA/3/2/1/25, 19/2/1801. Spencer referred to Saumarez's numerous applications and asked particularly that this matter be settled before he left the Admiralty; see Aspinall, *Correspondence of George III*, IV, #2366, 505–506, 19/2/1801.

63 SRO SA/3/2/1/25, 21/2/1801; the warrant is dated 25/6/1801.

64 Detailed in SRO SA/3/2/1/25.

65 SRO SA/3/1/2/1, 2/9/1801.

66 SRO SA/3/1/2/1, 7/9/1801.

67 SRO SA/3/1/2/1, 23/9/1801. The son, James, became a clergyman.

68 Aspinall, *Correspondence of George III*, V, #4142, 576–8, 1/6/1810.

69 Lady Saumarez's 'Retrospects', refers to 'flattering distinctions' her husband received; SA/3/2/7/2.

70 SRO SA/3/2/1/25, 15/6/1814; a draft but indicative of Saumarez's concerns.

71 SRO SA3/2/1/23, 11/9/1831; Admiral Sir Thomas Byam Martin, a political opponent of Graham, claimed Grey was a lukewarm supporter of Saumarez but also wrote that the peerage was awarded over the initial objections of the King; *Martin's Letters*, I, 30–1.

72 See Roger Morriss, *Cockburn and the British Navy in Transition: Admiral Sir George Cockburn, 1772–1853* (Columbia: University of South Carolina Press, 1997), 143ff and 193–8, for an account of the Plymouth election.

73 SRO SA/3/2/22, 15/9/1831.

74 C. Northcote Parkinson, *Edward Pellew, Viscount Exmouth, Admiral of the Red* (London: Methuen, 1934), 397–8.

75 Ibid., 410–11.

76 BL Add MS 31167, f 21v–22v, 7/3/1799.

77 BL Add Ms 31167, f5v, 20/12/1798.

78 *St Vincent's Letters*, I, 272, 273, 20/6/1801, 21/8/1801.

79 NMM DUC/25, 13/7/1801.

80 NMM MID/1/51, 13/5/1805.

81 NLS Ms 2571, f55, 27/3/1806.

82 BL Add Ms 31167, f 213, 19/5/1806.

83 Alnwick, Syon Miscellanea, G/5/1, 19/9/1807; James Ralfe, *The Naval Biography of Great Britain* (London: Whitmore and Fenn, 1828), II, 293.

84 NMM DUC/26, 30/4/1806.

85 Ibid., 22/5/106.

86 NMM DUC/27, 11/11/1806, 17/11/1806, 12/12/1806, 29/12/1806; DUC/28, 4/12/1807, 13/12/1807; DUC/15, 15/12/1809; DUC/27, 21/12/1806.

87 NMM DUC/19, 10/6/1814.

88 *London Gazette*, Supplement, #16972, 4/1/1815.

89 Tucker, *St Vincent*, II, 382; NMM DUC/19, 10/1/1815.

90 G. Cornwallis-West, *The Life and Letters of Admiral Cornwallis* (London: Robert Holden, 1927), 277–9.

91 Ibid., 514.

92 NA ADM 1/585, 5/1/1815; emphasis in the original.

93 Ibid., 6/1/1815, 11/1/1815, 13/1/1815.

94 Ibid., 7/1/1815, 24/1/1815.

95 *Collingwood's Correspondence*, 19, 1/1/18068; Newnham Collingwood, *Correspondence*, I, 227.

96 Richard Blake, *Evangelicals in the Royal Navy, 1775–1815* (Woodbridge: Boydell Press, 2008), 201–202. It is unclear why Gambier accepted a peerage under these circumstances, unless as a reward for past services.

97 See Lady Georgiana Chatterton, *Memorials of Lord Gambier* (London: Hurst and Blackett, 1861), II, 331.

98 NA ADM 1/579, 21/2/1795.

99 Michael Lewis, ed., *A Narrative of My Professional Adventure (1790–1839) by Sir William Dillon* (London: NRS, 1953), I, 160.

100 NMM Ms MKH/506, 15/8/1799; BL Add Ms 35201, f115, 27/7/1800.

101 NA PRO 30/8/146, ff20–1, 12/11/1798.

102 NMM Ms 52/060, 22/3/1806; *House of Commons Papers*, 1809, #281, 55–9.

103 NMM Ms 52/060, 12/9/1807, 19/9/1807; Dorothy Hood, *The Brothers Hood*, 159–60.

104 Aspinall, *Correspondence of George III*, III, #1685, 12/2/1798.

105 NWMS DUN/17, f49, 12/7/1803.

106 Naish, *Nelson's Letters*, 458, 18/10/1798.

107 Nicolas, *Nelson's Dispatches*, V, 47–9, 8/3/1803.

108 Ibid., 49.

109 Ibid., 48n6.

110 *St Vincent's Letters*, I, 229, 7/12/1801. This pension was never listed in *Steel's* but unlike Hood's does not appear in the parliamentary records either; it seems likely that Keith would have complained if it was not awarded and there is no record of that.

111 SRO SA/3/1/2/1, 23/9/1801.

112 *St Vincent's Letters*, I, 214, 6/8/1802.

113 See Tim Voeckler, *Admiral Saumarez versus Napoleon: The Baltic, 1805–12* (Woodbridge: Boydell Press, 2005), 30–1.

114 Devon Heritage Centre, Exeter, Hood Letters, 152M/c1795/ON3, 8/5/1795.

115 Morriss, *The Channel Fleet*, 148, 20/3/1796.

116 NMM WYN/104, 29/8/1799.

117 *Collingwood's Correspondence*, 269, 21/3/1809.

118 Ibid., 326, 17/7/1808, 9/1/1809.

119 BL Add Ms 31164, f104, 21/7/1807.

120 NMM MSS/94/034 f93, 12/12/1789.

121 *Spencer Papers*, II, 402, 12/5/1797.

122 A. D. Webster, *Greenwich Park: Its History and Associations* (Greenwich: Henry Richardson, 1902), 8–10.

123 BL Add Ms 75863, f27v, 1/7/1798.

124 Aspinall, *Correspondence of George III*, III, #1785, 94, 17/7/1798.

125 Parkinson, *Pellew*, 388.

126 Ibid., 402, 10/10/1812.

127 R. G. Thorne, *The House of Commons, 1790–1820* (London: Secker and Warburg, 1986), I, 47, II, 74.

128 See Parkinson, *Pellew*, 388.

129 Brian Lavery, *Nelson's Navy: The Ships, Men and Organisation 1793–1815*, revised edn (London: Conway, 2012) 96, 98, 322; Robert B. Burhan and Ron M. McGuigan, *The British Army against Napoleon: Facts, List and Trivia, 1805–1815* (Barnsley: Frontline Books, 2010), 16–17, 212.

130 *Naval Chronicle*, V, 226.

131 Aspinall, *Correspondence of George III*, IV, 440 and note 2.

Chapter 11

1 SRO SA 3/2/7/1/5, 3/4/1802; emphasis in the original.

2 NMM YOR/5, #12, 26/5/1806; Tracy, *Naval Chronicle*, I, 162–3.

3 BL Add Ms 58987, f70, 5/5/1806.

4 BL Add Ms 35196, f52, 13/7/1795, f99, 26/7/1795, f180, 24/8/1795.

5 Janet Macdonald, *Feeding Nelson's Navy* (London: Chatham, 2004), 129.

6 NA ADM 2/1090, f106, 17/9/1796; NMM, DUC/8, 11/12/1802.

7 NWMS DUN/19 f21, 15/1/1794.

8 NMM DUC/15, 11/8/1801, DUC/7/ Ms 83/089, 10/8/1801.

9 WSRO AM 760/1/115, 2/7/1811; emphasis in the original.

10 NMM MID/1/51, 13/5/1805.

11 Lady Bourchier, ed., *Memoir of … Admiral Sir Edward Codrington* (London: [sn], 1873), 125, 24/10/1806, 51, 30/9/1805.

12 Roger Knight, *The Pursuit of Victory* (London: Allen Lane 2005), 216–17, 470n.

13 Bourchier, *Memoir*, 49, 20/9/1805; Anne Parry, ed., *The Admirals Freemantle* (London: Chatto & Windus, 1971), 70, 12/9/1805.

14 Bourchier, *Memoir*, 49, 20/9/1805.

15 See Anne Petrides and Jonathan Downs, Jonathan, eds, *Sea Soldier: An Officer of Marines with Duncan, Nelson, Collingwood and Cockburn* (Tunbridge Wells: Parapress, 2000), 127, 13/1/1898, 114, 28/10/1807; emphases in the original.

16 C. H. H. Owen, ed., 'Letters from Collingwood', in Michael Duffy, ed., *Naval Miscellany*, VI (Aldershot: Ashgate/NRS, 2003), 167, 14/12/1798.

17 Matthew Sheldon, 'How to Re-fit an Old Admiral for Sea', *MM*, 87:4 (2001), 479.

18 Brian Lavery, ed., *Shipboard Life and Organisation, 1731–1815* (London: NRS, 1998), 631.

19 Edward Pelham Brenton, *Life of St Vincent* (London: Henry Colburn, 1838), I, 349.

20 Sheldon, 'How to Re-fit an Old Admiral', 479–81.

21 Macdonald, *Feeding Nelson's Navy*, 133.

22 Lavery, *Shipboard Life*, 616–21.

23 Ibid., 611, 616–21.

24 BL Add Ms 31167, f130, 22/7/1800, f143v, 28/7/1800.

25 See p. 98 above.

26 [Sir John Orde] *Copy of a Correspondence, &c* (London: R. Faulder, 1802), 109.

27 Bourchier, *Memoir*, I, 56, 16/10/1805.

28 *Spencer Papers*, II, 182–3, 184, 188, 27/7/1797, 7/8/1797, 11/8/1797.

29 NMM DUC/26, 24/7/1806, 31/7/1806.

30 BL Add Ms 58987, f68, 5/5/1806, f70, 6/5/1806.

31 See *Markham Letters*, 84–5, 88, for a reference to Duckworth's sale of furniture when he left Jamaica.

32 BL Add Ms 31164, f23v, 2/4/1806.

33 James Davey, *In Nelson's Wake* (London: Yale University Press, 2016), 117.

34 NA ADM 1/582, 7/4/1807, 1/584, 23/7/1814.

35 See Brenton, *Life of St Vincent*, I, 435.

36 SRO Saumarez Papers, SA/3/21, 12/8/1795, 8/9/1795.

37 Knight, *The Pursuit*, 330.

38 Colin White, *Nelson: New Letters* (Woodbridge: Boydell Press, 2005), 27, 2/12/1801; George P. B. Naish, ed., *Nelson's Letters to His Wife* (London: NRS, 1958), 608.

39 SRO SA/3/1/2/1, 5/3/1801, 18/3/1801; 31/1/1807.

40 NMM YOR/5, #13, 1807.

41 NMM YOR/3 #19, 31, 18/6/1810, 6/10/1810.

42 CRO 588/c.95, 27/8/1808.

43 Tracy, *Naval Chronicle*, II, 302.

44 NMM Duckworth Papers, DUC/25, 22/9/1800, 29/9/1800.

45 Keele UL, M 148/6 (53/6), October 1803. On the Whitbys and Cornwallis, see Barry Jolly, *Mrs. Whitby's Locket* (Milton-on-Sea, Milton-on-Sea Historical Record Society, 2011).

46 Keele UL M 148/6 (53/6), 4/6/1805; 16/9/1805.

47 Jolly, *Mrs. Whitby's Locket*, 42–6.

48 See p. 46 above.

49 Quoted Oliver Warner, *The Life and Letters of Vice-Admiral Lord Collingwood* (London: Oxford University Press, 1968), 180.

50 Ibid.

51 *Collingwood's Correspondence*, 291, 13/8/1809.

52 NWMS, DUN/17 M.1995.2.114, ff39, 15/5/1798, 11/9/1798, f45 16/7/1799, f49, 28/9/1799.

53 See Martyn Downer, *Nelson's Purse* (London: Bantam Press, 2004).

54 Nicolson, *Nelson's Dispatches*, VII, cxlix–cl, 5/4/1798.

55 Lans 6 (1)f259, 28/2/1800.

56 See Ellen Gill, *Naval Families, War and Duty in Britain, 1740–1820* (Woodbridge: Boydell Press, 2016), 47–67, for a recent treatment of this topic that focuses on two post captains.

57 See Margarette Lincoln, *Naval Wives & Mistresses* (Stroud: The History Press, 2007), 29–31, for an account of the postal services available to naval personnel.

58 WSRO AM 760/1/135, 27/2/1806.

59 *Collingwood's Correspondence*, 84, 3/6/1797, 87, 16/12/1797.

60 Ibid., 97, 4/5/1799.

61 Ibid., 129, 24/8/1801, 121–2, 4/1/1801.

62 WSRO AM 760/1/135, 27/2/1806.

63 *Collingwood's Correspondence*, 108, 5/12/1799.

64 Ibid., 213, 1/7/1807. See Warner, *Admiral Lord Collingwood*, 239–45, on Collingwood's attention to his daughters' education.

65 Ibid., 298, 298–300, 9/10/1809, 19/10/1809.

66 J. D. Hilton, 'An Admiral and His Money: Vice-Admiral Cuthbert Collingwood', *MM*, 95:3 (2009), 299.

67 Ibid., 306n1.

68 CRO 588./c.74, 22/7/1808, 30/6/1808.

69 Ibid., 588/c.68, 23–24/8/1799, 588/C69B, 12/5/1898.

70 *Morning Post*, 12/5/1810.

71 CRO 588/c.95, 27/8/1810.

72 SRO SA/3/1/2/1, 25/10/1799.

73 SRO SA/3/1/2/1, 6/3/1800; emphasis in the original.

74 SRO SA/3/1/2/1.

75 SRO SA/3/1/2/1, 22/3/1801; emphasis in the original.

76 Ibid., 20/4/1801.

77 SRO, SA 3/2/1/24, 3/4/1802, 27/4/1802; emphasis in the original.

78 Ibid., SA/3/1/2/1 22/2/1802, 26/4/1801.

79 Ibid., SA 3/1/2/1, 16/4/1801, 6/5/1801, 2/1/1802.

80 Ibid., 2/1/1802.

81 Ibid., SA 3/1/2/1, 16/4/1801.

82 Ibid., 5/3/1801; emphases in the original.

83 Ibid., 22/3/1801.

84 Naish, *Nelson's Letters*, 429, 15/5/1798; the case was reported in the *Times*. Lincoln (*Naval Wives*, 48) refers to it without mentioning the damages sought, or commenting

on the significance of the limited damages awarded. Dr Lincoln reports a later case in which damages of £10,000 were awarded for adultery against Collingwood's critic Captain Edward Codrington.

85   Naish, *Nelson's Letters*, 346, 15/2/1797, 358, 3/4/1797, 361, 10/4/1797, 428, 23/4/1797; 346, 8/2/1797, 15/2/1797.

86   Ibid., 252, 11/3/1797; emphases in the original.

87   Ibid., 357, 3/4/1797.

88   See p. 196 above.

89   Naish, *Nelson's Letters*, 421, 30/3//1798, 428, 6/5/1798, 439–40, 16/7/1798, 445–6, 26/8/1798.

90   Ibid., 447–8, 11/9/1798.

91   Ibid., 538, 13/11/1799.

92   Downer, *Nelson's Purse*, 268–70.

93   Keele UL, M148/6 (53/6).

Chapter 12

1   BL Add Ms 35195, f2, 1/7/1795; emphasis in the original.

2   The Society's website lists past members; for D'Auvergne's scientific interests, see Henry Kirke, *From the Gun Room to the Throne* (London: Swan Sonnenschein & Co, 1904), 31–4, and for Bentink's, see Castalia Countess Granville, *Lord Leveson Gower* (London: John Murray, 1916), I, 69.

3   R. G. Thorne, *House of Commons* (London: Secker and Warburg, 1986), I, 315–17, IV, 546–7, 695–6, 841–4.

4   CRO 588/F61 Income tax return, 5 November 1804; 588/A11, Accounts of Rents 1797–1811.

5   W. S. Lewis, ed., *The Yale Edition of Horace Walpole's Correspondence*, 48 vols (London: Oxford University Press, 1971), 25: 12 and n19.

6   Eliza Pakenham, *Tom, Ned and Kitty* (London: Phoenix, 2008), 16–17, 49.

7   *Journal of the House of Commons*, vol. 79, 1804, Appendix 60, 774. Eliza Pakenham's family history records his career in the Ordnance as having stalled at the surveyor generalship (which was resigned in 1797) and does not mention the compensation payments made to Sir Thomas and two of his sons who had clerkships in the office; see *Tom, Ned and Kitty*, xii.

8   Maria Edgeworth, who knew the family well, drew upon Pakenham's life ashore in depicting the 'witty profligate' Sir Ulick O'Shane in *Ormond*; see *Ormond*, ed. Claire Connolly (London: Pickering and Chatto, 1999), xiii.

9   *ODNB*, 28, 482.

10   Marcus Binney, *Sir Robert Taylor: From Rococo to Neo-Classicism* (London: George Allen & Unwin, 1984), 37–60.

11   BL Add Ms 29914, 4/10/1800.

12   HRO 19M61/4217, 4216, 2165.

13   NWMS DUN/17, f84, 13/10/1802.

14   Kevin D. McCranie, *Admiral Lord Keith and the War against Napoleon* (Gainsville: University of Florida Press, 2006), 183.

15   NMM MKH/502, 19/9/1807.

16   NMM MKH/502, Ms 52/060, 16/2/1802?

17   NMM DUC/22, 16/10/1805.

18 NLS MS 2571 f71, 6/5/1806.

19 James Greig, ed., *The Farington Diary by John Farington, R.A.* 5 vols (London: Hutchinson, 1925), V, 191, 19/6/1809.

20 NMM WDG/11/1/15, 29/12/1800; Alnwick, DNP, 64, f4, 31/1/1808; Getty Provenance Index Database: Phillips's auction on 19/4/1823 and Christie's sale of 12–13/5/1826. I am grateful to Dr Erin Griffey of the University of Auckland for directing me to this source.

21 See Philip MacDougal, *London and the Georgian Navy* (Stroud: History Press, 2013), 25–6.

22 *Bath Chronicle*, 12/11/1807, 30/11/1814.

23 Ibid., 11/3/102, 17/3/1802, 10/3/1803, 30/8/1804, 19/6/1806, 16/4/1807, 14/4/1808, 15/9/1808, 8/12/1808.

24 Ibid., 7/7/1808.

25 Ibid., 8/9/1808; see Michael Pembroke, *Arthur Phillip: Sailor, Mercenary, Governor, Spy* (Richmond, Victoria: Hardie Grant Books, 2014), 258.

26 SHC DD/CPL 43, 19/11/1809.

27 Richard Harding, 'Sir Charles Henry Knowles, 1754–1831', in Peter Le Fevre and Richard Harding, eds, *British Admirals of the Napoleonic Wars* (London: Chatham, 2005), 135–6.

28 Elsie Ritchie, 'The Moriartys of Ballineanig', 71–3, unpublished draft.

29 NA ADM 1/582, 17/4/1808.

30 WSRO AM 760/3/20,21. The probate documents are in two parts which seems to have misled Murray's biographer and the author of the *ODNB* entry. There is no evidence in his papers to support Aldridge's suggestion that Murray traded in wine, and that would seem a very unusual and degrading occupation for a half pay admiral; see Barry Aldridge, *My Dear Murray. A Friend of Nelson: The Life of Admiral Sir George Murray, KCB* (Chichester: Published by the author, 2014), 79–80.

31 Aldridge, *My Dear Murray*, 81.

32 Ibid., 85.

33 Ibid., 81, 83.

34 WSRO AM 760/1/134, 10/11/1802. See Roger Knight, *The Pursuit of Victory* (London: Allen Lane, 2005), 421–7, and John Sudgen, *Nelson: The Sword of Albion* (London: Vintage, 2014), 537–51, for the purchase of Merton Place and Nelson's life there between October 1801 and May 1803. A detailed account of the property, complete with floor plans, is provided in Peter Hopkins, *A History of Lord Nelson's Merton Place* (Merton: Merton Historical Society, 1998).

35 Quoted, Knight, *The Pursuit*, 421.

36 Quoted Hopkins, *Merton Place*, 7.

37 *Barham Papers*, III, 381, 4/4/1806.

38 Ibid., xxxvii, 25/7/1810.

39 Barry Jolly, *Mrs. Whitby's Locket* (Milford-on-Sea: Milford-on-Sea Historical Record Society, 2011), 58–59, 62 note. Cornwallis's estate in 'cash and stock' is reported as £50,000 exclusive of land and the house.

40 Keele UL M148/6 (53/6), late summer? 1807, 6/7/1809, nd Aug 1813, 2/6/1814, nd Oct 1817.

41 ADM 1/582, 20/9/1810.

42 ADM 1/583, 27/2/1813, 28/2/1813.

43 See Roger Knight, 'Politics and Trust in Victualling the Navy, 1793–1815', *MM*, 94:2 (2008), 139–40.

44 NA ADM/2/1090, f99, 18/8/1796.

45 NA ADM 1/582, 18/7/1897, 21/7/1807.

46 *Barham Papers*, III, 381, 4/4/1806.

47 NA ADM 1/580, 22/12/1802, 1/583, 19/4/1811, 9/8/1812, 1/1/1813, ADM 1/584, 27/8/1814.

48 NA ADM 1/579, 14/5/1798, 31/4/1798, 5/7/1798.

49 ADM 1/582, 8/6/1808, 7/10/1809, 18/4/1810, 31/5/1810, ADM 1/584, 10/4/1814.

50 NA ADM 1/584, 16/10/1814, 12/12/1814.

51 NA ADM 1/581, f566, 8/7/1806.

52 NA ADM 1/582, 7/4/1809.

53 Ibid., 2/4/1808, 23/4/1808, 4/5/1808, 6/5/1808, 17/10/1808; ADM 1/583, 26/4/1809, 11/6/1810, 3/3/1812,8/6/1812; ADM 1/584, 1/3/1814; ADM 1/585, 22/5/1815.

54 See Nicholas Rogers, 'The Sea Fencibles, Loyalism and the Reach of the State', in Mark Philp, ed., *Resisting Napoleon: The British Response to the Threat of Invasion, 1797–1815* (Aldershot: Ashgate, 2006), 45–8.

55 NA ADM 1/582, 5/4/1809; 1/583, 7/3/1811.

56 NA ADM 1/583, 4/5/1812, 5/5/1812.

57 NA ADM 1/583, 7/12/1812, 8/12/1812, 8/12/1812.

58 *Collingwood's Correspondence*, 132, 8/11/1801; ADM 1/582, 16/7/1809.

59 NA ADM 1/582, 23/7/1810.

60 See p. 195 above.

61 See Lynda Pratt, 'Naval Contemplation', *Journal for Maritime Research*, 2:1 (2000), 84–5.

62 NA ADM 1/579, 15/12/1797.

63 *The Times*, 2–3, 20/12/1797.

64 See p. 75 above.

65 NA ADM 1/581, f434, 5/1/1806.

66 Knight, *The Pursuit*, 534.

67 BL Add Ms 29915, f67, 22/12/1805. In his reference to this alleged controversy, Martyn Downer assumes mistakenly that St Vincent was still first lord; see 'Nelson and His "Band of Brothers": Friendship, Freemasonry, Fraternity', in David Cannadine, ed., *Admiral Lord Nelson: Context and Legacy* (Houndmills: Palgrave Macmillan, 2005), 38.

68 NMM MID/1/135, 24–30/12/1805.

69 NMM MID/1/135, 5,6/1/1806.

70 NMM MID/1/135, 8/1/1806, 16/1/1806. These telling details are not recorded in Kathrin Orth's biographical essay on Orde; 'Sir John Orde, 1751–1824', in Le Fevre and Harding, *British Admirals*, 88; or in Denis Orde's *Nelson's Mediterranean Command* [1997] (Barnsley: Pen & Sword, 2014), 196. The *London Gazette*, 18/1/1806, perpetuated the polite fiction that Orde was always seen as a late substitute, but Sir John's complaint to Barham makes it clear that the received account is inaccurate.

71 Knight, *The Pursuit*, 532–3; Castalia Countess Granville, *Lord Granville Levinson-Gower* (London: John Murray, 1916), II, 155, 9/1/1806.

72 Tracy, *Naval Chronicle*, IV, 330.

73 *Times*, 12/5/1810, 4.

74 *Morning Post*, 12/5/1810; Horace Twiss, *The Public and Private Life of Lord Chancellor Eldon, with Selections from His Correspondence*, 3rd edn, 2 vols (London: John Murray, 1846), I, 431.

75 NMM MKH/505, nd 1808.

76 BL Add Ms 35199, ff191–2, 195–6, 213, 28/9/1798, 1/10/1798, 12/10/1798, NMM MKH/505, nd 1808, 4/4/1808, 19/4/1810.

77 Dorothy Hood, *The Admirals Hood* (London: Hutchinson & Co, 1934), 222.

78 BL Add Ms 31167, f29v, 24/4/1806, f98, 15/12/1806, f101, 1/1/1807, f100v, 23/12/ 1806, f104, 21/1/1807.

79 BL Add Ms 29915, f133v, 14/5/1807.

80 BL Add Ms 31165, f31, 29/4/1806.

81 Keele UL M148/6 (s 3/6) nd? August 1807, July/August 1814.

82 Ibid., M 148/6 (53/6), 14/7/1808.

83 WSRO AM 760/1/38 nd 1809; emphasis in the original.

84 Ibid., 760/1/39, 31/3/1810, 31/1/1810.

85 Ibid., 760/1/39, 40, 31/1/1810, 31/3/1810, AM 760/1/14, 10/11/1810, AM 760/1/46, 16/7/1811; emphasis in the original.

86 Anne Salmond, *Bligh. William Bligh in the South Seas* (Auckland: Penguin, 2011), 397–406, 414–17.

87 WSRO AM 760/1/59, May 1810.

88 Ibid., 760/1/44, 30/4/1811, 760/1/46, 16/7/1811; emphasis in the original.

89 Ibid., 760/1/64, 28/10/1810, 760/1/117, 24/5/1811.

90 BL Add Ms 29915, f140, 8/6/1807, f195, 25/121805, f201, 20/1/1808; James Ralfe, *The Naval Biography of Britain* (London: Whitmore and Fenn, 1828), II, 403.

91 Alnwick, DNP 64, ff19–20, 1/2/1807; Northcote Parkinson, *Edward Pellew, Viscount Exmouth, Admiral of the Red* (London: Methuen, 1934), 245–6, notes that the Troubridges shared £26,000 from a single action.

92 WSRO AM 760/1/9, November 1809; emphasis in the original.

93 Ibid., 760/1/82, nd July/August 1810, 760/1/83, 15/10/1810.

94 NLS MS 2265, f152, 6/2/1811.

95 WSRO AM 760/1/84, 28/10/1810, 760/1/80, 28/10/1810, 760/1/64, 28/10/1810; quoted James Davey, *In Nelson's Wake* (London: Yale University Press, 2016), 77n.

96 WSRO AM 760/1/84, 28/10/1810.

97 Ibid., 760/1/137, 27/10/1815.

98 BL Add Ms 29915f235, 18/4/1808.

99 BL Add 29915, f230v. 10/4/1808.

100 BL Add Ms 29915, f154v-155, 20/8/1807, f245, 6/5/1808.

101 Ibid., f234v, 18/4/1808.

102 Ibid., f234, 18/4/108.

103 Ibid., f235–235v, 18/4/1808.

104 Joseph Allen, *Memoirs of the Life and Services of Admiral Sir William Hargood* (Greenwich: H. S. Richardson, 1841), 213–14.

105 Knight, *The Pursuit*, 424, puts them at £1,500pa but the collection of printed documents on which he draws lists bills averaging £69 per week for 21 weeks which suggests a total of just under £3,600pa, split with Sir William Hamilton; see Alfred Morrison, *The Hamilton and Nelson Papers*, 2 vols (Private circulation, 1894), II, 28/ 6/1802–4/4/1803. Sugden puts the figure at £800: *Nelson: The Sword of Albion*, 551.

106 See p. 106 above for Nelson's income and Sugden, *Nelson: The Sword of Albion*, 524–5, on the Bronte estate.

107 Quoted Hopkins, *Merton Place*, 34.

108 Sugden, *Nelson: The Sword of Albion*, 546–7, points out that while the company was mixed it did not warrant the barbs of some of Emma's enemies.

109 Knight, *The Pursuit*, 426.

110   Keele UL M148/6 (53/6), April? 1818.

111   Ibid., nd August 1813, nd July 1813.

112   Ibid., nd 1817.

113   Ibid., nd 1818, 1816.

114   Ibid., nd August 1813, nd 1817.

115   *ODNB*, 13, 484–5.

116   NLS MS 7296, f106, 8/8/1812.

117   NLS MS 7296, ff103v-4, 8/8/1812; emphasis in the original.

118   NLS MS 2265, f104v, 26/12/1809, f107, 22/9/1810, f183, 18/12/1811, Ms 2297, f30v, 30/6/1809, ff113–114v, 22/10/1812.

119   NLS Ms 2297, f99, 26/4/1812.

120   BL Add Ms 29915, f147, 30/7/1807, 156, 11/9/1807.

121   BL Add Ms 29915, f220, 14/3/1808, f224, 27/3/1808, f242, 28/4/1808.

122   Evelyn Berckman, *Nelson's Dear Lord: A Portrait* (London: Macmillan, 1962), 227–8.

123   Add Ms 29914, ff144–144v, 6/7/1807.

124   Tucker, *St Vincent*, II, 321–32.

125   BL Add Ms 29919. Knight was the author of a number of similar effusions preserved in this collection.

126   *Saumarez Papers*, 262 and n1, 22/101812.

127   Lady Martha Saumarez, 'Retrospect', SRO, SA/3/2/7/2, not paginated.

128   The family biography appended to Ross's work gives only a sentence to Carteret's life and death claiming that she 'died young'. In fact, she died at about the same age as her older sister who receives a paragraph's notice; see Ross, *Saumarez*, II, 417–20.

129   SRO SA/3/1/2/1, SA/3/2/7/1/8, 21/6/1814.

130   Lady Saumarez, 'Retrospect'; emphasis in the original.

131   See Martin Wilcox, "'These Peaceable Times Are the Devil': Royal Naval Officers in the Post-war Slump, 1815–1825', *International Journal of Maritimes History*, 26:3 (2014), 471–88, for a recent account of the challenges facing commissioned officers and how they responded to them.

132   *Steel's List*, November 1814.

133   Wilcox, '"Peaceable Times"', 473.

134   NMM MKH/502, 5/4/1814.

135   See pp. 2–3, 168–9 above.

136   From 1815 half pay increased by two shillings a day for admirals and two and six a day for vice and rear admirals. Annual amounts were £705, £546 and £420 for each rank; NA ADM 25/169.

137   Allen, *Memoir of Admiral Sir William Hargood*, 212–15.

Bibliography

Manuscript Sources

Alnwick Castle, Northumbria

  Duke of Northumberland Manuscripts (DNM MS G/4/60–141) and Duke of
    Northumberland Papers (DNP Ms 63–8): Duke of Northumberland, Sir Edward
    Pellew and Sir John Duckworth
  Syon Miscellanea G/5/1–23: Duke of Northumberland to Sir John Duckworth

Bowood House, Wiltshire (BH)

  Lord Keith: Lans

British Library (BL)

  Althorp Papers: Add Ms 75863–4
  Bridport Papers: Add Ms 35195–8, 35199–351201
  Collingwood Papers: Add Ms 40096–8
  Dropmore Papers: Add Ms 58987
  Grenville Papers: Add Ms 41852
  Jervis Papers: Add Ms 29914–5, 29919
  Martin Papers: Add Ms 41364
  St Vincent's Letterbooks: Add Ms 31164–7, 36708

Caird Library, National Maritime Museum, Greenwich (NMM)

  Barham Papers: MID/1–2
  Bridport Papers: MKH/501, 502, 505, 506
  Collingwood Papers: COL/14–15
  Duckworth Papers: DUC/5–29
  Pole Papers: WYN/103–5
  Rainier Papers: RAI/6–12
  St Vincent: MSS 94
  Thompson Papers: THO/2–5
  Waldegrave Papers: WDG/3–11
  Warren Papers: WAR/18, 35, 52–4, 82, 85, 90
  Yorke Papers: YOR/2–10

Cambridgeshire Records Office, Cambridge (CRO)

  Cotton Papers: Ms 588

Derbyshire Records Office, Matlock (DRO)

Gell family papers: D3311/1/1

Dundee City Archives (DCA)

Duncan: Letter Books, 1795, 1798–1800

Hampshire Records Office, Winchester (HRO)

Kingsmill Papers: 19M61/2162, 2165, 2167, 2588, 4204–206, 4216–17, 4395

Keele University Library (KeeleUL)

Admiral Cornwallis's correspondence with Captain and Mrs Whitby: M148/6

Melford Hall, Suffolk

Sir Hyde Parker Papers: F42, 64, 75, 76, 86, 94, 98

National Library of Scotland (NLS)

Berkeley Papers: MS 9932–8
Cochrane Papers: MS 2264–5, 2295–7, 2327, 2340, 2345–9, 2569, 2571, 3022
Keith Papers: MS 3420
Lynedoch Papers: Ms 3595–8
Melville Papers: Ms 3841, 9734

National Museum of the Royal Navy, Portsmouth (NMRN)

Earl St Vincent: MSS 259/1–4

National War Museum of Scotland

Duncan Papers: MI995; DUN/17, 19, 20, 23, 32,

Somerset Heritage Centre, Taunton (SHC)

Hood Papers: DD/AH 3
Nelson-Duckworth: DD/DU 234
Sir Richard Keats: DD/CPL 30–47

Suffolk Records Office, Ipswich (SRO)

Saumarez Papers: SA3/1–2
Standing Orders: HA93/6

UK National Archives, Kew (NA)

ADM 1/107: Channel Command, 1797
ADM 1/248: Jamaica Command, 1797–8
ADM 1/341–44: Lisbon Command, 1811–12
ADM 1/405: Mediterranean Command, 1801
ADM 1/473: Newfoundland Command, 1797
ADM 1/579–585: Admirals Unemployed to Admiralty, 1791–1815
ADM 1/728–9: Nore Command, 1797
ADM 1/5359: Sir William Parker's Trial; 1/5369: Sir John Duckworth's Trial; 1/5371: Sir Robert Calder's Trial; 5442: Vice Admiral Stirling's Trial
ADM 2/932: North American Command, 1808–13
ADM 2/1090–6: Admiralty to Admirals Unemployed, 1795–1815
ADM 3/110–126, 144, 256: Admiralty Minutes and Rough Minutes, 1793–1801, 1805–1808
ADM 7/51: Mediterranean Command, 1810–11
ADM 7/675: Administration
ADM 12/15: Flag Officers Commanding Stations and Squadrons, 1793–1808
ADM 25/125–69: Half Pay Lists 1793–1815
PRO 30/8/146: Chatham Papers
PRO 30/11/275: Vice Admiral and Lord Cornwallis
WORK 6/362/2: Nelson's Funeral

West Sussex Record Office, Chichester (WSRO)

Sir George Murray Papers: AM 760

Printed Primary Works

Aspinall, Arthur. *The Later Correspondence of George III*. 5 vols. Cambridge: Cambridge University Press, 1962–70.

Baring, Mrs Henry, ed. *The Diary of the Right Hon. William Windham, 1784–1810*. London: Longmans, Green and Co., 1866.

Bonner-Smith, D., ed. *The Letters of Lord St. Vincent, 1801–1804*. 2 vols. London: NRS, 1922, 1927.

Buckingham and Chandos, Duke of. *Memoirs of the Court and Cabinets of George the Third*. 4 vols. London: Hurst and Blackett, 1853–55.

Collingwood, Newham, G. L. *A Selection of the Public and Private Correspondence of Vice-Admiral Lord Collingwood: Interspersed with Memoirs of His Life*. 2 vols. London, 1837.

Corbett, J. S., ed. *Private Papers of George, 2nd Earl Spencer, 1794–1801*. 4 vols. London: NRS, 1913, 1914, 1924.

Craig, Hardin, Jnr. 'Letters of Lord St. Vincent to Thomas Grenville 1806–7', Christopher Lloyd, ed., *The Naval Miscellany Volume IV*. London: NRS, 1952, 470–93.

Freemantle, Anne, ed. *The Wynne Diaries 1789–1820*. London: Oxford University Press, 1952.

Grainger, John D., ed. *The Royal Navy in the River Plate, 1806–1807*. Aldershot: Scholar Press/NRS, 1996.

Greig, James, ed. *The Farington Diary by John Farington, R.A.* 5 vols. London: Hutchinson, 1922–25.

Hamilton, R. V., ed. *Letters and Papers of Admiral of the Fleet Sir Thomas Byam Martin, 1733–1854.* 3 vols. London: NRS, 1903, 1898, 1901.

Hodges, H. W. and Hughes, E. A., eds. *Select Naval Documents.* Cambridge: Cambridge University Press, 1927.

Hughes, E., ed. *The Private Correspondence of Admiral Lord Collingwood.* London: NRS, 1957.

Jackson Surges, T., ed. 'From the Letterbooks of Sir Charles Thompson, Bart, Vice-Admiral', J. N. Laughton, ed., *Naval Miscellany II.* London: NRS, 1911, 297–322.

Laughton, J. K., ed. *Letters and Papers of Charles, Lord Barham, 1758–1813.* 3 vols. London: NRS, 1907, 1910, 1911.

Lavery, Brian. *Shipboard Life and Organisation, 1731–1815.* Aldershot: Ashgate/NRS, 1998.

Lewis, Michael, ed. *A Narrative of My Professional Adventure (1790–1839) by Sir William Dillon, KCH, Vice-Admiral, of the Red.* 2 vols. London: NRS, 1953, 1956.

Leyland, J., ed. *Dispatches and Letters Relating to the Blockade of Brest, 1803–1805.* 2 vols. London: NRS, 1899, 1902.

Mark, William. *At Sea with Nelson: Being the Life of William Mark, a Purser Who Served under Admiral Lord Nelson.* London: Sampson Low, Marston & Co, 1929.

Markham, C. R., ed. *The Correspondence of Admiral John Markham, 1801–1807.* London: NRS, 1905.

Morrison, Alfred. *The Hamilton and Nelson Papers.* 2 vols. Printed for Private Circulation, 1894.

Morriss Roger, ed. *The Channel Fleet and the Blockade of Brest, 1793–1801.* London: NRS, 2001.

Naish, George P. B., ed. *Nelson's Letters to His Wife and Other Documents 1785–1831.* London: NRS, 1958.

Nicolas, Nicholas Harris, ed. *The Dispatches and Letters of Vice Admiral Lord Viscount Nelson.* 7 vols. London: Henry Colburn, 1844–46.

[Orde, Sir John]. *Copy of a Correspondence, &c Between The Right Hon. The Lords Commissioners of the Admiralty, The Right Hon. The Earl of St.Vincent, K.B., The Right Hon. Earl Spencer, K.G. and Vice-Admiral Sir J. Orde, BART.* London: R. Faulder, 1802.

Owen, C. H. H. 'Letters from Vice-Admiral Lord Collingwood, 1794–1809'. Michel Duffy, ed., *The Naval Miscellany VI.* Aldershot: Ashgate/NRS, 2003, 149–220.

Perrin, W. G., ed. *The Letters and Papers of Admiral Viscount Keith.* 3 vols. London: NRS, 1927, 1950, 1955.

Petrides, Anne and Downs, Jonathan, eds. *Sea Soldier: An Officer of Marines with Duncan, Nelson, Collingwood and Cockburn.* Tunbridge Wells: Parapress, 2000.

Ryan, A. N., ed. *The Saumarez Papers: The Baltic 1808–1812.* London: NRS, 1968.

Steel's List of the Royal Navy. London: Steel, 1793–1815.

Thursfield, H. G., ed. *Five Naval Journals.* London: NRS, 1951.

Tracy, Nicholas, ed. *The Naval Chronicle: The Contemporary Record of the Royal Navy.* 5 vols. London: Chatham, 1999.

White, Colin, ed. *Nelson: The New Letters.* Woodbridge: Boydell Press, 2005.

Secondary Works

Adams, Max. *Admiral Collingwood.* London: Weidenfeld & Nicholson, 2005.

Aldous, Grahame. 'Lord Nelson and Earl St Vincent: Prize Fighters'. *The Mariner's Mirror,* 101:2 (May 2015): 135–55.

Aldridge, Barry. *My Dear Murray. A Friend of Nelson: The Life of Admiral Sir George Murray, KCB*. Second edition. Chichester: Published by the author, 2014.

Allen, Joseph. *Memoir of the Life and Services of Admiral Sir William Hargood*. Greenwich: H. S. Richardson, 1841.

Anson, Walter Vernon. *The Life of Admiral Sir John Borlase Warren*. London: Simpkin, Marshall, Hamilton, Kent & Co, 1914.

Aspinall-Oglander, Cecil. *Admiral's Widow, Being the Life of Hon. Mrs Edward Boscawen from 1761–1805*. London: Hogarth Press, 1942.

Atkins, Gareth. 'Christian Heroes, Providence and Patriotism in Wartime Britain, 1793–1815'. *Historical Journal*, 58 (2015): 393–414.

Atkins, Gareth. 'Religion, Politics and Patronage in the Late Hanoverian Navy, c1780–c1820'. *Historical Research*, 88 (2015): 272–90.

Barrow, Sir John. *The Life of Richard, Earl Howe, KG, Admiral of the Fleet and General of Marines*. London: John Murray, 1838.

Barrow, Tony. *Collingwood's Northumbrians: Old and Valuable Officers*. Rainton Bridge: Business Education Publishers, 2010.

Barton, Mark. 'Duelling in the Royal Navy'. *The Mariner's Mirror*, 100:3 (2014): 282–306.

Berckman, Evelyn. *Nelson's Dear Lord: A Portrait of St Vincent*. London: Macmillan & Co, 1962.

Blake, Nicholas. 'The Wardroom Mess Account for HMS Leyden, 1809'. *The Mariner's Mirror*, 99:4 (2013): 444–54.

Binney, Marcus. *Sir Robert Taylor: From Rococo to Neo-Classicalism*. London: George Allen & Unwin, 1984.

Blake, Robert. *Evangelicals in the Royal Navy, 1775–1815*. Woodbridge: Boydell Press, 2008.

Bond, Gordon C. *The Grand Expedition: The British Invasion of Holland in 1809*. Athens: The University of Georgia Press, 1979.

Bourchier, Lady, ed. *Memoir of the Life of Admiral Sir Edward Codrington, With Selections From His Public and Private Correspondence*, 2 vols. London: [sn], 1873.

Breihan, John R. 'The Addington Party and the Navy in British Politics, 1801–1806'. Craig L. Symonds, ed., *New Aspects of Naval History*. Annapolis: United States Naval Institute, 1981, 63–189.

Brenton, Edward Pelham. *Life and Correspondence of John, Earl St Vincent*. 2 vols. London: Henry Colburn, 1838.

Burhan, Robert B. and McGuigan, Ron M. *The British Army against Napoleon: Facts, List and Trivia, 1805–1815*. Barnsley: Frontline Books, 2010.

Byrn, John D. *Crime and Punishment in the Royal Navy: Discipline on the Leeward Islands Station, 1784–1812*. Cambridge: Scholars Press, 1989.

Campbell, Lorna M. and Noel-Smith, Heather. 'You Are a Very Naughty Admiral Indeed'. *The Mariner's Mirror*, 101:2 (May 2015): 220–1.

Camperdown, Earl of. *Admiral Duncan*. London: Longmans, 1898.

Chatterton, Lady Georgiana. *Memorials, Personal and Historical of Lord Gambier GCB*. 2 vols. London: Hurst and Blackett, 1861.

Christie, Cary. 'The Royal Navy and the Walcheren Expedition of 1809'. Craig L. Symonds, ed., *New Aspects of Naval History*. Annapolis: United States Naval Institute, 1981, 190–200.

Clowes, W. L et al., eds. *The Royal Navy: A History from the Earliest Times to the Present*. Vols III, IV, V. London: Samson Low, Marston and Company, 1898–1900.

Consolvo, Charles. 'The Prospects of Promotion of British Sea Officers'. *The Mariners' Mirror*, 91:2 (2005): 135–59.

Cornwallis-West, G. *The Life and Letters of Admiral Cornwallis*. London: Robert Holden, 1927.

Creswell, John. *Generals and Admirals: The Story of Amphibious Command*. London: Longmans, Green & Co, 1952.

Crimmin, Pat. 'Sir Thomas Troubridge, c1749–1807'. Peter Le Fevre and Richard Harding eds, *British Admirals of the Napoleonic Wars: The Contemporaries of Nelson*. London: Chatham, 2005, 295–322.

Dancy, J. Ross. *The Myth of the Press Gang*. Woodbridge: Boydell Press, 2015.

Davey, James. *In Nelson's Wake: The Navy and the Napoleonic Wars*. London: Yale University Press, 2016.

Davey, James. '"Within Hostile Shores": Victualling the Royal Navy in European Waters during the French Revolutionary and Napoleonic Wars'. *International Journal of Maritime History*, 21:2 (2009): 241–60.

Dickinson, H. W. *Educating the Royal Navy: Eighteenth- and Nineteenth-Century Education for Officers*. London: Routledge, 2007.

Dickinson, H. W. 'The Portsmouth Naval Academy, 1733–1806'. *The Mariners' Mirror*, 89:1 (2003): 17–30.

Downer, Martyn. 'Nelson and His "Band of Brothers": Friendship, Freemasonry, Fraternity'. David Cannadine, ed., *Admiral Lord Nelson: Context and Legacy*. Houndmills: Palgrave, 2005, 30–48.

Downer, Martyn. *Nelson's Purse*. London: Bantam Press, 2004.

Duffy, Michael. *Soldiers, Sugar and Seapower: The British Expeditions to the West Indies and the War against Revolutionary France*. Oxford: Clarendon Press, 1987.

Dugan, James. *The Great Mutiny*. London: Andre Deutsch, 1966.

Gilbert, Arthur N. 'The Nature of Mutiny in the British Navy in the Eighteenth Century'. Daniel Masterman, ed., *Naval History: Sixth Symposium of the US Naval Academy*. Annapolis: US Naval Academy, 1987, 111–20.

Gill, Conrad. *The Naval Mutinies of 1797*. Manchester: Manchester-Victoria University Press, 1913.

Gill, Ellen. '"Children of the Service": Paternalism, Patronage and Friendship in the Georgian Navy'. *Journal for Maritime Research*, 15:2 (2013): 149–65.

Gill, Ellen. *Naval Families, War and Duty in Britain, 174–1820*. Woodbridge: Boydell Press, 2016.

Gordon , Iain. *Admiral of the Blue: The Life and Times of Admiral John Child Purvis, 1747–1825*. Barnsley: Pen & Sword Maritime, 2005.

Gwyn, Julian. *Frigates and Foremasts: The North American Squadron in Nova Scotia Waters, 1745–1815*. Vancouver: UBC Press, 2003.

Hall, Christopher D. *Wellington's Navy: Sea Power and the Peninsular War*. London: Chatham, 2004.

Hamilton, C. I. 'John Wilson Croker: Patronage and Clientage at the Admiralty, 1809–1857'. *Historical Journal*, 43:1 (2000): 49–77.

Hamilton, C. I. *The Making of the Modern Admiralty: British Naval Policy-Making, 1805–1927*. Cambridge: Cambridge University Press, 2011.

Hamilton, C. I. 'Naval Hagiography'. *Historical Journal*, 23 (1980): 381–98.

Hanny David. *Naval Courts Martial*. Cambridge: Cambridge University Press, 1913.

Harding, Richard. *Modern Naval History: Debates and Prospects*. London: Bloomsbury, 2015.

Harding, Richard. 'Sir Charles Henry Knowles, 1754–1831'. Peter Le Fevre and Richard Harding, eds. *British Admirals of the Napoleonic Wars: The Contemporaries of Nelson*. London: Chatham, 2005, 113–38.

Harling, Philip. *The Waning of 'Old Corruption': The Politics of Economical Reform in Britain, 1779–1846*. Oxford: Oxford University Press, 1996.

Heppe, David, J. *British Warship Losses in the Age of Sail 1650–1859*. Rotherfield: Jean Boudriot, 1994.

Hill, Richard. *The Prizes of War: The Naval Prize System in the Napoleonic Wars, 1793–1815*. Stroud: Sutton/Royal Naval Museum Publications, 1998.

Hilton, J. D. 'An Admiral and His Money: Vice-Admiral Cuthbert Collingwood'. *The Mariners' Mirror*, 95:3 (2009): 296–300.

Hood, Dorothy. *The Admirals Hood*. London: Hutchinson & Co, 1934.

Hubley, Martin and Malcolmson, Thomas. '"The People from Being Tyrannically Treated, Would Rejoice in Being Captured by the Americans": Mutiny and the Royal Navy During the War of 1812'. Craig Lantle, ed., *The Apathetic and the Defiant: Case Studies of Canadian Mutiny and Disobedience, 1812*. Toronto: Dundurn, 2007:

Jenks, Timothy. *Naval Engagements: Patriotism, Cultural Politics, and the Royal Navy, 1793–1815*. Oxford: Oxford University Press, 2006.

Jesse, John Henge, *Memoirs of the Life and Reign of George the Third*, 2nd edn, 3 vols. London: the author, 1867.

Jolly, Barry. *Mrs Whitby's Locket. The Story of Captain John Whitby – England's Youngest Ever Naval Captain – and His Redoubtable Wife*. Milford-on-Sea: Milford-on-Sea Historical Record Society, 2011.

Jordan, Gerald and Rogers, Nicholas. 'Admirals as Heroes'. *Journal of British Studies*, 28 (1989): 201–24.

Kirke, Henry. *From the Gunroom to the Throne: Being the Life of Vice-Admiral Philip D'Auvergne, Duke of Bouillon*. London: Swan Sonnenschein & Co, 1904.

Knight, Roger. *Britain against Napoleon: The Organization of Victory*. London: Penguin, 2014.

Knight, Roger. 'Politics and Trust in Victualling the Navy, 1793–1815'. *The Mariners Mirror*, 94:2 (2008): 133–49.

Knight, Roger. *The Pursuit of Victory: The Life and Achievement of Horatio Nelson*. London: Allen Lane, 2005.

Lambert, Andrew. *Admirals: The Naval Commanders Who Made Britain Great*. London: Faber & Faber, 2011.

Lambert, Andrew. *The Challenge: Britain against America in the Naval War of 1812*. London: Faber and Faber, 2012.

Lambert, Andrew. 'Sir William Cornwallis, 1744–1819'. Peter Le Fevre and Richard Harding eds, *Precursors of Nelson: British Admirals of the Eighteenth Century*. London: Chatham, 2000, 353–76.

Lavery, Brian. *Nelson's Navy: The Ships, Men and Organisation 1793–1815*, revised edn. London: Conway, 2012.

Le Fevre, Peter. '"Little merit will be given me": Admiral Sir Hyde Parker (1739–1807) and the Diplomatic Build-up to the Battle'. Stephen Howard, ed., *Battle of Copenhagen 1801 200 Years*. Shelton: The 1805 Club, 2003, 1–30.

Lincoln, Margarette. *Naval Wives and Mistresses*. Stroud: History Press, 2010 [2007].

Lincoln, Margarette. *Representing the Royal Navy: British Sea Power, 1750–1815*. Aldershot: Ashgate/NMM, 2002.

Macdonald, Janet. *Feeding Nelson's Navy: The True Story of Food at Sea in the Georgian Era*. London: Chatham, 2004.

Macdonald, Janet. 'Two Years Off Provence: The Victualling and Health of Nelson's Fleet in the Mediterranean, 1803–1805'. *The Mariners Mirror*, 92:4 (2006): 443–54.

Mackay Ruddock F. and Duffy, Michael. *Hawke, Nelson, and British Naval Leadership*. Woodbridge: Boydell Press, 2009.

Mackesy, Piers. *British Victory in Egypt, 1801: The End of Napoleon's Conquest*. London: Routledge, 1995.

Mackesy, Piers. *The War in the Mediterranean, 1803–1810*. London: Longmans, Green & Co, 1957.

Malcolmson, Thomas. *Order and Disorder in the British Navy, 1793–1815*. Woodbridge: Boydell Press, 2016.

Manwarring, G. E. and Dobreé, Bonamy. *The Floating Republic*. London: Penguin Bks, 1937.

Marshall, John. *Royal Naval Biography*. 8 vols. London: Longman, Rees, Orme, Brown and Green, 1823–35.

Matthews, H. C. G. and Harrison, Brian, eds. *The Oxford Dictionary of National Biography*. 61 vols. Oxford: Oxford University Press, 2004.

McCranie, Kevin, D. *Admiral Keith and the War against Napoleon*. Gainsville: University of Florida Press, 2006.

Morriss, Roger. *Cockburn and the British Navy in Transition: Sir George Cockburn 1772–1853*. London: Exeter University Press, 1997.

Morriss, Roger. *Naval Power and British Culture, 1760–1850*. Aldershot: Ashgate, 2004.

Namier, Sir Lewis and Broke, John. *The House of Commons, 1754–1790*. 3 volumes. London: HMSO, 1964.

Nicholson, Adam. *Men of Honour: Trafalgar and the Making of the English Hero*. London: Harper Collins, 2006.

Orde, Dennis. *Nelson's Mediterranean Command*. Barnsley: Pen & Sword Maritime, 2014.

Orth, Kathrin. 'Sir John Orde, 1751–1824'. Peter Le Fevre and Richard Harding, eds, *British Admirals of the Napoleonic Wars: The Contemporaries of Nelson*. London: Chatham, 2005, 67–90.

Padfield, Peter. *Broke & The Shannon*. London: Hodder and Stoughton, 1968.

Pakenham, Eliza. *Tom, Ned and Kitty: An Intimate Portrait of an Irish Family*, 2nd edn. London: Phoenix, 2008.

Parkinson, Cyril Northcote. *Edward Pellew, Viscount Exmouth, Admiral of the Red*. London: Methuen, 1934.

Parry, Anne, ed. *The Admirals Freemantle*. London: Chatto & Windus, 1971.

Pope, Dudley. *The Black Ship*. London: 1988 [1963].

Pratt, Lynda. 'Naval Contemplation'. *Journal for Maritime Research*, 2:1 (2000): 84–105.

Ralfe, James. *Historical Memoirs of Admiral Charles Stirling with Notes and Observations by Vice-Admiral Stirling*. London: L. Harrison, 1826.

Ralfe, James. *The Naval Biography of Great Britain: Consisting of Historical Memoirs of Those Officers of the British Navy Who Distinguished Themselves during the Reign of His Majesty George III*. 4 vols. London: Whitmore and Fenn, 1828.

Rodger, N. A. M. *The Admiralty*. Lavenham: T. Dalton, 1979.

Rodger, N. A. M. *The Command of the Sea*. London: Penguin, 2005.

Rodger, N. A. M. 'Commissioned Officers' Careers in the Royal Navy, 1690–1815'. *Journal for Maritime Research*, 3:1 (2001): 85–129.

Rodger, N. A. M. 'Nelson and the British Navy: Seamanship, Leadership and Originality'. David Cannadine, ed., *Admiral Lord Nelson: Context and Legacy*. Houndmills: Palgrave, 2005, 7–29.

Rodger, N. A. M. 'Patronage and Competence'. *Les Marines de Guerres Europeénes XVII-XVIIIe Siécles*, 237–48.

Rogers, Nicholas. 'The Sea Fencibles, Loyalism and the Reach of the State'. Mark Philp, ed., *Resisting Napoleon: The British Response to the Threat of Invasion, 1797–1815*. Aldershot: Ashgate, 2006, 41–60.

Ross, Sir John. *Memoirs and Correspondence of Admiral Lord de Saumarez*. 2 vols. London: Richard Bentley, 1838.

Ryan, Alan. 'An Ambassador Afloat: Vice Admiral Sir James Saumarez and the Swedish Court, 1808–1812'. Jeremy Black and Philip Woodfire, eds, *The British Navy and the Use of Naval Power in the Eighteenth Century*. Leicester: Leicester University Press, 1988, 237–58.

Salmond, Anne. *Bligh. William Bligh in the South Sea*. Auckland: Penguin, 2011.

Sheldon, Matthew. 'How to Re-fit an Old Admiral for Sea'. *The Mariners' Mirror*, 87:4 (2001): 479–82.

Spencer, C. Tucker and Reuter, Frank, T. *Injured Honor: The Chesapeake-Leopard Affair June 22, 1807*. Annapolis: Naval Institute Press, 1996.

Stirling, A. M. W. *Pages & Portraits from the Past, Being the Private Papers of Sir William Hotham, GCB*. 2 vols. London: H. Jenkins, 1919.

Sugden, John. *Nelson: A Dream of Glory*. London: Pimlico, 2012.

Sugden, John. *Nelson: The Sword of Albion*. London: Vintage, 2014.

Sutcliffe, Robert K. *British Expeditionary Warfare and the Defeat of Napoleon 1793–1815*. Woodbridge: Boydell Press, 2016.

Syrett, David. 'The Role of the Royal Navy in the Napoleonic Wars After Trafalgar, 1805–1814'. *Naval War College Review* (September–October 1979): 71–84.

Syrett, David and DiNardo, R. L., eds, *The Commissioned Sea Officers of the Royal Navy, 1660–1815*. Aldershot: Scholar Press/NRS, 1994.

Talbott, John E. *The Pen & Ink Sailor: Charles Middleton and the King's Navy, 1778–1813*. London: Frank Cass, 1998.

Taylor, Stephen. *Storm and Conquest: The Battle for the Indian Ocean, 1809*. London: Faber and Faber, 2007.

Thorne, R. G. *The House of Commons, 1790–1820*. 3 vols. London: Secker and Warburg, 1986.

Tracy, Nicholas. 'Sir Robert Calder, 1744–1818'. Peter Le Fevre and Richard Harding, eds, *British Admirals of the Napoleonic Wars: The Contemporaries of Nelson*. London: Chatham, 2005, 197–217.

Tracy, Nicholas. 'Sir Robert Calder's Action'. *The Mariners' Mirror*, 77:3 (1991): 259–70.

Twiss, Horace. *The Public and Private Life of Lord Chancellor Eldon, with Selections from His Correspondence*, 3rd edn, 2 vols. London: John Murray, 1846.

Voelcker, Tim. *Admiral Saumarez versus Napoleon: The Baltic, 1805–12*. Woodbridge: Boydell Press, 2005.

Voelcker, Tim. 'Victories or Distractions, Honour or Glory'. Tim Voelcker, ed., *Broke of the Shannon and the War of 1812*. Barnsley: Seaforth Press, 2013, 57–73.

Warner, Oliver. *The Life and Letters of Vice-Admiral Lord Collingwood*. London: Oxford University Press, 1968.

White, Colin. 'The Battle of Cape St Vincent 14 February 1797. Stephen Howard, ed., *Battle of Cape St Vincent 200 Years*. Shelton: The 1805 Club, 1998, 38–67.

White Colin. 'A Man of Business: Nelson as Commander in Chief Mediterranean, May 1803– January 1805'. *The Mariners' Mirror*, 91:2 (2005): 175–94.

White, Colin. 'The View from Nelson's Quarterdeck'. Stephen Howard, ed., *Battle of Copenhagen 1801 200 Years*. Shelton: The 1805 Club, 2003, 30–63.

Wilcox Martin. "'These Peaceable Times Are the Devil": Royal Naval Officers in the Post-war Slump, 1815–1825'. *International Journal of Maritimes History*, 26:3 (2014): 471–88.

Wilson, Evan. *A Social History of British Naval Officers 1775–1815*. Woodbridge: Boydell Press, 2017.

Woodman, Richard. *A Brief History of Mutiny*. London: Robinson, 2005.

Index

Lightning Source UK Ltd.
Milton Keynes UK
UKHW051111150320
360285UK00007B/13

9 781350 127777